INSIDE STORY

THE FIRST TEN YEARS

INSIDE STORY

THE FIRST TEN YEARS

EDITED BY
PETER BROWNE
WITH
KATE MANTON

Published by Grattan Street Press, 2018
Introduction copyright © Peter Browne, 2018
Collection © Inside Story Publishing Pty Ltd, 2018
Cover by Rachelle Moulic © Grattan Street Press, 2018

Grattan Street Press is the imprint of the teaching press
based in the School of Culture and Communication
at the University of Melbourne, Parkville, Australia.

THE UNIVERSITY OF
MELBOURNE

Grattan Street Press
School of Culture and Communication
John Medley Building,
Parkville, VIC 3010
www.grattanstreetpress.com

Printed in Australia

ISBN 978-0-6482096-0-7

A catalogue record for this book is available
from the National Library of Australia

CONTENTS

POWER AND POLITICS 149

CLASS AND CRISIS 225

CREATORS 305

INTRODUCTION

PETER BROWNE

aunching a new magazine just as a recession was beginning to bite
might seem careless, at least in retrospect. Or perhaps it could be
seen as a plucky attempt to test the old adage that the media does
best when there's plenty of news around. Either way, Inside Story went
up online on 28 October 2008. Ten years later – and after a few near-death
experiences – the plenty-of-news theory has had a thorough workout and
we're still standing.

Not surprisingly, the global financial crisis was the subtext of the
first article we published, which was based on a chapter about the Great
Depression by the economic historian Erik Eklund in a new book called
Turning Points in Australian History. The piece was illustrated with an
arresting black-and-white photo of an unshaven but neatly dressed
man offering pencils for sale in the streets of Brisbane, a reminder of
how unequally the effects of an economic downturn can fall but also
of how far Australia's welfare system had developed in the intervening
decades.

Inside Story's own safety net was a salary and a grant of $30,000 from
the vice-chancellor of Swinburne University of Technology, where we
were based at the time, and support from the university's Institute for
Social Research. We began publishing three or four new articles each
week, usually in time for an email newsletter every Thursday morning.
Although we weren't bound by the news cycle, we had some early luck: by
chance, we had a correspondent on Christmas Island when Kevin Rudd's
government faced its first boat arrivals; another correspondent had been
invited to the World Economic Forum's latest summit; and another was in
Austria after the far-right BZÖ party had performed unexpectedly well in
the October election.

We were aiming to fill a gap in the daily papers' coverage of politics,
policy and culture. Somewhere between the 800-word opinion piece and
the Saturday feature, there seemed to be an opening for deeper but no
less accessible writing by the best-informed academic researchers and
freelance journalists. Although the media was changing quickly, The
Conversation, *The Saturday Paper,* and Guardian Australia weren't yet on
the scene, so the field was wide open.

Among the earliest pieces in Inside Story was the one that opens this collection: Shino Konishi's beautifully written account of an irascible French anthropologist's visit to Tasmania in 1802 ('François Péron and the Tasmanians: An Unrequited Romance'). We were delighted to publish the work of a young Indigenous scholar with such a fresh approach to the complexity of those early contacts between Europeans and Indigenous Australians. It was around this time that Kate Manton joined Inside Story as deputy editor, adding a new level of professionalism to the magazine.

Shino's essay introduces one of Australia's earliest European 'witnesses,' and the remainder of the opening section of this anthology is made up of the first-hand experiences of the authors themselves or their subjects. Subsequent sections step back a little, exploring issues from a biographical and historical perspective ('Lives and Times') and in terms of power relativities ('Power and Politics'). The fourth section ('Class and Crisis') focuses on the legacy of the global financial crisis and the pressures created by increasing migration and growing demands for Indigenous recognition, and the anthology closes with essays from our cultural coverage. Generally, but not always, the articles appear in chronological order.

•

Education policy was a priority from the beginning; Chris Bonnor, Dean Ashenden ('The Educational Consequences of the Peace', in this collection) and later Tom Greenwell ('The Piccoli Prescription') helped us to track the debate that would culminate in the first Gonski report, and then to analyse the backsliding and muddled thinking that culminated in the Morrison government's political fix in September 2018. Also among our earliest pieces was historian Tom Griffiths' essay about the February 2009 Black Saturday bushfires ('We Have Still Not Lived Long Enough'), which went on to win the Alfred Deakin essay prize in the Victorian Premier's Literary Awards. Tom wrote two further challenging essays about bushfire, and over the years contributed essays on the Antarctic, archaeology, Tony Abbott's political legacy, and the death of Harold Holt.

Our resolve to publish international features and analysis alongside Australian material was boosted when The Canberra Times agreed to publish a 2500-word world news feature from Inside Story every Saturday. Maria Tumarkin ('Remembering and Forgetting'), John Besemeres and Robert Horvath analysed changing conditions in Russia; Fred Fletcher, who had been a visiting professor at Swinburne University, sent us a profile of the new leader of Canada's Liberal Party, Michael Ignatieff; Tessa Morris-Suzuki looked at Japan's prospects after the failure of Fukushima No. 1 nuclear plant. We smuggled some local stories into the paper, too, including Brett Evans' profile of the philosopher David Chalmers and Charles Gent's report on the worrying southward movement of Goyder's Line in South Australia.

As we had hoped, other newspapers and magazines also began paying us to republish pieces. One important part of our plan for self-sufficiency seemed to be falling into place: we would commission reportage, essays and reviews; newspaper and magazine editors would pay us handsomely for the rights to reprint them. But then the global financial crisis – deftly anatomised by Timothy Sinclair in 'The Queen and the Perfect Bicycle' – really started to bite.

•

During those tumultuous early days we were fortunate to have the historian Frank Bongiorno writing for us from one of the crisis' epicentres, London. As the recession deepened and prime minister Gordon Brown's problems intensified, Frank sent a series of vivid dispatches, not only examining politics and the economy but also exploring other matters, including the success of London's congestion tax, the threat to the National Health Service, and Britain's buttoned-up attitude to breastfeeding.

While Australia rode out the global financial crisis relatively comfortably, Britain elected a government that seemed determined to make it worse. Despite all the evidence that 'austerity' was the wrong way to reverse the downturn, David Cameron's Conservative government slashed spending on welfare and services, and largely let the villains off the hook. With Frank back in Australia, David Hayes, one of the founders of openDemocracy, took over the job of illuminating the political and cultural crisis – and the blunders on both sides of politics – that eventually led to the Brexit vote.

In the midst of that inexorable slide came a well-timed biopic about Margaret Thatcher, who had transformed British politics back in the eighties and continued to transfix many on the left and the right. David used the film as a point of departure for his reappraisal of her government and its long shadow ('Margaret Thatcher, Between Myth and Politics'). Much of the left, he wrote in January 2012, 'remains deeply in love with its hatred of Thatcher, unaware that thirty years on this is the most conservative of emotions ... The outcome is a form of self-entrapment that corrodes the capacity to begin to understand the political experience of the last four decades in all its many-sidedness, contingency and complexity.'

Across the Atlantic, Lesley Russell – a long-time health policy analyst and former adviser to Julia Gillard – was chronicling the early Obama years from Washington (where she'd once worked for the US Surgeon General), alive to the complexity of a period that no one dreamed would end with the election of Donald Trump. Our other regular correspondent during those early years, Xan Rice, wrote about East Africa from the Kenyan capital, Nairobi, but also reported from South Sudan as refugees began returning, and from Benghazi and Misrata after the fall of Muammar Gaddafi. There, 'the frustration of not being able to observe the war in the east [of Libya was] replaced by the exhilaration of experiencing it at close quarters. And by fear.'

Back home, Tony Abbott was well entrenched as opposition leader. Despite Labor's capable handling of the global financial crisis, Abbott's ruthless opportunism brought down a prime minister, Kevin Rudd, who had his own flaws. When news started leaking out on the momentous evening of Rudd's demise in June 2010, crime writer Shane Maloney happened to be killing time in Canberra, his own business at Parliament House complete. 'Reports of an imminent spill are getting more feverish by the minute,' he wrote in a piece that didn't stick strictly to the conventions of press gallery reporting ('Shoulder-Deep in the Entrails'). 'Journalists are interviewing journalists about what other journalists think might be happening. Arms are shoulder-deep in the entrails; reports arrive of a calf born with two heads; flights of vultures have been sighted in the evening sky.'

Julia Gillard's incautious rush to the polls; three years of minority government; the brief return of Kevin Rudd – time rushed by, and suddenly Tony Abbott was prime minister. Almost as suddenly, the bottom fell out of the Coalition's poll figures, and it has rarely done better than Labor since then. Peter Brent, one of our earliest and most frequent contributors, had been blogging at *The Australian* for the duration of the Gillard government (in circumstances described in 'Mitchell, Murdoch and Me') but returned to Inside Story in mid 2014 to resume puncturing the conventional wisdoms of the pundits. Soon after, we were joined by Tim Colebatch, the prolific former *Age* economics editor and columnist, who dissected economic indicators and analysed psephological data, and made a sharp diagnosis of the Liberal Party's troubles ('A Former Leader's Advice ...').

Other historically informed analysis came from long-time contributor Norman Abjorensen, whose sweep is evident in his description of a little-noticed but decisive transition in Australian party politics ('Australia's Great Political Shift'). During Julia Gillard's prime ministership, James Panichi investigated whether MPs were spending too much time running advice bureaus for their constituents and not thinking enough about the big challenges ('The Everyday Politics of Perpetual Electioneering'). Reviewing the ABC's documentary series on the fall of Kevin Rudd, Jane Goodall considered whether political life exacts too great a toll on politicians ('Personality as Destiny'). Stepping back from day-to-day politics, Andrew Leigh examined how and why inequality persists through generations ('The Remarkable Persistence of Power and Privilege'), while John Quiggin described 'The Coming Boom in Inherited Wealth'.

•

Along with Google and Apple, the growing reach of Facebook and Twitter delivered a final blow to the old business model that had sustained publishing houses like John Fairfax and Sons (whose last chair, James Fairfax, was recalled for Inside Story by Andrew Dodd in 'Now, Where Were We ...?'). A less-noticed effect of the immediacy and influence of social media was a blurring of the geography of political debate. Suddenly, voting patterns and political trends in Britain and the United States seemed directly and immediately relevant to Australian politics and public policy.

Australia certainly shared some of the conditions that had fuelled right-wing populism in Britain and the United States: high and increasingly controversial immigration levels, signs of growing inequality, an onset of wage stagnation. But in many ways these similarities were outweighed by the differences. As Peter Brent argued in Inside Story, Donald Trump became president only by hijacking one of the two major American parties. (Bernie Sanders had tried unsuccessfully to do the same to the other.) If Trump had run as an independent, his own support base wouldn't have got him any closer to the White House than Ross Perot got in 1996. Australian political parties are pretty good at blocking or disposing of leaders who are too far out of step with the mainstream, as Tony Abbott learned in 2016. (The subsequent removal of Malcolm

Turnbull pointed to a deeper problem within the Liberal Party that could take years to resolve.)

But the differences are much broader than that. We don't have the race-inflected suspicion of the welfare state that divides the United States, or that country's deep cultural mistrust of government. We have accommodated a proportionally larger immigrant community over a much longer period than Britain has, and on that measure we have done better than the United States in recent decades as well. We're not a former imperial power having to face up to the first signs of decline (America) or its late stages (Britain). Our welfare state works better, and yet more cheaply, than America's, and our governments – even, thanks to the Senate, the Abbott government – didn't follow Britain's socially disastrous campaign of austerity.

All of this means – as Tim Colebatch noted in Inside Story after the 2016 election – that Pauline Hanson's One Nation, the most successful of the new parties of the far right, gets so far and no further. Hanson's party managed 4.3 per cent of first-preference Senate votes in 2016 – and less than 10 per cent in its heartland, Queensland – but then received a backhander six months later in the WA election. The Liberals, who had struck a controversial preference deal with the party, suffered a landslide defeat.

That's not to say that Australia doesn't share problems with other Western countries – our variety of liberalism has many of the flaws that Rob Hoffman discusses in 'Has Liberalism Forgotten What It Does Best?' – but it's important to get the diagnosis of these problems right.

That diagnosis should include our biggest piece of unfinished business, a settlement with Indigenous Australians. Along with Shino Konishi's essay, this anthology features Bronwyn Carlson's wrenching account of her growing understanding of her own Aboriginality in the Australia and New Zealand of the seventies and eighties ('Who's Counting?'). Later in the collection, Jack Latimore describes the debate within the Indigenous community – little noticed in the mainstream media at the time – that led to the Uluru Statement from the Heart ('Jumping the Gate').

The debate about refugees, and increasingly about migration in general, has continued to generate enormous heat, despite the evidence that its significance to voters at election time has been vastly overrated by the political parties. Over the decade, our contributing editor Peter Mares tracked the frequent shifts in government policy, identifying the dramatic change in Australia's migrant intake towards temporary rather than permanent arrivals, a theme he developed in his 2016 book, *Not Quite Australian*. And recently, after 'African gangs' in Melbourne captured headlines for weeks, Margaret Simons spent time in the suburb at the centre of the debate to write a nuanced account of the intersection of migration, crime and the media ('Looking for Trouble').

Our coverage of climate change began in November 2008 with a report on the role of an Australian company in California's path-breaking carbon-reduction strategy; nine years and eleven months later Mike Steketee reminded readers that Margaret Thatcher advocated action on climate – for impeccable conservative reasons – as far back as 1990. In this anthology, Tom Griffiths looks at an extreme weather event of the kind that will become more common as the impact of climate change intensifies, and Tim Colebatch explores the policy paralysis that has prevented effective action on this and other challenges.

From the United States came the #MeToo movement, which Sophie Black and Jane Goodall discussed for Inside Story, with David Hayes also reporting on its impact on British politics. Jeremy Gans tracked the unfolding implications of section 44 of the Constitution – the citizenship saga – and then (in 'The Great Assenters') turned his attention to an emerging decision-making troika on the High Court bench.

Uneasiness about the power of the United States – not a new phenomenon, but supercharged by the election of Donald Trump – has been mirrored by growing concerns about the increasing economic and strategic power of China. Inside Story's China-watchers Antonia Finnane ('Sam Dastyari and the Thousands of Years of Chinese History') and John Fitzgerald were among the earliest to raise questions about the relationship between Australian and Chinese universities, while Frank Bongiorno used the occasion of the publication of Clive Hamilton's much-publicised book *Silent Invasion* to sound his own note of caution about how the debate was unfolding ('Up to a Point, Professor Hamilton').

This collection closes with nine pieces from our books and arts coverage. For most of the decade, Sylvia Lawson ('Silence Made Visible') reviewed films for Inside Story, and composer Andrew Ford ('Peter Sculthorpe, a Composer in Australia') wrote about music. Later, Susan Lever ('On Literary Awards') and Jane Goodall joined them, writing about Australian literature and TV. Another reviewer, Richard Johnstone, created a sparkling series of essays about photography, including the appreciation of the work of a prolific Sydney photographer ('The Humane and Sympathetic Eye of Sam Hood'). All are represented in this anthology, along with Jill Kitson's sceptical look at the emerging Jane Austen self-help industry ('Women Behaving Badly'), Matthew Ricketson's appreciation of one of New Zealand's greatest exports ('John Clarke and the Power of Satire'), and Diana Bagnall's personal account of the changing magazine industry ('Between the Covers').

•

Diana's piece brings us up to 2018, and the tenth anniversary of Inside Story's launch. Our aims have stayed the same, but some things have changed. Since the beginning of 2017, the magazine has been published independently, with Mark Baker, a former senior Fairfax writer and editor, joining us as publisher. Swinburne University still contributes funds, and it has recently been joined by the University of South Australia. We have also benefited from a generous bequest from our much-admired film reviewer Sylvia Lawson, who died in late 2017 after a remarkable career as a critic, journalist and academic. Also vital throughout the decade have been well-timed grants from the Copyright Agency's Cultural Fund.

Our back-of-the-envelope business plan took a blow from the financial crisis, but we nevertheless reached our ten-year mark, and are publishing more articles and reaching a bigger audience than ever before. Many writers and readers have valued Inside Story enough to support the publication with their time and attention. Like all magazines, we rely on a wide network of advisers, regular and occasional contributors, and readers – inside and outside universities, in Australia and overseas – and we've benefited enormously from their enthusiasm, ideas and wise counsel.

The environment in which we publish Inside Story has also changed significantly. With The Conversation, *The Saturday Paper* and Guardian Australia now among our friendly rivals, the media landscape has become more crowded and more complex. Print, which was being treated as a doomed format when we launched, isn't looking quite so dispensable now, and we're working on plans to launch a new print edition in 2019. If 2008 was the worst and best of times to launch Inside Story, 2018 is an uncertain but exciting moment to be embarking on our second decade.

WITNESSES

FRANÇOIS PÉRON AND THE TASMANIANS: AN UNREQUITED ROMANCE

SHINO KONISHI

29 January 2009

François Péron was my first. A slight man with a sickly aspect, blind in one eye and possessing a long patrician nose that gave him an imperious air, he had a tendency to be self-indulgent and was not averse to plotting against anyone he disliked. He could easily bend the truth if he saw any benefit in it, and could never be accused of mincing his words. His dedication to self-justification was exasperating, to say the least.

I first encountered Péron's writings as an undergraduate. It was what he said about Indigenous people and how he perceived women that offended me. He could be callously clinical in his descriptions. He never refrained from running his cold eye over the body of a black man or woman, focusing on any physical quality he saw as lacking, aberrant or simply unattractive. He lacked self-awareness and humility, and never missed an opportunity to present himself as a hero, a role that rested precariously on his slender frame.

I was only interested in refuting him, dissecting his words and proving that he was an ignorant egomaniac. Yet François Péron significantly changed my life. He was the first to make me want to become a historian. He was my first primary source; his writings, the first object of my study. Over the years I began to humour his pomposity and look beyond the oft-cited descriptions that sparked my ire. Slowly, my opinion of Monsieur Péron changed. Where once I dismissed him, now I try to engage with him. Without realising it, I have developed a relationship with him, and like all romances it is turbulent. At times, he appals me and I detest him. At other times, I affectionately imagine I can see through his facade and see him as he truly is.

In a way, I have cast myself in the role of tragic heroine, and want to redeem my man. While I have since developed relationships with others, they can never be the same. I have journeyed to the other side of the world to see his handwritten letters and journals and to touch the same paper on which he spent the last years of his short life writing, to feel whether he left any remnant of himself imprinted on the surface. I have walked through the town from which he departed on his epic voyage, whose people he imagined had wished 'may you ... return once more to your country, and the gratitude of your fellow citizens!'[1] as he set sail for my side of the world. I have done all this in order to understand him better; to grasp exactly what it was that made him say those terrible things.

In 1800, at the tender age of twenty-five, Péron was the last man to join the French scientific expedition to *Terra Australis*. Devised by the veteran seadog Post Captain Nicolas Baudin, its scale and cost had surpassed his humble amateur naturalist fantasies when it was co-opted by the newly formed Société des Observateurs de l'Homme and sponsored by Napoleon Bonaparte. But I am jumping ahead of my story, and must return to Péron's life before the expedition so you can understand how he became that self-confessed 'irresponsible, scatter-brained, argumentative, indiscreet', opinionated and alienating man, 'incapable of ever giving way for any reason of expediency'.[2]

Péron was not born into a wealthy family, and his father died at an early age. He was guided on the usual trajectory of an intellectually curious, eighteenth-century French man from the lower orders: he was encouraged to join the seminary. But in the course of Napoleon's numerous campaigns, he was forced to enlist and became a prisoner of war at the age of nineteen. After his release, he moved to Paris and, under the patronage of Monsieur Petitjean, enrolled in a medical degree, becoming a student of the esteemed men of science and members of the Société, Antoine-Laurent de Jussieu and Georges Cuvier. Upon hearing of the expedition to *Terra Australis*, Péron abandoned his studies and immediately entreated his mentors to recommend him. He was given the posts of anthropologist and zoologist. Anthropology was a science then in its infancy. An artefact of its recent inception was the disparity between the two treatises that served as his instructions: Cuvier's were inspired by the new science of comparative anatomy, while Joseph-Marie

---

1   François Péron, *A Voyage of Discovery to the Southern Hemisphere, Performed by Order of the Emperor Napoleon, During the Years 1801, 1802, 1803, and 1804* (London: Richard Phillips, 1809).

2   Nicolas Baudin, *The Journal of Post Captain Nicolas Baudin, Commander-in-Chief of the Corvettes Géographe and Naturaliste, assigned by Order of the Government to a Voyage of Discovery*, trans. Christine Cornell (Adelaide: Libraries Board of South Australia, 1974).

DeGérando's reflected the eighteenth-century philosophical approach of Jean-Jacques Rousseau.

In order to best describe Rousseau's significance in this story, I need to jump ahead, skipping over the departure of Baudin's ships, the *Géographe* and the *Naturaliste*, from Le Havre, and their stop at the Île de France (Mauritius) where they lost a significant proportion of their crew, disaffected by the slow journey and scant provisions. I pass over the brief visits to Western Australia, including the French's first encounters with Aboriginal people, and their longer sojourns in Tasmania and Port Jackson. In fact, I skip over all the events on the journey that changed him. Instead, I want to introduce you to Péron as he was about halfway through the expedition, just after his departure from Port Jackson on 18 November 1802, when the ships were about to return to France via Western Australia.

By then, Péron's writings reveal, he was already a disappointed man. He had recently concluded volume one of his four-volume journal, *Voyage of Discovery to the Southern Hemisphere*, in which he described the results of his experiment comparing the physical strength of Indigenous men and European men using a newly invented mechanical device known as Régnier's dynamometer. Within this ostensibly objective and empirical context, Péron launched into a derogatory and bitter description of the Tasmanian people.

He began with a minutely detailed disquisition on their bodies, easing into his subject matter by stating that the Tasmanians' height was similar to that of Europeans. The head warranted fuller description because Péron thought it 'uncommonly large' and oddly proportioned, being much longer than it was wide. His comprehensive survey then moved down the length of the body, pausing at the torso, which appeared to merit more positive, albeit economically worded, praise. The Tasmanian men's shoulders were broad, their loins 'well formed' and their buttocks 'sizeable'. It was when he scrutinised the men's legs, however, that Péron's aim became clear. He elaborated the muscular stockiness of their torso only to heighten the apparent feebleness of their extremities: his eye discerned 'scarcely any muscle' and he thought their scrawniness was accentuated by their abdomens, which bulged like a 'balloon'. This vignette is classic ethnography à la Péron, and widely quoted.

But it was not just the Tasmanians' bodies that came under attack; he also dismissed their society, polity, abode, arts and diet. Péron's entire description was damning. It inexorably led to his pronouncement that 'the inhabitant of these regions unites all the characters of man in an unsocial state, and is, in every sense of the word, the *child of nature*'. This is a familiar sentiment to any student of Aboriginal history, but Péron's pointed use of italics suggests the reason for his ire: it was a rebuke against those 'vain sophists' who 'attribute to savages all the sources of happiness and every principle of virtue'.

Now Rousseau can enter the story. As a student, Péron had been influenced by the eminent philosopher's thesis on the state of nature. He was seduced by the fantasy of the 'noble savage', a child of nature not only more virtuous than civilised man but physically superior in both form and function. My first impression of Péron's vitriolic attack on the body of the Tasmanians was that it was fuelled by the bitter disappointment of a former acolyte – by the realisation that his deeply held faith was a fantasy.

My first sympathetic understanding came from believing that Péron's disillusionment with 'J.J', as he intimately called Rousseau in his notes, was heartfelt, perhaps enflamed by having lost his own father. His filial misfortune led me to suspect that he did not take the disappointment of a fallen patriarch such as Rousseau lightly. I believed then that there was a tragic romance between Rousseau the mentor and Péron the disciple. Naturally, I concluded that the Tasmanians were merely innocent unfortunates caught in the crossfire, purely a means to Péron's end of proving that Rousseau was a charlatan *philosophe*. The idea that the Tasmanians themselves played almost no role in shaping these derogatory European attitudes was compelling, and widely held by other scholars.

But re-reading Péron again and again I have come to question this belief for, although it is not often acknowledged, Péron was not always damning in his appraisals of the Tasmanians. It seems that his vitriolic fire was not sparked by Rousseau alone, but also fanned by the Tasmanians. Not by their inferiority and physical degradation as Péron implies, but rather by their cool indifference to him, their reluctance to play the foil to his heroic self-imaginings. After acquiring a more intimate knowledge of his writings, I have come to the conclusion that Péron's unrequited romance was not with Rousseau at all, but with the Tasmanians.

•

Let us return to Péron as he was on 13 January 1802: a prodigy in the science of natural history, idealistic and expectant. His enthusiasm was partly attributed to the relief of finally catching sight of Tasmania after an arduous sixty-one-day journey from Timor marked by dysentery, death and despair. To Péron, the Tasmanian coastline was an Arcadian vision.

Despite the brisk temperatures he stood on the deck of the *Géographe* transfixed by the sight of the 'lofty mountains', the inland plains which rose 'in amphitheatres' over the whole island, and the 'immense forests'. He listened to the calls of the seabirds that circled the ships and the dolphins' splashes as they danced in the ship's wake. All the sights and sounds contributed to his solemn feeling that he had 'touched the extreme boundary of the southern world'.

Péron's admiration of the landscape grew as the ships sailed into the d'Entrecasteaux Channel in search of fresh water. Observing the lush green of the vegetation and prodigious mountains, and the beautiful plumes of the local parrots and majestic swans, he declared that it was the 'most picturesque and pleasant' place they had seen during their long voyage. It was in this halcyon environment that Péron first glimpsed the Tasmanians.

As the ships approached the shore two men appeared on the beach, disappearing as the ships neared. Then, after the French disembarked, another two men appeared, the braver of them immediately bounding down the rise to greet them. This young man captivated Péron with his athleticism, for he 'seemed rather to spring from the top of the rock than to descend from it'. His physicality made him appear 'strong' and the only defect he appeared to have was a looseness to his joints. Péron scanned the Tasmanian's face and, seeing that his eyes were 'lively and expressive', concluded that his 'physiognomy had nothing fierce or austere' about it.

This figure bewitched the young anthropologist. Here was his noble savage, a man of impressive physical strength and dexterity with an open and guileless demeanour. Péron's compatriot Freycinet immediately embraced the man, and he followed suit. It was in this fleeting caress that Péron got his first inkling that his admiration was not reciprocated. The aloof Tasmanian received the strangers' embraces with an 'air of indifference', but Péron, in his excitement at finally beholding this fabled noble savage, was willing to overlook the minor rebuff. Instead, he interpreted it as a sign that physical displays of affection had little meaning to the man. Later, he would apply this theory to all Tasmanians, but for the time being, Péron was enchanted by the man's insatiable curiosity.

The Tasmanian ran his hands over the strangers' clothes, marvelling at their white skin and layers of attire. Opening their jackets and lifting their shirts, perhaps even rolling up their sleeves and tugging at their waistbands, he inspected their skin, punctuating his fervid manoeuvring with 'loud exclamations of surprise' and stamping his feet. Then the boat caught his eye, and he rushed over to inspect it with the same zeal. Ignoring the men seated aboard, he jumped in and immediately began running his hands along its wooden boards.

The young man was then distracted by a bottle of arrack given to him by one of the bemused sailors. Holding the bottle in the sun he slowly turned it, catching the rays of light that glinted off its surface. Suddenly, his attention again seized by the boat, he threw the bottle overboard, much to the chagrin of the sailors. The loud splashes as one of the Frenchmen dove after the bottle did not distract the Tasmanian, who was then attempting to push the boat off and sail it by himself. Péron was charmed by the man's display of energetic inquisitiveness and impressed by his deductive reasoning. He would later write that they were 'the most striking demonstrations of attention and reflection which we had ever seen among savage nations'.

While this scene was being played out in the water, Péron and Freycinet wandered further ashore to meet the second Tasmanian in a somewhat less frantic exchange. This man's salt-and-pepper hair and beard suggested that he was more than fifty years old, and while he was obviously frightened by the strangers' sudden appearance he gave an impression of 'kindness and candour'. Once he too had dishevelled their strange clothes and scrutinised their white skin, he beckoned two women to join them on the beach.

After some deliberation, the women approached with the elder leading the way. The skin on her belly was marked with 'furrows' and ridges, a telltale sign for Péron that she had mothered many children. The younger woman nursed a baby girl, giving Péron an excuse to linger over the shape and fullness of her bosom in his written description. But when he lifted his gaze to her face he was taken aback by her expression as she openly returned his stare. Unlike the 'kind and friendly' countenance of the older couple, this young woman had 'fire' burning in her eyes. Yet when her eyes flitted back to her baby they changed, becoming warm with affection as she fondled and cared for her infant in a display of 'maternal love' that Péron could only assume was a peculiarity of women the world over. Again, his delight at beholding real-life noble savages led him to overlook the woman's momentary flintiness.

After this meeting Péron's fellow naturalists wished to move on to begin their scientific studies, but he opted to stay with the two women and the Tasmanian patriarch so he could 'collect some words of their idiom'. Meanwhile the young man remained with the sailors, gathering wood and lighting a fire when he realised that they were cold. As both parties converged at the fire Péron had another opportunity to delight in the innocence of these 'children of nature'. When one of the sailors removed his glove the young woman suddenly screamed, fearing that this strange man could simply detach his hand 'at pleasure'. Realising her mistake, the Frenchmen all laughed heartily at her naivety. It was during this first stage of the romance that the ill-fated bottle of arrack re-entered the story.

Under the cover of this distraction, the elderly patriarch took the same bottle of arrack that had been given to his son and headed off towards his camp. The loss of such a valuable resource, comprising 'a great part' of their 'stock', incited the sailors to roughly reclaim the bottle. The Frenchmen's erratic behaviour over this supposed gift sparked the old man's ire, and he immediately led his family away from the strangers, ignoring their subsequent gestures of appeasement and requests to stay. Despite this hiccup in the budding relationship, Péron was confident that he could regain their affections, so he joined his fellow naturalists for a spot of shell collecting.

Later that afternoon some explorers ventured further along the shore looking for specimens and discovered a hut and canoes, which they keenly inspected. After deciding that they lacked sophistication and workmanship, they met the same family, whose number had since swelled to nine. The Tasmanians rushed forward with cries of delight and joy, the earlier altercation seemingly forgotten. They took the sailors back to their hut and prepared a simple meal of broiled shellfish, which the Frenchmen found to be 'succulent and well-flavoured'. The happy guests hoped to repay their hosts' hospitality by regaling them with a spirited rendition of *La Marseillaise*. Péron thought the song would serve an anthropological purpose by revealing 'what effect our singing would have on our audience'. The Tasmanians did not appear surprised by the sudden rendition, though they responded to the music with 'diverse contortions' and 'odd gestures', which greatly amused the explorers. The Tasmanians' immediate 'exclamations of admiration' at the conclusion of the stirring anthem encouraged Péron to entertain them with more song.

Changing the mood somewhat, he led his fellow voyagers in crooning some of their 'tender airs'. Even though the Tasmanians appeared to 'comprehend the sense' of these romantic ballads, they remained unaffected, much to the dismay of the amateur troubadours. After what could only have been an uncomfortable period of silence, the awkward atmosphere was broken by the sudden appearance of Ouré-Ouré, a Tasmanian belle. She was about sixteen or seventeen years old, thought to be the younger sister of either the energetic young man or his flinty wife, and attracted the strangers' keenest attention. Her nakedness and 'delicate' form could not be ignored, but Péron, in a moment of chivalry, refrained from clinically describing her body, and thought her beguilingly unaware that there could be anything indecent or immodest about her 'absolute nudity'. Even though she paid Freycinet the most attention, Péron thought her glances towards all of them were 'affectionate and expressive'.

To Péron, Ouré-Ouré was a natural coquette. Yet, when she behaved in a more forward manner, Péron was taken aback. 'Taking some burnt charcoal in her hands, she crushed it so as to reduce it to a fine powder' then daubed it all over her face, expressing a confident and satisfied attitude towards her beauty regimen. The Frenchmen were flattered by her attentions and amused to discover that 'fondness for adornment ... prevails in the hearts' of all women, but Péron was also distressed by how 'frightfully black' it made her. Evidently, Péron found her coy preening simultaneously enticing and disturbing. Yet he accepted Ouré-Ouré's new look and later seized the opportunity to try to usurp Freycinet in her affections. Noticing that she owned a bag made of rushes, he thought to himself that 'as this girl had also shewn me some marks of regard' he would venture 'to ask her for this little trifle'. She happily gave him the bag, accompanied by 'an obliging smile' and 'some tender expressions' that he lamented not being able to understand. In response to this flirtation Péron inundated her with presents, including a handkerchief, a hatchet and a hammer, disregarding Baudin's orders to be sparing with gifts.

Péron was enamoured not only of the Tasmanians' hospitality and camaraderie, and Ouré-Ouré's affections, but also of the playful mischievousness of the children, and the ease with which he seemed to converse with the Tasmanians, despite not sharing a common language. Upon bidding their adieus the French were accompanied back to their boat by the Tasmanians, where they met the French sailors, most of whom also noticed Ouré-Ouré's considerable attractions and festooned her with even more gifts. The Tasmanians' seemingly mutual feelings of affection were evident in their reluctance to allow the Frenchmen to leave.

•

This day would be Péron's most romantic with the Tasmanians, full of laughter and warmth. He was impressed not only by how the family had embraced their visitors but also by the tenderness they had shown one another. Later he would reflect that on that day he 'saw realised with inexpressible pleasure, those charming descriptions of the happiness and simplicity of a state of nature, of which I had so often read, and enjoyed in idea'. Yet only two days later, on 15 January, Péron would begin to rethink this evaluation.

On that fateful day Péron was completely oblivious to how events would play out. In fact he was not even thinking of the Tasmanians, but was instead charting the Port of Swans in a small boat, marvelling at the countryside and wildlife. The naturalists had discovered a river, which they named after the celebrated hydrographer Fleurieu, and Péron decided that a European colony should be established there, as the river would supply the settlement with water all year round.

Meanwhile, hostilities flared on Bruny Island. That day some sailors had ventured out on a fishing expedition, and shortly after landing had encountered a group of Tasmanians. Péron later learned that a burly midshipman by the name of Jean Maurouard, perhaps anticipating the study Péron would later conduct with his dynamometer, had decided to test the strength of the infamously physically adept noble savages. After presenting the 'natives' with gifts and finding them to be friendly, Maurouard felt at liberty to try something new. Selecting the one who 'appeared to be the most robust' he indicated his desire to engage in a little roughhousing. Planting his feet firmly in the sand, the Frenchman grabbed the Tasmanian's wrist and gestured that both should 'pull as hard as possible'.[3] Assuming that his gestures were fully comprehended, the midshipman engaged in numerous feats of strength, repeatedly toppling or throwing his opponent into the sand. Mighty Maurouard won out every single time, but as the game was played amid much laughter and frivolity he did not anticipate the Tasmanians' reaction.

Tired of wrestling and collecting fish, the Frenchmen decided to withdraw to the ship. They said their goodbyes and presented more gifts. With his back turned to the Tasmanians as he pushed the boat out into the water, Maurouard was suddenly speared in the shoulder. The Frenchmen immediately sprang into action: Sub Lieutenant Saint Cricq drew his pistol, and together with the irrepressible Maurouard charged back up the rise to find the attacker. They later reported to Baudin that they came upon seven or eight armed men who did not react upon seeing the Frenchmen. Struck by their peculiarly impassive demeanour, Saint Cricq and Maurouard decided that it was most prudent to return to the ship, so retreated back down the rise without further incident.

Péron reported the story differently, however. When he heard news

---

3   Baudin, *Journal*, 305.

of this attack a few days later he was filled with horror. How could those noble savages whose company he had so thoroughly enjoyed only days earlier have behaved so barbarically? But then perhaps he recalled those brief incidents during his first day when their response had been cool or indifferent, not to mention their attempt to steal the arrack. Perhaps those minor rebuffs by the Tasmanian men preyed on him. He certainly remembered the hostile attacks that they had suffered on the west coast of New Holland. Possibly the Tasmanian men were not as different from their mainland neighbours as he had first thought. Péron judged this attack to be a 'perfidious and cowardly' display of brutality. He immediately assumed that it was a vindictive response to their resounding defeat at the hands of Maurouard.

It never occurred to him that the Tasmanians might have been demonstrating their own Indigenous game of skill, the art of spear dodging, or that the Tasmanians might have tired of the strangers' presence and wanted them to leave. In fact, Péron did not even entertain the notion that the Tasmanians had any motivation other than an inherent 'destructive instinct', because to him they were little more than a cipher for his fanciful projections. His penchant for melodrama, which became more pronounced over the course of his journey, revealed itself in his retelling of this incident. According to his narrative the French immediately gave pursuit, and he claims they would have 'punished them as they deserved' had the cowardly locals not already 'escaped among the rocks, or hid themselves among the brambles'. This would not be the only time that Péron allowed his fantasies to obscure the truth.

After a reprieve of only a few days, the French had another encounter with the Tasmanian men that played out in a similar fashion, again resulting in 'violent aggression'. For a second time Péron missed out on the action, but at his request the botanist Jean-Baptiste Louis Claude Leschenault wrote him a report, so he had all of the important details. That is to say, the report described the violent actions, mentioning neither how the Tasmanians were encountered nor what their attitude had been, because after the spearing of Maurouard the French could only see the Tasmanian men's actions as inexplicably and instinctively violent.

Leschenault reported this second attack to Péron, who included it in the official journal of the voyage. The report contained the critique of Jean-Jacques Rousseau which would come significantly to influence Péron: 'I am astonished,' wrote Leschenault, 'to hear sensible people aver, that men in a state of nature are not wicked', adding that it was preposterous to believe that the natives never played the role of aggressor. Two attacks were evidently enough for him to reject the claim that the Tasmanians were noble savages. Péron, on the other hand, with lingering memories of Ouré-Ouré, still had a soft spot for the women.

On the last day of the month, after almost two weeks with little contact, Péron came across a group of Tasmanians. Following Leschenault's advice to the letter, he turned back 'without hesitating a moment'. Beating a hasty retreat along the shoreline, he happened to meet Sub Lieutenant François Antoine Boniface Heirisson. Bolstered by this extra support, he decided to return to where he had seen the 'natives'. Realising that they had no chance of catching the Tasmanians if they chose to avoid them, Péron and Heirisson signalled their good intentions by calling out, holding up their presents so they could be seen, and 'waving their handkerchiefs'. The group eventually submitted to these entreaties and stopped, allowing Péron and Heirisson to catch up. It was as they approached that Péron realised that 'they were women, and that there was not a single male among the party', which instantly lifted his spirits. Unfortunately, these women were not to live up to Péron's fantasies, for they were hardly shy and malleable coquettes.

•

From the outset of their encounter the women were in control. It was the women who allowed the Frenchmen to draw near, the women who instructed them to sit, and the women who made them disarm. The Frenchmen not only had to submit to the women's instructions but also had to tolerate their interrogations and mockery. Péron thought that they seemed 'often to criticise our appearance' and laughed 'heartily at our expense'. When the surgeon Jérôme Bellefin attempted to repeat their earlier success with the Tasmanians by singing to them, the women again seemed to appreciate it, but one, who they later learned was called Arra-Maida, mimicked his 'action and the tone of his voice'. Her singing had such an unfamiliar melody that Péron thought it difficult to 'give any idea of music', and her dancing plainly shocked him. Her contortions and 'attitude' bordered on 'indecent', forcing him to primly note that these savage people were still absolute 'strangers to all the delicacy of sentiment and conduct' that was a natural 'consequence of complete civilisation'.

Péron's earlier ambivalence regarding Ouré-Ouré was only exacerbated by these seemingly brazen paramours. Having been tantalised by Ouré-Ouré and entranced by demure flirtations that allowed him to play the role of chivalrous seducer, he was clearly taken aback at being forced into the role of blushing coquette himself. But his surprise at this inversion of roles paled in comparison to the women's attempt to transform the Frenchmen's appearance. Once Arra-Maida had finished her performance she approached Péron, taking from her rush bag some charcoal, which she crushed between her hands just as Ouré-Ouré had done. But instead of powdering her own face she applied it to Péron's and then Heirisson's. Though both men 'submitted to this obliging piece of caprice', and Péron even recognised that the Tasmanians might have the same disdain for white skin that Europeans had for black, this meeting with the women further cooled Péron's ardour for the Tasmanians.

In contrast to his chivalrously discreet account of the delectable Ouré-Ouré, Péron openly scrutinised these women, describing their bodies in clinical and derogatory detail, picking out any flaw, no matter how minor, in his exhaustive catalogue of imperfections. Even the young girls, who possessed an 'agreeable form and pleasant features', were criticised because their 'nipples were rather too large and long'. He concluded that 'in a word, all the particulars of their natural constitution were in the highest degree disgusting'. In Péron's eyes, signs of the women's brazen behaviour were now physically apparent in their bodies.

Even though Péron's opinion of the Tasmanians had become jaded, he was not the one to end the romance. Despite his ambivalence towards the women Péron stayed with them as long as he could, playing the dupe to their 'many tricks' and 'drolleries' and enjoying a 'merry' time. As he followed them home from their fishing expedition, musing on the unjust burdens imposed on savage women, he was suddenly roused from his reflections by one woman's 'loud cry of terror'. The women had just caught sight of the manned French boats. The realisation that there were more intruders waiting just off the shore ignited their fears, and all but one of the women fled towards the forest. The indomitably courageous Arra-Maida hectored her fleeing sisters and eventually convinced them to escort the party back to their boat. As they neared the shore Péron realised that the 'husbands' of these women had also converged where the boats were moored, and instead of being fearful they appeared to be filled with 'malevolence' and suppressed anger, which Péron assumed to be consequent to their 'inability to contend' with the superior Europeans. Yet the Tasmanians seemed to have decided that the best way to contend with the French trespassers was to spurn their advances by evading them and giving the Frenchmen an apparently unambiguous sign of their disdain.

On 3 February, only a few weeks after their first meeting, the French returned to Bruny Island. On seeing two women walking down the mountain to the sea, two of the explorers who had yet to encounter the Tasmanian women immediately ran towards them hoping for a closer look. When the women realised they were being pursued they sprinted off, disappearing before the men could catch them. Disappointed, the entire party continued along the coast and eventually spied a huge bonfire that appeared to have been burning since the night before. As they approached the pyre they realised that it was surrounded by 'almost all the presents' that the French had given the Tasmanians. Like any jilted lover, Péron was in denial. Instead of recognising that the Tasmanians had rejected the French explorers' overtures, he imagined that this bonfire and deliberate return of their gifts was just a manifestation of their 'puerile curiosity'. He deluded himself by thinking that 'these uninformed men threw away what no longer pleased or amused them', and refused to recognise that it was actually he and his compatriots who no longer pleased the Tasmanians.

Had this romance been a fiction rather than being based on historical events the story would have ended here, perhaps with Péron mourning the end of the affair, or moving on to look for another race of impossible noble savages. But the harsh and prosaic reality of the situation was that Péron and the French lingered in Tasmania, unwanted, for a few more weeks, meeting other Tasmanians and making further futile attempts to study these children of nature. Their attentions were frequently rebuffed, and encounters usually ended in violent or aggressive altercations, with the French having to resort to drawing their weapons.

So why did I develop some sympathy for Péron, this vindictive, 'irresponsible, scatter-brained, argumentative' and 'indiscreet' man? It was not because he lost his father at an early age, nor because he was a prisoner of war. My change of heart was because, after years of reading him again and again, I recognised that he had been searching and longing for something that did not exist. He had adopted such a passionate faith in a singular idea that it bordered on religious zeal. He was desperate to find the perfect noble savage, a tabula rasa on which to project his fantasies of an ideal human society. When he finally found it on the temperate shores of Tasmania he did not anticipate that things would play out the way they did. He never expected that his offerings and paternalistic guidance would be rejected, that the noble savages would refuse to do his bidding and be model objects of study, and that they would fail to behave as Rousseau had led him to believe. So he reacted with the vindictiveness of a jilted lover.

So, you may ask again, why do I sympathise with Péron? The answer is simply because his quest mirrored my own. As an Indigenous historian

I have combed these first contact narratives for any accounts and revelations about pre-contact Aboriginal people in order to understand the heartbreaking experiences and momentous changes that colonisation wrought for Indigenous Australians. Despite seeing myself as standing at the opposite end of a temporal and colonial abyss from François Péron, I now realise that we are in some instances uncomfortably aligned. For I too have idealistic fantasies about Aboriginal society and have attempted to impose this romanticised vision on the historical record. In doing so I have come to realise that I have inadvertently glossed over the complexities and idiosyncrasies of pre-contact Aboriginal society, and ignored the playful and amicable relations that were formed in those first moments of contact. I have been blind to the power that the Indigenous people had in those early colonial encounters. Like Péron, I made the mistake of misinterpreting and misjudging the agency of eighteenth-century Aboriginal people and treated them as mere ciphers for my postcolonial theories. I sympathise with Péron because I eventually recognised this, and unlike him, I am now free to be intrigued and enthralled by the real complexities of the Tasmanians and other Indigenous historical figures all over again.

WE HAVE STILL NOT LIVED LONG ENOUGH

TOM GRIFFITHS

16 February 2009

W
e should have seen this coming. We *did* see this coming. Yet we failed to save lives. We have still not lived long enough.

They had not lived long enough were the words that Judge Leonard Stretton used to describe the people who lived and worked in the forests of south-eastern Australia when they were engulfed by a holocaust wildfire on 'Black Friday' in 1939. The judge, who conducted an immediate royal commission into the causes of the fires, was not commenting on the youthfulness of the dead: he was lamenting the environmental knowledge of both victims and survivors. He was pitying the innocence of European immigrants in a land whose natural rhythms they did not yet understand. He was depicting the fragility and brevity of a human lifetime in forests where life cycles and fire regimes had the periodicity and ferocity of centuries. He was indicting a whole society.

In 1939, Australians were deeply shocked by what had happened in their own backyard. Rampant flames had scourged a country that considered itself civilised. As well as shock, people sensed something sinister about the tragedy and its causes. Judge Stretton tried to find the words for it in his fearless report. Of the loss of life at one sawmill settlement, he wrote: 'The full story of the killing of this small community is one of unpreparedness, because of apathy and ignorance and perhaps of something worse.' The 'something worse' that he tried to define was an active, half-conscious denial of the danger of fire, and a kind of community complicity in the deferral of responsibility.

There is something sinister also about the dreadful tragedy of 2009, although the character of it is different. Those of us who know and love these forests and the people who live in or near them are especially haunted. In 1939, some of the ignorance and innocence was forgivable, perhaps. Black Friday was a late, rude awakening from the colonial era of forest exploitation and careless fire use; it demanded that people confront and reform their whole relationship with the bush. When the

1939 fires raged through the forests of valuable mountain ash (*Eucalyptus regnans*), settlers did not even know how such a dominant and important tree regenerated. In the seventy years since 1939, we have lived through a revolution in scientific research and environmental understanding and we have come to a clearer understanding of the peculiar history and fire ecology of these forests. We have fewer excuses for innocence. We knew this terrible day would come. Why, then, was there such an appalling loss of life?

•

Victorians live entirely within what the international fire historian Stephen Pyne calls 'the fire flume'. It is the most distinctive fire region of Australia and the most dangerous in the world. When a high pressure system stalls in the Tasman Sea, hot northerly winds flow relentlessly down from central Australia across the densely vegetated south-east of the continent. This fiery 'flume' brews a deadly chemistry of air and fuel. The mountain topography of steep slopes, ridges and valleys channel the hot air, temperatures climb to searing extremes, and humidity evaporates such that the air crackles. Lightning attacks the land ahead of the delayed cold front and a dramatic southerly change turns the raging fires suddenly upon its victims.

There is a further ingredient to the chemistry of the fire flume. Across Australia, eucalypts are highly adapted to fire. Over millions of years, these trees have turned this fragment of Gondwana into the fire continent. But in the south-eastern corner – especially in the forests of the Victorian ranges – a distinctive type of eucalypt has evolved. Ash-type eucalypts (the mountain and alpine ash) have developed a different means of regeneration. They do not develop lignotubers under the ground like other eucalypts and they rarely coppice. They are unusually dependent on their seed supply – and, in order to crack open those seeds high in the crowns of the trees and to cultivate the saplings successfully, they need a massive wildfire. Ash-type eucalypts generally grow in even-aged stands. They renew themselves *en masse*. These particularly grand and magnificent trees have evolved to commit mass suicide once every few hundred years – and in European times, more frequently. Not all the communities that were incinerated in 1939 and 2009 were in or near the forests of ash, but many were, and the peculiar fire ecology of the trees is another deadly dimension of this distinctive fire environment. These are wet mountain forests that only burn on rare days at the end of long droughts, after prolonged heatwaves, and when the flume is in full gear. And when they do burn, they do so with atomic power.

The 2009 fires were 'unprecedented', as many commentators have said. They erupted at the end of a record heatwave and there seems little doubt that this was a fire exacerbated by climate change. But it is the recurrent realities that are more striking. For those of us who know the history, the most haunting aspect of this tragedy is its familiarity. The 2009 bushfires were 1939 all over again, laced with 1983. The same images, the same stories, the same words and phrases, and the same frightening and awesome natural force that we find so hard to remember and perhaps unconsciously strive to forget. It is a recurrent nightmare. We know this phenomenon, we know the specific contours of the event, and we even know how people live and how people die. The climate change scenario is frightening. But even worse is the knowledge that we still have not come to terms with what we have already experienced.

The Bureau of Meteorology predicted the conditions superbly. The premier issued a warning. Fire experts knew that people would die that day. History repeated itself with uncanny precision. Yet the shock was, and still is, immense. It is the death toll, not the weather, which makes the event truly unprecedented.

The recommended survival strategy of 'leave early or stay and defend your home' was a death sentence in these Victorian mountain communities on a forty-something degree day of high winds after a prolonged heatwave and a long drought. There is no identifiable 'early' in this fire region on the fatal days. We understand why this policy has evolved and it has much to recommend it. It is libertarian; it recognises the reality that people prefer to stay in their own homes and defend them if they can; it seeks to minimise late evacuation which is so often fatal; it encourages sensible planning and preparation; and it has demonstrably saved lives and homes. It will continue to guide people well in most areas of Australia. But I fear that it has misled people in this distinctively deadly fire region to believe that they could defend an ordinary home in the face of an unimaginable force.

We need to be wary of 'national' fire plans and to develop ecologically sensitive, bioregional fire survival strategies. We need to move beyond an undifferentiated, colonial sense of 'the bush' as an amorphous sameness with which we do battle, and instead empower local residents and their knowledge of local ecologies. The quest for national guidelines was fatal for the residents of these Victorian mountain communities on such a day; it worked insidiously to blunt their sense of local history and ecological distinctiveness. Clearing the backyard, cleaning the gutters and installing a better water pump cannot save an ordinary home in the path of a surging torrent of explosive gas in the fire flume.

A 'stay and defend' option is only realistic in such places and conditions if every property has a secure fire refuge or bunker. A bunker at the shire hall or at the end of the street is not good enough – people will die getting to it. I welcome the Prime Minister's promise to rebuild these communities 'brick by brick' – and I would like him to add: 'and bunker by bunker'. Many people built bunkers in their backyards in the Second World War and most, thankfully, were not used. But we know for certain that any secure bunkers built in these Victorian forest towns *will* be used in the next generation, and they will save lives. This is an appropriate challenge to the design and construction industries of the fire continent.

Fires inflame blame. Arsonists will be rightly condemned, but they will also distract us from addressing the reality of fires mostly caused by lightning. There were arsonists in 1939 and 2009 and there will be again in 2069; they are a sickening factor mostly beyond our predictive control. Water-bombing helicopters will again be promoted and in some areas they will be effective. The environmental and protective impacts of systematic control burning of our forests will be debated even more vociferously. Climate change will be correctly identified as a new factor in fire behaviour. But none of these policies or issues will ultimately save lives in these Victorian mountain communities on a holocaust day. Deep in the forests on Black Friday, 1939, with flames leaping kilometres ahead of the fire front, there was only one way to go – down. Well-built dugouts saved lives.

•

There was another meaning to Judge Stretton's declaration that *they had not lived long enough*. He was saying that lived experience alone, however vivid and traumatic, was never going to be enough to guide people in such circumstances. They also needed history. They needed – and we need it too – the distilled wisdom of past, inherited, learned experience. And not just of the recent human past, but of the ancient human past, and also of the deep biological past of the communities of trees. For in those histories lie the intractable patterns of our future. There is a dangerous mismatch between the cyclic nature of fire and the short-term memory of communities. These bushfire towns – where the material legacy of the past can never survive for long – need to work harder than most to renew their local historical consciousness. The greatest challenge in fire research is cultural.

There is a perennial question in human affairs that is given real edge and urgency by fire: *do we learn from history?* Testimony from the 1939 and 2009 fires suggests that there is one thing that we never seem to learn from history. That is, that nature can overwhelm culture. That some of the fires that roar out of the Australian bush are unstoppable. As one fire manager puts it, 'there are times when you have to step out of the way and acknowledge that nature has got the steering wheel at the moment'. It seems to go against the grain of our humanity to admit that fact, no matter how severe are the lessons of history.

SHOULDER-DEEP IN THE ENTRAILS

SHANE MALONEY

28 June 2010

I t's four on Wednesday afternoon and I'm wandering the corridors of Parliament House trying to figure out where I am. The place is vast, a world entire, and its navigation presents a considerable challenge for the non-denizen on a temporary visa.

I arrived yesterday, come for a bit of a sniff around, collecting background for a novel way beyond deadline. I've already got what I came for – a few minutes with a handful of members, people who can draw diagrams of processes and describe situations that will become grist to my fictive mill – and I'm wondering if I can trade my cut-price ticket for an earlier flight back to Melbourne. What I don't yet know is that an accident of timing has put me in the dress circle for the biggest show in town.

Anthony Albanese is coming towards me, flanked by a pair of suits. I've met Albo, eaten with him. Something about him makes me think of a kid with a slingshot, scabby knees and a billycart you wish you were game enough to ride, a big winner in the marbles ring, bit of a jostler. He gives me a nod as we pass, not quite placing me. He doesn't look like he's plotting a coup, but what do I know?

My spirit guide finds me. A repository of Labor Party history, a fountain of discretion, he wheels me around, introducing me, identifying the invisible proprieties, minding my manners, borrowing from the library on my behalf. He knows where my interests lie, in the nooks and crannies of potential happenstance that can be woven into a plot. He smooths my path into the offices of ministers and the cubicles of invisible minions, those messengerial attendants who pass unremarked through the sealed doors of confidential conclaves.

It's six-ish now and I'm back in Lindsay Tanner's office, my temporary *pied-à-terre*. This is ministerial row, heavy-hitters territory, and not a mouse stirs in the corridor. If skulduggery is afoot, it treads very softly indeed.

The day is winding down and the staff in the office engine room are keeping an amused eye on the television monitors streaming Sky News. Reports of an imminent spill are getting more feverish by the minute.

Journalists are interviewing journalists about what other journalists think might be happening. Arms are shoulder-deep in the entrails; reports arrive of a calf born with two heads; flights of vultures have been sighted in the evening sky.

Tanner's chief of staff shambles into the room, watches for a while, shrugs, joins the general badinage, does a little light job allocation, wanders out. Mary Day, his political major-domo, lends me her desk to check my email. Nothing to see here, folks.

The television commentators keep gnawing their bone. The South Australian right is organising the numbers, the Victorian left ... Julia Gillard has been seen going into Kevin Rudd's office. The PM and deputy PM are having a meeting. Hold the presses.

In breaking news, Lindsay has joined Kevin and Julia in the PM's office. Not bad, considering he's three metres from me and we're off to dinner. If something doesn't happen soon, the Australian media will burst like a festering boil. Time to get out of there.

So it's down to the basement car park and into the Prius and off to a pub in O'Connor. Lindsay's driving, letting his phone go unanswered. By now, it's vibrating like a blowfly with the DTs.

We join Maria Vamvakinou, the member for Calwell, and a crew of young staffers. Lindsay does a quick check of his messages, somebody wanting to know if he'll be attending the press conference. Shrugs all round. What press conference? Lindsay doesn't bother to reply. For the next two hours, we talk about ... books. Recent reads, swapped recommendations, shared authors, the problem of finding enough time for history and fiction. He helps me shape a particular scene in the novel that I've been sweating. Lucky he's only the federal finance minister. Back in Brumbyland, this amount of frontbench face-time would cost me thousands.

He gives me a lift to my rented room. On the way, I quiz him about the Greens' challenge to his seat. He triangulates the electoral demographics, won't be drawn on tactics. I leave him parked at the kerbside, phone to his ear.

The Victor Lodge has neither TV nor radio but the coin internet has ten minutes left on the meter. While his finance minister was helping me plot a chapter, Rudd had announced a caucus meeting for the next morning. Lindsay's car is no longer at the kerb.

So now it's nine-thirty the next morning and I'm standing behind the media scrum outside the party room. Feral cats at a mouse hole, they await their prey. Bob Ellis, X-ray visionary, is framing his cadences into a dictaphone: '... an atmosphere of desolate pity ...' The door opens and the pack lunges at the party's emissary. Gillard, unopposed. Swan, deputy.

Hurble-burble, hurble-burble. No further information is forthcoming. Heave and surge. The caucus doors open on an empty room. They've escaped, gone out the other door. The flackery departs, stringing out along the corridor, bound I know not where. I'm not in the loop.

Ah-ha. The prime minister's courtyard. Security men are checking passes. Press only, and PH staff. My day visitor tag won't cut it. I pull out my notebook, merge into a cluster of pundits and sidle through. We wait in the damp air, voices muted. A historic moment. I seek portents and symbols. On cue, the cawing of a crow pierces the winter sky.

Michelle Grattan and Paul Kelly join the crowd, waxy and wrinkled as exhibits in some glass case at Madame Tussauds. What ponderous platitudes must Kelly's gigantic intellect be distilling from this moment, I wonder? What quotidian punditry is Grattan incubating? Polonius and old lace.

Rudd appears. He looks numb. He speaks slowly. The lip quivers. We watch, transfixed. He has a list, dot points of his achievements. Let it be recorded that he made worthwhile things happen, that he helped people, improved and prolonged lives. I'm proud of this, proud of that. He tries to speak from the heart. It is too late. The carapace of jargon cannot be thrown off so easily. His voice catches. The pauses grow longer. His eyes moisten. His ticker falters, replaced valve and all. We gotta zip, he finishes. Zip? Zip?

There is scant satisfaction in this. Not much pity, either. It's too late. Anyway, it's Gillard's turn. Toward the waterhole lumbers the herd.

Eleven o'clock and the party room is chockers. Press, MPs, you name it. Julia sweeps in. Swan combines the gravity of a cardinal with the air of a man who just found a fifty-dollar note on the footpath.

Gillard speaks, ticks all the boxes in our bright and admirable democracy of alarm clocks and open minds, harnessed talent and harnessed wind, teamwork and hard work, surplus budgets and brave soldiers, pulled government advertising and invitations to reciprocity. There's mention, too, of sanctuary.

A very elastic word, that.

And now the press are shouting, baying like brokers in the bourse. Fran Kelly is a corgi, straining at the leash. Barking, barking. 'Juliagillard, juliagillard, juliagillard.'

Each must have their turn, no matter that the question has already been asked and answered. Every child wins a prize. Nobody cares if the lolly has already been sucked. Gillard's full sentences are chopped into bits. It's the only language these people understand. Then it's Julia's turn to zip. She's off to see the GG, get her chit signed.

Back in Tanner's office and everybody is closeted in a meeting. Next thing we're staring up at the office television, watching Lindsay call it quits. Nobody can doubt his explanation because he is, quite simply, exactly what he appears to be. A mensch.

On the plane back to Melbourne, I find myself sitting beside a Channel 10 news presenter and her producer. They'd arrived too late for the Kevin and Julia shows and spent the afternoon doing live links to camera.

I hope I'm home in time for the late news so somebody can explain it all to me.

BEYOND THE EASY LIFE OF GODS

ANNIKA LEMS

12 July 2011

One day in July 2003 I found myself waiting for a bus in inland Ghana, somewhere between Cape Coast and Kumasi. It was the height of the rainy season, drenched in humidity, and we were stranded in a small village whose name I can't remember. Our *tro tro*, as the Ghanaians call their privately run minibuses, had broken down and all its passengers, including the five goats on the roof, had been unloaded and told to wait.

Our group soon attracted the curiosity of the villagers, who took a break from their work in the surrounding fields to greet us and discuss our transport problem. A woman with a baby on her back brought plastic chairs and sat down with us to hear more about the country my friend Dani and I came from. All the while, her baby cried heartbreakingly.

The woman told us that she and the baby had been sick for a few days now. In an attempt to distract the child from its sorrows, I began to swing the colourful bracelet I was wearing. In no time the baby stopped crying and began to giggle. Its mother, visibly relieved, planted the child on my lap and said, 'She likes you. You can take her with you.' Dani and I laughed at what we thought was a joke and so did the other women around us. But the baby, glowing hot from a fever, refused to go anywhere else and spent the next few hours on my lap, playing, sleeping and cuddling up to me.

When our *tro tro* was repaired and we got ready to say goodbye, I turned towards the mother to hand her baby back. But she refused to take the child. 'You take her with you,' she said. 'Take her to your country. You can be her mother and look after her.' Shocked at what seemed to be a serious proposal, I asked if she wouldn't miss her daughter if she were sent off with a stranger. 'Look,' she said, 'my child is ill, she has a very high fever and I don't have any medicine. There's nothing here in this village, but where you come from she will have happiness and a good life. She wants to come with you.'

I left the village without the baby. Its heart-rending cry as I boarded the *tro tro* and waved goodbye has disturbed my dreams ever since, and I'm still baffled by the readiness of this woman to give away her only child to a stranger for a supposedly better life. Was life in the village really so miserable? Would there be no happiness in the baby's future life? How was I to explain that in the part of the world where I came from people's paths weren't necessarily paved with happiness? And these thoughts led me to the underlying question: what, in the end, makes life worthwhile?

In *Life Within Limits: Well-being in a World of Want,* anthropologist and author Michael Jackson sets off on a journey to explore exactly this feeling of existential dissatisfaction, this deeply human belief that life should offer us more than what it currently does. Returning to visit the Kuranko people in the village of Firawa in Sierra Leone – the place where his first ethnographic fieldwork took him more than thirty years ago, and where later he lived for a time – he tries to understand what constitutes human well-being. Sierra Leone frequently appears in lists of the world's 'least liveable' countries and is usually represented as a place of poverty, hopelessness and conflict. Using ethnography as a tool to look deep into people's everyday lives, Jackson shows that well-being is about more than financial or material stability.

Since Jackson first went to Sierra Leone, much has changed. On a political level, the country has been through a bloody civil war, traditional belief systems have been challenged, religious observance has changed and migration to other parts of the world has left its traces. The Kuranko people with whom Jackson has established long-lasting relationships have also changed – and so has the ethnographer himself. But he has stayed in touch with them through thick and thin, and it is the accounts of everyday life that he has collected along the way that make this poetically written book so gripping.

For an anthropologist, the technique of ethnography is, as Jackson puts it, 'a way of thinking oneself through in the place of another'. During his thirty years of fieldwork the New Zealander, who is currently a visiting professor at Harvard University, has shown that the themes that preoccupy scholars can be communicated to a wider audience. His books engage readers by presenting the stories yielded by relationships he has built with people during his fieldwork, and it is through the way they see the world that broader existential questions are raised and illuminated. As a phenomenologist, he never imposes ideas or frameworks on people's realities; instead, he focuses on 'things as they are' and on the way they unfold in front of our eyes when we engage with others and their experiences. But his large body of work looking at 'others' in order to reflect on 'ourselves' is never simply a cultural critique of 'the Western world'. In unfolding the struggles, heroic deeds, victories and losses of people's everyday lives, he touches on the very basics of a shared humanity that he aims to look at in the light of its connections rather than its disparities.

At times, *Life Within Limits* reads almost like a travel essay. The anthropologist isn't moving around in the way one would imagine the classic solitary researcher on a mission to observe how 'others' define well-being. Instead, Jackson is accompanied by his seventeen-year-old son, Joshua, and his young Kuranko friend, Sewa, who migrated to London some years ago. The company of the two young men, one making his first visit to Africa and the other visiting his home country, enriches the journey. Joshua's experiences reconnect his father to his own early travels through the country; Sewa, whose story as a migrant in London featured in Jackson's previous book, *Excursions*, allows the anthropologist to look at the topic of well-being through the 'double lens' of someone who was born into Kuranko society and left it behind in the hope of a better life in Europe.

For Sewa, everything in his home country is different from how he remembers it. The characterisations of mutual regard, solidarity and friendship, which he had so often used in London to describe life in his childhood village, have disappeared. Jackson takes Sewa's story as a starting point to think about the role of the past in our existential longing for something that goes beyond what life can offer us. This common human characteristic – the belief that the world was once a happier place but has fallen apart – shows that well-being, rather than being a simple and achievable goal, is a necessary fiction to keep us believing that there is something to live for. 'Like the idea of utopia,' Jackson writes, 'the idea of well-being captures a universal yearning to be more than we presently are and to have more than we presently possess.'

While material poverty plays an important role in the longing many young people feel for another, better place, it isn't necessarily the decisive factor. In Firawa, social harmony has traditionally been of greater importance and – at least during Jackson's first travels to Sierra Leone – poverty was accepted by people as being in the nature of things. But this view has changed radically. People now believe that poverty is the fault of those in power who have become wealthy at the expense of others. According to Jackson, this material scarcity translates into an existential feeling of being *without*, of being outside the same potentialities of other people's lives.

It is with the story of ten-year-old Sira from Firawa that Jackson comes close to the heart of the complexities that surround human well-being. One evening, when he is sitting around the campfire with Sewa, a group of young girls approaches them to sing a few songs. The anthropologist is immediately fascinated by the poetic and thoughtful lyrics. Later he finds out that one of them, Sira, had composed all the songs. Jackson becomes interested in the girl's story and visits her home. He is struck by the poverty. Sira and her mother live in a house that was burnt down during the war and has only partly been repaired. Her mother's only belongings are a mortar and pestle, a winnowing tray, a water pot and a fishing net. Sira used to be an excellent student, but she had to leave school after four years when her father left them and her mother could no longer afford the fees. As well as her talent for storytelling, the little girl also has the gift of divining. Twice a week she is visited by two djinns, she says, who show her how to collect medicinal plants from the bush and prepare herbal medicines to cure illnesses.

Although Sira doesn't have enough to eat she complains not about a lack of food but about the lack of love, recognition and opportunity. This makes Jackson wonder what his own response to her plight should be. Would enabling her to go back to school help her or would raising her hopes for a better life simply complicate things further? Perhaps she has already worked out a way of coping within the limits of her situation through the stories she tells in her songs? As Jackson remarks, it is never possible to know a situation so fully that one can judge with certainty how to respond. 'We act with good intentions, but the road to hell is paved with good intentions,' he writes. 'We think we choose, but our situations also choose us.' But these thoughts don't stop him from choosing to enable Sira to go back to school by paying her school fees.

For the Kuranko people the most important thing is to find the best way to bear the burdens of life. Drawing on this perspective, Jackson comes to the conclusion that well-being is not so much a reflection of hopes as a matter of learning how to live within limits. In Sira's case, this means 'making a virtue of her lot by singing on an empty belly'. Learning how to deal with the obstacles of everyday life entails more than the dream to escape or to be rescued. The difference between traditional and modern societies is first and foremost a difference between the limits humans have to struggle with. What really matters is that humans need to have a sense that they are not mere victims of whatever situation life throws them into. Rather, they need the feeling that their actions and thoughts make a difference.

The real value of Jackson's books lies in the way he manages to hold a mirror to ourselves by examining the way others perceive the world. Ours is a time in which happiness is seen as a measurable state to which everyone is entitled. Countries like Sierra Leone not only appear at the very bottom of international rankings of 'happiness' or 'quality of life' but have come to represent places where life is almost 'unliveable'. By dismissing suffering, pain and effort – those necessary counterparts of happiness – we risk losing the tools to deal with constraints; any deviation from monotonous happiness is perceived as a major disruption.

Anthropologist Arthur Kleinman once met a seventy-eight-year-old American artist who suffered from leukaemia. Tired by the attempts of people around him to make him hope for a happy ending, he asked, 'Do I have to go with a smile on my face? That seems to me ridiculous, and insulting.'[4] I think this man's question helps to explain why the Ghanaian woman's drastic call for my help was so disturbing. I was about to return to a highly individualised world in which people are led to believe that anything is possible and there are no borders or limitations – a view of life drastically out of step not only with life in that village, but also with human life in general. As Hannah Arendt writes in *The Human Condition*, pain and effort are not simply symptoms that can readily be removed from our lives; they are modes in which life makes itself felt. Referring to Greek mythology, she concludes that the 'easy life of the gods' would be a lifeless existence for humans. What marks us as genuinely human is exactly our ability to move amid the limits of the world we are born into.

That knowledge won't stop me from hoping things have changed for the better for the girl and her mother. Nor will it stop me from thinking that limitations are distributed unfairly. We mustn't demand that the poor and desperate simply accept these constraints. The people whose stories we hear in Jackson's book show that, despite everything, humans never cease to push the boundaries and will go on hoping for the easy life of the gods.

---

4   Arthur Kleinman, "'Everything That Really Matters': Social Suffering, Subjectivity, and the Remaking of Human Experience in a Disordering World," *Harvard Theological Review* 90, no. 3 (1997): 332.

THE HUMANE AND SYMPATHETIC EYE OF SAM HOOD

RICHARD JOHNSTONE

24 March 2014

S am Hood began his photographic apprenticeship in the mid 1880s, when he was barely into his teens. He was still working as a photographer on the day he died, at the age of eighty-one. That adds up to a long career, and it made for a lot of photographs, many of which can be seen on the websites of the State Library of New South Wales and the Australian National Maritime Museum, among others, and on Trove and Flickr. The State Library's Hood archive alone – evocatively described in the catalogue as 'Sydney streets, buildings, people, activities and events' – comprises some 11,400 images. This sounds like a large number, and if Sam Hood had been a painter rather than a photographer, it would have been a very large number indeed.

But photographic legacies routinely run into the tens and even the hundreds of thousands. The recently rediscovered Chicago street photographer Vivian Maier is survived by an archive of 100,000 images, saved from probable destruction by sheer chance. The photographer and photographic historian Jerry L Thompson, in his recent polemic *Why Photography Matters*, tells us that the archive of Garry Winogrand, whom many would nominate as the best of all twentieth-century street photographers, runs to almost a million items, not a few of which Winogrand has never seen.

Yet archives of even these astonishing proportions can blend, unremarked or overlooked or passed over, into the vast cache of photographs already in existence, or about to be brought into existence by people whose careers are photography and by the many more people who just like taking photographs. And as we take more and more photographs, on our compact cameras and our smartphones, we are taking less time to look at them. The contemporary photograph is no longer so much a record of the moment as a part of the moment itself, an integrated component of whatever it is we happen to be doing. Taking a photograph is something you do when you're already doing something.

At the other end of the photographic spectrum is the singular photograph, the work of art that might hang on a gallery or a lounge room wall. It is made with the intention of engaging us, persuading us to pause and reflect on its content, to look at it more than once, and to remember it. Unlike the smartphone photo, which typically favours for its subject the spontaneity (or apparent spontaneity) of the fleeting moment, the photograph-as-art will often highlight its own contrivance, by being elaborately and obviously staged, for example, or by juxtaposing people and objects in ways that emphasise the stylised formality and artificiality of the image. This kind of juxtaposition can be seen in the work of the many contemporary photographers whose elaborate 'sets' and staged incongruity seem designed to distance the work from the smartphone culture and the inherent forgettability of the typical digital image.

Contrivances like these are an attempt to give substance to our casual, and often misleading, habit of describing photos as 'memories' by staging and photographing an event that is not part of the flow of life but a deliberate and striking intrusion into that flow, something that will be remembered for its very intrusiveness. Sometimes this can work to undeniable effect, as in Richard Renaldi's photographs of complete strangers – strangers to him and to one another – who have been persuaded to pose in attitudes of intimacy, with arms linked or wrapped around shoulders or encircling waists, in imitation of a relationship that does not exist. It sounds faintly gimmicky but it can also produce some affecting – and memorable – images.

Not everyone would agree. Jerry Thompson, for one, has little patience with this kind of consciously artistic or staged photography. He dismisses those photos that imitate iconic paintings as 'decorative self-indulgence', for example, which seems a bit harsh, but the question he then asks is one that goes to the heart of our expectations of photography and of photographs: 'Shouldn't photography – which began as a hyperdetailed record of our shared visible world – provide a close, critical examination of that world, the kind of jarring irritant able to rouse viewers out of a complacent, forgetful slumber, and into a wakeful regard of *what is*?'

It is a plea for the kind of photograph that sits – perhaps somewhat uncomfortably these days – in the middle of the photographic spectrum, with the smartphone snap at one end and the photograph of complete strangers touching one another, or the super-saturated tableau of people dressed up in renaissance costume, at the other. It's the kind of photograph that manages to bring an artistic eye to the world as it is – or was, at the time when the photograph was taken. It assumes a world that can never be completely contained or managed by a photograph or a photographer, however skilled he or she may be. Chance always plays a part. 'Pictures by even the greatest photographers,' observes Thompson, 'insist on containing elements of the outside world that just happened to be there.'

•

Sam Hood was that kind of photographer – perhaps the most common kind in the history of photography – the kind who brought a photographic eye to the 'world as it is'. As Alan Davies describes in his 1991 book about Sam Hood and his work, *Sydney Exposures*, he grasped whatever opportunities there were to take photographs and be paid for it. He photographed ships in Sydney Harbour and sold the images to sailors as mementoes of their voyage. He took studio portraits, and he supplied images to a dozen or so different newspapers in the twenties and thirties. He undertook commissions to document buildings and events – public ceremonies, sporting matches, first nights, weddings. In all this, it is doubtful that Hood ever thought of himself as an artist rather than as a working photographer whose work was his life.

Two young girls holding hands (c. 1920). Australian National Maritime Museum

And yet in many ways he behaved like an artist. He was obsessive about every aspect of photography, overseeing the entire process to ensure that the final image was as it should be. He survived many setbacks, including the prospect of re-establishing his studio after it was burnt down on two separate occasions. He pressed on, inseparable from his camera – the same one for forty years, as Davies reports, despite opportunities to upgrade. It reached a point where the camera had been repaired and patched so often, and had acquired so many tics, that 'no one else could use it'.

It is difficult to know how to 'read' Hood's photographs today, just as it is difficult to know how to approach any photographic collection or archive. We are caught between our habit of scrolling through the albums on our screens – usually so quickly that it can almost be like watching a film – and the demand of the single iconic image that we pause and contemplate in isolation. But there is also a middle way. Sam Hood, and photographers like him – artisanal rather than consciously, or self-consciously, artistic – are best appreciated and understood by means of a hybrid of these two extremes, a kind of slow scrolling.

Individual photographs by Hood don't generally stand out immediately, at least not in a way that invites us to brand them as particularly representative or 'iconic', as we might brand a Max Dupain or a David Moore, for instance. They need to be taken as a whole or, given that tens of thousands of images are difficult to take in as a whole, in chunks, further defined and refined by subcategories of chronology or genre or subject. In this way, we can build up a sense of a particular time and place, as captured by a particular photographic sensibility.

Admittedly, not all of Hood's photographs encourage us to scroll slowly. There are, for all but the most enthusiastic of maritime enthusiasts, only so many ships one can look at in one session. Hood also had a weakness for photographing people with animals – women with cats, men with elephants, a girl with an Angora rabbit, images that fit neatly now with the web's fascination with cuteness, but don't encourage us to linger.

On the other hand, Hood had a special talent for observing and photographing people, and especially people in groups; sometimes in their hundreds, lined up in quasi-military formation or squashed together at a town hall hop, but more often in compositions of two to a dozen figures. The photographs are posed, reflecting the technical capacities and photographic conventions of the time, but for all that they convey a sense both of natural intimacy and of an occasion shared, while preserving the individuality of the people who make up the composition.

In the photograph of 'two young girls holding hands' which forms part of the Samuel J Hood Studio Collection at the National Maritime Museum, the young girls of the caption, who are clearly twins, are posing face-on to the camera. In his characteristic way, Hood conveys naturalness within formality, individuality within likeness. The background is quite geometric – a long strip of an unidentified and unidentifiable building forms the upper border. Below that is a hedge and some vegetation, carefully clipped and tamed, that stretches across the frame. In the foreground, in contrast to these vaguely modernist horizontal lines, are the two girls, barely containing their exuberance and enjoyment of life. Most strikingly – and against the long tradition of photographing twins and look-alike siblings that owes so much to Hood's near contemporary, the great August Sander, who emphasised likeness and encouraged the viewer to spot the subtle differences – the girls here, while dressed alike and, as far as we can guess, identical, have quite different facial expressions. They are together but also themselves.

Politicians lolling on the grass at Canberra (1927).
State Library of New South Wales

The same mixture of naturalness and formality is struck in Hood's photograph of 'politicians lolling on the grass at Canberra', taken in 1927 and now held by the State Library of New South Wales. At first and perhaps even second glance it is not an especially remarkable or distinguished photograph. And yet, in looking beyond its undoubted historical interest – the figure second from the right is the Indian politician Sir RK Shanmukham Chetty, who was visiting Australia as part of a Commonwealth parliamentary delegation and only a few years later became India's representative at the League of Nations – we can see a number of Hood's characteristic touches. These politicians lolling on the grass of Lanyon Homestead – particularly the two in the middle – have clearly been directed, but for all that there is a relaxed if sober conviviality about the scene, and a humanising contrast between the important business that brings them together and the fact that they are sitting on the grass, chatting, staring into space, smoking a cigarette or drinking tea.

Charles Parsons & Company (1935). State Library of New South Wales

As is often the case with Hood, the background is formal, with a structured, almost geometric feel to it. The view of the verandah is divided, along classical lines, into three panels; there is even a column two-thirds of the way across to break the horizontal flow, in a way that is pleasing to the eye. In the middle panel, seated on a sofa, are two men observing the main subject of the photograph from behind. Their presence sets up a mild visual joke, as these two rather more conventionally seated and suited figures observe their comparatively frivolous (these things are relative) colleagues lolling on the grass. The right-hand panel contains a set of French doors; we can see nature reflected in the glass. Against the formal background and complex perspective, we can also spot, to the right of the frame, a detail that seems to have crept in unnoticed: a lone briefcase and a hat, also lolling on the grass but bereft of their owner. No one is looking directly at the camera, or indeed at one another. And yet the overall impression – reinforced by the domestic touch provided by the teacups – is one of amiability and professional goodwill.

•

Hood's way with photographing groups can also be seen in an image featured in Alan Davies' monograph. It shows six men, all quite formally dressed, engaged in their work at a fabric warehouse in Sydney in 1935. The long line of a cutting desk stretches diagonally across the bottom third of the frame. In the upper background we see more long lines, in the form of rows of shelves extending into the left-hand distance, each shelf piled high with neatly wrapped bolts of material that rise to the very ceiling and threaten to push their way through. In front of the shelves are the men, going about their business.

What strikes us first in this photo is that none of them is looking at any of the others. They are shown engaged in their various tasks – measuring and cutting material, making entries in a ledger. One man is retrieving a bolt of material from the top shelf. Another man – a buyer, a customer? – appears to be examining a sample. Some elements of the photograph's composition seem to work against any suggestion of intimacy or camaraderie, and yet that is precisely what is conveyed. This impression is helped, perhaps, by the fact that on the faces of three of the men, particularly the one who is cutting material, there are signs that laughter may not be far away.

This sense of enjoyment, or ease, in one another's company is characteristic of Hood's group photographs. Sometimes the enjoyment and the relaxation are palpable, sometimes implied. Either way, we as viewers don't feel as if we could enter easily into the group, becoming its next member. Instead we witness, and almost envy, its cohesiveness, which seems to spring from the kind of naturalness and lack of affectation that is difficult to replicate in these more knowing times. There is nothing 'knowing' about Hood's photographs, despite the often sophisticated nature of his compositional sense. For that reason alone, they belong quite clearly to another age.

Jack Gacek, wrestler (1938). State Library of New South Wales

This is not simply a function of the times in which the photographs were made; old photographs can sometimes feel surprisingly contemporary. Hood's photographs, however, do not give us a clear line to the past. If anything, they announce their pastness, if only because they come so clearly from an age in which people's self-consciousness in posing was an essential part of their naturalness. In Hood's world, people seem connected with each other rather than with us as viewers; groups provide consolation; individuality is downplayed. Although Hood's portraits of individuals can sometimes express uncomplicated good cheer, as in his engaging photograph from 1938 of the wrestler Jack Gacek, it is also noticeable how often the individual in a single, observant portrait by Hood will seem lonely and uncertain, displaying rather less of the strength and vitality that seems to come from being photographed in company.

Bourke & Fitzroy Streets corner grocery store (1934). State Library of New South Wales

In one of Hood's better-known photographs, a portrait of a woman standing in the doorway of her corner shop, the woman is almost secondary to the shop itself, which takes up most of the frame. Her stance is a combination of assertiveness and defensiveness – she has one hand on her hip; her other hand rests protectively against her neck, in a once-common social gesture that betrayed anxiety. The inside of the shop behind her is in near darkness, while the outside, including the windows and even the footpath, is covered with handwritten signs, advertising the goods within. All this visual chatter threatens to dominate the image, quelling the figure of the woman who, despite her squared-on stance, seems in danger of being overwritten by the words that have her surrounded.

But if we move on, continuing to scroll slowly through the photographs of Samuel Hood, we will soon tack away from such sobering thoughts. In his group photographs in particular, Hood's subjects appear with a kind of awkward confidence, their general optimism, and ease in one another's company, captured by a remarkably humane and sympathetic eye.

MITCHELL, MURDOCH AND ME

PETER BRENT

13 October 2016

When I answered the phone on 11 July 2007 it was Chris Mitchell's personal assistant on the line. It turned out to be a courtesy call from *The Australian*'s editor-in-chief to inform me that I would be starring in the next day's editorial – and not pleasantly. It would consist of a demolition of online critics of the newspaper – mostly me, complete with photo – in retaliation for the horrid things I'd written on my website about how the paper reported its fortnightly opinion poll, Newspoll.

This wasn't the first phone conversation I'd had with Mitchell. That had been the previous December, after I'd emailed him out of the blue about a Newspoll pitting a hypothetical Kevin Rudd–Julia Gillard Labor leadership team against the incumbents, Kim Beazley and Jenny Macklin (why were there no figures on voting intentions?). That email had resulted, to my surprise, in an hour-long chat, in which Mitchell schmoozed and flattered and tried to get me to see things his way. He obviously spent a lot of time reading online opinions about his newspaper. Any dividends from that December charm offensive were short-term, because here we were eight months later. Rudd was leading Labor and rampaging against the Howard government in the polls, and *The Oz* was still clutching at Newspoll straws. You can read the comments that sparked the call online.[5] That July conversation got quite heated and ended, I think word for word, like this:

Me: 'Oh, come on, Chris.' (As in, 'Don't be ridiculous.')

Mitchell: 'I'm going to go you so personally!'

Me: 'See ya.'

Mitchell: 'Bye.'

For the rest of the day my imagination ran wild, conjuring up visions of an investigative unit digging up embarrassments from my distant past. But when the editorial was uploaded early the next morning, the long rant – the social media are parasites; we are the best in the business;

---

5   Peter Brent, "Oh Martin, What Are You Doing?," *Mumble* (blog), July 11, 2007, http://www.mumble.com.au/index_oldish32.html#martin.

we know Newspoll – pulled its punches in its treatment of me. Mitchell explained later that he'd cooled off. There was no photo.

This event, which academic Sally Young calls the 'July 12 incident', has been described as 'indicative of the emerging crisis in professional journalism as the traditional "gatekeeping" prerogatives of large media organisations are challenged in an age of Web 2.0 technologies and internet journalism.'[6] Maybe. It led, I believe, to the resignation from the paper of blogger Tim Dunlop, after his response was pulled from *The Oz*'s website. Since then, editorials like that have become a regular feature of the paper, only these days the target is Twitter.

Correspondence between Mitchell and me continued for several years; my email folders contain sixty-nine emails from him between 2007 and 2010, the large bulk in response to requests I'd sent about Newspoll. Sometimes these elicited phone calls instead (always through the personal assistant). He regularly sent me Newspoll results on the night before publication and allowed me to post them even before the newspaper did. Was I bought off? I did largely stop criticising Dennis Shanahan's Newspoll coverage.

•

Fast-forward to Budget morning 2010. Chris and I are having breakfast at Canberra's Hyatt Hotel and he's hiring me to join the paper as a blogger. Charm setting dialled up, he drops several confidences: that the 2006 leadership Newspoll I'd criticised had come after a request from Rudd, phoning from the Great Wall of China where he was in the company of Simon Crean and Kim Carr (since revealed to the reading public by Mitchell himself); that Rudd, after becoming prime minister, had wanted Shanahan to be his chief of staff (later revealed by Peter van Onselen); that Mitchell had wanted to hire Annabel Crabb but reckoned he couldn't compete with the ABC's financial largesse. I, of course, was much more affordable, and would start in July. Just do what you've been doing, he said, write whatever you want, 'but don't bag Dennis'.

I got a floating desk in the Canberra bureau and became, more or less, just another employee several rungs down. Regular email correspondence was no longer appropriate. But I did retain some special privileges. At

---

6 Axel Bruns, "The active audience: Transforming journalism from gatekeeping to gatewatching," in *Making Online News: The Ethnography of New Media Production*, ed. Chris Paterson and David Domingo (New York: Peter Lang, 2008).

that May breakfast, Mitchell said I should go to him with any work issues that couldn't be resolved to my satisfaction. In 2011 I took up this offer when a directive arrived from the editor (one rung down from Mitchell) that I should stick to writing about polls and numbers and leave the wider commentary to others. An email from me to the editor-in-chief boss saw the instruction comprehensively and emphatically reversed within hours.

And aside from requests for particular stories for the print edition during the 2010 campaign, and one during Barack Obama's 2011 trip (about previous Newspoll boosts after presidential visits), I did enjoy carte blanche. Self-censorship, conscious and otherwise, is of course another matter; I certainly didn't disparage the paper's reporting of Newspoll (or of anything else, but my self-imposed purview had always been quite limited). Any conflict of interest had greater influence on my words on Twitter, where comments tend to be more wide-ranging. When, for example, Rupert Murdoch started tweeting, I regularly had to bite my tongue. Anyway, Mitchell retired last December after almost fourteen years as the paper's editor-in-chief and then wrote a book called *Making Headlines*, published this month. Most of the interesting gossipy titbits, about his interactions with prime ministers, have already been excerpted or reported. Of course it's a self-serving tome – why else do people write books about themselves? – but it's not an especially self-aggrandising entry in the genre. Compared to, say, former *Sunday Times* editor Andrew Neil's *Full Disclosure* (1996), Mitchell's memoir is a paragon of modesty.

Unsurprisingly, Mitchell re-argues various controversies, starting with Manning Clark's alleged Order of Lenin, from his time as editor of the Brisbane *Courier-Mail*. Then there's the invasion of Iraq, which Mitchell says he personally opposed:

> [It was] a tricky time to be a newspaper editor. Management ran very tight controls on all the paper's coverage, but I wanted to make sure that, whatever our position in editorials, the news accounts were accurate and not politically skewed towards George W Bush.

This sits inside a general assertion that 'avid readers of *The Oz* would accept that the paper's news pages are straight down the line, even if the opinion page and editorials are dominated by an economically liberal point of view at odds with left-wing collectivism'.

'Straight down the line' is a jaw-dropping assertion few would agree with; and while the editorials might have been 'economically liberal', that was only part of it, sitting as they often did inside more comprehensive culture war paraphernalia. Naturally, there's much in the book about *The Australian*'s reporting of climate change, but how do you defend the indefensible? By arguing that rival organisations are captured by progressive orthodoxy, contaminated by social media, estranged from ordinary Australians, and so on. Only *The Australian* was appropriately inquisitive and enquiring. Apparently, '[t]he latest polling in the northern hemisphere now suggests that more than half of all voters in the United States and Europe are sceptical about the science'. It would be useful to know the source of this surprising finding, but it's not provided. As with Mitchell's columns in *The Australian* since his retirement, the most interesting parts of *Making Headlines* deal with media matters. The least interesting are suck-a-lemon-and-let-rip missives fired at 'the left' and the progressives in Fairfax and the ABC, who are out of touch with 'middle Australia' and captured by Labor and the Greens – you know how it goes.

In *Man Bites Murdoch*, former News Corp editor Bruce Guthrie made quite a fuss about Rupert Murdoch's comment that he valued loyalty in an employee above all else. It's actually an unexceptional sentiment from a business leader, but when that business is the media it can be very tricky. Murdoch has long been accused of aligning his coverage with his business pursuits, and Mitchell's book contains a no doubt carefully composed acknowledgement of 'the possibility that Rupert Murdoch's commercial interests might at times play out in the journalism of his products. Undoubtedly this is the case for all media proprietors.' The book drips with great affection for two public figures: Murdoch and ex–prime minister John Howard. The former is understandable, given the long relationship under which Mitchell's career flourished; the second, given Howard's long stint in power, provides vindication of Mitchell's political worldview. It's the big ideological battles again: cue references to rival journalists underestimating that colossus's connection with blue-collar workers, and so on. Rudd, Julia Gillard and Tony Abbott aren't fit to lick Howard's boots, nor Bob Hawke's or Paul Keating's for that matter. Malcolm Turnbull just might be, but since the book was written that's not turning out so well. Some of the cognitive dissonance jars. Mitchell reckons politicians really must not stray from the aspirations of mainstream Australians – that was Rudd and Gillard's mistake – yet the leaders he most admired were those prepared to take difficult, unpopular decisions.

It is vital that media players similarly remain in touch with the interests of ordinary people, yet many of *The Australian*'s battles – Gillian Triggs, the ABC, climate change – were surely a huge yawn to anyone outside the

5 per cent interested in politics, and to many inside. There's something or other about Pauline Hanson, and now Donald Trump, suggesting that lefties shouldn't criticise them as it only adds to their appeal – or something – you know how it goes; it doesn't really make sense. And, needless to say, Howard got it exactly right when he refused to condemn Hanson. We know that a decade ago Mitchell was getting worked up about blogs; in the final years it was Twitter. Those editorials pummelling a particular segment of society must leave the bulk of the readership scratching their heads.

•

Still ... There have always been idiosyncratic, biased newspapers and always will be. Mitchell's accusations of progressive groupthink inside the ABC and Fairfax aren't without foundation, and his diagnosis of *The Age* and *The Sydney Morning Herald* business plans – so much clickbait fluff and stories based on tweets, driven by traffic numbers and shrinking advertising revenue, behind a highly porous paywall, 'reverse published' the following day, all spiralling downwards – is persuasive. You could make an argument that *The Australian*'s (and News Corp's) top-down enforced right-wing skew provides a useful balance to the bottom-up left-wing tendencies of the others. This online world of ours does contain no shortage of self-ordained media 'experts' who, it seems from their writing, believe all media products should (a) reflect their own personal beliefs and (b) be provided free of charge.

Many who know these things say *The Oz* under Mitchell – the regular vindictiveness and ideological indulgences aside – was supremely well edited. I'm no media expert but to me it remains generally authoritative and hard-edged – and the home page is Kardashian-free. It does investigations, breaks stories and is what Murdoch most desires: influential in the press gallery and among the wider political class. And he had the good sense to hire me.

In 2014 I was downsized; this time my entreaties to up high came to nought. Mitchell left the building in December 2015 and the following month my marching orders arrived.

That editor I'd had put in his place was now editor-in-chief.

THE PICCOLI PRESCRIPTION

TOM GREENWELL

7 March 2018

He's the Nat who gave a Gonski. In charge of schools in New South Wales from 2011 to 2017, Adrian Piccoli was a sometimes-lonely conservative voice championing needs-based school funding. Whether his stance was inspired by the experience of representing a rural seat in the state's south-west, or by a Catholic sense of social justice, or simply by a temperament inclined to consensus, it's almost impossible to imagine the Gonski reforms without him.

Consider two critical moments in the unfolding of school funding policy this decade. The first is in 2013. The Gillard government is in its dying days and the shadow education minister, Christopher Pyne, is attempting to sabotage the prime minister's signature reform by calling on state Coalition counterparts not to sign Gonski funding agreements. Queensland, Western Australia and the Northern Territory heed Pyne's call. Victoria wavers. A national initiative with just South Australia, Tasmania and the Australian Capital Territory on board won't amount to much.

But then, in April, New South Wales signs on and Gillard now has the largest jurisdiction in the country, led by a Coalition government, on her side. And a National Party minister, Adrian Piccoli, is spruiking her policy, giving it serious bipartisan credibility. The centre holds and, a month before the 2013 federal election, opposition leader Tony Abbott feels enough pressure to join a purported 'unity ticket' on the issue. When Pyne attempts a backflip only four months later, the public outcry quickly forces him into a humiliating reversal.

Fast-forward to May 2017, and the second moment. The Turnbull government resurrects Gonski, and the man himself appears in the flesh at a press conference for the benefit of the sceptics. The not-so-subtle subtext is that the government is jettisoning Pyne's 'money doesn't matter' mantra. Money clearly does matter – otherwise the government wouldn't be announcing a commitment to spend more of it. Again, Christopher Pyne is humiliated. Again, Piccoli's role is critical.

For the past four years he had been calling on his federal Coalition counterparts to make an announcement just like this one: to commit to delivering the final two-thirds of Gonski money. Throughout that time, he consistently argued that getting the funding right is a precondition for a successful school system. In his own state, he implemented the needs-based Resource Allocation Model. And now, the new federal education minister, Simon Birmingham, clearly wants to be less like his predecessor and more like Piccoli.

Given Piccoli's influence on the national conversation, it's fitting that the new research outfit he is heading at the University of New South Wales has been called the Gonski Institute of Education. 'It's going to sit in between the academic world and the practice world,' Piccoli explains to me when I meet up with him at the National Library in Canberra. 'Let's take what schools and systems and leaders often need and then use research to address what they need. And the other way round.' If researchers are 'doing really good stuff that has a distinct application, part of our role is to turn it into something that is actually usable by schools'.

Piccoli has come to Canberra to speak at an event hosted by the influential Grattan Institute looking at what the federal government should do to 'drive improvement' in school education. The occasion has been prompted by the new review David Gonski is conducting into Australia's schools, announced when Gonski joined Malcolm Turnbull and Simon Birmingham at that May 2017 press conference. Where Gonski's 2011 report was on funding (how much and who gets it), his new review will make recommendations on 'how money is best used' to 'achieve educational excellence'.

Total government funding to NSW public schools increased by $1073 per student between 2012–13 and 2015–16, and by $586 per student in private schools, according to the Productivity Commission's 2018 *Report on Government Services*. This is the tangible part of Adrian Piccoli's legacy. Disadvantaged children in New South Wales are now receiving a substantially better-resourced education. But has it made a difference? Given the current Gonski review's emphasis on spending educational dollars efficiently and effectively, I ask Piccoli if there's anything to show yet for the extra money. Piccoli replies:

> Last year's NAPLAN results were the best results that New South Wales has ever had … Perhaps not across every testing domain but across quite a few of them. We had the premier's priority, which was increasing the number of students in the top two [NAPLAN] bands by 8 per cent over the four years from 2015 to 2019. And now we're already at that, two

years ahead ... just the other day the *Closing the Gap* report came out and it showed that since 2011, they've doubled the retention rate for Indigenous students in New South Wales. I think it's still below the state average but it's a doubling. So we're seeing lots of improvement.

These results aren't definitive, but when many indicators show Australian schooling stagnating or even going backwards, the NSW data can only be seen as promising. So what does Piccoli – as the former minister who got a lot right when it came to the nexus between funding and outcomes – believe is the key to driving improvement in Australian schools?

His response is a surprising one. He suggests that maybe the real change needs to happen outside the school gates:

I think we have a cultural problem in Australia when it comes to education ... This is one of the things that is actually worthy of research. Is Australia suffering from twenty-five years of uninterrupted economic growth? Are we becoming complacent about how hard it is to get a job? Are we saying, 'It doesn't matter how well you do at school because, you know, you can [still] get a job'?

Getting more pointed, he adds, 'I think parents, I think the public – even the way that adults reflect upon schools and teachers in front of children, generally speaking, doesn't respect schools and doesn't respect teachers.' He presented the same view at the public forum that evening, eliciting a headline in *The Sydney Morning Herald*: 'Former Education Minister Blames Complacent Parents for School Results'. That might be an oversimplification, but he surely knew what he was doing. He clearly sees a role for himself as a provocateur, prepared to tell the community, in effect, 'Sure, you want schools to deliver all these things. And do it better than ever before. But it's a two-way street.'

It's an interesting – and potentially valuable – way to position himself. But, it's not immediately clear where he hopes this kind of conversation might lead. Reassuringly, he is not suggesting that 'you deliberately throw the economy into a recession' as a wake-up call to parents. And he recognises that complacency may be better than being 'in the situation of some of these other countries where kids' stress levels are through the roof'.

So, what exactly is he suggesting?

Piccoli is clearly frustrated about a range of signals that invite students (and their parents) to take school less seriously than he believes they should:

> A number of universities don't even require maths [at school] to do maths at university. I mean, to me, that just kind of does my head in ... Now, a big chunk of the kids in Year 12, in New South Wales, get a place at university before they even do the HSC exam. I've had lots of principals tell me that we should change the rules.

Equally, Piccoli is concerned about the relative ease of entry into the teaching profession:

> When you think about professions that are highly regarded, it's pretty closely aligned with how difficult they are to get into ... You know, doctors, lawyers – you must be smart because they're hard to get into. Whereas teaching – you know, 'I didn't get into anything else. It was my last option. Didn't get into physio, so I went into teaching.'

The result, Piccoli believes, is that teachers are not accorded the respect they deserve:

> I mean if you sit around a table and say, 'Oh yeah, what do you do for a living? I'm a school teacher.' You'll most likely hear somebody say, 'Oh aren't you lucky you get all those school holidays?' But if you say, 'I'm a doctor,' they'll go, 'Oh wow.'

If Piccoli's views of education – and human motivation – rely too heavily on instrumental self-interest, there's an undeniable kernel of truth in what he is saying. And as minister he took significant steps to enhance the standing of the teaching profession. He instituted more demanding prerequisites for undergraduate teaching courses. To study to become a teacher, NSW school leavers now need to have three Band 5 HSC results (meaning that they must have ended up in the top 20 per cent of their cohort in at least three subjects, including English). 'So we introduced a minimum standard,' he says, 'which I hope is one of the things Gonski recommends.'

Piccoli thinks it is an example of where the Commonwealth can play a useful role in supporting the state and territory governments that run schools:

> Where the federal government does it, you get more consistency nationally ... We now have the situation in New South Wales where we have higher standards than our neighbouring states, so some universities are getting round it by enrolling students from other states.

The Commonwealth's responsibility for tertiary education means it doesn't have to use the blunt instrument of HSC results and can allow universities some discretion about the criteria (academic results, aptitude tests, interviews, principal recommendations) they use to select the teachers of the future.

When Piccoli talks of a cultural problem in Australia, he is clearly thinking of high-performing Asian nations (as well as high-performing Australian children from Asian backgrounds), but he also appears to have Finland in mind. In December came the news that Piccoli would be joined at the Gonski Institute by the man who has done the most to spread the word about Finland's success, Pasi Sahlberg. Thinking about a country like Finland helps make Piccoli's point clearer. To take one example, Sahlberg has written about how his niece missed out on entry to a teaching degree. 'Finnish primary school teacher education programs that lead to an advanced, research-based degree are so popular among young Finns,' he writes, 'that only one in ten applicants is accepted each year.'[7]

And yet Finnish teacher salaries differ little from Australia's or those in comparable countries. There seems to be something else going on in relation to how the culture thinks about the importance of education. And it's that 'something else' that Adrian Piccoli wants us to think more deeply about.

•

On the eve of the release of a new Gonski report, the politics of school education involve the interplay of three distinct but related questions.

---

7 Pasi Sahlberg, "Q: What Makes Finnish Teachers So Special? A: It's not Brains," *The Guardian*, March 31, 2015, https://www.theguardian.com/education/2015/mar/31/finnish-teachers-special-train-teach.

How much do we need to spend? Who gets it? And what's the smartest way of spending it?

The Turnbull government's narrative is that the school funding wars are over. This time, it really is on a unity ticket. Everyone supports needs-based funding now, it says, so let's move on (to the conversation about return on investment, which the new Gonski review is intended to engender).

Unfortunately, it's not that simple. Struggling schools are still a very long way from entering needs-based funding nirvana. Gonski 2.0 delayed delivery of the full needs-based Schooling Resource Standard, or SRS, until 2027. And even more disconcertingly, most public schools may continue to be underfunded even then.

The crucial technicality is that the Commonwealth has taken responsibility for delivering 80 per cent of the SRS of private schools but only 20 per cent of public schools' SRS, leaving the states and territories to make up the difference. The problem, as Piccoli acknowledges, is that 'some states fund above 20 per cent of the SRS to non-government schools and below 80 per cent of the SRS to government schools'. In fact, on the current trajectory, public schools in New South Wales are on track to receive 91 per cent of their SRS in 2027, while Victorian public schools will be at just 86 per cent of their needs-based entitlement, Northern Territory public schools at 87 per cent, and public schools in other jurisdictions will also remain underfunded.[8] Hundreds of private schools will continue to be overfunded. If that scenario unfolds, school funding in Australia will be neither nationally consistent nor needs-based nor sector-blind.

I ask Piccoli – as somebody with a deep commitment to equity, whose time in government focused on advocating and implementing needs-based funding – whether the states should respond to the Commonwealth's 80–20 rules by realigning how they are allocating their funds to public and private schools. He bats the question away, saying, 'This is what the Commonwealth is requiring states to do.'

The Commonwealth is negotiating funding agreements with the states that would require them to deliver 75 per cent of the SRS for public schools (not the full 80 per cent). It has not signalled any intention to require states to bring funding of private schools back down to 20 per cent of the SRS.

At this point, Piccoli only offers generalities:

---

8   Trevor Cobbold, "Gonski 2.0 Is the Best Special Deal Private Schools Have Ever Had," Save Our Schools, December 10, 2017, http://www.saveourschools.com.au/funding/new-figures-confirm-more-private-schools-will-be-over-funded-under-gonski-20.

Everyone goes, 'We love needs-based funding.' Well, that's what it is. You can't say, 'I like needs-based funding for somebody else and not for me.' It doesn't work that way. You're either for needs-based funding or you're not for needs-based funding.

That's true. And the trouble is, unless we get all three things right – the right spending on the right students in the right way – we're unlikely to change Australia's educational culture. As head of the Gonski Institute, Adrian Piccoli is set to play a fascinating role in debates on all three questions. It's only to be hoped that he directs his provocations at politicians as well as parents.

BREAKFAST IN AMERICA

GRAEME DOBELL

10 October 2017

An Australian in the United States is branded on the tongue. The moment you speak, they know you're not from around here. In previous decades, the question was usually whether you were English or Irish. As a bloke in Maryland joked the other day, taking me for a Pom, 'We Americans think you people speak our language real good.'

On this front, I can report progress. These days, Australia is often the first guess. And this time I haven't once had the comic confusion over Austria and Australia.

One other big difference has been noticeable during these six weeks in Washington, New York and up the east coast. On previous visits – under Reagan, Clinton and Obama – being identified as not from around here never once triggered a question about what we thought of the president. The United States is a world confidently unto itself, so there was only mild interest in outsider views. And the personality of the president never came up. It does now.

Grappling with the meaning of Donald Trump has trumped questions about kangaroos and what season it is in Oz. That's why it was no surprise to see a glum Malcolm Turnbull as one of the faces on the cover of *Foreign Affairs* magazine's September–October edition, 'The View from Abroad', reporting on how allies are responding to Trump.

My random sampling finds that viewers within America are just as mystified as we are. Some are amazed and scared and outraged. Some, though, love what they see: the Donald 'flipping the bird' at the system via tirades and tantrums; the tweeting, trumpeting troll-in-chief.

•

The lore and the laughs of the travelling-correspondent game decree that a hack arriving in a country afresh should make all grand pronouncements within weeks of landing. After that, the gradual growth of understanding and accumulation of facts tend to get in the way of sweeping assertions.

Sending this letter after six weeks means I'm just covered by the impressions/pronouncements rule. My conclusions:

> • Despite all its moving parts, or perhaps because of them, the American system is working well under the Trump pressure test.
> • US economic indicators are really starting to glow after eight slow years; the engine is pumping.
> • Americans are as positive as ever about themselves and their country. This is a nation of gusto, from its arguments to its eats. For gastronomic gusto, order the Texas ribs anywhere, but go to Maryland for the crab cakes. For a good argument about anything, just find a New Yorker.
> • If Trump doesn't eat himself to a heart attack with all those extra helpings of dessert, he's got every chance – based on the economy and the way America treats sitting presidents – of getting a second term. To be rejected by two-thirds of Americans and embraced by one-third could be enough – he's done it once.

On the system working as it should, one of the great pleasures of eating breakfast in America is still the chance to consume *The New York Times*, *The Washington Post* and *The Wall Street Journal*. For an old hack, this is bliss. After forty-five years as a journo, I've a simple answer to that question about which books most influenced my life: newspapers.

The Donald is a magnificent challenge for American journos. The *Times* and the *Post* have been exemplary. New players like *Politico* are doing lots of lifting. Hard times demand hard news. Strange times can be strangely stimulating for hacks, and they are serving America well.

The crumbling foundations and facades of the media world may mean this is the last great newspaper war between the *Times* and the *Post*. But what a great and worthy war, fought for, and with, the best traditional weapons.

The walk down Pennsylvania Avenue between the US Capitol building and the White House takes you past Newseum, a museum dedicated to the role of a free press in a democracy. Carved into the front wall, a couple of storeys high, are the words of one of the most profoundly revolutionary texts ever proclaimed by government: the US First Amendment, guaranteeing freedom of religion, speech, the press and assembly, and the right to 'petition', or argue against, your own government.

It's emblematic of the afflictions of American newspapers that the Newseum is in financial trouble. The America of the First Amendment, though, is doing fine, despite the Trump stress test.

On any given day, the *Times* or the *Post* can make you confident about both America and its journalism. Indeed, the Sunday *New York Times* shines as a weekly expression of the American experience; on a good weekend, make that the American civilisation in all its hues.

While the *Post* and the *Times* are feeding on the richest of meat, the poor old *Wall Street Journal* is on a leash. Its owner, Rupert Murdoch, isn't going to have his newspaper upset his regular telephone conversations with the president.

The *Post* and the *Times* are living out the injunction of the playwright Arthur Miller: 'A good newspaper, I suppose, is a nation talking to itself.' The *Journal* is a good newspaper that won't say 'boo' to the president – it's much the same as Australia's own policy in dealing with him.

•

In fact, seeking to accommodate rather than confront Trump is shaping up, unfortunately, as good long-term planning. Americans do one great favour to sitting presidents – they re-elect 'em. Landing the top job is extraordinarily tough. Doing it is nigh impossible. Getting re-elected is the oft-recurring gift.

Dating the modern superpower presidency from Franklin D Roosevelt, the re-election prize has been granted to FDR (thrice), Truman, Eisenhower, Nixon, Reagan, Clinton, George W Bush and Obama. The 'oncers' were Kennedy (denied by a bullet, not the voters), Ford (never elected in the first place), Carter and George HW Bush. Carter and George HW were beaten in their second-term quests by the US economy and better political campaigners.

More than three years from the next election, Trump's qualities as a politician, plus the healthy economy, have him well placed to be a 'twicer'. Sorry about that. Prepare for seven more years.

The economic part of the equation looks good for Trump because it's so positive for America. The recovery has entered its ninth year and is no longer limping; humming can be heard. Unemployment is below 4.5 per cent and labour shortages mean that after decades of stagnation, workers' median earnings have been rising for a couple of years.

With more than two million jobs a year being created, the optimistic view is that America's workers are coming into a 'new golden age'.[9] Imagine what the Trump megaphone could do with a golden age: a perfect period of platinum perfection, perhaps?

The scariness of Trump as a leader shouldn't obscure his qualities as a politician. As he was beginning that extraordinary run, back in January 2016, he boasted, 'I could stand in the middle of Fifth Avenue and shoot somebody and I wouldn't lose voters.' Turns out, that's kind of true.

Indeed, if two-thirds of the electorate hate him, that passion reinforces Trump's electoral base. As long as one-third of voters stay solid as Trump's core support, he can build to repeat his electoral performance in November 2020. Constantly taunting myriad enemies is Trump's pleasure, doing dual duty as political strategy.

He doesn't have a political agenda that normal politicians recognise. The agenda is the glory of the Donald. Trump has done more than make a hostile takeover of the Republican Party – he aims to turn the base against the Republicans, plus gather a lot of equally disgruntled Democrat voters.

The Republicans created the conditions for Trump's rise – nativist, even nihilistic – and now the president uses those conditions against the party. This is not so much 'reap what you sow' as 'ride your own whirlwind'.

•

One of the strange safety valves of the Trump style is that none of his courtiers are yet able to do much of the deep stuff either. To survive in the Trump court, the courtiers must court the king. Lots of key middle-level and upper-level jobs in the administration are still vacant. Running the White House as reality soap opera takes a lot of time and energy. If you spend most of the day just handling the king, what else can you handle? Trump's only steady vision is reserved for the mirror.

Railing against 'the system' – the promise to drain the Washington swamp – got him elected. Now he can't give up the habit. Consider the strange sight of a president ranting against his own powers and berating his own party. He will happily wreck a lot of stuff in Washington – what I call structural damage – but he shows little ability to build much new.

---

9   Eduardo Porter, "Unemployment Is So 2009: Labor Shortage Gives Workers an Edge," *The New York Times*, September 19, 2017, https://www.nytimes.com/2017/09/19/business/economy/labor-shortage.html.

Well into the first year in office, we have plenty of episodes to understand the stock scripts of this reality show. Trump's actions can be nasty and dangerously random, yet Trump's temperament tics are becoming wearily familiar. We don't know what the forty-fifth president will do, but we do know how he does it.

The narcissist loves himself by loving an argument with anybody. The volume is set to maximum – whether it's to argue with North Korea about nuclear war or with NFL footballers kneeling in protest during the national anthem.

Nuclear annihilation or NFL knees: in Trumpland, the tone and temper are the same. Maximum Donald. Always. It's dark and mordant stuff, as bizarre comedy dances on the edge of apocalyptic tragedy.

The world is a giant TV, and Trump sits in front of the screen, zipping through channels, yelling his responses at the shifting images.

The political mantra about letting the candidate be genuine, to be a true expression of his or her own personality – rendered in the stock line, 'Let Donald be Donald' – has reached a weird epiphany. The Donald being Donald is about little else but Donald; much lies beyond his standard range (or rage). The limits of the personality offer some hope about limiting the damage. He is better at invective than invention. He does chaos, not creation.

America is set to lose much – not least, a lot of its standing as an international leader. But it's a diverse and dynamic nation. The economic and legal foundations are deep and strong, even as the society and the politics morph and mutate and shift and sizzle. The place is so robust it can even survive Donald Trump at the helm. God bless America – because, by God, it's going to need all the strength it can muster.

LOOKING FOR TROUBLE

MARGARET SIMONS

18 May 2018

I t's a Saturday afternoon in Tarneit, twenty-five kilometres west of central Melbourne. The streets are mostly empty, the parks full of parents with pushers. The houses are closed up, cars parked in the driveways, residents appearing occasionally and driving away. The feeling is not fear but containment. There are no kids kicking balls in the street, no neighbours hanging over the fence.

A few hundred metres away at McDonald's, two large central tables are occupied by a group of teenagers whose recent origins lie in Africa. Only one of them is a girl, and the boys are jockeying for her attention. Their Bantu knots make their heads seem knobbly. They touch each other's heads and punch each other's arms. The girl shows off her tight braids. The boys are in tracksuit pants and hoodies, and they are very tall and very dark.

They swarm outside, and take turns to ride a hoverboard around the carpark. Customers coming and going from the restaurant have to navigate around them. Snatches of conversation float by: it's fuck this and fuck that. Someone messages them from Werribee station and suggests they catch the bus over there. Suddenly one of the boys starts chasing the girl around the table inside, everyone laughing. A bag of chips and a thickshake go skittering across the floor.

It's here on the westernmost edge of Melbourne, according to last summer's headlines, that Australia fractured. *The Australian* described it as a 'summer of hate'. The reporting of this supposed crisis took in Tarneit and other suburbs across Melbourne, roping together terrifying home invasions in a number of suburbs, a party out of control in the south-western suburb of Werribee, and violence thirty-three kilometres east on St Kilda beach. What each incident had in common were 'African youths'.

Writing in the *Herald Sun* in December, Andrew Bolt used offences ranging from a central-city mugging to an attempted murder to argue that 'integration' has clear limits 'when the intake is of poorly educated people from a tribal and warlike culture'.

It was Tarneit, according to the *Herald Sun*, that best symbolised the state's 'youth gang crisis'. Nine Network's *A Current Affair* screened shocking CCTV footage of young black men beating up one of their number in a local street. Locals, said the two outlets, were living in fear of violent, rampaging African gangs.

At the dawn of the new year, home affairs minister Peter Dutton weighed in with a blast for the state's Labor government. He claimed that people in Melbourne were scared to dine out at night because they were followed home by gangs. Prison sentences were a joke, he said, and the police were acting on 'politically correct' instructions from the state government. Gang violence was out of control and growing.

Premier Daniel Andrews and the Victoria Police denied there was a crisis but responded as if there were. Andrews said crime was under control but then went on television to condemn thuggery and promise firm action. The police rejected the idea of 'gangs' but set up a task force of African community leaders.

People in the inner suburbs protested on social media at Dutton's apparent racism and lampooned any suggestion that they were afraid to go out at night. They loved going to restaurants. They even went to *African* restaurants. But, for once, the inner suburbs – those safe Labor seats populated by the knowledge class – were completely irrelevant to this furore.

It was a long silly season last summer: no catastrophic bushfires, no floods, and the Sydney-to-Hobart yacht race passed without mishap. Perhaps it wasn't surprising that the media discerned another kind of newsworthy trouble and made the journey west to Tarneit.

Four months later, after the summer of hate had disappeared from the headlines, I went to Tarneit and spent many hours there at all times of the day and night. I was looking for trouble.

•

To get to Tarneit from the city you drive west on a highway that runs swift and wide between concrete sound barriers. Along the broad, walled-off river of traffic, trucks have left strips of shredded tyres like hard black lizard skins. Turn off after twenty-five kilometres and the first buildings you see are supersized warehouses and factories that dwarf the people who work in them.

Massive billboards rise out of abandoned farming land, offering three-bedroom house-and-land packages from $435,000 (or, as the local council's website puts it, 27,800 smashed avocadoes). Earthmovers perch dinosaur-like over the skeletons of houses under construction, pine frames awaiting plasterboard, cladding and render.

There's a mosque, and a new grammar school. A plain brick house serves as an evangelical church; a pub-and-pokies palace offers a bland rendered wall to passing traffic.

This is the City of Wyndham, the fastest-growing local government area in Victoria, and one of the fastest-growing in the country. Thirteen babies are born each day in this sprawling municipality, and more than 13,000 extra people move here each year. In just five years, the population has grown by 37 per cent. It is Australia under construction, and Tarneit is its newest product.

From the new Tarneit Central shopping centre, opened just six months ago, the skyscrapers of the city are visible across the ancient lava plain. They are the distant point against which everything – housing prices, commuting times, job opportunities, visibility and power – is calibrated. Opposite the shopping centre, the Tarneit railway station looks like a spaceship landed in the paddocks. Here you can catch a fast regional train to the city for the same price as a suburban fare. On the opposite corner is the new Julia Gillard Library, and just down the way the promisingly named Prosperity Street travels past warehouses and piles of earth before ending at a farm gate.

The new suburb spreads out on the other three sides of the shopping centre. Each spanking new house has a little portico relieving its box-like features. The gardens are newly planted, and some of the neatest lawns, on closer inspection, are astroturf. There hasn't been time to put down roots, not only because of migration but also because of stretched lives.

This is not a particularly poor suburb. On indices of social disadvantage it is in line with the rest of Melbourne, and it is ahead of Wyndham as a whole and several of its surrounding areas. The unemployment rate is slightly higher than Melbourne as a whole, but so too is the workforce participation – those in work or looking for work. Almost all families have two incomes and most people over the age of fifteen are employed full-time, most commonly in healthcare, social assistance, transport, warehousing and retailing. These are the shift workers who service the city and look after the ageing. The cars start early in the morning and late at night as people travel to work, dropping their children at childcare centres at all hours.

If you're on the street in the evening or the early morning you can be startled by garage doors opening suddenly, triggered by remotes. A car appears and drives in, the door closes, the house lights up and the blinds are drawn. The street is empty again.

On Poplar Boulevard, a few hundred metres away from the shopping centre, a house has been vandalised or has met with some other misadventure. The portico has been stove in and the render is lying in sheets, the structure revealed. The walls are made of foam blocks held together by render and welded rods. One knock, and half the house is collapsing.

Half a century ago, the folk singer and activist Pete Seeger sang a song, 'Little Boxes', about the development of suburbia. But that was a song sung by a white middle-class man about the white middle class – a satire about conformity. This is different. Apart from the ticky-tacky of rampant property development, and behind it the cold, hard calculations of cost, price, profit and compromised building standards, it could hardly be more different.

More than half of the residents here were born overseas, and they come from 162 different countries. Combine that with the fact that it has the youngest population in Victoria – a median age of just thirty – and it means almost all the adults and most of the youth are new Australians. Fewer than half of the residents here speak English at home. The dominant ethnic group is not Africans or Sudanese, but Indians, who make up about 23 per cent of the population. After Australians and British migrants, Filipinos come next, at 4 per cent of the population, closely followed by Chinese. From there the ethnicities are more or less even in proportions – Italians, Irish, Māori, Maltese, Punjabi. Sudanese are the biggest African group and well down the list of population groups, at just under 2 per cent, or about 500 people at the last census.[10]

•

In January, in the midst of the 'summer of hate', a scuffle at the Tarneit shopping centre appeared on *The Daily Mail*'s website as 'the latest gang flare up' involving African teenagers. 'EXCLUSIVE: Police SPAT ON and Abused as Officers Arrest African Teenagers Outside a Shopping Centre in Melbourne's West in Broad Daylight – in Latest Gang Flare Up' read the headline. Pictures showed black youths being restrained by police.

Two days after the article was published, the Victoria Police executive director of media and corporate communications, Merita Tabain, wrote

---

10   These figures are derived from data collected by the Australian Bureau of Statistics' 2016 Census of Population and Housing.

a confidential email to the editors of Melbourne's main media outlets expressing concern that aggressive behaviour by journalists might 'exacerbate the current tensions'. She used the incident at the Tarneit shopping centre as an example.

The incident, she said, had been provoked by the photographer's decision to 'move in to take close-up photos of a group of African teenagers socialising.' The teenagers, she went on, 'had been doing nothing of public interest prior to the photographer's decision to move in and take the photos and [the group] reacted to the photographer and what he was doing. This led to police being called in and a scuffle ensued in which police were spat on and arrests were made.'

The photographer had apologised for provoking the incident, Tabain reported, but the published article makes no reference to this.

Today, on a warm weekend in April, the most noticeable people gathering outside Tarneit Central shopping centre are men in immaculate suits and gleaming shoes. They are real estate agents. On any weekend, they are among the most prominent people in Tarneit, erecting open-for-inspection signs in seconds and ferrying young families – women in headscarves, men in turbans, all kinds – around the quiet streets.

Inside, the centre is gleaming. The signs in the shops speak of lean meats and fresh vegetables. Anglo faces are in the minority. Many women wear headscarves. It seems as though every shopper has a toddler at foot or in a pusher, and as though every second woman is pregnant. If this is Australia under construction, then it is possible to feel proud. It is busy, diverse, moderately prosperous and harmonious.

If it differs from older shopping centres in established suburbs, it is in the degree of sociability. Dutton worried about people going to restaurants, but the truth is there aren't many restaurants in Tarneit, other than the fast-food chains. There are cafes in this shopping centre, and they are almost empty. People come here, do their shopping, and leave.

Two cops stroll through in high-vis vests, with truncheons, pepper spray and all the other accoutrements of the modern police officer on the beat. They are looking at their mobile phones as they walk. If this place was not flat, bright and neat, they would surely trip over. They could hardly be more relaxed.

What do people here think about the media attention their suburb received over summer? Is this a safe place to live?

A couple living on the improbably named Camelot Drive, about a kilometre from the shopping centre, arrived from the Philippines five years ago. She works in aged care. He drives a truck. Their children are cared for by an enormous new childcare centre a suburb away. In the mornings they wake early to juggle shifts and responsibilities. Their evenings are spent inside, sleeping, watching television or Skyping with relatives in the Philippines.

Australians, they say, don't know how lucky they are. Here there are no shootings in the street, no armed war on drugs, no homes lacking toilets or running water. The gangs? There were some teenagers who got out of control. It's quiet now.

Mr and Mrs Fletcher are doing their shopping at Tarneit Gardens. They have lived in Wyndham all their lives, and they don't like the way it is changing. Chief among their complaints is traffic congestion, the amount of time it takes to reach the highway from home. But they are also concerned by all the different groups, and the feeling that the newcomers don't socialise. They are living adjacent to, rather than with, these new Australians. And the African youths – yes, they are frightening.

A short walk away, in Rippleside Terrace, estate agent Rajesh Kumar has a seven-year-old town house for sale, a 'stunning' residence 'enjoying a lakeside view' over what the maps call Sayers Drain, an agricultural drainage channel now made the centre of a big, grassy park. The town house is one of the oldest residential buildings in Tarneit and is part of a high-density, two-storey cluster. The sign says, it's 'perfect for executives, busy families or investors'.

The sellers are a Chinese family with young children looking to move to something larger. Is there ever any trouble in the park over the road? I ask. Kumar tells me that the park is fine. Tarneit is fine. Then, unprompted, he mentions Ecoville Community Park. The trouble, he says, was over there. Perhaps I read about it in the papers. The African teenagers wrecked it. 'But now there are police there all the time. I live in Tarneit. Tarneit is fine.'

•

All human stories take place in a landscape. All are partly about land – how we use it, usurp it, mould and are moulded by it.

The focus of media attention in Tarneit over summer was on one piece of land, Ecoville Community Park: the 'heart of darkness', as one media report described it; the 'symbol of the state's youth gang crisis' according to the *Herald Sun*.

This very local story made it into *The Australian*'s national affairs section:

A gang of youths have vandalised the community centre and park at a new Victorian estate, terrorising families with nightly crime sprees ... The youths, mostly of African appearance, have trashed the Ecoville Park in Tarneit ...

And on it went, linking the vandalism in this park with the out-of-control party in St Kilda and an assault of a police officer at another western-suburban shopping centre.

Responding to the incident, premier Daniel Andrews vowed that those responsible for the damage would feel 'the full force of the law'. *The Australian*'s editorial writers weren't reassured:

It should be abundantly clear by now that a zero-tolerance approach that puts the public interest first is sorely needed to bring order back to Melbourne's suburbs. Yes, most of the offenders are young. But they are old enough to accost shopkeepers with knives and shotguns, and commit armed robberies and indecent assaults, cause serious injuries and endanger lives, and kick police officers in the face.

The paper's coverage was illustrated with pictures of the Ecoville community centre showing broken windows, bashed-in walls, torn-apart furniture and walls scrawled with graffiti. The paper concluded:

Like many other incidents in Victoria, the young Africans' recent rampages are the work of a small percentage of immigrants from less civilised societies, where violence is routine. But their backgrounds are no reason for authorities to turn a blind eye to their criminality.

The park has its own story, which began back when the Ecoville housing estate was first conceived by the Resimax Group. The company's website once carried the advertisement for housing sales, in which the park's 'community pavilion' features prominently beneath an impossibly blue sky. Soaring white sails shelter a sparkling building:

The architecture of this community pavilion creates a strong statement about the progressive nature of the municipality it belongs to. The designers have embraced the ideals of eco-sustainability with a contemporary approach to outdoor establishments. The design is intended to create a landmark feature and to become a beacon for future property developments in Australia.

Today, driving past the little boxes to the community centre, the white sails soar over the houses, but they are grubby and scrawled with graffiti. The skatepark, the tennis court and the basketball court are strewn with rubbish. The grass is unmown. The community centre is boarded up. But young people are clearly still gathering in what the developers grandly described as an 'amphitheatre' – a neglected sunken area in front of the community centre.

What went wrong? The story emerges from the minutes of the Wyndham City Council. Once the suburb was built and the houses sold, the park was abandoned by the developer. Officially it belonged to the owners' corporation, to which all the recently arrived owners of the surrounding houses belonged. It was private space, which meant council had no power or responsibility for its upkeep. But the owners are owners only in law, not as a lived reality. They do not gather, they do not associate. The owners' corporation is run by a group that specialises in such things, based far away in Port Melbourne. When council ordered clean-ups, the owners' corporation complied. But now the owners' corporation has asked council to take over the park. Council has refused.

The park was a modern-day folly, a developer's marketing device. It has no part in council's open-space plans. It is too small to be a 'district park' and not modest enough to be cheap to maintain.

It was in even worse condition back in summer, says Wyndham councillor Kim McAliney, who holds council's portfolio for community safety. When the 'African gangs' crisis hit the headlines in summer, she took it personally. She visited Ecoville Park and was 'not happy'. An abandoned car body was sitting in the middle, rubbish was everywhere and the community centre was wrecked. It might still look dreadful, she acknowledges, but it is better than it was.

Some of those who hung around the park and caused the trashing were certainly Sudanese youth, she says, but the problem was longstanding. The vandalism had been happening for at least eighteen months. Of course young people gathered, says McAliney. There were toilets, water, electricity and free wi-fi.

And, of course, the Sudanese stuck out. 'They are tall. They are thin. Shopkeepers worry when they hang around in a way they wouldn't worry if they were Italians, for example.'

After the attention given the park by the national media, police began to patrol it constantly. Council cleaned it and boarded it up. More importantly, council organised for the owners' corporation to turn off the services and free wi-fi that had encouraged young people to gather.

McAliney is concerned about law and order in Wyndham. She has been campaigning for a long time for a new police station at Point Cook – an initiative that was funded in the recent state budget. But the main safety issue in this suburb, she says, is not gangs but family violence. 'And in that we are not alone.'

And the attitude of the police themselves? Until the day I interviewed him, Russell Barrett was commander of Victoria Police's north-western region, which includes the City of Wyndham. For months before the *Herald Sun* discovered Ecoville Park, he says, police had been talking to council and the owners' corporation about 'the way we are using that space, the way suburbs like this get constructed, and what the developers leave'. Police had brought the parties together to try to resolve the issues it was causing.

Then the *Herald Sun* discovered it. Barrett is reluctant to criticise the media. The offences they reported across Melbourne did occur, and some of them were serious. 'Victoria Police has never shied away from the fact that serious crime was happening. I think that when they highlighted areas like Tarneit and Ecoville it placed pressure on the totality of the community, and made them feel, I suppose, a little bit more vulnerable and on edge. That then really challenges the strength and fabric of community.' He doesn't say this, but part of the problem is surely that there is not much fabric there.

The police began to get a new kind of phone call from people in Tarneit. One night there was a call at eleven o'clock complaining that there was a group of 'African' youths playing basketball in the school grounds at Tarneit – just a stone's throw from Ecoville Park. The police attended. The young men were not doing anything wrong. The court was well lit, and it is understood that students can use it after hours. The police spoke to them, and that was that.

It is possible, thinking of this incident, to feel sympathy for everyone involved. Imagine the schoolyard at Tarneit on that hot summer night. Like the whole suburb, it is new. Take a wrong turn around here and you end up in farming land still in the process of being subdivided.

At night, the sound of crickets is so loud that you need to raise your voice to be heard. You can see foxes on the streets. The suburb has yet to entirely obliterate its rural origins.

The young Sudanese men gather to play basketball. It is hard to imagine anything less antisocial for them to do in this suburb of deserted-after-dark streets. But the neighbourhood is frightened. It has been told it is in crisis. And the crisis is just over there, it seems, just a street away ...

A call is made. Then, out of the blue, the police are there. They talk to the young men but make no arrests. Perhaps they suggest that 11 pm is not the best time to be playing basketball.

The neighbours have rung the police because they are scared. The police have responded because that is their job. The young people have done nothing wrong. Yet all it takes is a few incidents of this kind and the police will be accused of racial prejudice and racial profiling.

But who is racially profiling? The police, or the neighbourhood?

Stories like this abound in Tarneit. I spoke to three brothers who caught the train at Tarneit station. They are tall young men – tall enough to have to duck as they enter the carriage. When they got on board, three families moved to another carriage. Or there are the two young men, sitting in a car in a driveway, not doing anything wrong, just talking. The police pulled up. Someone had rung saying that there was an African gang outside.

•

On the day I interviewed Barrett, he was promoted to assistant commissioner for police complaints. The post had fallen vacant after it was revealed that his predecessor, Brett Guerin, had been making social media posts, under a pseudonym, laced with sexually explicit comments. It was the end of a month in which the media had also carried reports of brutality by police – a disabled pensioner pepper sprayed, an African man beaten and kicked while lying handcuffed on the floor.

Barrett didn't want to talk about the challenges of his new post. I asked him for his response to allegations that the police racially profile.

He replies smoothly. The police focus on the offence, he says, not the race of the offender. 'You know, in terms of policing, if offending is taking place in a geographical area, and the intelligence points to a cohort of young people, then we will talk to those young people. Not all of them will be committing offences.'

Barrett doesn't believe there is a crisis among Africans. Many of them are already doing very well, he says, and in twenty years they will be an accepted part of the community, just like the Indochinese and the Greeks and Italians before them.

Meanwhile, they have shallow roots. Barrett thinks about how his own children found their first jobs, their first footholds in society. It was through family friendships and connections, something the Sudanese, so recently arrived, clearly lack. Not surprisingly, some young people become alienated and go astray.

Over the past few decades, Victoria has moved away from the idea of a police *force* and towards a police *service* – community policing. Police are community workers, bringing in social services to try to change the circumstances that lead to crime. But can that possibly work when at the same time police must do the gritty, frontline tasks of finding and arresting offenders?

Barrett acknowledges a tension. The 'interface,' he says, is 'challenging.' He tells his people to do their jobs – arrest the offenders and begin the processes of criminal justice. But after that, he says, 'They should be looking for the causal factors for this crime. What are the vulnerabilities within their family network? And start to link that person with other support agencies who actually provide the necessary services.'

A large part of his job is interacting with state and federal government policy, to try to talk about what is needed in the way of such support.

But for police to be able to do this on-the-ground community work, he says, they must have the trust of the community they are dealing with. That is difficult when it is also their job to prosecute offenders. 'Ultimately we can do a lot but if the young person isn't willing then we're not going to be effective.'

And in that difficult relationship, incidents like the young men playing basketball and being spoken to by police don't help.

Nyadol Nyuon is an example of what Barrett describes as a Sudanese young person doing incredibly well. She came to Australia as a teenager straight from a Kenyan refugee camp. She graduated from Victoria University and then the University of Melbourne, and now works for the law firm Arnold Bloch Leibler in the heart of the city's legal district. She is a community leader. She has appeared on the ABC's *Q&A*.

She hears all the time about racial profiling by police. It is hard, she says, to be constantly called on to express gratitude to Australia – to be conspicuously thankful – while facing implicit racism.

Nyuon lives in the south-eastern suburbs, far from Tarneit. But has she, with her professional qualifications and her confident manner, been subjected to racial profiling here where she works in the centre of the city? It is hard to know. In the past year, she tells me, she has been stopped three times by police and charged with jaywalking. This could be because she is black. And it's true, she *was* jaywalking. 'I was in the wrong. I was doing the wrong thing. It's hard to know.'

•

So are there African gangs, or is the whole thing a media invention? The coarse net of crime statistics is not, by itself, very helpful. The figures have been used by both those who want to create a sense of crisis and those who want to quieten the fears.

Those who say there is no problem point to the fact that overall crime fell in Victoria over the last year – the period in which some media outlets would have had us believe Victoria was in a crisis of violence and fear. Crime dropped by 6 per cent, the biggest drop in twelve years. The crimes that so many people fear – home invasions and burglaries – were also down, by 15 per cent, to 46,311.[11]

But this decline followed a long period of a slightly upward trend, meaning that the state is now back to roughly where it was in 2014. For crimes against the person – assaults and other violence – though, the picture is slightly different. Numbers had been relatively steady for years, but rose last year by 1.5 per cent, driven by an increase in sexual offences, and with domestic violence a key factor.

On one reading of the statistics, Sudanese-born people are over-represented – and this is how the numbers have been reported. Sudanese make up just 0.1 per cent of the state's population, or about 6000 people, but the data shows that they are responsible for more than 1 per cent of all crime in Victoria and are particularly over-represented in several categories. In the year to September 2017, among alleged offenders aged between ten and eighteen, Sudanese-born Victorians were involved in 3 per cent of serious assaults, 2 per cent of non-aggravated burglaries, 5 per cent of motor vehicle thefts and 8.6 per cent of aggravated burglaries.

But statistics can lie. First, they record only country of birth, not ancestry. Those of Sudanese background who were born in Australia show up as Australian offenders. If Sudanese ethnicity is a problem, the statistics probably under-represent it. On the other hand, the statistics reflect arrests and charges, not convictions. Some of those caught in the mesh may not have been guilty of the offences with which they were charged.

Finally, and most significantly, there is the age of the Sudanese population. The deputy director of the Centre of Social and Population

---

11   The statistics on crime have been obtained from the Victorian Crime Statistics Agency.

Research at Monash University, Rebecca Wickes, describes as a 'brute fact' a concept criminologists call the age-crime curve. It represents what every parent knows – that people are most likely to get into trouble with the police between the ages of fifteen and twenty-four. Combine this with another fact – that the Sudanese are the youngest ethnic community in Australia – and their apparent over-representation in the crime statistics becomes not so much a brute fact as a questionable one.

Surprisingly, nobody has done the detailed modelling that would tell whether Sudanese – or any other ethnic group – are offending at greater rates than other populations of similar age distribution. 'It's a complex thing to do,' says Wickes. 'You'd have to age standardise and you'd have to do a whole bunch of funky statistical tricks.' But without this work, she says, it is simply not possible to say with confidence that Sudanese youth are more likely to break the law than other young people. The apparent over-representation in the statistics would certainly be reduced and might even disappear if age distribution was factored in.

Meanwhile, the total number of offences in which Sudanese youth are involved is numerically small. 'There is nothing in the statistics to support the idea that we have a crisis of African gang activity such as what's been reported in the media,' says Wickes. 'There's just simply no evidence base for that whatsoever.'

Police and criminologists agree that a small number of young men of African appearance are responsible for repeated violent offences. 'It's a drop in the offender bucket,' says Wickes:

> It's serious, though, and it has consequences. If anybody has ever been held up at night or invaded in their home [they know] it's terrifying and dangerous. It's particularly terrifying in a country like Australia, where serious violence is not the norm.

Russell Barrett agrees that the serious problem is not vandalism at Ecoville but 'a very small cohort of young people from African-Australian backgrounds who we are seeing continually, and they are committing really high-harm crime'.

How big is this cohort? Wickes says the data doesn't allow an accurate figure to be discerned, but her experience and contacts in law enforcement lead her to the conclusion that it is a few dozen – perhaps around forty. Her impression is that the police are pursuing these groups hard. 'They want to see them locked up and off the streets.' Barrett declines to confirm that figure of forty explicitly, but says, 'I wouldn't argue with it.'

It is this group, overwhelmingly, that is committing the serious home invasions and assaults. Added to this are parties that get out of control, the minor crimes like vandalism, and the fact that some of them involve young men of African appearance. 'We see parties that get out of hand in policing all the time,' says Barrett. The use of Airbnb properties for parties has made the problem worse. This is a Melbourne-wide problem, but he has observed that such incidents usually make the media only if African youths are involved.

Are the serious offenders of African origin forming gangs? Wickes and Barrett say that it depends partly on definition. There is no hierarchy or organisation within the groups, as there usually is in 'gangs'. They don't wear distinctive colours or move as a unit. A lot of the crimes are opportunistic, sparked by an unlocked house, for example.

Barrett prefers the term 'networked youth offending'. In other words 'young people who communicate with each other by social media and come together for a purpose, which might be entertainment or sporting events or crime. They're all using the same methodology.'

When the groups commit crime, he finds that the young people involved had often not met each other before:

> They've communicated somehow. They've come together through a loose social connection for a short period of time and they've gone out and committed a crime together and it could be a really serious high-harm crime. But they don't actually know each other. They might not have met each other till half an hour beforehand, but they've had a connection through social media.

•

Early last summer there was a spike in the number of assaults and home invasions committed by such groups. This was the nugget of truth in media reports of crisis. Barrett says there is no discernible reason for that spike, which has now subsided. Summer school holidays are often a period of trouble, with young people on the streets. But the Easter school holidays passed without any increase in crime. As for the rest of the media's talk of crisis, it was mostly breathless reporting of routine incidents such as out-of-control parties and vandalism.

But what about the fear in a place like Tarneit, with its shallow roots and its lack of places in which the people might come together to form a common understanding of the nature of their suburb?

Rebecca Wickes says that international research on perceptions of safety consistently finds that people's fear of crime and perception of personal safety has little to do with the actual crime levels. The research has used every plausible measurement, including researchers driving slowly around a neighbourhood recording incidents. Overwhelmingly, the research shows that the most powerful driver of people's perception of risk is the level of poverty and ethnic diversity in a neighbourhood. 'So I think we have a very strong "worried well" population in Victoria. I think this is absolutely a crisis of perception,' says Wickes.

And Tarneit in particular? The state's Crime Statistics Agency provided me with crime and country-of-birth figures, both for the City of Wyndham as a whole and for Tarneit specifically. (For privacy reasons, given the small number of offences, the agency would not provide a detailed breakdown of offences by country of birth for an area as small as Tarneit, but it provided that data for Wyndham as a whole.)

In 2017, the period that includes the 'summer of hate', people of Sudanese birth committed ninety-two crimes against the person and sixty-nine property and deception offences in the City of Wyndham. In Tarneit, the Sudanese-born were responsible for 7.2 per cent of all offences, which sounds bad – but the total number of offences was just fifty-one over the year, and it was down on the previous year.

On the other hand, the long-term trend shows sharply increasing percentages of offences committed by the Sudanese-born. At first sight it is alarming – until you match it with the Australian Bureau of Statistics census data. In 2011 there were just eighty-four Sudanese-born people living in Tarneit, and 112 who described their ancestry as Sudanese. By the 2016 census, it was 345 born in Sudan and 621 with Sudanese ancestry.

Match this with the crime statistics, and a rough analysis suggests that the apparent leap in Sudanese crime in Tarneit is exactly in line with the increase in the Sudanese population.

•

It was easy, watching the group at McDonald's that weekend, to imagine how their boisterousness, their egging each other on and their domination of space could get out of hand. It was easy to imagine them gathering at Ecoville Park before the constant police patrols began and the wi-fi was cut off. It is easy to imagine Ecoville getting trashed.

But in the two hours I watched and stalked these teenagers, they might have been a nuisance, but they did nothing illegal. Apart from their colour, there was nothing to mark them out from any other group of teenagers with nothing to do on a Saturday afternoon.

This was the closest thing to trouble I found in Tarneit during three weeks of visits.

I stayed in Tarneit until late that night. Peter Dutton had said that people in suburbs like this are scared to go to restaurants. There aren't any restaurants in Tarneit other than fast-food outlets, but they were doing a good trade. The kebab shop at the shopping centre had a United Nations of ethnicities queuing up to be served.

As midnight approached, Ecoville Park was in darkness, but something was going on. Voices echoed from the 'amphitheatre'. A laugh, a string of swearing, the sound of broken glass being kicked.

It was a warm night. It took a while, but finally two figures emerged into the street light – teenagers, a girl and a boy.

It was clear what they were here for. They were flirting and snogging and feeling each other up, out of sight of parents. Who knows what happened on this night, what memories and futures they created in this liminal space, this social hole in this brand-new suburb?

The boy was very tall. He was of African appearance. The girl was white.

LIVES AND TIMES

REMEMBERING AND FORGETTING

MARIA TUMARKIN

22 October 2009

In mid October, a Russian historian researching the treatment of Germans in the Soviet Union during the Second World War was arrested and charged with breaching privacy laws. *The Guardian* reported that Mikhail Suprun was detained by Russian security service officers, who searched his apartment and confiscated his research archives. His arrest came as a reminder of how the Stalinist era remains a live issue in post-Soviet Russian politics.

As if reminders were needed. Last year the Russian Academy of Sciences and the government-owned television network, Russia Channel, instituted a nationwide search for the historical figure that best represents the Russia of today. Modelled on the BBC's *100 Greatest Britons*, the project commenced with 500 potential candidates for the title of 'The Name of Russia'. By the end of the process, Joseph Stalin had gathered enough votes to finish third, and rumours strongly suggested that the organisers had resorted to tampering with the votes to avoid the scandalous possibility that the Soviet leader would finish at the top of the list.

On the broadcast itself, Stalin was presented as a flawed and ambiguous character. ('Flawed' must be the euphemism *du jour* of the early twenty-first century.) Yes, viewers were told, the man was known for occasionally pillaging and plundering, but let us not forget that he also turned a backward, agrarian and deeply dysfunctional country into an industrialised superpower. He was making an enormous omelette so can we please stop counting the broken eggs. Then, of course, the extra-heavy weaponry was wheeled out – the Stalin-led Soviet victory in the Second World War. As achievements go, you can't beat stopping Hitler from enslaving Europe and wiping the Soviet nation off the surface of the earth. In Britain, by the way, *100 Greatest Britons* was won by Winston Churchill, who beat Diana, Shakespeare and Charles Darwin to the title.

The millions of votes cast for Stalin would have been simply inconceivable in the late 1980s and early 1990s. But by 2008, seventeen years after the collapse of the Soviet Union, things had changed. There were, of course, protests from democratic and human rights organisations and historians, who argued that the very fact that Stalin was on the list was completely unacceptable, particularly while his victims and their families were still alive. In Germany, as protesters pointed out, no Third Reich figures were allowed to be nominated in a comparable contest because they had long since been recognised as criminals. Not so in Russia. The organisers responded by appealing to the always handy principles of democracy. Surely an open discussion of Stalin's significance in the history of his country was a sign of a healthy and robust civic society. As a Russian saying goes, 'you cannot throw words out of a song'.

How do we make sense of the rehabilitation of the Soviet regime – and particularly the figure of Stalin – in present-day Russia? In the independent Russian media and in the Western media, this phenomenon is rarely explained without reference to some kind of caricature. It may be the supposed masochistic craving for an iron fist deeply ingrained in the Russian psyche, or a case of a nationwide uber-forgetting of mythic proportions. Or it might reflect the power of mass hypnosis attributed to the government of Vladimir Putin and Dmitry Medvedev.

•

There is no denying that the current government is engaged in a concerted campaign of rehabilitating all things Soviet – its leaders, its achievements and its legacy – minus, of course, the regrettable 'excesses' of purges and forced collectivisation. After all, Putin famously described the collapse of the Soviet Union as 'the greatest geopolitical catastrophe' of the twentieth century. This campaign of rehabilitation can be seen in government rhetoric and in messages laundered through government-controlled media outlets, in the shutting down of archives and culling of history textbooks, and in the unlawful raids on the offices of the human rights and historical preservation society, Memorial – the most important voice for preserving the memory of Stalinism in Russia.

The rehabilitation of the Soviet era is also evident in the emergence of youth movements such as Mishki, the Russian word for teddy bear. Mishki's full name is the Youth Organisation for the All-Round Development of Personality, Patriotic and Moral Education of Children and Youth. Yulia Zimova, its twenty-something-year-old founder, has told journalists that the movement's aim is to teach children pride in their town and country, responsibility, independence and concern for others. It would sound like a harmless version of the Scouts if it had not been set up by members of Nashi, a youth organisation with strong links to the Kremlin, conceived as a Russian response to the Ukraine's 'Orange Revolution'. Some journalists who do not share Nashi's devotion to Putin as Russia's saviour have referred to the young members of the movement as 'nashists', and references abound to fascism and Hitler-Jugend, as well as to Soviet-era youth groups such as the Octobrists, Young Pioneers and Komsomol.

What does Nashi want? They want a full and swift restoration of Russia's greatness. They want people to be dripping with pride in their country. They want the rest of the world, America and Britain in particular, to sit up and listen. (Shaking in fear will be the next step, of course, all things going to plan.) They want a 'clean', 'strong' and 'united' Russia, and that means sweeping the country with a big, long broom to rid it of all kinds of scum – ethnics, democrats, prostitutes. Nashi does not limit itself to ideological warfare; the movement offers paramilitary training to give its members the important life skills for breaking up opposition rallies. As a phenomenon, Mishki is both obscene (forced political participation of children is illegal even in Russia, to say nothing of being deeply immoral) and unintentionally hilarious, especially in its infantilisation of the political sphere. In all seriousness, Mishki has asked Putin to become the head of their movement – the Chief Teddy Bear.

One of Mishki's slogans proclaimed, 'Thank you Mr Putin for our stable future.' As the journalist Lev Rubinstein noted, this time Putin had outdone even Stalin. In Stalin's times, the slogan was 'Thank you to Comrade Stalin for our happy childhood.' Now Putin was being thanked for the future he apparently has rendered stable.

In fact, analogies between Putin and Stalin abound in popular culture. As do the jokes.

Stalin's ghost appears to Vladimir Putin in a dream. Troubled by the crippled economy, Putin asks the Great Dead Leader for advice. 'Round up and shoot all the democrats, and then paint the inside of the Kremlin blue,' Stalin replies. 'Why blue?' Putin asks. 'Ha!' says Stalin. 'I knew you wouldn't ask me about the first part.'

or

Putin gets up in the middle of the night and goes to the refrigerator. When he opens the door, a dish of jellied meat begins to tremble. 'Don't worry,' says Putin, 'I've only come for a beer.'

It is, of course, all too tempting to think of Putin as the direct heir to Stalin and his brand of neo-totalitarianism as a far more moderate, modern and ideologically savvy version of Stalin's iron fist. But like most historical analogies, this one is not particularly illuminating. As the

Russian writer and journalist Dmitriy Bykov argues, 'In the case of Putin we are dealing not with the cult of personality – since the personality barely manifests itself and, plus, it is hermetically sealed from strangers' eyes – but with the cult of substance.'

This substance is virtually impossible to define. Because it encapsulates 'collective expectations which are greater than any kind of logic', it is 'a phantom of mass self-hypnosis'. The way Bykov sees it, Putin's rule is not comparable to Stalin's cult of personality because Putin is not a personality but the archetypal *man without qualities*, the medium for the masses.

Arseniy Roginskiy, the chair of Memorial, argues that the rehabilitation of Stalin, as such, was not the objective of the current government. Rather, it was a by-product of the rehabilitation of the idea of Russia as a great nation and of the concerted campaign to re-legitimise the authority of the state, which began in the early 1990s. The vacuum left by the collapse of the Soviet regime was filled by certain heavily mythologised moments taken from Soviet history, with the Soviet victory in the Second World War foremost among them. Sociologist Lev Gudkov points out that the victory of 1945 is, in fact, 'the only positive reference point for the national consciousness of the post-Soviet society'. Surveys show that the identification of the war and the Soviet victory as the most important historical event of the twentieth century has only grown (and grown significantly) in the last decade or so. And the war is so inextricably linked with the figure of Stalin that any growth in its symbolic power is bound to increase Stalin's legitimacy. In fact, the more the figure of Stalin is associated with the war, the weaker his links appear to be to the history of political terror and mass repressions.

Russian sociologist Boris Dubin suggests that contemporary Russia is 'a society lacking in depth, characterised by flatness'. Quick to tire of anything complex or burdensome, it has been unable to hold on to a historical awareness of the crimes committed by the Soviet leadership, which were revealed under Gorbachev. Dubin believes that the outpouring and wide public circulation of memories of Stalinism in the late 1980s and 1990s were tools of political confrontation between the reformers and the old regime. Once the Soviet Union collapsed, this confrontation was essentially exhausted and the urge to remember and to bear witness seemed to lose its cultural and social imperative. The idea that a strong and self-aware civic society is dependent on the active historical consciousness of its members has, he says, become an abstraction.

And, indeed, in a country in which, if you so much as scratch the surface of most family histories, you are likely to discover first-hand experiences of gulags, deportations and state terror, there are no legal processes by which the atrocities of Stalinism can officially be recognised and condemned as crimes against humanity. Unlike, say, South Africa or Argentina, Russia has had no Truth Commission, no *Never Again* report, no mechanisms to enable the nationwide work of testimony, witnessing and mourning. Russia has had nothing like the wholesale memorialisation of its traumatic history that we have seen in Germany or the United States. There is no central monument to the victims of terror. The location of most mass graves remains unknown, and streets across the nation still carry the names of Stalin's henchmen. That victims of Stalinism and their families could receive an official apology like the one delivered by Kevin Rudd to Indigenous Australians is unimaginable.

•

On the surface, this looks almost like a clinical picture of collective amnesia or, in psychoanalytic terms, the mass repression of mass repressions – only this is not quite the case. On the contrary, in today's Russia can be found not an absence of memories of totalitarianism and Stalinism but a profound surplus. There is an incredibly rich, voluminous and constantly growing body of highly credible literature that painstakingly chronicles both specific experiences and the broader historical narratives underpinning the fate of millions of Soviet citizens killed, imprisoned, deported, sent to gulags or forced to live in constant terror. There is so much material, much of it available freely on the internet, that you could spend a lifetime reading. The historical legacy of Soviet terror, in other words, is being painstakingly remembered and just as painstakingly forgotten.

It must be said that the situation in Russia is markedly different from that in many other post-Soviet nations (and in countries of the former Eastern Bloc more broadly). Ukraine and the Baltic states, for instance, are experiencing the process Ukrainian historian Gregoriy Kasyanov calls the 'nationalisation' and 'privatisation' of history. This kind of oppositional national history is used as the cornerstone for the revival of national consciousness and identity, an argument first for sovereignty and then for an unbroken tradition of a unified (and invariably democratic) national consciousness. And with historical narratives so firmly ensconced in the 'politics' corner (however noble we may judge all aspirations of sovereignty and self-determination to be), what people choose to remember in public or semi-public forums very quickly becomes a question of allegiances and loyalty.

In Russia the picture is significantly more complex. While claims about the past are an integral part of political debates, the vast body of testimony and historical documents relating to the Soviet regime, and specifically to the history and legacy of Stalinism, has not been able to counter widespread forgetting or misremembering. By and large, attempts to mobilise this massive and constantly growing repository of private memories, public documents and historical work to act as an effective antidote to the falsification of historical accounts have failed. In the late 1980s and early 1990s it seemed as if social memory was the force that was going to put an end to the deployment of history as pure ideology – and then something went awry. It seems clear that the outpouring of people's memories about what happened under Stalin did become part of Russia's civic culture through the publication of survivor accounts, archival documents and serious works of history, through TV programs and films, but ultimately this *outpouring* has not been able to reconfigure Russia's public sphere in any profound or lasting sense. The hardware has remained the same.

Russian historians based at Memorial point to the need to counter the persistent immateriality of the memory of Soviet totalitarianism as one of the most important historical battles they are facing today. For any true social change to occur, the victims of Stalinism, they say, need to be named. Their families need to know where their loved ones are buried. The material remains of gulags, prisons, mines and other types of industrial projects built on the slave labour of the camp inmates and special deportees need to be identified and marked. A central museum needs to be built. Memorials need to spring up in city centres rather than on the outskirts or as part of cemeteries. Plaques need to be put on the buildings where people were tortured and from which they were taken. Nothing, historians say, will stop people from forgetting until the memory of Soviet totalitarianism becomes part of the material fabric of Russian cities and towns, until children simply bump into things on their way somewhere and feel compelled to ask questions of their parents. It is a tragedy that at present their wish list seems outrageously implausible – almost as implausible as Stalin narrowly missing out on becoming 'The Name of Russia'.

FROM UBIQUITOUS TO OBSOLETE

SHAKIRA HUSSEIN

30 March 2011

The title of Kwame Anthony Appiah's latest book, *The Honor Code*, sent a shudder through my gut, probably because I've read too many reports lately in which the word 'honour' was immediately followed by the word 'killing'.

It stirred memories of a conversation I once had with Shahtaj Qazilbash at the office of the law firm in Lahore where she worked as a paralegal. Qazilbash had more reason than most to recoil from the debased use of the word 'honour'. A year before our discussion, a client called Samia Sarwar had come to the office for a meeting with her mother. Samia had been estranged from her family ever since she'd sought help from prominent lawyer Hina Jilani to divorce her abusive husband. Her parents had initially refused to countenance the shame of a divorce in the family, but the meeting between mother and daughter was meant to be a first step towards reconciliation.

The reunion was short-lived. Samia's mother was accompanied by her uncle and a driver. Once inside, the driver shot Samia dead and threatened to kill Hina Jilani before being killed by a security officer. Samia's uncle took Qazilbash hostage at gunpoint and used her as a shield as he and Samia's mother retreated to the hotel where her father was waiting to be told that his wayward daughter would bring no further shame on the family.

Samia's death received more publicity than most such killings, partly because it happened so publicly and partly because her family belonged to the urban elite. Wealthy and well connected, they were never held to account for her death, and their crime was defended by the political establishment of their home state.

As Appiah relates, thousands of women are murdered every year in the epidemic of honour-related violence that he describes as a 'war on women'. Samia Sarwar's death plays a central role in his discussion as he asks why her killers went unpunished and, most crucially, whether honour killings can be consigned to history, not by attributing less value to honour but by reframing the definition of honourable conduct.

Appiah's purpose in *The Honor Code* is to suggest that apparently deeply entrenched practices such as honour killing need not be regarded as regrettable but insurmountable social ills. He precedes his discussion of honour killing with analyses of duelling, foot-binding and slavery – long-established social practices that relatively quickly made the transition from ubiquitous (at least in the social circles that upheld them) to obsolete. Just as honour may have been the underlying rationale behind these customs, honour also became the reason for abandoning them, as once-honourable practices came to be seen as shameful, primitive or, in the case of duelling, ridiculous to the point of embarrassment.

Appiah's opening anecdote certainly does sound comically ridiculous to contemporary sensibilities. In 1829, the Duke of Wellington, prime minister and hero of Waterloo, was accused of deceptive conduct during the debate over Catholic emancipation. The *Roman Catholic Relief Act 1829*, which would allow Catholics to sit in parliament, was strenuously opposed by the Earl of Winchilsea, who claimed that Wellington was using his support for the Anglican King's College as a distraction from his 'introduction of Popery into every department of the State'. This slur on Wellington's honour couldn't be allowed to stand, and the prime minister demanded satisfaction. After all, Wellington and Winchilsea were both gentlemen, and duelling was the recognised means of resolving questions of honour.

After a token exchange of gunfire in a field near Battersea Bridge, Winchilsea's 'second' handed over a pre-prepared apology and the two gentlemen retreated, with Wellington's honour redeemed to his own and his peers' satisfaction. Neither gentleman faced any legal consequences, and Wellington's political career was secure. Yet duelling was technically illegal and widely regarded as immoral. Appiah asks how a practice that was openly tolerated would become practically obsolete a few decades later.

In fact, the factors that would lead to the duel's demise were already visible in the confrontation between Wellington and Winchilsea. The honour code was still powerful enough to support Wellington's claim that he had no other choice but to defend his honour against Winchilsea's outrageous slur. Yet, Appiah suggests, while Wellington was able to portray himself as a gentleman forced into a regrettable situation in which he had no option but to demand satisfaction, he was also deploying the defence of his honour as a political tactic – an altogether less elevated motive.

The somewhat ritualistic nature of the Wellington–Winchilsea encounter is another indication that the duel had become a less serious affair. Honour dictated that Wellington issue the challenge and Winchilsea accept it, but only two shots were fired. Wellington's shot went wide and Winchilsea fired into the air – not really in the true spirit of duelling, as observers of the time noted.

Suggestions from some quarters that Winchilsea ought to have been beneath Wellington's notice undermined the assumption that gentlemen met on the duelling field as equals. At the same time, the aristocrats for whom duelling was an accepted social practice were losing their elevated social position as the middle class assumed an ever more important role. Gentlemen's foibles became more visible and open to ridicule, with the Wellington–Winchilsea encounter the subject of mockery and cartoons. Over the following years, duelling ceased to be the exclusive preserve of 'gentlemen', as disputes among the lower orders came to be framed in its language. A social norm that allowed the aristocracy to break the law and transgress accepted moral standards was no longer sustainable. And as the duel lost its social cachet, the gentlemen in question no longer wished to engage in it. Honour was no less important, but duelling had ceased to be honourable.

Appiah draws a connection between duelling in Europe and foot-binding in China, describing both of them as elite honour practices that withered under external scrutiny. Foot-binding effectively crippled women and girls, which meant that the practice was confined to those who didn't need female labour. But bound feet were also an essential attribute for the wife of an upper-class man, thus ensuring that the practice was adopted by families that aspired to raise their social rank. As with duelling, foot-binding lost some of its sheen as it was taken up by the lower orders. Its prevalence lowered its value and provided a mechanism for its abolition.

Foot-binding was criticised within China even before it was denounced by American and European missionaries. These criticisms made few inroads while China remained self-confident and self-contained; but as China redefined itself as a member of the global community – and a member that was facing decline – foot-binding came to be seen as a source of national shame. No longer associated with prestige, it was increasingly viewed through the lens of international scrutiny, and the tiny feet that had been extolled as beautiful instead appeared barbarous and embarrassing.

Appiah cites the slave trade as another practice that was widely seen as morally abhorrent but was resilient in the face of criticism until it also came to be seen as shameful. He acknowledges but dismisses the argument that slavery was abolished because it no longer made economic sense. In his opinion, honour was more than just a cover for self-interested motives. It was a means by which abolitionists could not only frame their cause in terms of virtue but also portray inaction as a source of shame. The British abolition movement harnessed support from both the middle and the working classes, tying the struggle for the emancipation of slaves in America to their own claims for an appropriate level of respect. '[Slavery's] unequivocal meaning was that manual labor was to be equated with suffering and dishonour,' writes Appiah. 'That was why it could be used to speak of the suffering of those who were not literally enslaved.' Slavery, then, dishonoured even those who were only indirectly implicated.

Remembering the shelves of files in Shahtaj Qazilbash's office, each folder containing a story of tragedy and injustice, I hope that Appiah's optimistic belief in the power of honour to achieve liberation as well as oppression proves justified in the case of honour killings. 'There is no honour in honour killings,' campaigners repeat, but even those who claim to oppose the practice often blame the activists who publicise the violence, rather than the perpetrators who commit it, for the dishonour it brings to Pakistan's name.

Appiah closes his book with the story of Mukhtaran Bibi, a Pakistani village woman he calls a 'model of honour'. Mukhtaran was sentenced to be gang-raped by the upper-caste men of her village in retribution for her brother's alleged transgression, but rather than buckle beneath the shame she reported her attackers to the police. Her case was eventually taken up by the lawyers who had represented Samia Sarwar.

Once her story gained the attention of the international media, Mukhtaran was held responsible for causing Pakistan international embarrassment. Explaining why she had been denied an exit visa to receive an award in North America, then-president Musharraf told *Washington Post*, 'This has become a money-making concern. A lot of people say if you want to go abroad and get a visa for Canada or citizenship and be a millionaire, get yourself raped.' But, as Appiah relates, Mukhtaran continues to speak out and used the compensation she eventually received to establish a girl's school in her village.

•

The Honor Code is a narrative of human progress, and its account of 'moral revolutions' means that it is an optimistic book, despite the sometimes-grim stories it has to tell. I was cheered, but also left wondering whether honour simply demands that oppression should be kept out of sight or presented in a more palatable form. Little girls in China no longer suffer the torture of foot-binding, but more and more women around the world undergo sometimes dangerous cosmetic surgery in pursuit of self-worth. We no longer tolerate institutionalised slavery, but we continue to purchase mass-produced clothing even while knowing that it is probably manufactured in slave-like conditions. As Appiah notes, morality in itself is an insufficient force to generate social change.

In current political discourse the word 'honour' generates cynicism. It's a word treated with appropriate seriousness on Anzac Day and after national tragedies such as bushfires or floods, particularly in relation to those whose actions have gone beyond the call of duty. As Appiah says, honour provides motivation and reward for deeds that could not be either demanded or purchased. The word's indiscriminate use devalues it, however, which perhaps explains why it sounds so cheap when used for political purposes.

Among the more recent moral revolutions, the apology to the stolen generations seems like an exercise in re-attributing honour. Australians gained a heightened awareness of the forced removal of Indigenous children from their families following the 1997 publication of the *Bringing Them Home* report. The damage inflicted on the stolen generations and their families and John Howard's steadfast refusal to acknowledge them in the form of an apology had both become a source of national shame. Kevin Rudd opened his 'Sorry Day' speech with the words, 'Today we honour the Indigenous peoples of this land,' but the apology that followed was first and foremost an attempt to redeem the honour of non-Indigenous Australians. In those terms, it was highly successful, but the continued vulnerability and disadvantage experienced by too many Indigenous people indicate that we redeemed our honour at a bargain-basement price.

As I read *The Honor Code* I began to speculate about which contemporary, taken-for-granted social practices might crumble in the face of moral revolution. We have no moral consensus over how (or whether) the sex industry should be regulated. The commodification of human body tissue seems to be gaining rather than losing acceptance, with governments under pressure to allow payment to surrogate mothers and organ and bone-marrow donors. Support for euthanasia seems to be gaining momentum. Environmentalism seems ripe for a transformative moral revolution – or perhaps not. In a century or two, people may need to strain to imagine what life was like before the moral revolutions that transformed these issues – or they may find it hard to believe that a change to the status quo was ever seriously suggested.

'There is no honour in honour killing.' There is honour, however, in Shahtaj Qazilbash's courage in returning to work in the office where she had witnessed a murder and been kidnapped at gunpoint. Sadly, as Pakistan descends further into chaos, violence against women is increasing, and much of it is committed under the banner of honour. And women are not the only casualties. The most high-profile recent victim is Salmaan Taseer, the blunt-spoken governor of Punjab who had come to the defence of a woman accused of blasphemy – the sin of dishonouring God. Taseer's uncompromising stance against the blasphemy laws cost him his life. He was gunned down by one of his own bodyguards – and his assassin was 'honoured' by a crowd of lawyers who garlanded him with flowers when he was taken to court.

In retrospect, Taseer's determined stance against the blasphemy laws seems quixotic – but then, Don Quixote was nothing if not a man of honour.

UNLUCKY IN LOVE

ANNA CRISTINA PERTIERRA

9 October 2012

W e like to see love as the purest of feelings, an antidote to the cold calculations of work life, government or finance. In a society where the market rules, personal emotions – of which love must be the most intense – are often portrayed as among the few things that lie beyond economic incentives. People who confuse love and money are derided for being gold-diggers or worse, and when sex is mixed up with the market – in pornography, prostitution or sexualised advertising – it causes great consternation.

What are we to make, then, of sociologist Eva Illouz' new book, *Why Love Hurts: A Sociological Explanation*, which tells us that the suffering caused by love as we know it is actually the product of modern capitalism? When life is painful in the modern, secular world, we are taught to look inwards to overcome our problems. Rather than turning to God or to traditions, we turn to psychologists, financial planners, personal trainers and others who can help us to help ourselves. 'Throughout the twentieth century,' writes Illouz, 'the idea that romantic misery is self-made was uncannily successful, perhaps because psychology simultaneously offered the consoling promise that it could be undone.' Entire self-help industries are underpinned by the premise that we must look within ourselves to understand and overcome the flaws that cause us to find love painful.

Like any sociologist worth her salt, Illouz pushes readers to consider how our experience of love might largely be created by the kind of society we live in. Tracing a sort of history of emotions through archives and literature since the Regency era, she argues that in earlier times people's feelings about love and sentiment were quite different from those we take as self-evident. Although we think of love as entirely spontaneous and natural, the way we speak of love, and the problems that love creates for us, are more a historical formation than a natural occurrence.

Take, for example, this set of clichés: a woman who is sexually active and carefree in her twenties gets to her thirties and starts looking for a serious relationship, suddenly aware of her closing window of fertility. But all she can find is men who claim to be looking for love, and who think of themselves as good guys, but refuse to settle down. Some people might think it has ever been this way, but history and the social sciences suggest that these styles of behaviour are a recent invention. In the wake of a generation of new sexual freedoms, men no longer see women's sexuality as something that is scarce, and this decreases women's value in a market of love and sex. There are always more and younger women around the corner, which in itself makes women both more desirable in the abstract and less desirable in the concrete:

> The modern situation in which men and women meet each other is one in which sexual choice is highly abundant for both sides; but while women's reproductive role will make them end the search early, men have no clear cultural or economic incentive to end the search early.

The detached modern man of this stereotype is probably not deliberately being caddish, says Illouz. He simply tries, in avoiding attachment, to find value in a process of looking for love within which he happens to control the field. Recent decades have brought all sorts of social changes that affect how and when we seek love. Women wait longer to have children, men no longer feel the pressure to marry young, women and men start careers quite late in life – these are not so much natural or biological phenomena as social and political shifts. Modern capitalism changes how we love as much as it changes how we work.

•

If our experience of love is shaped by, or even created by, capitalism, then a modern emblem of capitalist love must be the world of online dating. This is the subject of Jean-Claude Kaufmann's *Love Online*, a sociological meditation on the practices and problems of looking for love and sex via dating sites that form a 'hypermarket of desire'. Women and men can browse apparently endless profiles without risk. They can chat online to potential dates and are free to be direct, romantic, sexual or daring without any great consequence. But, as Kaufmann shows, when people come to set up face-to-face dates, they seem overwhelmed by uncertainty. Love and sex are a complicated combination, and deciphering how much of each anybody is looking for is one of the many hazards of online dating. People can turn out to be different from what they promised. Sometimes they don't turn up at all. Even when a meeting works well, the rules for progressing from an initial coffee or drink can be fraught with miscommunication and unknown intentions. Kaufmann takes us through the problems that both men and women face in navigating the murky waters of cyberdating, although women often seem to have more to lose emotionally in this uneven market.

While internet dating is a recent phenomenon, Kaufmann locates it within a brief history of the modern courtship rituals through which a culture of dating emerged in twentieth-century United States and Western Europe. Dance halls established spaces where young people could meet more freely and choose their partners. In the twenty-first century, this process of choosing a partner sped up and spread out with the arrival of the internet. 'The whole of society has become a huge dance hall where anyone (boy or girl) can ask anyone else (boy or girl) to dance,' writes Kaufmann:

> As in the past, the ritual is reassuring because it is so well-oiled and gives the impression that the rules of the game are clear. But what we make of a date is not predetermined and can vary a great deal, more so than ever now that sex is part of the equation and may even be the most important thing about it.

For Kaufmann, although love online increasingly looks like a hypermarket, it doesn't offer all the ease and convenience promised. We remain all too trapped by our own passions and humiliations when we try to build relationships with the real people on the other side of an internet exchange. Internet daters must learn the courting rituals of our age: first sending some messages, perhaps a photo, then having an initial drink, followed by 'real' dates. But internet daters are disappointed to find that the new rules of dating solve few of the problems that engulf someone looking for love. As Kaufmann puts it, 'the rules relate to the formalities and the setting. They tell us nothing about the content of the game. On the contrary, the issue of sex/love is now more confused than ever. Sex has not become just another leisure activity.' Now that sex has become so commonplace, it is love that Kaufmann sees as truly radical. Love is what people struggle to realise: 'We were deluding ourselves when we believed, as we often did in the 1960s and 1970s, that it is sexuality and not feeling that has a revolutionary import.'

•

Kaufmann and Illouz want readers to understand the very specific and recent changes that have made men and women what they are today. Readers looking for an explanation grounded in evolutionary theory can turn to *The War of the Sexes* by Paul Seabright. Although he is an economist by training, Seabright's work draws from evolutionary biology and evolutionary psychology to explore what he sees as the riddles of modern sexual inequality. Describing the process of natural selection as like moving through a long tunnel, he suggests that:

> During the passage through that evolutionary tunnel, men who could acquire economic resources were able to coerce or bribe their way into sexual reproduction and left more descendants than those who could not. Those conditions have changed beyond recognition today, but if we are to make economic inequality between men and women a thing of the past, we need to understand the psychological marks that the tunnel has left on us.

Far from arguing that women are 'naturally' less capable of succeeding in the modern economy, Seabright says that the data shows that any sex differences in ability pale in comparison to real-world differences between male and female economic success. Instead, he suggests that a more important difference between women and men (as well as the males and females of other species) is in how they collaborate and compete: how they network.

In modern capitalism, we are supposed to prize efficiency above all else. But biology shows us that what is important – even more important than efficiency – is success, which is achieved through collaboration as much as through competition. Evolutionary theory says we seek success in sexual selection: women seek to make the best choice of partner for a considerable investment in fertilising their eggs, while men must work hard to ensure that their plentiful sperm can have a chance of reaching any eggs at all. Seabright says that this battle of sexual selection has effects in most other arenas of life as well, and he is particularly interested in the arena of paid employment. He argues that modern workplace research provides many examples where what should be efficient fails to happen. Women, whose labour should be very valuable, continue to be under-represented at the top end of business. While men fill out the top bracket beyond their due, they also dominate the most marginalised sectors of society, including the homeless and the imprisoned.

Such inefficient differences, for Seabright, are partly explained by the fact that our prehistoric wiring tends to make men and women work within certain kinds of networks in ways that are overlooked in the modern era. Women tend to create strong ties through relationships in which they invest a lot, while men tend to create weak ties across a wider field. While strong ties are important for maintaining a family (you need people to help you in a very committed way when you have mouths to feed), a wider range of weak ties can be much more useful in seeking jobs across a dispersed employment market. To complicate this idea, both women and men tend to prefer working with members of their own sex, which not surprisingly leads women to be shut out of the boys' clubs that continue to dominate elite groups. We need to understand such differences, says Seabright, if we want to help both women and men reach their full potential economically, creating an economy that is both better and fairer.

The War of the Sexes begins with a wide-ranging discussion of prehistory and evolutionary biology before jumping, quite suddenly, to contemporary differences between male and female economic power. The gap would have been nicely overcome by readings of anthropology and history as careful as those Seabright presents from evolutionary biology and psychology. But this economist does not make the claim so hated by those of us at the more 'cultural' end of the social sciences, that all of our social behaviour can only be explained by market mechanisms or by biology. He deeply disapproves of people, from the left or the right, who argue against scientific findings on a political or moral basis, and clearly believes that the answers to explosive debates about sexual difference and gendered abilities can best be found using the superior weapon of science. But he also takes obvious pleasure in revealing findings from biological research that confound conservative views of sexual behaviour, arguing, for example, that 'the view that natural selection has made men promiscuous and women monogamous is factually incorrect'.

These are three quite different books: Kaufmann looks at practices of love and romance, Illouz prefers to unpack the structures underneath such practices, and Seabright tends to be more interested in sex differences than in sexuality. But all three concentrate on the difficult intersection of love, sex and gender. They all argue that love, sex and gender are inherently problematic in the contemporary age. All three see that the distance between men and women creates pain and suffering and, perhaps more importantly, that such misunderstandings have wide-ranging social consequences well beyond individual psyches – consequences for what we earn, when we work, and how and when we raise our children. Presumably, these consequences also deeply affect people who do not live within the heterocentric models of love and sex that are the focus of all three books (a limitation they acknowledge to varying degrees).

Whether the problem is caused by the evolutionary need to care for children much longer than most other animals or the historical formation of women as emotional and men as detached, all three books aim to unpack the truths and the myths that seem to have left women with the short end of the dating stick, not to mention the working stick. Eva Illouz tries to console the reader by writing, 'If there is a non-academic ambition to this book, it is to "ease the aching" of love through an understanding of its social underpinnings.' It is not our own fault love hurts, Illouz tells us; it is inherent to our modern condition.

Understanding exactly why love is guaranteed to be miserable is certainly illuminating. But it hardly makes for cheerful reading for a thirty-something reviewer in the early twenty-first century.

DICK CASEY'S FORGOTTEN PEOPLE

STEPHEN MILLS

25 July 2012

Sick of negative political ads? Turned off by the screaming match that election advertising has become? Had enough scare campaigns about inflation and the cost of living? Thanks to the restoration of a remarkable collection of water-damaged gramophone records, more than sixty years old, you can now experience the political advertising your grandparents listened to. Make up your own mind if they enjoyed a higher level of electoral discourse than we do today.

A collection of thirteen gramophone records was recently exhumed from the University of Melbourne Archives. Damaged by dirt, water and sheer old age, the 33 rpm discs were cleaned, conserved and digitised and are now on the archives' website. That they can now be downloaded as MP3 files is a remarkable story of survival in itself. More than that: these rescued recordings plunge us back into one of Australia's most important and innovative – and expensive – political advertising campaigns.

These are campaign advertisements, but not as we know them today. Broadcast on radio in 1948 and 1949, they formed part of the Liberal Party's long-running campaign to weaken the Chifley Labor government. Adapting the popular format of a radio serial into a sort of political satire, the fifteen-minute broadcasts ran twice-weekly for about twenty months in the lead-up to the 1949 election campaign. In total, about 200 episodes went to air on more than eighty commercial radio stations in every state. Many of the scripts have survived, but the broadcasts themselves were believed lost until these gramophone records, containing twenty-two episodes, came to light. Their existence allows us to experience the complete aural environment of the original broadcasts – voices, accents, music, sound effects – and appraise once again a pioneering propaganda campaign that helped defeat Labor and install Robert Menzies as prime minister.

The star of the show – host, commentator and animating spirit – was 'John Henry Austral'. Played by actor Richard Matthews, Austral is a complex figure. With his smooth voice, educated accent and cool cynicism about life under the Labor government, Austral is the embodiment of the Liberal Party's political philosophy and values. To have a fictitious persona, rather than a politician, as party spokesman was itself unusual – indeed, Austral rarely endorsed or even named any Liberal politician. Instead, as his name suggests, Austral's political affiliations arise from his national identity: his is the voice of commonsense, home-spun wisdom and native morality; he speaks repeatedly of 'your land – and mine'; and the show's theme song is a soaring orchestral version of 'Waltzing Matilda'. Austral's accent is cultivated – he might be a solicitor or doctor, and like any professional he assumes that his client-audience will defer to his authority. But the effect is moderated by an easy Australian vernacular, and he seems careful not to speak down to, but to share his concerns with, his fellow citizens, 'lovers of democracy, lovers of Australia':

> The air is thick today with plans and blueprints for social reconstruction. In all walks of life there are enthusiasts with ready-made answers to all the questions. And 'isms' are two a penny. But – healthy sign as this may be – it doesn't itself mean that problems are solved. We can argue till we are blue in the face about the merits and demerits of a planned economy, bureaucratic controls, nationalisation of this or that. But we'll never get away from the fact that development of any country depends at bottom on the character and outlook of its people.[1]

That said, Austral is a determined and, to modern ears at least, slightly sinister propagandist. He pulls his punches against 'the amiable Mr Chifley' and his predecessor, 'the late John Curtin', but unreservedly damns their 'socialistic government', with its 'repressive officialdom', 'political oppression', 'regimentation' and affiliation 'with a minority which owes its allegiance to a foreign, anti-British, anti-Australian power'. Most of the episodes end with what in marketing terms is his 'call to action': sometimes he invites listeners to write to him with their comments; more often he reminds them about the impending election:

> We complain about high taxes – but keep electing the blokes who stand behind them. It's time to stop grumbling and do

---

1 The recordings can be accessed through the John Henry Austral Collection in the University of Melbourne's digitised archives.

something! Our opportunity is just around the corner. Let's make the most of it!

Joining Austral is a diverse cast of characters who act out the daily dramas that are the principal stuff of these ads. The point of this campaign was to undermine confidence in the Labor government by illustrating the difficulties and anxieties of life under Chifley. Food prices were rising. Shoppers queued. Essential goods were still rationed through coupons, just as they had been during the war. A black market thrived, 'dragging decent people down into the mud' and 'degrading this land of ours – your land, and mine,' as Austral reminds us. Teenagers wasted their evenings. And somewhere not too far away, the communists were secretly plotting their revolution.

These themes were all deftly conveyed in little scenes: men discussing black-market whisky in a pub, wives chastising their husbands in the living room for going on strike, teenagers lounging on a street corner, shoppers quizzing shopkeepers about the groceries. Through clever use of accent and tone, the actors underline the political message. A soapbox speaker loudly condemns big business with a rich working-class accent: 'Why should rich men loll in luxurious idleness while you toil and sweat?' His critic responds with the facts, in an upright, prim voice: 'Big business is owned by small shareholders.' Austral asks us, 'Who do you choose to believe: men of calibre or the ill-informed spielers of socialism?' The communist plotters, of course, all mutter and splutter in heavily accented (German? Russian?) tones, and call each other comrade with a capital 'K'.

And then there are the women. Almost without exception, the women characters are heard in the home or the shop. These are not income earners, but mothers and wives. But it is precisely from these roles that, in Austral's world, they derive practical wisdom and moral authority, which in turn gives them a legitimate and in fact powerful political voice. Managing household budgets, they understand the impact of inflation; they are the 'chief sufferers' of strikes because (they argue) such disputes cause price increases; raising children they understand education policy. In the privacy of the living room, they cajole and persuade their husbands with common sense and moderation – while reminding them not to drop ash on the carpet.

The political strategy is clear. John Henry Austral represented the middle class in all its solidity and anxiety. He speaks as they do, promotes their values, articulates their concerns and unflinchingly attacks those who threatened them: communists, indolent workers, and centralised planners in Canberra: 'Unless we produce more and keep on saving our savings, all our over-centralised economic planning cannot save Australia from disastrous inflation!'

•

Six years before the Austral broadcasts, before the Liberal Party had been created and while the Second World War still raged, another radio broadcast had invoked the middle class in a similar way. Former United Australia Party prime minister Robert Menzies, a member of a fragmented and dispirited opposition, delivered his landmark statement of political values, 'The Forgotten People':

> The time has come to say something of the forgotten class, the middle class, those people who are constantly in danger of being ground between the upper and nether millstones of the false class war; the middle class who, properly regarded, represent the backbone of this country … the kind of people I myself represent in parliament: salary-earners, shopkeepers, skilled artisans, professional men and women, farmers and so on.[2]

As the political scientist Judith Brett has observed, although there is an attractive quality about Menzies' praise for the family and the home-centred life and his defence of values beyond the material and utilitarian, it also has a hard, unforgiving quality, a smug sanctimony and an authoritarian moralising reminiscent of a headmaster or vicar. Like 'The Forgotten People', the John Henry Austral series embodies a mix of inclusive and exclusive values, extolling a society made up not of classes or organisations, but of families in their homes and consumers in their shops; a society in which ideology shrinks before individual moral character; a society of freedoms rather than rights. Big business is nothing more than the small shareholders who own it, while organised labour is a collection of conscientious working Australians under the sway of union officials or organisers who are ignorant rabble-rousers, many of them communists.

---

2   Robert Menzies, *The Forgotten People: And Other Studies in Democracy* (Sydney: Angus and Robertson, 1943), 1.

Like Menzies' broadcast, too, the John Henry Austral series constitutes a political strategy dressed as a disinterested statement about national interest – a party-political statement that does not mention parties. Where Menzies had spoken to the middle class in 1942 about the long term, John Henry Austral had an immediacy about his message to them, explicitly focusing their attention on the electoral opportunity, which in 1948 lay just ahead of them. In one episode, Austral asks, 'And who is the public?' His rhetorical question is met with an anthem of responses, the voices of the Forgotten People:

> I, the housewife and the mother of a family.
> I, the factory worker.
> I, who work in an office, or nurse in a hospital.
> I, the clerk – the bank teller – the man at a desk or a counter.
> I, the school teacher – business executive – doctor – dentist
> – family man.
> I, the man on the land, whether farmer, grazier or labourer.
> I, the returned soldier.
> I, the woman who also served.
> I, the wharf labourer, miner, sleeper cutter, the trade
> unionist everywhere!

The political strategy behind these broadcasts is pursued relentlessly and consistently – but also with a light touch. Entertainment was a necessary path to instruction, and the audience gathered around the wireless sets was presented with diverse offerings of historical fare – such as pioneer stories about John Batman and John Forrest – as well as what we might think of as comedy sketches. To convey the impact of price rises, for example, Austral introduces a story about 'the strange adventures of Mr William van Winkle'. This 'highly respectable' man falls asleep in 1937 – only to wake up eleven years later. A kookaburra laughs at him as he struggles with his long beard and when he gets to the barber shop, he is astounded to find the cost of a haircut has risen; train fares and greengrocer prices have doubled as well. He tells his solicitors that he is living in a 'nightmare' and, as they explain the modern economy, with its producer subsidies and black markets, they smoothly reassure him that we all get used to that feeling. Finally, as he works out what has happened to him, Mr van Winkle tells anyone who will listen, 'I've been asleep for ten years – but you're all still asleep!'

In another elaborate story about rising prices or, as it was understood then, the falling value of the pound, Mrs Buyer goes shopping in 1908 in 'Mr Golden Quid's Emporium' (the series was strong on eponyms). She orders a long list of household goods. Mr Quid tells her the price of each – adding up columns of shillings and pence in a miraculous feat of mental arithmetic that gives a handy reminder to modern listeners about the virtues of decimal currency – and informs her that her basket of goods will cost seven shillings. But then, in a trick of time travel achieved through simple sound effects, Mrs Buyer is transported four decades into the present day, 1948. She walks into the same shop, 'but imagine her surprise when, instead of the sovereign-like figure of Mr Golden Quid, she was confronted by a thin and weedy gentleman with a paper-like complexion and a green wrinkled look'.

This papery Mr Quid – modern listeners may need reminding that the £1 note was green in colour – is surly, his service is truculent and his prices strike Mrs Buyer as astronomical. Her basket of goods now costs – after more mental arithmetic – sixteen shillings and seven pence! And this includes coupons for the butter and the tea! Mrs Buyer cannot pay, so Mr Quid goes through her shopping and throws out most of her goods, including chopping the leg of lamb (now, mutton) in half right there on the counter. 'There,' the new Mr Quid declares with malicious triumph, 'is seven shillings of goods at present-day values. You can't have been here for forty years – certainly not for the past eight' – that is, since Labor came to power.

Perhaps the strangest episode to modern ears is the one promoting the Liberal Party's idea of funding community centres 'for the advancement of culture and the awakening of public spiritedness among our younger men'. In this sketch, four young men meet after work and are bored: they do nothing more edgy than smoke cigarettes and go to the pictures. But the joke is that their fathers all fear they are up to mischief or, in the exasperated words of one of the lads, having 'the odd spot of marijuana, or whatever they call it'. Later that evening, quizzed by his father, another one declares:

> Well, I met the lads. First thing we did was to have a shot of cocaine all round. Then while Bill and Tom went off to one of those houses – you know – Dick and I went to the back door of the Trumpeters Arms and sank six double brandies in quick succession, prior to murdering a policeman and doing a couple of hold-ups. Then we went home.

This kind of humour is not what we expect in a political broadcast these days – whether from the Liberal Party or anyone else.

•

How these disc copies of the broadcasts survived is not entirely clear. Indeed, it's not clear why they were made in the first place. They have lain undisturbed in the archives of the University of Melbourne and it is only recently that their unique status has been recognised; certainly no other major collecting library possesses anything like this. They were packaged for the post in Phillip Street, Sydney – home of the Macquarie Broadcasting Network and its production arm Artransa – and addressed to station 2GN in Goulburn, New South Wales. It seems unlikely that the discs were distributed to every station for the original broadcast; perhaps this collection was assembled after the campaign was over and distributed in this more durable format. Even so, it is an odd sample, covering the first five episodes of the series, broadcast in February–March 1948 as well as a selection from much later, in 1949.

And did the discs ever reach Goulburn? A one-shilling railway freight stamp stuck on the package suggests they did. But at some point, somehow, they ended up with Richard Casey, federal president of the Liberal Party, and – according to another sticker on the package – he sent them off to London to an acquaintance, the prominent Australian businessman Sir Clive Baillieu. Casey and Baillieu had overlapped in Washington during the war, Casey as Australian ambassador and Baillieu as a British government representative on the purchasing commission. Perhaps the discs never made it to Goulburn, but were handed back to the Liberal Party whence Casey thought they would make interesting listening in London. After Baillieu died in 1967, the discs made their way back to Australia and were ultimately handed over, soiled and travel stained, to the archives which are accessible, after all, in the university's Baillieu Library.

Dick Casey was the brains behind the Austral campaign. Gallipoli veteran, diplomat, member of parliament and then wartime governor of Bengal, he had tried unsuccessfully to return to politics via Liberal preselection for the new party's first electoral contest in 1946. He settled for the federal presidency. A convert from his Washington days to the emerging practice of public relations, Casey saw merit in a series of radio talks that would run not during the election campaign but well before the campaign, aimed at shaping public opinion at the very time it was not actively focused on an electoral choice. Moreover, Casey turned out to be a brilliantly successful party fundraiser. Using his connections into the business community in Australia and London, and riding the tide of alarm at Chifley's bank nationalisation plans, Casey raised huge sums – at least A£250,000 – and could fund a lavish campaign. Precise figures are not possible, but the Canberra journalist Dick Whitington later reported claims that Casey had raised A£1 million and had spent A£800,000 on the 1949 campaign. Adjusted for inflation that is a campaign budget of $40 million in today's terms, which would buy a very competitive quantity of market research, TV advertising and campaign websites.

Casey's biggest contribution to the campaign, however, was poaching Labor's entire advertising agency to run the Liberal campaign. South African born, Sim Rubensohn had successfully run his own commercial advertising agency in Sydney, the Hansen–Rubensohn Company, since the late 1920s. By the early 1930s he had won the account to manage political advertising for the state Labor Party and, in short order, for federal Labor as well. He was well connected, shrewd and good at his work. Advertising was a sometimes-murky business: in a sensational court case in 1935, it emerged that Rubensohn had assisted police in arresting an advertising salesman, Douglas McConnell, in possession of a brown paper parcel containing 500 one-pound notes, in Rubensohn's own office. McConnell was charged with inciting Rubensohn to bribe an alderman of Sydney County Council to win the council's advertising account; he was ultimately acquitted. Rubensohn's advertising for the Labor Party had attracted the admiring attention of Menzies who, after the Liberals were defeated in their first federal election in 1946, bemoaned his party's lack of a 'clever set of advertising tradesmen at work in the centre' like Labor had. Salvation was near at hand, however: with bank nationalisation, Rubensohn split from federal Labor; when Casey heard of the row, he was quick to offer him the Liberal Party account.

It is not clear who was more shocked at the switch. Chifley, initially at least, accepted the departure of Labor's ace with remarkable equanimity; the Liberal Party state branches, on the other hand, were nervous about taking on a new and unknown talent 'at the centre' of the party and beyond the reach of their parochial interests. For Rubensohn's part, the deal was irresistible. Like Casey, he was convinced of the political merits of a long-run radio series and believed he could not only knock over Chifley's bank plans but perhaps also win lucrative concessions for his other clients from a new Liberal government. And he negotiated a 15 per cent commission on all campaign outlays. In a peculiar display of egotism or arrogance, Rubensohn took to illegally parking his luxury car in the street outside his city office; within three years he had racked up 183 parking fines.

If Rubensohn was the successful 'suit', then his 'creative' was also critical to the success of the agency. Pip Cogger, an Englishman who had been wounded in Mesopotamia while serving with the Royal Field Artillery, had decided to switch to copywriting while convalescing in a London hospital in 1919. He made his way to New Zealand and thence to Sydney, telling journalist Gavin Souter in 1953 that he had served as 'advocate-in-written words' for virtually everything 'from the damnation of Communism to the deification of deodorants'. Rubensohn and Cogger were to switch back to Labor almost immediately after the Liberals' 1949 triumph, and Rubensohn continued to manage Labor's campaigns until finally eased out in 1974. But for now, Cogger had the task of crafting the mellifluous, ardent words of John Henry Austral and the varied dialogues of the shoppers, housekeepers, farmers and pioneers who populated his world.

•

It should be pointed out, though it is perhaps obvious, that the John Henry Austral campaign was launched entirely without the benefit of market research. No focus groups were hurt in the development of the Liberals' strategy. Nor was there any targeting of marginal seats. Aiming for the unconverted majority middle class was as targeted as things got in the 1940s, as the Liberal Party's federal executive noted in early 1949:

> Propaganda should not be designed to please those who will support us anyway. It need not waste time trying to wean diehard Labor supporters from their allegiance. It should be aimed at the greatly expanded middle class.

The John Henry Austral campaign should not be held up as some paragon of virtuous political communication. It played on emotions rather than the rational mind. It was deceptive in presenting its little dramatisations as factually accurate. It was negative in its own sly way. And Austral was as remorseless a propagandist as they come, wedging his opponents at every opportunity. But looking back at the campaign from the great distance of more than sixty years, and listening once more to these sounds, one significant merit is apparent. This advertising represented a concerted, extended effort to present voters with a coherent and complete worldview – a political philosophy. John Henry Austral was middle-class, market-based, anti-communist, anti-Canberra and nationalist because that was the view and ideal of the Liberal Party he represented. At a time when party campaign advertising has abandoned platforms to focus almost exclusively on manoeuvring over short-term issues and attacking the character of rival leaders, that is not a bad example to look back on.

FLETCH, MUSCLES AND THE ROCKET

JOCK GIVEN

26 February 2013

Ken Rosewall must have spent more time on Australia's centre courts this summer than any Australian player. He was at Ken Rosewall Arena in Sydney when Bernard Tomic thanked 'Mr Rosewall' for his first ATP Tour tournament trophy. He was at Rod Laver Arena when Andy Murray was too good for Roger Federer in a semifinal of the Australian Open, and he was there two nights later when Novak Djokovic was too good for Murray. Australians see a lot of this in January. There are many more Australian tennis champions in the stands than on the courts and it has been that way for a long time. Rosewall will turn eighty next year; Rod Laver will turn seventy-five in August, the day after Roger Federer's birthday; Margaret Court is seventy. Australia's last winner of an Australian Open singles title was Chris O'Neil in 1978. In six of the ten championships before that win, both the female finalists were Australian.

Australia's golden age has produced a book bubble lately, with the release of Rosewall's *Muscles: The Story of Ken Rosewall, Australia's Little Master of the Courts* (as told to Richard Naughton), Laver's *The Education of a Tennis Player* (with Bud Collins), and Hugh Lunn's *The Great Fletch: The Dazzling Life of Wimbledon Aussie Larrikin Ken Fletcher*. These players come from an era when future champions lived with ironic nicknames from their early days on the court: Rosewall became 'Muscles' because he didn't have any; Laver, the 'Rocket' because, as a boy, he wasn't one. The two of them ended up in one of the great rivalries in the history of tennis, its duration, intensity and closeness masked by the invisibility of many of the matches they played as professional one-night stands all over the world, often in makeshift venues, in the 1960s and early 70s.

Laver came from country Queensland, Rockhampton, about 650 kilometres north of Brisbane; Rosewall from Rockdale in Sydney's south. Neither was tall even by the standards of the time: Laver 1.73 metres (five feet, seven inches); Rosewall, four years older, an inch shorter. Rosewall and his almost exact contemporary, Balmain boy Lew Hoad, were teenage stars. Chosen for the Davis Cup training squad in 1951 at seventeen, they travelled overseas the following year with an Australian team whose star, Frank Sedgman, won the singles and the men's and mixed doubles at Wimbledon. In 1953, at nineteen, Rosewall won the Australian singles title at Kooyong and then the French title on clay in Paris. Back at Kooyong between Christmas and New Year, Rosewall and Hoad became national heroes when Australia won the Davis Cup from the United States. Down two matches to one after the doubles, both won their reverse singles, Hoad over just-crowned US singles champion Tony Trabert and Rosewall against reigning Wimbledon champion Vic Seixas.

Davis Cup coach Harry Hopman might not have thought Laver the quickest kid around the court but he saw enough in him to select him as one of two youngsters for the Australians' overseas tour in 1956. Laver lost the Wimbledon junior final but won the junior US and was at Forest Hills to see Hoad fall one match short of the Grand Slam Laver would win twice – the Australian, French, Wimbledon and US singles championships in the same year. Hoad made the cover of *Sports Illustrated* and the US final, but his Sydney mate Rosewall got through as well, played better in the windy conditions and won in four sets.

•

Players now measure their achievements by the number of 'slams', or major tournaments, they win. Margaret Court won twenty-four in singles, the record, including all four, the Grand Slam, in 1970. Roger Federer has seventeen, the most by a man. In three separate years he has won three of the four, but has never won all four. Rod Laver's two Grand Slams came first as an amateur in 1962, then in 1969 as a professional, the first calendar year professionals were allowed to play in all four major tournaments. It was the chance of a Grand Slam in 1969 that *Boston Globe* tennis writer Bud Collins says gave him his book about Laver, first published in 1971 and re-released in 2009 for the fortieth anniversary of the achievement. Laver's agent had approached Collins about a memoir. Publishers Simon & Schuster were interested but only if Rod won the four tournaments: 'No Slam, no book', though Collins didn't tell Laver that.

The fact that he won a Grand Slam of mixed doubles with Margaret Court (Margaret Smith at the time) in 1963 is what makes Ken Fletcher's disappearance from the list of Australian tennis champions of the era so puzzling. Explaining 'the dazzling life' of this 'Wimbledon Aussie larrikin' is the job former journalist with *The Australian*, Hugh Lunn, sets himself in *The Great Fletch*. With Grand Slams in singles, Rod Laver and Margaret Court have got arenas named after them at Melbourne Park, where the

Australian Open gets played each January. With plenty of Grand Slam singles tournament wins but no Grand Slam, Ken Rosewall's Arena is in Homebush. Ken Fletcher has a park on the river outside the Pat Rafter Arena in Brisbane.

•

The authors of these three books have different relationships with their subjects. Lunn was the oldest of old mates with Fletcher, who died in 2006. They were 'in the playpen together as babies', at different schools a few hundred metres apart in the Brisbane suburb of Annerley, young men travelling the world together and, in 1965 and 1966, tennis player and cheerleader at Wimbledon.

This is a much more personal story than the other two. Fletch, we learn, didn't like people who were tight with their money, people with no personality, and skites. 'No Australian man was ever more upfront about his feelings for others.' There is plenty of tennis, because that was what Fletcher was best known for – as well as his mixed doubles Grand Slam in 1963, he won another five major mixed doubles titles, won men's doubles titles at Wimbledon and in the French Open, and made the singles final of the Australian Open in 1963, losing to Roy Emerson, and the Wimbledon or French quarterfinals five times. But there is just as much of the anguish of falling short in an era when those around him were climbing higher, of the difficulties of piloting his own prodigious talent – 'the greatest and purest tennis shot I have seen in my life, and I have seen them all, was Fletcher's forehand', says a contemporary, Jim Shepherd. There is a lot about life beyond tennis courts, sometimes rich and raucous, at other times troubled and impecunious. A park by the Brisbane River, just outside the courts, with swings and barbecues and lots of people, seems a much better memorial for Fletch than an arena.

Bud Collins is the voice of Rod Laver in *The Education of a Tennis Player*, credited as 'Rod Laver with Bud Collins'. The reader gets Laver's story, peppered with wisecracks that sound more Boston than Rockhampton. Cliff Drysdale is 'a good-looking South African who could talk a Kruger Park lion into becoming a vegetarian'. On one Laver backhand: 'You don't plan a shot like that, not unless you're on marijuana, and the only grass I'm partial to is Wimbledon's.' But Collins, Laver's choice of biographer, gives a strong sense of the distance a kid from Rockhampton traversed to become a world champion. He worked out very early what he wanted to do and set about doing it. It meant leaving home, travelling constantly, living everywhere at once, eventually mainly in California, grinding out tennis matches when he was exhausted or injured or just not playing his best, getting himself ready for the ones that really mattered. Collins doesn't give us a neat linear tale of Laver's career or even of his second Grand Slam year. The rough chronology of tournaments and matches is there, but he detours for the backstories and twenty-five 'Lessons' on topics like 'The Crisp Volley' and 'Playing Against Familiar Opponents'.

Rosewall's biographer Richard Naughton – credited 'as told to ...' – is an academic lawyer and tennis lover, a senior fellow in the law faculty at Monash University and author of *Australian Labour Law: Text, Cases and Commentary*, as well as a biography of Australia's first Wimbledon champion, Norman Brookes. His story is relentlessly chronological, but it seems exactly the right way to write about Rosewall's long quest, match after match, set after set, serves, returns, approaches, passes, handshakes at the net. Rosewall just kept doing it and in a way he still does. You can't summarise 'Muscles' without diminishing him.

•

All three books are centrally about the era when becoming a professional tennis player meant not being able to play the four major tournaments. Rosewall turned pro at the start of 1957, aged twenty-two, Laver in 1963, at twenty-four. Fletcher, two years younger than Laver, stayed an amateur. John Newcombe, younger still, won Wimbledon as an amateur in 1967 and turned professional right at the beginning of the Open Era. This was not a split like World Series Cricket or Super League that blew sports apart for a couple of years before they got back together again and lived happily ever after. It went on for decades. Pancho Gonzales turned professional after winning the US championships in 1948 and 1949 aged twenty and twenty-one. He got to play his country's national championships again at forty. Two-time Wimbledon champion Laver got a letter from the All England Tennis Club after he turned professional advising him he could no longer wear the club tie.

When professionals were finally allowed to play the major championships again, they were called 'Opens' but separate playing circuits continued for most of the year. Queensland's amateur tennis boss Bill Edwards, no supporter of pro tennis, put on an embarrassing Australian Championships in January 1969, apparently heading to the races one afternoon rather than watching the tennis. This was how Queensland welcomed the Rocket back to Milton. The International Lawn Tennis

Federation banned Rosewall, Laver and members of the professional World Championship Tennis circuit from the French Open and Wimbledon in 1972 and the professionals boycotted Wimbledon the following year over a different issue. Australia's professionals could play the Opens from 1968 but weren't allowed back to play the Davis Cup until 1973.

The pro tours were rough and hard, small groups of fine players up against each other over and over again on all kinds of weird, temporary surfaces – canvas stretched over boards or even ice rinks – and only occasionally getting access to the established tennis venues. They drove themselves from one town to the next each day after treasurer Rosewall had counted the money, set up again, and faced up to the same opponents. If you got injured you played on because if you didn't there'd be no crowd and no pay next time the troupe came to town.

We know how the story ends now, in an Open Era when professionals got to play in the great championships again, but there was never any certainty about that. The pros were better, and if you wanted to be the best and make decent money without taking a PR job with Dunlop or Slazenger then you had to turn your back on the great trophies and accept it might be forever. When Rosewall turned pro, Pancho Gonzales whipped him, although Rosewall eventually turned that around. When Laver turned pro at the start of 1963, having just won his first Grand Slam against the amateurs, Lew Hoad beat him in their first seven matches and Rosewall in four of their first six. Meanwhile, the next generation of 'amateurs' were winning the major championships the pros couldn't enter.

•

Laver says Rosewall is the 'least appreciated great player in the history of tennis'. He – Rosewall – 'was the player we all had most trouble with'. In the French Pro Indoor final in 1963, Laver says he played 'the finest tennis I believe I've ever produced' and still got beaten by Rosewall. Fred Stolle said he'd 'rather play Laver any day than Rosewall. If the Rocket's hitting his shots there's no chance for me ... But there's always the chance he'll be a bit off and then you're right in the match. Rosewall was never off.' Harry Hopman said the initially 'scrawny and slow' Rocket 'worked harder at it than anybody else'. 'The dangerous thing about Laver is he hits the impossible shot when he's out of position – the time you least expect it,' said Pancho Gonzales. Rosewall thought – and Laver doesn't deny – that the Rocket always found something special when there was big money at stake.

One tennis historian scores the many Laver–Rosewall matches 80–67 Laver's way, another 79–71, also Laver's way, including 22–7 in the Open Era. On his way to his two Grand Slams, Laver met and beat Roy Emerson in five of the eight tournaments, but Rosewall only once, in the French final in Paris in June 1969. They'd met in the final a year earlier, in the 1968 Paris Spring; Rosewall had prevailed. This time at Roland Garros, the Rocket put Muscles down in straight sets. The tennis jury is still out on what happened: some thought it was Laver's day, Laver's year; others that it was just Laver. With two legs of his second Grand Slam secured, Laver won thirty-one straight matches between July and September, including Wimbledon, the US Open and five other tournaments. After winning the four major tournaments in a single year for the second time, he never won another one.

•

The stories of Fletch, Muscles and Rocket are about the long, hard work required to get to the top of tennis and stay there. But tennis, more than most other sports, is also about moments and these books feast on them. There's Rosewall in his first Wimbledon final in 1954, his best chance it turned out, getting a strange soft serve on match point from the Czech Drobný and pushing it into the net. And Laver, match point down against Marty Mulligan in the quarters at Roland Garros in 1962; getting a crucial line call against Tony Roche late in the fifth set of the semifinal at the 1969 Australian Open, the first tournament in his 1969 Slam; hitting a backhand slice across court to pass John Newcombe, who was serving at a set apiece, 4–2, 0–15 in the 1969 Wimbledon final – a point Laver later thought to be 'the whole match'. For Ken Fletcher, it's a different kind of moment: playing the Hungarian István Gulyás in the 1966 French, unable to put away three smashes in a row, fed another by the scrambling Gulyás, choosing to belt it over the stands and into the Bois de Boulogne, shouting, 'Get that one, you Hungarian bastard!' It's Fletcher's response to the relentlessness of top tennis – or maybe just a grass court specialist's frustration at how often the ball comes back on clay.

If you were starting to watch a bit of sport on TV in the early 1970s, after live satellite broadcasts began but before colour, you might have seen the Davis Cup final in Cleveland Ohio in late 1973, when all the pros were finally allowed back. Australia picked the apparently ageless Rosewall (thirty-nine), Mal Anderson (thirty-eight), Laver (thirty-five) and Newcombe (twenty-nine). The younger Geoff Masters and Ross Case, who later won a Wimbledon doubles, were there too, but it was a sign that Australia's golden tennis era was almost done. They all had to earn their spots. Laver showed he was ready at the Sydney Indoor tournament, beating Rosewall and recently crowned US Open champion Newcombe. Picked for the semifinal against Czechoslovakia at Kooyong, he beat Jan Kodeš in straight sets, won a marathon doubles with Rosewall, and beat Jiří Hřebec – surprise conqueror of Newcombe on the first day – in five sets.

For the final in Cleveland, the triumphant return of Australia's greats to the Davis Cup, Newcombe and Laver got all the work. Both won their opening day singles in five sets, Laver coming back from two-sets-to-one down to beat Tom Gorman. Then captain Neale Fraser chose Newcombe ahead of Rosewall to partner Laver in the doubles. They made short work of the Americans and the Cup was Australia's. Two decades after his and Lew Hoad's teenage heroics at Kooyong, Rosewall didn't get the chance to put on his whites. The next year, astonishingly, the thirty-nine-year-old Rosewall made the finals of Wimbledon – twenty years after his first final there – and the US Open, five years after Laver's last wins there, but had to play the tough young superstar of the moment, Jimmy Connors, in both. Rosewall won just eight games over six sets in the two finals. Fans came away from Forest Hills, according to *Tennis World*, wearing 'the glazed expression of those caught too near an exploding bomb'. It felt like the cruellest luck that Rosewall had been extraordinary enough to be on the court at all. To be so good for so long, to want it so much ... and that was the reward.

Whether or not Connors really demanded that his manager 'Get me Laver!' after that 1974 US Open, as was reported, Jimmy got him. The Rocket turned up at Caesar's Palace, Las Vegas, in February 1975 for a match billed as '$100,000 Winner-take-all', though Laver tells Bud Collins he got $60,000 for it, his biggest ever single payday. The twenty-two-year-old American was too good for the thirty-six-year-old Australian, but Laver did manage to get a set off him.

Laver also hit a shot that has stayed with me, a running forehand from way, way out of court. I didn't know then what it took to play that shot – the left forearm as big as Rocky Marciano's and the seven-inch wrist, the legs to get to the ball, the head to believe it was possible, the heart to want it. But something about it stuck. It was a moment and you were so lucky to see it. Jimmy couldn't reach it, it was in, it was the Rocket.

FORTY MILLENNIA OF INDIGENOUS HISTORY AT THE BRITISH MUSEUM

MARIA NUGENT

8 May 2015

The wide press coverage of the opening of the British Museum's *Indigenous Australia: Enduring Civilisation* exhibition was as much a result of Prince Charles' quips about Prince Harry on 'walkabout' in Australia as it was of the exhibition itself. The formal reception, held in the museum's Great Court, was a memorable event – and not just because one museum trustee, Grayson Perry, attended as his alter ego Claire in full Victoriana garb, or because Kathy Lette was swanning about in a dress styled on the Aboriginal flag, or even because Prince Charles asked me whether I had submitted my chapter for the exhibition book on time. (I had, nearly.) It was memorable also because it felt momentous – as ceremonial occasions for landmark events often do.

And there is little doubt that the exhibition is a landmark event. This is the first time the British Museum has staged a major exhibition devoted to Indigenous Australia, a fact that Neil MacGregor, the institution's soon-to-be-former director, acknowledged more than once. He also observed what an anomalous and unacceptable state of affairs this was, given that Indigenous Australians are considered the 'oldest continuing civilisation' in the world and the British Museum is an institution dedicated to telling the stories of the world's great civilisations. Promises have been made to remedy the situation, with a permanent display of Aboriginal and Torres Strait Islander culture and history one possibility. It is late coming, but it is a start.

Indigenous Australia has been skilfully curated by Gaye Sculthorpe, a Palawa woman whose ancestors were from north-east Tasmania. Sculthorpe, who led the development of the Bunjilaka Gallery at Museum Victoria before spending a decade or so with the National Native Title Tribunal, is responsible for the Oceania part of the museum's Department of Africa, Oceania and the Americas. She was enticed to the British Museum in 2013 by another Australian, Lissant Bolton, who heads up the Department of Africa, Oceania and the Americas (or what is sometimes dubbed 'the rest of the world'); by the time she arrived, the decision to mount an Indigenous Australia exhibition had already been made.

Since around 2007, the National Museum of Australia and the British Museum have been slowly developing a partnership that has included staff exchanges and collection research. Some foundational research was undertaken by Ian Coates from the National Museum of Australia, and that work, which had an emphasis on the collectors and the conditions under which objects were collected, has been bolstered by Sculthorpe and others since. This partnership eventually led to a successful Australian Research Council grant application for a project called 'Engaging Objects: Indigenous Communities, Museum Collections and the Representation of Indigenous Histories', led by anthropologist Howard Morphy, involving the British Museum, the NMA and the Australian National University. Along with anthropologist John Carty, also from ANU, I have been involved in the project since it commenced in late 2011.

The future dimly glimpsed in 2007 has arrived. On taking up the position at the British Museum, Sculthorpe was immediately faced with the considerable task of pulling together an exhibition in a reasonably short time with limited labour and resources. *Indigenous Australia: Enduring Civilisation* is largely due to her energy, unfailing efforts, and ability to bring people together. Early in the process, she developed a strong vision for the exhibition, which she envisaged would present an account of Indigenous Australia spanning 40,000 years and incorporate a component dealing with the almost 250 years since Captain Cook.

Her commitment didn't falter, even though it was not common for British Museum exhibitions to deal with such 'recent' history, and even when early audience research indicated that some museum-goers didn't want to be reminded of the terrible deeds done in Britain's name. At the same time, Indigenous Australians were adamant that the truth should be told about violence on the frontier. The exhibition would need to be not only clear-eyed about the violence of that encounter and the dispossession and destruction it caused, but also attentive to Indigenous people's agency, resilience and creativity. It is this doubled perspective that is captured in the exhibition's subtitle, 'enduring civilisation', which signals the remarkable persistence of Indigenous Australian civilisation even as Indigenous Australians endured the imposition of European civilisation.

Since the media in Britain and Australia were told back in January that the exhibition was to be staged this year, much of the discussion in print, especially in Australia, has focused on the issue of repatriation of museum objects to Indigenous people. While few gainsay the repatriation of human remains, when it comes to 'ethnographic' or cultural objects the matter is less clear-cut. For those advocating immediate return, some familiar themes have been rehearsed, including the portrayal of the British Museum as an unreconstructed and irredeemable imperialist institution and its collections as little more than colonial loot.

Indeed, over lunch recently, Gaye Sculthorpe told me that the first review she read the morning the exhibition opened to the public was written by Zoe Pilger (daughter of Australian filmmaker and writer John Pilger) for *The Independent*. In a blustering piece, Pilger the younger criticised the exhibition in rather simplistic terms as little more than a piece of colonial denialism, described the objects as stolen and called for their immediate return, and was indignant about various other matters on Aboriginal people's behalf. Huffing and puffing about the inclusion of a *larrakitj* (memorial pole) by Gawirrin Gumana, which incorporates an image of both Barama and Captain Cook, and objecting to the wall text describing the object as 'a gesture of historical and political generosity', Pilger asked, 'But why should the artist be generous?'

A righteous, moralising anger on behalf of Indigenous people has sustained the Pilger family output for some time. In a thoughtful rebuttal of the 'review', art critic Jeremy Eccles suggested in the online forum *Aboriginal Art Directory* that the comments demonstrated very little appreciation of 'the remarkable Yolngu capacity for generosity in the face of white rapacity'. Instead of grasping the subtle politics of generosity and exchange within which much Indigenous art production is embedded, Eccles wrote, 'Zoe oppresses them with a simplistic binary obsession with race and her assumption that Yolngu philosophy is as racist as her own.'

•

Generosity was much on display during the week of festivities surrounding the exhibition's opening. In attendance were the young filmmaker and director Ishmael Marika and the artist Wukun Wanambi, director of the Buku-Larrnggay Mulka Arts Centre, who are both from north-east Arnhem Land. After visiting the British Museum and its collection in 2013 and seeing the crowds of people swarming around the Reading Room in the Great Court, Wukun Wanambi produced a remarkable memorial pole, or *larrakitj*, covered in his ancestral designs of fish. 'The fish are swimming from creek to creek, river to river, searching for their destiny,' he explains. 'Just like all these people from all over the world coming to the British Museum here. Everybody is searching for their own story.' This pole is on show in a small room (Gallery 3) off the main entrance of the British Museum, complementing the larger exhibition, which is upstairs in a gallery carved out of the old Reading Room. Ishmael and Wukun were present throughout the week of the opening, welcoming VIPs and others with song and music, patiently introducing them to their art and culture and thanking the British Museum for showing it to the world.

Few of the reviews of the exhibition that followed, and there have been many, have endorsed Zoe Pilger's views. Sculthorpe was relieved that the second she read was by *The Guardian*'s art critic Jonathan Jones (not to be mistaken for the Wiradjuri artist of the same name). He gave the show five stars, appreciating a focus on Indigenous art and culture that doesn't shy away from history and politics. Acknowledging the ever-present repatriation debate, Jones ended by saying that 'the only thing to be said for museum ownership is that it makes it possible to put on an exhibition as enlightening as this'.

Other reviews that appeared around the same time engaged more directly with the section of the exhibition that deals with history since Captain Cook. *The Times*' reviewer noted, for instance, that '*Indigenous Australia* represents more than just a fascinating jumble of artefacts':

> It sets out to present a wider, more subtly nuanced picture of the relationships between Aboriginal people and their colonisers ... Even as it presents a confrontational history of fierce resistance to the relentless advance of the occupiers, of bloody attacks on settlers followed by even bloodier reprisals, it also speaks to two cultures coming together, attempting to understand one another.[3]

It is easy to criticise an interpretation of Australia's colonial history that conceives of it as a 'shared' or 'entwined' history. (Pilger fulminated at the use of metaphors like this in the exhibition.) Some believe that it risks playing down the larger structures of colonial authority and domination that intruded into almost every aspect of Indigenous Australians' lives, and within which Indigenous people were ultimately powerless. Yet,

---

3 Rachel Campbell-Johnston, "Indigenous Australia: Enduring Civilisation at the British Museum," *The Times*, April 21, 2015, https://www.thetimes.co.uk/article/indigenous-australia-enduring-civilisation-at-the-british-museum-mlmnrccszxw.

an overriding emphasis on dispossession and destruction also has limitations, playing down Indigenous people's agency as they sought to engage with the colonisers, to persuade them of the value of their own civilisation, and to seek redress for the destruction of their rights and freedoms. These twinned historical themes are covered in the exhibition – but not, of course, to everyone's satisfaction.

•

It is no easy task to negotiate the intricate politics of history and memory when it comes to Australia's colonial past, and critics and visitors can sometimes underestimate the challenge. One way in which the curatorial team led by Sculthorpe has sought to tread the thorny path between telling histories of domination and histories of determination has been to work with the dynamism that is so often produced by putting together the old and the new. Contemporary art becomes especially powerful here.

There's a corner (literally) of the exhibition where this works, in my view, in particularly productive ways. I might not be impartial here, because it is a 'module' focused on the encounter between Captain Cook and Indigenous Australians, about which I have written a great deal. The display occurs at a pivotal point, where the exhibition's narrative moves into a section covering post-contact history. It draws together an assemblage of objects that are all associated in some way or another with Captain Cook – the memorial pole, which Pilger mentioned; the shield believed to have been used by a Gweagal man in defence against Cook's landing party at Botany Bay in 1770; a copy of Cook's original chart of Botany Bay and the drawing made by the Ra'iatean man Tupaia (who had joined the voyage in Tahiti) showing three Gweagal people fishing with hand lines and spears from two canoes. Two other contemporary artworks are featured as well: Michael Cook's photograph, *Undiscovered #4*, which shows an Aboriginal man dressed as Captain Cook standing on the beach with his ship behind him, and Vincent Namatjira's painting, *James Cook – With Declaration*, in which the 'proclamation' Cook writes to take possession of the territory appears as an extension of his naval uniform.

In various clever and subtle ways, each of these 'objects' works to destabilise the meanings embedded in other pieces and to enrich and multiply the possibilities for the interpretation of this history. Tupaia's sympathetic drawing, for instance, points to interactions other than the violent one (which the shield symbolises) that occurred during the *Endeavour*'s time in the bay in 1770. Michael Cook's photograph and Vincent Namatjira's painting draw attention to the historical myth-making that Cook, as settler foundational figure, has come to represent. Gumana's pole, by contrast, acknowledges Cook's law, but shows that it did not displace Barama's law in Yolngu country. It is not possible to convey all of these potential interpretations in the space of the exhibition, but nonetheless the exhibition provides the resources for interpretative work of this kind. Later this month, I have the opportunity to present a lunchtime lecture at the British Museum on Indigenous Australian interpretations of Captain Cook in which these ideas and arguments can be presented more fully.

So, for all of their educative qualities, exhibitions can only do some of the work of communicating complex ideas and difficult histories to audiences. They are constrained by limitations on the amount of text that can be included, the size and shape of the room (in this case an awkward dogleg) and other contingencies. The book accompanying the exhibition compensates to some extent by providing greater detail and contextual discussion. But other forms of interpretation and dialogue, and other forums, also play their part. Indeed, what is often overlooked in critiques of exhibitions is what goes on around them, and the ways in which they work to provide occasions – and create spaces – for other kinds of history-telling and history-making to occur. This includes, it must be said, the history-making and claim-making that occurs as part of discussions about repatriation that exhibitions like this one provoke.

Among the activity that took place in and around the *Indigenous Australia* exhibition during the week of the opening are some powerful examples of this expanded sphere of historical interpretation and debate, and these contributed to my growing sense that something momentous was taking shape. A number of Aboriginal and Torres Strait Islander people had travelled to London to participate in the festivities, including members of the National Museum of Australia's Indigenous Reference Group and many of the artists whose work is included in the exhibition.

Early one morning midweek, we gathered, along with invited media, at the exhibition to witness a gift-giving ceremony the National Museum of Australia delegation had arranged. They presented the museum director Neil MacGregor with a beautiful glass-blown sculpture in the shape of a dilly bag, made by the award-winning Canberra-based artist Jennifer Kemarre Martiniello. The gift was an expression of the relationship that was growing with the British Museum, and mediated in no small way through the exhibition-making process. On receiving the gift, Neil MacGregor acknowledged not only its sheer beauty, but also its significance in commemorating the exhibition and marking the beginning of a new friendship.

There was obvious symmetry between this event, which was conducted with a powerful grace and reminded us yet again about the subtle arts of the diplomacy of generosity, and some historical episodes featured in the show. A good example from 1863 involves the Coranderrk people of Victoria presenting Queen Victoria and her family with a cache of gifts as part of their efforts to engage diplomatically with the highest authority in Britain. This early-morning performance served to animate such episodes, drawing them into the present and pointing towards continuities that are not so easily captured or appreciated, but are a crucial part of the multi-layered idea of 'enduring civilisation' explored by the exhibition.

Among the visiting dignitaries to London last week was Bunuba woman June Oscar, from the Kimberley region in Western Australia. The British Museum, with the support of the Menzies Centre for Australian Studies at King's College London, under the new directorship of Ian Henderson, brought Oscar over to help open the exhibition. On the evening before the formal reception, she delivered a powerful public lecture in which she took the audience on a journey into her ancestral country and people's history by starting out from the place where we were. From the vantage point of the River Room at the university's Strand campus, overlooking the Thames, she reflected on two histories of violence and impoverishment that come together on Australia's many colonial frontiers. It was a masterclass in telling 'entwined' histories.

Oscar treated the objects in *Indigenous Australia* – including a boomerang believed to have belonged to the Bunuba resistance fighter, Jandamarra, and objects collected from 'native camps' by the local policeman on that frontier and sent to the British Museum in the belief that they 'might be of value and interest' – as mere props for her story. Here she reversed the usual order of things within exhibitions, in which objects take the privileged place. What was important in her lecture were the true stories of the frontier, the country that was the Bunuba people's museum, and the contemporary performances through which contemporary Bunuba keep Jandamarra's memory and legacy alive.

•

Despite the depth of engagement, the sustained critical response, and the energy and excitement that is palpable around the exhibition, the Australian press has quickly become fond of saying that the exhibition has received 'mixed' reviews. This is, it seems to me, a lazy assessment of the reaction to date. It is indicative of the ways in which the Australian media seems intent on finding controversy for the exhibition's present run and for its upcoming iteration at the National Museum of Australia.

Rather than engage with the exhibition's interpretative themes and arguments, the default position is to raise the spectre of repatriation. Calls for the return of cultural material will always attract more notice than other modes of engagement between Indigenous people and museums. As important as it is, and for some communities more than others, the preoccupation with repatriation in the Australian press is often at the expense of other issues and questions, not least of which are the interpretative challenges and possibilities involved in using a collection like the British Museum's as a resource for telling true histories of the encounter between Indigenous Australians and British settlers in ways that reach new audiences.

Much important work went on in opening week, both at public events and behind the scenes. There have been meetings with the British Museum's director and members of the Board of Trustees. There have been visits to the collection storeroom. There have been public lectures, a conference and various diplomatic and ceremonial performances. The British Museum has rung with the voices of a diverse group of Aboriginal and Torres Strait Islander people, all with different views about it and about museums in general. And many different statements about the repatriation issue were voiced, underscoring just how complex the issue is.

When, for instance, Ishmael Marika from Yirrkala was asked by an audience member at a panel discussion how he felt about his people's things in the British Museum, he said that it meant that his culture and people were appreciated. For her part, June Oscar concluded her Menzies Centre lecture by suggesting that the objects in the British Museum, which speak to the shared history of Indigenous Australia and Britain, will be ready to return home only 'when we have learnt from our mixed heritage and accepted our equal Indigenous and non-Indigenous nationhoods'.[4] The idea that the objects will come home only when this mutual

---

4   June Oscar, "Encountering Truth: The Real Life Stories of Objects From Empire's Frontier and Beyond" (Menzies Centre lecture, London, April 29, 2015), *Australian Institute*

recognition of fundamental equality is achieved, and the continuation of Aboriginal law is acknowledged, in the way that Gumana's memorial pole suggests, is a provocative one. Given the current state of affairs, it is hard to put a time frame on it.

Peter Yu, a member of the Council of the National Museum of Australia and chair of its Indigenous Reference Group, also advocated for a go-slow approach to the issue. 'Many Indigenous people and supporters demand that Indigenous property held by the British Museum be repatriated to the descendants of those who once owned it,' he said in a public presentation since published in *The Australian*. 'I deeply respect that view and support the right of people to make that argument. But to move forward and advance the interests of Aboriginal and Torres Strait Islander peoples requires sophisticated dialogue.' Moreover, he argued:

> A mature discussion would appreciate that repatriation is sensitive and problematic. Contemporary Indigenous ownership of the material is often not clear and in all honesty we should not shy away from this; rather we should challenge ourselves on how to retrieve the situation. This reality must be recognised.

This diversity of viewpoints won't satisfy those who call for the immediate and wholesale return of objects. It complicates and unsettles the simple approach taken by much of the press, as journalists continue to canvass the issue as simply a choice between 'preservation' and 'plunder'.

Museums are complex institutions and exhibitions are productive and provocative events. Occasionally, a museum exhibition is staged that does much more than present new interpretations and stories to new audiences. Sometimes, perhaps only rarely, such an exhibition can change how the conversation about relationships between Indigenous people, museums and collections is conducted. *Indigenous Australia: Enduring Civilisation* might well be one of those.

---

of Aboriginal and Torres Strait Islander Studies. https://aiatsis.gov.au/explore/articles/encountering-truth-real-life-stories-objects-empires-frontier-and-beyond.

WHO'S COUNTING?

8 March 2016

For as long as I can remember, my parents never missed an opportunity to accuse each other's family of having been 'touched by the tar brush'. My father would pass comments like, 'It's your mother's side that are the Abos.' My mother would in turn accuse my father of being the 'guilty' one.

I learned a number of things from these everyday expressions of domestic tension. One was that 'being Aboriginal' must not be a good thing. Another was that any reference to being Aboriginal was an insult. But I also learned at an early age that the colour of a person's skin carried meaning – it signified something. For me, knowing we were 'touched by the tar brush' meant we were not white. But in that era, not being recognisably black also meant I was not Aboriginal. This was an early source of anxiety about who I was, and how I was to represent myself.

I remember as a young girl being asked if I was Aboriginal and replying that my maternal grandmother was. My answer was based on my lived understanding of Aboriginality as somehow signified by skin colour or 'look'. Nana was 'dark' and therefore could be called Aboriginal. But could I? All I knew was that our family were 'part-Aboriginal'. It was not until I was much older that I was able to establish with certainty the facts of my mother's ancestry from a long line of Aboriginal women who originated in South Australia. In the interim years, the way our Aboriginality was *not* discussed at home had as much effect on me as did the way it was used as a tool of insult.

But it was not just domestic tensions that produced confusion about what it meant to be 'part-Aboriginal'. My childhood in the 1960s and 1970s was overlaid by a range of commentaries about what being Aboriginal signified out in the world beyond our home, and these infiltrated my self-awareness. I cannot recall any positive message about being Aboriginal. In school, the media and everyday interactions I was faced with frequent assertions that 'Aboriginal people' were a passive lot who lived in the bush and were dirty. We were bombarded with images of semi-naked children with fly-infested noses. For the most part, I was positioned to see Aboriginal people as wanting and in need of help.

In my childhood mind, one exception to this negativity was the TV show *Boney*, in which 'full-blood' Aboriginal people were portrayed as mystical 'beings' and were to be feared as sorcerers. Little did I know that the main Aboriginal character was played by a white person covered in black paint. Nevertheless, some of these representations connected with my own experiences and reflected some things that I already knew. 'Pointing the bone' was a common saying in my childhood, as was a fear of the 'Kadachi Man', who wore feather boots and couldn't be heard approaching. It was common for our parents to caution my brother, sisters and me that if we didn't behave the Kadachi Man would get us.

Throughout my childhood, our family moved regularly from town to town, and from state to state. I attended schools in Geelong, Victoria; in Oodnadatta, South Australia; in Katherine, the Northern Territory; and still others throughout the Illawarra in New South Wales. Later, I came to understand that our frequent moves, which my mother called 'moonlight flits', were about having outstayed our welcome. In the middle of the night we would pack our possessions into an old Falcon and depart on another 'journey'. For a young child, this developed into an unsettling feeling of not belonging or being welcome anywhere.

Then, when I was seven years old, my father took us to New Zealand, which was the mother of all moonlight flits. All I knew about New Zealand was what I had learned at school – that Māori people were scary natives who ate people and, like savages, would kill without cause. Needless to say, my sisters and I were petrified by the time the plane landed in New Zealand, and really concerned as to whether we would be safe living in grass huts. Although I came to understand how and why Indigenous people are portrayed as primitive savages, at the age of seven it was a terrifying experience, such was the power of those unmediated images on my young mind.

Life in New Zealand mirrored our lives in Australia. 'Relocations' were frequent. Drunken parties were commonplace, as were fights and arguments. We were no strangers to poverty, but as young children we didn't understand that we were poor or that we had nothing; that was just the way it was. I do remember my mother making the most out of what we had, which was a lot of empty wooden beer crates. In our lounge room we had beer crates covered in old blankets for seats. In our bedrooms we had mattresses on beer crates, and to store our clothes we had more beer crates. My sisters and I used to entertain ourselves with beer bottle tops, building toy houses, and making up all sorts of games.

After two years of living in New Zealand, my father returned to Australia. If we thought we had nothing until then, we were mistaken. He left us with no money and no possessions, and soon we were served an eviction notice. As Australians, we were not entitled to government assistance in New Zealand, so we lived on handouts from church groups and other organisations, and learned over time that it was good to avoid those to whom we owed money.

As we struggled from day to day, I realised that not everyone lived like we did, and I began to resent that fact. My younger sister and I began rebelling and soon ran into trouble with the police, eventually earning a reputation for being 'uncontrollable'. I spent some time in Bollard Girls' Home in New Zealand and, at the age of fifteen, I was deported to Australia with my younger sister in tow. As part of our punishment the court ordered us to live in Australia with our father and not return to New Zealand for a period of twelve months.

When we arrived in Katherine in the Northern Territory, I felt we were neither welcomed nor wanted by my father and his new family. Further rebellious behaviour was the inevitable result. I remember getting into trouble for hanging out too much with the 'blacks'. Katherine in the 1980s was a racist town. I recall once overhearing a conversation between some men on the street who were commenting that if you ran over a black, you should then reverse over them to ensure they were dead as it would mean less paperwork. That way, they also contended, the death could more easily be attributed to the victim's being drunk. In those days, most people kept shotguns with salt pellets to shoot at the blacks if they came onto their property. At night, it was common for the local white teenagers to drive their Mini Mokes through the blacks' camp yelling abuse, just for a laugh.

It was not long before I was sent to Wollongong to live with my aunty. I loved Wollongong because my nana also lived there. Although I had become a very angry person, I loved being near my nana and I cherished those times with her. Her house was the only place I recognised as a home, and she was the only stable element in my life growing up. After I turned sixteen I returned to live with my mother in New Zealand; Nana died not long after.

Through my schooling in New Zealand I learned about Māori people and their culture in a similar way to how I was taught about Aboriginal people in Australia. In all my social studies classes, both Māori and

Aboriginal people were portrayed as having lived in the past. I learned that Māori were warriors and that their warrior status was the difference between them and Aboriginal people in Australia – Māori fought for their land, Aboriginal Australians did not. I was also taught that Māori were defeated.

Social studies also helped me begin to uncover some of the mystery of my own ambiguous status. I learned about blood quantum as a measure of differences between 'full-blood', 'half-caste', 'part-Māori' and so forth. In New Zealand, 'half-caste' people were positioned both outside the Māori community and outside the white community, just as Aboriginal people were in Australia. Those of us who were 'touched by the tar brush' seemed to be quarantined, perceived as not being of any place or any group. These ideas filled my head. I came to believe that as a 'half-caste' or less, a person was not entitled to be considered Māori or, in my case, Aboriginal. I recall watching a television show that showed Māori protesting, and someone commented that 'they' (Māori) were as white as 'us' – 'they cannot be Indigenous'.

•

I returned to Australia again in my early thirties, now with a family of my own. It was 1998 and Pauline Hanson was gaining ascendancy with her provocative views on the 'privileges' of being Aboriginal in contemporary Australian society. Aboriginal protesters were prominent in the media and I remember the same types of remarks being made about Aboriginal protesters as I'd heard made about Māori protesters. Many comments referred to the lightness of most Aboriginal people's skin colour. Some commentators suggested that 'the real Aboriginal people' were the ones still on the land and that these urban 'white' Aboriginal people were somehow fraudulently passing as 'Aboriginal' to receive benefits denied to other Australians.

Now, as an adult, I became interested in exploring the firmly planted, but rarely discussed, family assertion of being 'touched by the tar brush'. I spoke with my relatives, including an old great-aunt, my nana's sister, who has since passed away. I was told stories of Nana's mother, who was commonly referred to as Kit. Another aunt confirmed that indeed Nana Kit was Aboriginal, but added that such things were not really spoken of in the family.

So, despite open confirmation of this knowledge, not all the family accepted that they were of Aboriginal descent. Even today, there are members of our extended family who still see Aboriginality as singularly a factor of colour or looks, and, therefore, don't see themselves as being Aboriginal, or don't feel confident with publicly identifying as Aboriginal. My cousin commented that I was lucky my hair and eyes are dark because that made it easier for me to identify as Aboriginal. I understand this, as I was also conditioned to think that Aboriginality was only afforded to those who were dark-skinned or 'looked' Aboriginal. I also understand that in many ways my generation had it far easier than my nana's or aunties' difficult circumstances, when it came to identifying, accepting and acknowledging our Aboriginal lineage. Historical circumstances had conditioned previous generations of our family to avoid the attention of the authorities.

I recognised that my search for information needed to extend past the family level. I needed to understand how and why I was understood as not being Aboriginal enough. I wanted to know how and why historical legacies continued to assign such weighted meaning to black/white lines in the everyday, given the history of dispossession and the subsequent administration of Aboriginal lives in Australia. I wanted to know why so many of us were suspended in the land of not belonging.

THE EDUCATIONAL CONSEQUENCES OF THE PEACE

DEAN ASHENDEN

28 July 2016

In July 1966, a special federal conference of the Australian Labor Party voted, in dramatic circumstances, to abandon its opposition to 'direct state aid' for non-government schools. The decision was seen at the time, and often since, as a radical reversal of Labor's historical attachment to 'free, compulsory and secular' education; as the beginning of the end for Australia's 'oldest, deepest, most poisonous debate'; and as the harbinger of a great leap forward in Australian schooling. Each of these estimates is half-right at best.

By 1966 Labor governments had been dispensing state aid for a decade or more. One state (Queensland) had been doing so ever since 1899, and another (New South Wales) since 1912. Labor had gone to two federal elections (1961 and 1963) with significant offers of aid. And while it is true that the 1966 decision led directly to the famous Karmel report of 1973, with its new deal for schooling, it also led to serious deformities in the structure of the schooling system – deformities that generated significant educational and social difficulties, and frustrated their solution.

Much in this ambiguous legacy was defined by the Byzantine politics within and between the Australian Catholic Church and the Labor Party, institutions so similar in many respects, and so deeply entwined, that politics often took on the character of a civil war, much of it fought on the battlefields of state aid.

The Catholic–Protestant sectarianism that had riven schooling for a century or more was about to disappear, but not the acrimonious division and controversy that accompanied it. That was simply transposed to a new, secular ground.

•

The second half of the nineteenth century saw the end of the decades-old system of public support for religious schools, and the creation of a government school system. But the Catholic Church was no hapless victim of the campaigns that brought this change. It did every bit as much as the most ardent exponents of 'free, compulsory and secular' education to split Australian schooling into what became three 'sectors': government, Catholic, and 'independent' or 'private'. It was angrily determined to go it alone, unaided. And, by combining modest fees with the low-cost labour of nuns and brothers shipped in from Ireland and elsewhere, it did.[5]

Some Catholics hankered after a restoration of state aid, but others did not. With aid would come conditions and controls, and the risk of secular pollution. In any event, right up until the eve of the Second World War, the question – leaving aside the small bursary schemes in New South Wales and Queensland – was hypothetical. Governments weren't going to stir up sectarianism all over again, even if they wanted to help, which most didn't, and the bishops weren't going to ask for aid, for the same reason.

The war had scarcely ended before aid became both possible and necessary. Numbers of students rose as rapidly as the supply of nuns and brothers fell. Classes swelled to sixty or even seventy or more, often taught by poorly educated teachers in schools that, as demonstrated by a famous and farcical incident to which we'll return, could not even provide enough toilets.

What could be done? State governments had trouble enough finding money for their own bulging institutions. Federation had left them with the responsibility for schools, but wartime legislation had taken away the taxation powers they needed to pay for them. The Church needed the money, though, and politicians needed the votes.

The solution was an under-the-counter trade conducted within boundaries well understood by both sides. Aid to meet educational expenses, yes; for staffing or building costs, no. To families and students, yes; to schools or school authorities, no. 'Indirect' and covert aid, yes; 'direct' and explicit aid, no. From state governments, yes; from the federal government, no.

A patchwork of arrangements made within these distinctions gave Australia in the mid 1950s something reminiscent of pre-abolition reality combined with post-abolition appearance. Aid ranged from the relatively straightforward (scholarships, bursaries and allowances, tax

---

5   Craig Campbell and Helen Proctor, *A History of Australian Schooling* (Crows Nest, NSW: Allen & Unwin, 2014).

deductions, free milk, stationery and bus passes) to the truly ingenious and obscure, such as grants for Catholic parent associations to match those given to their state school equivalents, and subsidies for school pianos.

At first the management of aid-that-wasn't proceeded smoothly enough, particularly with Labor governments. Labor was almost as Catholic as the Church itself. Most Catholics were Irish and therefore working-class and therefore Labor, and Labor governments – particularly in the two big states of Victoria and New South Wales – were often dominated by Catholics. On the Church side, all was in the hands of the hierarchy. Neither the laity nor the teaching orders had any say or role in the matter (nor, it followed, did women). As Michael Hogan put it in his definitive history, the bishops set out not to change public opinion but to go around it, and they succeeded.[6] This cosy arrangement was blown to smithereens by three explosions, one after another.

THE LABOR SPLIT, 1955

Victorian anti-communist Catholics, abetted by archbishop Daniel Mannix and his protégé Bob Santamaria, marched out of the Labor Party to form what would become the Democratic Labor Party, or DLP. Hogan likens the post-split relationship to a soured romance, but that was in New South Wales. In Victoria it was a vicious divorce.

One of many consequences was the revival in the Labor Party of the old battle cry of 'free, compulsory and secular'. In Victoria particularly, and in the national machinery of the party, anti–state aid feeling and forces mobilised. Long-serving federal powerbroker Joe Chamberlain, hitherto content to leave backroom deals to the state branches, became a ferocious opponent of state aid in any form, determined to choke off supply to the treacherous Catholics. That was, of course, directly contrary to what was needed to get the Catholic vote back from the DLP.

The politics of the Church, the Labor Party and their relationship in the decade that followed was dominated by the state aid question. They were rancorous, perverse, doctrinaire and extraordinarily complex. Labor was a tangle of cross-cutting divisions – between left and right, pro- and anti-aid, and Catholic and Protestant; between the states (again,

---

6   Michael Hogan, *The Catholic Campaign for State Aid: A Study of a Pressure Group Campaign in New South Wales and the Australian Capital Territory, 1950–1972* (Sydney: Catholic Theological Faculty, 1978).

New South Wales and Victoria especially), the state party machines and governments, and the federal office; and between an old guard led by Arthur Calwell and a new guard dominated by Gough Whitlam, twenty years younger than Calwell and a rising star.

As for the Church, differences among the bishops, particularly those from Victoria and New South Wales, were greatly complicated by rising agitation among the laity, and especially among those who had the thankless task of running schools and a school system careening towards collapse, who were fed up with the ineffectual bishops and their backroom manoeuvres. But the laity, too, was divided, between militants and gradualists, and between those loyal to Labor and those whose loyalties lay elsewhere.

GOULBURN, 1962

In July 1957, the New South Wales Department of Education issued a 'certificate of efficiency' to Our Lady of Mercy Preparatory School in Goulburn, in south-central New South Wales, conditional upon the installation of another seat in the boys' toilet. (Accounts differ on this and other details. It was just one seat according to Hogan, three according to political historian Jenny Hocking, and an entire toilet block according to *The Bulletin*'s man on the spot, Peter Kelly.)

The parish was beyond broke; its expenditure on schools had sent it into heavy debt. It temporised and fudged. The government authorities turned a blind eye for as long as they could, but then registration inspections came around again. The department told the parish that there would be no registration this time without the toilet upgrade. The local bishop, recently installed in office at the unusually early age of forty-two, got his back up. After consultation with a small group of (male) laity, he decided to go public. In the course of a speech on St Pat's Day, and in the presence of the local (Labor) member of the state (Labor) government, he said that the school might have to be closed. The certificate was promptly issued, pending advice that toilet facilities met requirements.

The Goulburn Catholics now asked to see the minister. The minister said no, he wouldn't see them. The bishop said that if the government wanted the school to stay open it could always pay for its requirements to be met. More fudges and deals were attempted, without success. The bishop then wrote to the minister, inviting him to attend a public meeting arranged for four days hence. Seven hundred people – not including the minister – turned up, and voted 500 to 120 to close not just Our Lady but Goulburn's five other Catholic schools as well. Two thousand children would be instructed to seek enrolment at their local state school. The next day, the 'Goulburn Strike' (or 'Lockout') was on front pages around the country.

The strike moved state aid from the backrooms to the middle of the political agenda. Initial media hostility soon turned to consensus that 'something had to be done'.[7] The Catholic schools could not be allowed to collapse. Goulburn's state schools were stretched to accommodate even the one-third (or a half – reports vary) of the 2000 applicants they were able to enrol, leaving the rest with nowhere to go. Imagine that scenario across the country! Governments were getting exactly the intended message. Perhaps most significant, but least noticed, was that the Catholic parents and students of Goulburn had made their requests for enrolment courteously, and the state schools responded in that same spirit. Some of those enrolled in state schools stayed there after the strike was over. Sectarianism was dying.

The strike put almost as much heat on the bishops as on the government. They had lost control to the laity, and their sotto voce requests for bits and pieces of aid were increasingly seen as craven as well as ineffectual. On the government side, the New South Wales premier, RJ Heffron, made a great show of refusing to be bullied and then let it be known that he would be open to representations from the Church. The Church rolled out its heavy artillery, a delegation headed by the cardinal himself, and made a list of its requirements available to the media. The list comprised more scholarships, help with teacher training and salaries for lay teachers, as well as support for capital works, including science labs.

Heffron had the advantage of a (Protestant-dominated) conservative opposition, unfriendly to Catholics and to aid, plus more than two years to the next election – plenty of time to get the party onside. His optimism was misplaced. The state conference endorsed aid of the science laboratory kind, only to be slapped down by its federal counterpart, urged on by the man Whitlam's speechwriter Graham Freudenberg called the 'self-appointed keeper of the conscience on this matter', Joe Chamberlain.[8] The New South Wales government was instructed to 'recast' its plans.

---

7 Emma Macdonald, 'The Genesis of State Aid', *Canberra Times,* July 14, 2012, https://www. canberratimes.com.au/national/act/the-genesis-of-state-aid-20120713-2212s.html.

8 Graham Freudenberg, *A Certain Grandeur: Gough Whitlam's Life in Politics* (Camberwell, VIC: Viking, 2009).

New South Wales resisted, and met with an even more stinging rebuke. It was required to submit all decisions on state aid to the federal secretary (aka Joe Chamberlain) 'for consideration and advice'. The lesson for the Church was that Labor could not be trusted to deliver.

Menzies – Protestant, no enthusiast for state aid, firm opponent of any federal involvement in schools – saw his chance. Two weeks after Chamberlain's diktat, Menzies called an early federal election with a centrepiece policy of providing science laboratories to all schools, government and non-government alike.

The Liberal leader had scraped home by just one seat in 1961, and Calwell believed that this time he would be prime minister. Instead, he lost ten more seats, seven of them in New South Wales. Then it was the state party's turn to be hammered. In May 1965, the New South Wales Labor government fell. It had been in office since 1941. The shift in the Catholic vote, and the Church's allegiance, away from Labor and towards the conservatives, which had commenced with the 1955 split, was accelerating. First the Church found that it couldn't trust Labor, then it discovered that it no longer had to.

The writing was on the wall, or two lots of writing actually, one about state aid, the other about the control and leadership of the Labor Party. Calwell couldn't or wouldn't read either. Whitlam could read both.

SHOWDOWN AT SURFERS, 1966

The sharp end of the Menzies wedge fell first on Labor's federal MPs. Come the next election, would they promise to cancel the science labs? In May 1965 caucus decided, albeit by a narrow margin, that no, it wouldn't. It would not undo 'existing arrangements'.

The wedge now pointed at the federal conference of the party, held a few months later. Calwell supported a move to dodge the question by having it referred to a national advisory committee on education.

The committee was dominated by Chamberlain, with Calwell in support. Its majority report to the federal executive six months later proposed that there would be no aid for school buildings or staff *and* that Labor's federal members could support existing federal aid, including, of course, Menzies' science labs. But on the very day of the report's presentation, Calwell announced that he had had an epiphany. He would withdraw his opposition to direct state aid. He had been much moved by a letter from his old friend (and friend of Labor) James Carroll, auxiliary bishop of Sydney, which documented the parlous conditions for students and teachers in Catholic schools, and protested against the iniquity of denying them financial support on the ground of their religion.

Chamberlain wasn't going to have it. Calwell was prevailed on to change his mind, again, and the Labor executive did a U-turn of its own. Not only would parliamentary members be bound to oppose state aid but, even more startling, the possibility of a High Court challenge to its constitutionality would also be investigated.

Whitlam had been a member of the advisory committee on education, and was scathing about the majority report's internal contradictions. Now he was apoplectic. He famously determined to 'crash or crash through', labelling the federal executive 'extremists', and then (on national TV) declaring them to be 'twelve witless men'. Calwell was jubilant. The upstart Whitlam had signed his own death warrant.

Calwell's move to have Whitlam expelled by a meeting of the national executive; a desperate phone call from Queensland MP Rex Patterson (beneficiary of Whitlam's phenomenally successful campaigning in a recent by-election) to state secretary Tom Burns; an equally desperate call by Burns to the two Queensland delegates at the meeting of the executive; the last-minute switch by those delegates as the noose was being placed around Whitlam's neck; and Whitlam's consequent escape by the narrowest of margins (seven votes to five) – all these are the stuff of Labor legend.

As important to history as the decision to let Whitlam off with a reprimand was the accompanying decision to send the whole business back whence it came, to federal conference. Even that took two goes, one in March, and another in July, at Surfers Paradise. There came a denouement less dramatic than the events that had led up to it. Joe Chamberlain was out of the game for once, laid up in hospital, and anyway, delegates' minds were concentrated by a looming federal election. It was agreed that Labor would not oppose existing aid, a crucial vote coming from Calwell, who had changed his mind yet again.

One view of that decision is that it was a volte-face, a reversal of a long-held policy. Another view, not quite the opposite but close, is that Labor had merely abandoned an old policy without deciding on a new one. A third view is that 1966 was not a reversal; it was another step down a long and tortuous path. And while 1966 didn't decide on a new policy, it very nearly arrived at one by default. To mix the metaphors, since the early 1950s Labor had been the frog in the pan, and by 1966 it was too late to jump. It would have to live with what a tangled history had provided, which included Menzies' 'direct' federal aid as well as the many and varied devices of the states.

By 1966 Whitlam was (as he himself had pointed out) Labor's leader in waiting, and it was his conceit that he knew how to rise above this history. What had long been seen as a question of religious versus secular schooling he had reconfigured as a question of meeting *need* in the interests of equal opportunity for all Australians. In place of a dog's breakfast of measures, he would put aid on a systematic basis across the nation. Against the push by a conservative–Catholic alliance for per capita grants, his aid would be according to need in government as well as non-government schools (which meant that expensive private schools would have to fend for themselves). All this would be worked out in detail and carried into practice by a grand new edifice, the Australian Schools Commission.

It is not hard to see why Whitlam believed that his plan changed everything. Amid an increasingly heated, confused and intractable debate, his proposal had cut through. It seemed lucid, sensible and practical, as well as bold. But it also changed much less than Whitlam imagined.

The 'needs' approach apart, Whitlam was effectively tagging along behind Menzies and the policy of direct aid, to be provided to all schools, by the Commonwealth. With that came a number of fundamental, structural realities: non-government schools would be 'aided', not funded. They would therefore continue to charge fees. Parents would have the right to choose between free and secular state schools or fee-charging religious schools. There would still be three school sectors, each run and funded in its own way, plus the additional complication of the involvement of a second layer of government. Implicit in the decision and the non-decisions of 1966 was the extension of an unfortunate history.

•

Among the very first actions of the Whitlam government was the appointment of an interim committee of the Australian Schools Commission, to be chaired by economist Peter Karmel. It handed down its report less than six months later (in May 1973). The report earned a rapturous reception for its trenchant support for equal opportunity, its encouragement of new approaches to teaching and curriculum, its preference for 'community participation' over authoritarian and centralised decision-making, as well as its special programs for disadvantaged schools, innovation, special education and the like. A generation of teachers, academics and administrators came to see the report, the Schools Commission, and the Commonwealth as sources of inspiration, salvation even.

The interim committee was serious in its advocacy of a more equal, humane and enlightening schooling for all, but that was not its core business. It was charged by Whitlam with working out the detail of his plan to bring the state aid question to a close, once and for all.

No part of Karmel's recommendations on implementation would have surprised Whitlam or, for that matter, many of the delegates to the 1966 conference in Surfers Paradise. The three school sectors would continue to operate in their familiar form; all would get support from both state and federal governments, one sector fully funded, the other two aided and therefore fee-charging; levels of funding and aid would be determined by need, which would in turn be tied to capacity to pay; distribution of those funds within the government and Catholic systems would be the responsibility of system authorities; parents would have the right to choose and, thanks to government subvention, choice would be more widely available.

The committee was clearly uneasy with the task it had been set and, by implication, with its own proposals. It was unhappy at being required to make recommendations 'in terms of structures which exist and which it has little direct power to modify [and which] may not be equally relevant for all time'. It fretted about how to ensure 'maintenance of effort' by both the states and the non-government schools in receipt of substantial new funding, about the 'role of fees in the financing of schools', and about the likelihood of a 'changed relationship' between government and non-government schooling. But there was no time to turn these and other concerns into proposals, and anyway they were scarcely heard in the clamour of approval. The state aid problem had been resolved, at last!

That illusion didn't last long. Less than two years on, an economic downturn restricted the massive outflow of federal funds needed to keep the many parties happy, leaving the realpolitik of the Karmel–Whitlam settlement exposed like coastal rocks after a storm.

One problem was inordinate complexity combined with confusion of roles and responsibilities: three sectors, each funded and controlled in its own way, two of them getting funds from three different sources including fees, a total of seven governments at different stages of three-year electoral cycles and of differing political persuasions. This was the genesis of a funding system described forty years later by David Gonski and his colleagues in the 2011 *Review of Funding for Schooling* report as uncoordinated, divisive and unnecessarily complex; containing overlapping responsibilities leading to duplication and inefficiency; and lacking any coherence, transparency, or connection to educational objectives.

A related problem lay in the interaction of 'need', 'capacity to pay' and arguments about reducing fees in the interests of 'broadening access'. The new system was an invitation to gaming and, on occasion, rorting. State education departments and Catholic school authorities both resisted Commonwealth efforts to attach conditions and purposes to its funds.

Moreover, almost everyone had a legitimate basis for complaint. One side could insist: we are open to all, and cater to most disadvantaged students and their families, so fairness requires that our schools have priority over schools that exclude. The other side could counter: it is not fair that those who choose a religion-based education should have to pay for that choice; parents who pay taxes and then make an additional contribution to the funding of schooling, year in, year out, are entitled to public support; and the lower the public support to non-government schools, the less able we are to enrol all comers.

For all these reasons, conflict over funding returned in full spate. The Schools Commission, attempting to arbitrate between lobby groups constituted or empowered by the Karmel–Whitlam settlement, was the first major victim of policies it was charged with administering. It was downgraded, and eventually (1988) scrapped. Other victims, in whole or in part, included a federal minister (Susan Ryan, author of the putative 'Ryan hit list',) a federal leader of the opposition (Mark Latham, of 'Latham hit list' fame), and the Gonski proposals, Julia Gillard's pre-emptive buckle ('no school will be worse off') notwithstanding.

More important than any of these disturbances in the corridors of power and in public forums were the consequences down on the ground. With three sectors funded and administered in different ways came very different levels of funding and very different regulation of rights and obligations. The Karmel–Whitlam settlement gave Australia both free *and* publicly subsidised fee-charging schools; schools lavishly funded *and* schools relatively impoverished; schools permitted to select on grounds of capacity to pay and/or religious affiliation and/or academic performance *and* schools prohibited from doing any of those things; parents who are required to pay when often they can't afford it *and* parents who aren't and can; and parents who are offered the full menu *and* others who must take whatever is put on their plate.

Unfairness is one part of the problem. The other is exacerbation of social and educational division. Parents in a position to choose have typically chosen schools where their children will find others just like themselves. In the doing, they make a choice for those who can't choose, for reasons of income and/or location, and/or because their child doesn't have what the choosy schools are looking for. Thus the non-choosers, like the choosers, increasingly find themselves among their own kind.

Australia now has an unusually high concentration of students at both ends of the spectrum, and a relatively small proportion of schools with socially mixed enrolments. One consequence of the massive sifting and sorting of the forty years since the Karmel–Whitlam settlement is a transformation of the Catholic sector. A school system established to help the poor and the excluded has off-loaded much of that task to the government schools in favour of catering to those already in the mainstream. One-quarter of students in Catholic schools are not Catholic, and half of all Catholic students – and almost certainly a relatively poorer half – are enrolled in government schools.

There is clear evidence to suggest that this segmentation, amounting in some respects and areas to segregation, has a depressing effect on the academic attainment of many, perhaps even most students. Its social and cultural effects go unmeasured and unreported.

•

What went wrong? In his celebrated denunciation of the 1919 Versailles peace conference, *The Economic Consequences of the Peace*, JM Keynes said of its protagonists that 'the future life of Europe was not their concern; its means of livelihood was not their anxiety'. Their anxiety was territorial settlement and reparations, with, Keynes correctly predicted, dire consequences to follow.

The analogy with the Karmel–Whitlam settlement is not exact in kind or, of course, in scale, but it is illuminating. Whitlam did have a concern for 'the future life of Europe' but it played very little part in shaping his thinking about the nature and terms of a state aid treaty, most of which had taken its final shape by 1966.

In 1991, Jean Blackburn, like Keynes a key player in the proceedings concerned (she was deputy chair of the interim committee and subsequently an important voice in the Schools Commission), looked back in anger:

> We created a situation unique in the democratic world. It is
> very important to realise this. There were no rules about stu-
> dent selection and exclusion, no fee limitations, no shared

governance, no common curriculum requirements below the upper secondary level ... We have now become a kind of wonder at which people [in other countries] gape. The reaction is always, 'What an extraordinary situation!'

Some of the omissions listed by Blackburn, to do with curriculum and accountability, have since been addressed, if not resolved, but others have not been addressed at all.

Both sides of politics are aware of structural problems in the school system. The Coalition has focused on dysfunctional governance arising from the involvement of two levels of government. Labor's concerns, larger in scope and spirit, concentrate on the (closely related) problem of complex and counterproductive distribution and use of funding. Neither seems aware of the importance of student selection and exclusion, of the consequences of the fee/free distinction, or of the relationship of all of the elements identified by Blackburn to each other. Neither has grasped how these dynamics are in turn related to Australian schooling's persistent inability to 'lift performance', and to the social and cultural effects of schooling.[9] Neither has been able to escape the power of interest groups formed in the 1960s to block structural change, and neither has been willing to confront some of those groups, on the reduction of decisions about 'the future life of Europe' to grabs for cash. Each seems to understand only parts of a big, complicated problem; each, like Labor in 1966, canvasses remedies which, if seen as solutions rather than steps towards a solution, will perpetuate more than they change.

---

9 Geoff Masters, *Is School Reform Working?* Policy Insights, no. 1 (Camberwell, VIC: Australian Council for Educational Research, 2014).

'NOW, WHERE WERE WE ...?'

ANDREW DODD

19 January 2017

In 2013, one of Australia's more exclusive schools was compiling profiles of its most notable alumni for an anniversary book. It asked me whether I'd write a few chapters and showed me a list of business-men, sportsmen, scientists and even prime ministers to choose from. They were all interesting people, but to my mind there was only one criterion. Whom did I want to meet?

There he was, James Oswald Fairfax AC, the one-time heir to a media empire and among Australia's greatest philanthropists. This was the person who usurped his father to take control of the country's oldest broadsheet newspapers, and who, in turn, was forced out by his half-brother, partly to avenge the way their father was treated. It's one of the epic sagas of Australian media history, involving a supposedly scheming wife who raised a son to resent his cousins and half-brother. It reads like the plot for a tragic opera, and the events shaped much of Australia's modern media landscape.

No question; I would profile him.

Before long I was on the phone to his home at Bowral, in country New South Wales. A kindly assistant answered and transferred the call, and a soft voice with a rather exaggerated plumminess came on the line.

'How lovely of you to ring,' said James Fairfax. He had been tipped off by the school and was already committed to an interview. The question was how it was to be done.

'Well, perhaps I could ask you some questions by phone,' I suggested.

'Yes, we could do that,' he replied, unconvinced. 'But I would rather like to do this in person ... Where are you living nowadays?'

It was as if we were old friends who had lost touch for a year or two.

'I'm in Melbourne,' I replied, assuming that would settle the matter and we could get on with a phone interview.

'Oh, well, I'll send the car,' he said, in a tone of absolute assurance, like he had solved a simple problem and, anyway, what was all the fuss about?

'Ah, thank you,' I offered. 'But it's a long way.'

'I would rather like to talk to you in person,' he repeated. 'You could come for lunch. You could stay the night if you like.'

Clearly, he had something important to say. Either that or he was very keen for someone to chat to. So I asked to be put back to his assistant, who I think sighed just a little as I explained Mr Fairfax's wishes. Did he do this for everyone? I wondered.

And so – I hereby declare – James Fairfax flew me to Sydney, and there his chauffeur was waiting to drive the one hundred kilometres to Retford Park, his grand, pink Italianate mansion on the edge of the country town.

The grounds had that imposing aspect you hope for when you approach a country estate along a winding driveway through manicured gardens. Only the lake was a little disappointing, more like a stagnant pond than a river of gold. Fairfax later gave the entire $20 million estate to the National Trust, with the adjoining land sold off to ensure the property's upkeep.

The chauffeur, who spoke of his boss with reverence, called ahead to signal the incoming guest, and so when we arrived he was standing on the verandah with his two perfectly groomed dogs. He was a little stooped in his comfortable slacks and casual shirt. We swapped pleasantries and he beckoned me onto the verandah, where we were served champagne and ate wafers and a selection of pâté and cheeses from a tray.

•

Now, you should probably know that the school in question was Geelong Grammar, which was a sandpit for a remarkable number of future media moguls. James' father Sir Warwick went there, as did his cousin John B. Fairfax. Kerry Packer was a student, along with members of the Holmes à Court family and Ranald Macdonald, who went on to run *The Age*. On one of his first days as a boarder at the junior school, James Fairfax was told that 'the commo' was waiting outside to see him. So out he went to find yet another future mogul, young Rupert Murdoch, standing on the lawn.

Murdoch was a couple of years ahead of Fairfax, and was known at the time for his left-wing views. It was the first time the heirs to Australia's two major newspaper companies had met. They would later become intense rivals, but at the time Fairfax appreciated the gesture of welcome. 'It was nice of him to do that,' he recalled.

'I am determined to be positive about Geelong Grammar,' James Fairfax wrote in his memoir, *My Regards to Broadway*. I asked him about that intriguing line and, as a cockatoo screeched in the trees and he poured us another glass, he explained how he had been the subject of 'ragging' during his school days. Nowadays, it's better known as bullying.

'They took it out on me from time to time. It was mainly verbal but they made things unpleasant.'

'In senior school,' he added, 'they had it down to a slightly fine art. I might have appeared reserved. They thought I didn't like them or want to be close to them. I didn't think I was all that different to anyone else.'

But it wasn't all bad. His headmaster deeply influenced him, and one particular art teacher, a postwar Eastern European refugee, changed the course of his life by exposing him to 1920s German art. 'He taught me to appreciate modern art going into abstract art,' Fairfax said.

By now we had moved inside to the dining room, where lunch was to be served. The dogs followed and lay on the floor. As he poured red wine, we admired a John Olsen painting on the wall and he explained he had 'no idea' how many pictures he had donated to galleries across the nation. 'Quite a few I'd imagine,' he said.

At least a couple of red wines later, the conversation made its way to the failed takeover bid by James Fairfax's younger half-brother, Warwick. It's the topic that's defined the Fairfax company, and family, since 1987.

Young Warwick is the son of James' late father, Sir Warwick, and Sir Warwick's third wife, Lady Mary. Instead of waiting for his inheritance, Young Warwick launched a reckless, debt-fuelled takeover bid, advised by the discredited Western Australian businessman Laurie Connell. For James and his two cousins, Sir Vincent and John B Fairfax, this was a complete shock. The bid coincided with the stock market crash and the family eventually lost control of the business. It ended James' career at the company, where he had been a director since the 1950s and chairman since 1977. He sold his shareholding for an estimated $168 million.

So, in the twilight of his life, how did James Fairfax reflect on both the destruction of the dynasty and the people he considered responsible, namely his half-brother Young Warwick and stepmother Lady Mary?

On one level, he seemed quite sanguine and forgiving: 'It's all in the past now. I really stopped thinking about it years ago, not that it kept me awake at night, but what's done is done and cannot be undone, can it?' But as the lunch meandered on, other feelings emerged, suggesting that those events still hurt a quarter of a century later.

He described the day Young Warwick visited his Darling Point home after lodging his bid with the Sydney Stock Exchange.

'He came to see me at Lindsay Avenue and he sat there motionless and [almost] speechless for about forty-five minutes, well it seemed like forty-five minutes, and then he went to cousins John and Vincent and we all fairly briefly rang each other and he pretty well said the same thing to all of us. Vincent was absolutely broken up, poor old boy. And, well, John and I felt the same thing about it and there was nothing to be done because the offer, whatever you do, was put into the Stock Exchange on the Monday morning and then the phones ran hot.'

He went on: 'I thought to myself, how ironic. My father used to refer to Young Warwick as "the hope of the side" and, one thing, Warwick said he would not have done it if his father was still alive. Well, that was fairly obvious, one would have to say, and I think it was several years before I really spoke to him again.'

Did he ever wonder, I asked, what might have been for the Fairfax company if Young Warwick hadn't made his bid?

'I think the family would still be owning it and controlling it. What he did was bugger himself and nearly bugger the company. To what degree his mother was either behind it or knew anything about it, well, your guess is as good as mine. I personally think he would have certainly spoken to her about it because anything to get me out and John out would have been an aim in itself.'

An aim of his or an aim of Mary's?

'An aim of Mary's. She could influence him any way she wanted.'

What would Sir Warwick have thought about it?

'It would have depended a little on how successful it had been or wasn't, and as it was a miserable failure he would have ... if he had been involved in it he would have accepted his own responsibility, which was the last thing Mary did of course. But he [Sir Warwick] was honest and he would have accepted, I think, that he had made a few misjudgements. I think he would have been absolutely horrified.'

Does Warwick now reflect on it and talk about it?

'Oh well, he'll talk about it up to a point and do his best to get out of any awkward questions, but at my age I frankly don't care anymore.'

And have you and Warwick reconciled?

'I never see him. It's that simple. We're polite to each other when we do. There's no point, when everything is over, in bearing old grudges. Well, what's the point of not speaking to him? Absolutely none. Not that he has ever apologised in a sense, but still, what's over is over, and we're never going to be buddies. But I say hello to him. I don't see him particularly. If he rang me up, I'd answer the telephone.'

Would an apology for the disastrous bid be appropriate?

'Well, again, if his mother let him, which she never would, his own inclination probably would be. But I'm not going to sit here for five years waiting for an apology because I'm not going to get one.'

After a short pause, and with perfect elocution, he continued, 'And I don't give a fuck, quite frankly.' The distinct articulation of 'give a fuck' was a little shocking. He was clearly done with this topic. 'I'm not going to let it worry me and I've long ceased to let it worry me,' he concluded.

•

On that day in Bowral I saw one of the last vestiges of the power and privilege associated with Australia's establishment media. James Fairfax was one of the last great patrician proprietors. While he was unashamedly conservative in outlook, he also valued and upheld the traditions of free speech and pluralism. He respected the craft of journalism and, as chairman of the family company, generally allowed it to prosper.

But I suspect that he and his cousins were saved from the inevitable. I suspect they would have been just as ill-prepared for the digital revolution that was about to sweep across the business. Instead, James Fairfax excelled at a life of splendid retirement, surrounded by the trappings of the wealth that he became so very good at giving away.

To end the interview, I thanked him for his hospitality and asked whether there was anything he wanted to add. My recording of that conversation cuts out with these words: 'Great pleasure. Now, I tell you what, if you give me a tiny bit more wine I'll endeavour to think of something ...' Sound of wine being poured. 'Thank you, that's fine. Now, where were we ...?'

SPEAKING INTO THE SILENCE

DRUSILLA MODJESKA

2 July 2018

'If we say it could have been me, shouldn't we ask who was she?' It's one of the many challenges Maria Tumarkin puts our way in her new book, *Axiomatic*, with its focus on trauma and the legacy of the past. It's a question that also hovers over Kate Rossmanith's *Small Wrongs*, which homes in on remorse and punishment. Who is she, weeping in the dock – or, more likely, not? Trauma and punishment, remorse and legacy: move the terms around, and there are elements of each in these two timely books. And what does any of it mean in a world of polarised narratives and gross inequalities? 'Curious thing,' Tumarkin continues, 'empathy via identification.'

'A few anecdotes placed side by side,' Rossmanith writes, 'can create an untruth.'

These books pose unsettling challenges, and necessary ones. Interestingly, both come to us from small independent publishers. This is not just the way of the future for publishing in this country, Tumarkin says, but already its formidable present. As is – I say with cautious optimism – this hybrid form of nonfiction written for a hybrid audience.

First, Rossmanith's *Small Wrongs*. In Australia, as in other common-law jurisdictions, remorse is 'a significant factor' in sentencing procedures. Deterrence, punishment and rehabilitation are core pillars in the complex sentencing matrix; remorse is a mitigating factor. If there's remorse, rehabilitation is assumed to be more likely and reoffending less likely. But what, exactly, is remorse? How, if at all, is it to be measured? How does the judge know if the court is witnessing remorse or merely the performance of remorse? What if remorse is there, but the accused is unable to express it? Can remorse be physically present but emotionally absent, or vice versa?

Early in the book, Rossmanith has coffee with a journalist. He's in his sixties when they meet, and he tells her that thirty years before, when he had a small child, he'd been in court on drug charges. In the group of heroin users he hung out with, the job of getting and supplying would move among them, not by design but by circumstance. It happened to be him on the day he was caught. He was young, and confident his middle-class credentials would get him off. He had no remorse at all. If it hadn't been him, it would have been one of the others; that's how things were. But he was smart and twigged in time. At his second hearing, he hung his head and uttered just two words: 'deep regret'. His sentence was suspended.

He says to Rossmanith:

> You know … I think remorse is an old person's game. It took me years to really regret selling heroin, and the regret mainly has to do with my family. My wife and I reconciled. We are still together. But even now I worry about my daughter. I still have a lot of remorse. What pains me most is that she got that protective thing kids get. She worried about me all the time … Kids take it on in some way. They feel responsible. So, anyway, as I said, remorse is an old person's game. The time it takes to align your personal view with a larger societal view – to align yourself with a larger consciousness – is really slow.

The comment stays with Rossmanith, and it stays with us as we go with her into courtrooms and parole board hearings, into judges' chambers and magistrates' rooms. While the alignment of the personal and the societal in sentencing is a realm for the court, for the accused remorse is entangled with fear and regret, denial and rage. Although she witnesses profound moments of remorse – that shift in posture and demeanour when the tears come – for the most part she watches how time plays against those in the dock. For a start, there's a disconnect between the way time moves in everyday life – its 'soupiness' she calls it; everyday time when things can slip, accumulate, hide, accelerate – and the event that lands someone in court, when time shudders and clangs, strangely arrested in that crisis moment. What happens then to the everyday time of the accused? Is there time between the event, the trial and the sentencing for remorse to raise even a glimmer?

In the higher courts, there can be weeks, even months between the trial, or the plea, and the sentencing. It may not be time enough for remorse, but it is time enough for the judge to pass sentence. In the magistrates' courts, there's rarely time. Magistrates may have to hear seventy matters in a day. It's sentencing on the run. Even the best of magistrates, the most experienced, the most compassionate, are moving against time, not with it. Month after month Rossmanith watches the array of offenders, some dressed for the occasion, as if that'd be enough, some out of it on drugs, some sullen and wretched, some without a clue what's going on. She watches as the parole board makes its way through the paperwork for dozens of prisoners caught in drawn-out punishment time. Some appear by video link from jail, not knowing which of the split screens to look at. A petulant young man who seems doomed ever to repeat appears in person before the board; no split screen for him, and somehow, somewhere, something breaks through – real feeling: fear, maybe, regret, hope, hopelessness. Remorse? Maybe. A young person's remorse tinged with anger and despair.

As she watches, Rossmanith focuses on the conundrum that faces every judge, every magistrate, every parole board member: how to assess and give objective weight to a factor that is crucial to the sentence but by its nature subjective. She reads the sentencing acts, the regulations that run to hundreds of pages, procedures that become more and more complex as if the process of sentencing can be nailed. A magistrate shows her the complex rubric she uses, and then says she moves the factors around until 'it feels right'. A Supreme Court judge tells her that as well as reading the psychiatric reports, he can pick up remorse, or its absence, across the courtroom. These are all thoughtful people. They take their role seriously. One judge mentions his own experience of remorse. These are the people you'd want to come before. They are also the ones who chose to speak to Rossmanith. Not all did.

As an ethnographer with academic guidelines and procedures to follow, Rossmanith also has to deal with the question of how to be objective when relying on the subjective. Ethnography as a discipline has grappled with this for decades. It's a paradox that requires her, she writes, to take notice not only of what is going on around her but also of what is going on inside her. A doubled perspective that is necessary 'if the nature of what has been observed is ever to be understood'.

She began this research as a new mother going through the stresses and strains that working couples of her generation are up against – career requirements, mortgages, child raising – which can take a toll on the best of marriages. There she is, studying 'remorse', while at home the mood darkens; she and her husband become 'expert' at avoiding the conversation they need to have, hardening themselves against the slights and hurts they inflict on each other. It doesn't help when she prangs his VW on the way home from court one day. In heavy Sydney traffic, she slams into the car in front. No one is hurt. Her husband's car is dented, but the other car is no longer driveable. Rossmanith immediately leaps to take responsibility, pressing money on the young driver to get the car towed. Remorse? Heaps of it. It's a comic moment, a naive rush into one form of remorse, yet still not taking on the issue at home, or the challenges of a daughter growing up. Spoiler alert: they make it in the end.

And so does her relationship with her father – a scientist, a kind man, but emotionally aloof in ways that were hard for her as a child. Kids take it on in some way, as that journalist said. Rossmanith's father was born in 1943 in war-torn Vienna, which meant his first experience of everyday time was in the ruins of a defeated city. A Lutheran child, he grew up surrounded by humiliated adults in shock, or denial. He was ten when he and his mother arrived in Sydney to find another language, another world, an Australian obliviousness best dealt with by letting the past lie low, lower still if such a thing were possible. And so Rossmanith and her siblings grew up with a loud silence beneath the boisterousness of their mother's family. It's the speaking into this silence, the revoicing of this past, delving into its meaning, that completes the woven threads of *Small Wrongs*.

•

Maria Tumarkin came to Australia in 1989 as a young teenager from Ukraine. Her Jewish parents and grandparents had lived through Nazi occupation, Soviet rule and the collapse of the Soviet Union. She knows about Australian obliviousness, the perils and attractions of conformity, not that she was ever much good at conforming. She hated school: the over-institutionalised version in Ukraine; the regulated classroom in Australia, hand up for the toilet, and outside, the unregulated playground. As a writer she pushes at the edges, and then pushes further; she wants to shout, and sometimes she does. *Axiomatic* is a bracing ride. At its heart is the big question of the past and its traumas. How do they play out? Where does trauma begin? In history? Genes? Family? Society? Is comfort to be found in the familiar truisms we're so quick to roll out?

Take the cliché 'time heals all wounds'. Does it? Does time heal those who witness suicide close-up? What about the teenage girl who finds her younger sister's body? At school the teacher hands her tissue after tissue as she sits there silent, refusing the offer of leaving if she'd prefer, of going home. How do you continue on with the everyday of teaching with that in the room? Especially if it's *Antigone* on the curriculum. And what about Bryn, who made friends with the wayward kids, and who spoke normally enough to his teacher the afternoon before he killed himself?

What was his story? It doesn't make sense. But sense isn't the point. Do the guidelines with their congested language help the teacher when she stands in front of that class the next day? Is there help to be given, and had? Do the bureaucrats really believe that such griefs can be 'managed'?

Bryn's teacher lets the students talk: talk that is only meaningful if it opens out way beyond any guideline. She's one of the good teachers, one of the teachers who spoke to Tumarkin. What about the teachers who don't, or can't let the students speak. Who don't care, or can't cope? Tumarkin knows the girl who found her sister. What is her story? Does time heal her, or does she just grow new parts? She asks Raimond Gaita about the suicide of his mother when he was a boy, which he wrote about in *Romulus, My Father*. He says he had to find pity for that boy. He talks of the Greek concept of pity, 'a sorrowing compassion that is marked through and through by awe at our vulnerability to misfortune'. What happens to pity when journalists come knocking at the door?

'I cannot take your past away,' a magistrate tells a man up before him on his second drink-driving offence. This is in a chapter titled 'History Repeats Itself'. Like Rossmanith, Tumarkin watches one offender after another as matters are quickly dealt with, and for every shattered person there's a shattered backstory and rarely the time to hear it, even if it were able to be told.

Tumarkin sits beside Vanda, a community lawyer in St Kilda. Most of her clients come from a 'tar pit', Tumarkin writes. 'People who don't get to do much choosing in their lives ... Poverty, abuse, addiction, mental health stuff, they are what's in the tar, the sticky parts.' Some of Vanda's clients are expert in self-sedation, arriving at court asleep on their feet. Drugs, drugs, drugs. Men who are desperate, suicidal, homeless. Girls for whom abuse is everywhere, women who lash out, spinning with an anger that tumbles back and fells them. She goes with Vanda to the funeral of a young girl in a church where the priest does the service for those whose deaths would otherwise go unnoticed. She thinks of Orwell's 'How the Poor Die'. All these years later, with all our wealth, is this how the poor must die, still, here, now, in Australia? Oblivious Australia. She sits with Vanda in her small, shabby office. No booklined chambers for her. How long can she keep doing this? she asks. Ten years, Vanda says, but then she thinks about all that she's gathered in, the relationships, the people she sees every day on the streets, on public transport. Could she let it all go, knowing what she knows?

Tumarkin uses the metaphor of the trucks. Most of us get hit by a truck sometime in our life, or are driving the one that causes the hurt and damage. For those of us with the backing, the education, the family and the time to recoup and rebuild, the crisis might be cathartic: a new starting point, often enough without having to stand in the literal dock in a literal court. And if the 'cushy middle-class' ones do find themselves in court, there are lawyers, psychiatrists. These are the privileged ones; they get to keep their lives. But if you are living on a highway, metaphorically speaking, as most of Vanda's clients are, it's one truck after another, there's nowhere to retreat or recoup. Just another truck. Society punishes people, Vanda says. 'Recurrence is the point,' Tumarkin writes. 'The point's the repetition.'

Not all the characters who inhabit *Axiomatic* are broken on the highway. Far from it. The book throbs with life: formidable characters, risk-takers, those who refuse to bow or be bowed. There's humour and resilience in the fury that swirls through the book, as well as moments of tenderness and unexpected disclosures. There's the grandmother who was sentenced for hiding her grandson from the drugged world of his mother. Okay, she lied to the police, she kept them off the scent. But a custodial sentence? Born a Jewish child in Nazi-occupied Warsaw, she knew about hiding, about not letting anything show. She stood, silent in court, no remorse to be seen. There was none; her silence was something else entirely. Why didn't she speak? Tumarkin asks. If ever there was a case to make, it was hers. Who would she speak to? That was her answer. Who could she talk to?

And then there is Vera Wasowski. This is 'Give Me a Child Before the Age of Seven and I Will Show You the Woman', the chapter that nearly breaks the book. Tumarkin comes close to losing control – as a writer, I mean – but she doesn't, not quite. It's also the chapter in which we encounter a vulnerability in Tumarkin that, despite everything she's let us see, or glimpse, is oddly unexpected. She'd known Vera for a long time; she'd been working on a book about her for years. The book never quite got there; there was something recalcitrant about it, as can happen with a book. And then Vera, who insisted she had no interest in telling her story, published a memoir. What to do with the swirl of emotion? What to do with the 20,000 words sitting there, all that work.

One of the reasons Vera's story is so difficult and compelling is that Vera is exactly that: a fiery woman who refuses all definitions, not just the stereotypes but the very words a writer might bring to her. Sharp and uncompromising, she has 'low tolerance' for polite society, polite anything. The word routinely used of her is 'outrageous'. Six years old when Germany invaded Poland, she's one of the very few Polish Jews alive at war's end. And, being Vera, she challenges every trope of the Holocaust survivor. She even manages to outrage a group of (mostly middle-class, conservative) Australians on the March of the Living from Auschwitz to Birkenau, by insisting on how much she loved the Polish countryside, Polish food. Poland. Her Poland. Did she have to repudiate everything Polish to refuse Polish anti-Semitism? She is Polish-Polish and Jewish-Jewish. Insistently, doubly both.

If Vera challenges Holocaust narratives, so too does Tumarkin. Is that what makes this chapter so scarifying? Or is it because it ranges over so much else, taking in characters, refugees from other worlds, other places, riffing on lives left behind, and shapes taken on, or resisted. The age of seven, Tumarkin tells us, is when the brain of the child first 'remembers' in ways they'll go on to remember. Before that it's moments, sensations. The grandmother who was given the custodial sentence remembers the joy of finding a doll in the bombed-out rubble.

And Vera? What does she remember, what has she put together since? What does the telling, or the not telling, do for her, do for a past, a present, too complex for a single narrative? What's she doing in Australia anyway? Oblivious Australia. How long will it be before Australian children say: 'The Holocaust? Oh yes, I saw the movie.' The Holocaust story that becomes sentimentalised. The heroic gentile saviour, the child innocent in the attic, the parents who do not turn towards the child watching from the window, resisting what Orpheus could not. Betrayal as salvation. Or the other way around.

How to tell this story again? Can Tumarkin avoid – can anyone avoid – the tarnishing that comes with the retelling? And what about us, the comfortable denizens of the West, with our placards? *Never Again.* Of course it could happen again, and one way or another right now it is, in this, our world. Not the same, but with as many refugees, displaced persons, traumatised children as there were back then, when that war ended. There are plenty of bombed-out cities; just not ours. That's my addition, but it's there. You can't read this chapter and not get the backwash from it.

And what are we going to do about it, any of it, all of it?

That's the question that hovers over both these books, as it does over all of us, readers and writers alike. The formidable face of the present.

POWER AND POLITICS

SWITCHING OFF

JUDITH BRETT

8 June 2010

Why, after being elected with such high hopes, has Kevin Rudd's star fallen so fast? We all know the events: the failure to negotiate the emissions trading scheme through the Senate and the decision to drop the policy until after the next election; the disastrously handled insulation scheme and the lesser disaster of Building the Education Revolution; the decision in an election year to take on one of Australia's most powerful interests, mining, with a new tax. And then there's the increasingly annoying manner, with the repeated taglines, the priggish, robotic delivery. It's only my professional commitment to following Australian politics that stops me from leaving the room when he appears yet again in a hard hat and fluoro safety jacket, or sitting in his shirt sleeves beside a hospital bed chatting with studied informality. And if, as the polls indicate, most Australians have switched off too, then his capacity to regain lost ground is very weak. It is as if he is fading from view before our eyes, still talking, a less and less substantial figure, like the Cheshire Cat but with pursed lips and a wagging finger.

The title of David Marr's June *Quarterly Essay*, 'Power Trip', points to some answers. Rudd began his maiden speech in federal politics with the words 'Politics is about power.' Well, yes and no. Power is complex. It comes in many forms, from coercive power, with its threats and bribes, to the authority to give orders and expect to be obeyed, to the power to persuade people to see a situation as you do and agree with your line of action. And in liberal democracies like Australia, the power of any one political officeholder, even the prime minister, is limited. Marr quotes a shrewd old bureaucrat who has worked with a few prime ministers and wonders if Rudd really understands the way power works at the top. 'He isn't afraid to pick a fight, but doesn't then behave like a prime minister: he involves himself so much; puts himself on the line so quickly; doesn't exercise authority by keeping at a distance.'

This is Rudd of 'the buck stops with me', who presents himself as the fixer of last resort of all the nation's problems. This is the Rudd who rushed in to take the blame for all the problems of the insulation scheme, and whisked his notebook out of his top pocket to note down the names of worried insulators, reassuring them that there would be another phase of government largesse once the problems were sorted out. Why did he think he had to take all the blame? There were a few other candidates – like shonky small business operators. And no one really expects the PM to act as everyone's local member, sorting out each person's problems with this or that government scheme. But having promised something he then found he couldn't deliver, and he only has himself to blame when he walks away and people are angry. There is a failure of judgement here as he promises too much and delivers too little, both in small things like the promise to the insulators and in large policy reversals like the emissions scheme. I am sure we will see a similar pattern in his attempt to fix the blame game in the nation's hospital system.

Implicit in these failures of judgement is a fantasy of concentration of power in the office of the PM. Bucks stop – or not – in many places in liberal parliamentary democracies like ours: in particular with individual ministers, with state premiers and, behind the scenes, with senior public servants. Marr shows convincingly that Rudd is driven by a genuine and deeply held commitment to making Australia a decent place for children to grow up in, a commitment forged in the hard years after his father died. Because his father was a tenant farmer, the family lost its home after he died, and he endured two terrible years as a boarder in a Marist College that instilled in him an icy hatred of the school. Rudd's determination to make Australia a place in which kids didn't have to suffer like he had was accompanied by a determination to remake himself from a fussy little kid on the margins of other people's lives into someone who was both unassailable and at the centre of things – which is where, he thinks, he now is.

But the problem is that, having got there, his hold on power is slipping faster than anyone could have imagined. He has become, Marr argues, the choke point in the government, just as he was in Goss's government when he ran the cabinet office. Rudd's micromanagement and need to be on top of every detail also has to do with owning all the outcomes of government; he treats senior public servants as underlings, patronises caucus, ignores advice and bypasses his ministers, hogging all the big announcements for himself. And, in the judgement of a former staffer, 'For all the effort he doesn't come up with particularly interesting solutions to problems. His policy positions aren't breakthrough, not particularly new or exciting. After all that work they are dull.'

Because he thinks power is all about him, he seems unable to give others the space to be creative, which means that he can't draw on the wisdom of those who are perhaps less clever than he is but have richer life experiences and more understanding of what makes others tick. And he seems to think that all he has to do is to make announcements. Power is also exercised through persuasion, and here he seems to have a major blind spot. As we know, he is very sensitive to voters' opinions, but seems little interested in that of stakeholders. It is mind-boggling that his government decided to introduce a new mining tax without any prior consultation with the industry. Ambushing Australia's most powerful industry in an election year is about as smart as Ben Chifley's taking on the banks. Doesn't he remember that the Australian Mining Industry Council's advertising campaign killed the Hawke government's commitment to national land rights legislation in the 1980s?

The battle with the miners has erupted since Marr finished his essay, but it is in character with the man Marr presents, a man for whom power is a brittle exercise in control and who has little understanding of the limits of what one person can do, even when he holds the highest office in the land. Perhaps Rudd will read Marr's essay and learn from it. He does have deep intellectual and emotional reserves. And with an unelectable opposition, we would all be grateful if he showed signs of a maturing political judgement. But the concluding scene does not bode well for such an outcome.

Marr and Rudd have been chatting and Rudd asks him about the likely argument of the essay. Marr tells him that he is pursing the contradictions of his life, and wonders aloud if his government will go the way of Goss's. Rudd explodes with controlled fury. It is, says Marr, the most vivid version of Rudd he has yet encountered. 'Who is the real Kevin Rudd?' he writes. 'He is the man you see when the anger vents. He's a politician with rage at his core, impatient rage.' Marr's essay is brilliant: it has all of the sharp observation and unexpected angles, and the lucid, supple prose, that make him such a fine interpreter of Australian political life.

THE EVERYDAY POLITICS OF PERPETUAL ELECTIONEERING

JAMES PANICHI

8 December 2011

L et's state the obvious: no Australian running for parliament would ever pledge to cut ties with his or her electorate after winning the seat. It's Politics 101: if you spend time and money ingratiating yourself with your potential constituents, the last thing you'd want to do is alienate them after the poll. It would be political suicide.

Or would it? In Ireland, the leader of the centre-right Fine Gael party did just that. Enda Kenny vowed that, if elected, he would direct his ministers to do no constituency work for their first one hundred days in office. Promising to end the 'circus' of ministers attending events in their constituencies, he made a deal: no unveiling of plaques, no kissing babies, no stump speeches, no constituent schmoozing. Nothing. Instead, a Kenny cabinet would 'hit the ground running' and focus on the country's battered and overexposed economy. It would be one hundred days of unadulterated delivery.

'If this becomes a reality, ministers will concentrate completely, to the exclusion of all works, on the national responsibilities of their portfolios,' Kenny said in February, shortly before the election. 'Their constituencies, I'm quite sure, will be happy to accommodate them.'[1]

These fighting words may well have helped Kenny become the country's new taoiseach (prime minister); yet within seventy days his pre-election commitment was in tatters. And the problem wasn't the constituents – their ability to accommodate the prolonged absence of their representatives was never put to the test. The issue was the politicians: they couldn't keep away from their electorates.

In May, the *Irish Independent* listed the functions Kenny had attended in his western electorate of Mayo since coming to power, and it added

---

1 Mary Minihan, "Kenny Says FG Ministers Would Avoid Constituency Work for 100 Days," *The Irish Times*, February 24, 2011, https://www.irishtimes.com/news/kenny-says-fg-ministers-would-avoid-constituency-work-for-100-days-1.580233.

up to an impressive level of local involvement. The taoiseach had raised a flag at the Galway–Mayo Institute of Technology, sounded the starting horn at the West of Ireland Women's Mini-Marathon, opened the Mayo ploughing championship, turned the first sod at May Abbey National School ... And his Spartan, outcome-focused cabinet members were doing the same around the country.

The take-home message is this: don't stand between an Irish politician and a constituent. The country's political reality has turned MPs into what columnist Fintan O'Toole described as 'demented ward-heelers'. And Ireland's multi-member electorates, in which politicians compete against both fellow party members and political opponents, are part of the problem.

'It is not war with the enemy but friendly fire that the Irish politician fears most,' O'Toole wrote earlier this year. 'That fear sustains the crazy system of doling out "imaginary patronage". Everyone does it because, if they don't, it's sure as hell that some hungry colleague will be out on the street corners pushing the drug.'[2]

In Australia that addiction is, if nothing else, out in the open. The substance has been legalised and the industry that is building up around its distribution has taken on an air of respectability. In fact, even without multi-member federal electorates the cult of being accountable to one's community has become the one constant thread in our political culture.

What Australian politician would claim to be anything less than a 'tireless worker' for his or her electorate? What kind of martyr would enter into a parliamentary debate without claiming to be in regular contact with the 'real Australia' of the constituency? (The vested interests and the elites, of course, live in ivory towers that have no postcode.)

Electorate offices are now outreach machines for politicians who have become travelling salesmen for themselves. On Saturday mornings you will find MPs sitting behind card tables at the local shopping centre, their rolled-up sleeves embracing the semiotics of suburban struggle. If you've had a tough night up with a crying baby, they feel your pain because they've been there themselves ('If I had a dollar for every nappy I've changed ...'); if your local council is driving you nuts, well, those jokers have been giving your local member headaches for years.

Accessibility, responsiveness and empathy are what we've come to expect from our politicians; they, in turn, have set themselves up to feed those expectations. Their staff numbers are growing and they pay

2   Fintan O'Toole, *Enough is Enough: How to Build a New Republic* (London: Faber and Faber, 2010).

commercial rates for offices in shopping strips to be certain of attracting through-traffic. They crave involvement.

In fact, the electorate responsibilities of many federal MPs are driving them to breaking point – and it's all self-inflicted. Particularly in marginal seats, our elected representatives are choosing to take on more work than ever before, and they are prepared to sacrifice their personal lives to deliver. Where does all that hard work go? What do the 150 members of Australia's House of Representatives actually achieve for their electorates? And how worse off would we be if our local MP skipped the odd community meeting and caught a movie instead?

•

Meet Bruce Billson, a gregarious forty-something guy with a volcanic laugh and an engaging personality. His busy diary and ridiculously overburdened desk exemplify the growing workload now faced by MPs in marginal seats.

Billson had a stint as veterans' affairs minister in the dying months of the Howard government, but he would readily admit that his greatest political achievement has been to keep the marginal seat of Dunkley, south-east of Melbourne, in Liberal hands since 1996 (at the time of writing he holds it with 2.04 per cent). His office in the bayside outer suburb of Frankston accommodates five members of staff (the standard four, plus one for his policy work as shadow small business, competition policy and consumer affairs minister). And everyone's busy.

'The design would be to say that you've got one staffer for the portfolio and the other staff to deal with the rest,' Billson says:

> In reality, it doesn't play out that way. In terms of constituent enquiries, there would be two-and-a-half of the team dedicating themselves almost entirely to that task. You then look at the community engagement relationship, the building-stakeholders-staying-in-touch activity – that's probably nearly another three-quarters of a person's role. And then the balance is the shift between what we call 'Canberra work', which isn't just in Canberra: that's the parliamentary debate, the legislation ... And what weaves through all of that is the portfolio work.

In other words, the bulk of the office's workload is centred on the electorate. When Billson's press officer shows me a large folder of the correspondence that has gone out over the past week, he's not doing so out of a sense of bravado. It's more of a horrified acknowledgement that this is what they do just to stay afloat.

'There is an expectation that you'll support, respond to and provide assistance to the electorate,' Billson says. 'If you don't do that well, you're failing to meet a very fundamental expectation that people have of you. If you do that quite well, people think "well, so you should".'

While many MPs are coy about the quid pro quo of electorate work, Billson is happy to acknowledge his state of 'perpetual electioneering'. 'I don't think you can win a lot of votes by being very responsive to the local electorate,' he says jokingly. 'But you can lose plenty if you're not.' And don't mention the emails: he gets over 800 of them in the course of a day. Billson lets me look over his shoulder as he goes through recent additions to his inbox, and while there are a couple of Google alerts, there are also forty genuine pieces of correspondence:

> This one's about Medicare funding for PET scans; here we've got some people talking about some internal party issues. There's something about what's going on in Sri Lanka and a problem with a memorial for a football team that drowned when its ferry came back to Mornington [in 1891]. There's a local CEO talking to me about infrastructure pressures on growth areas. More on the boating disaster. Something about changes to Fair Work; an issue of religious funding; a view on Bob Katter; a local sustainability centre …

Billson hasn't had to do anything. His mere existence as an MP in a marginal seat over the past hour has generated at least three hours' work for one of his staff. The internet has 'transformed' electorate work, he says. 'In some respects, in a positive way; in other respects – welcome to my nightmare.'

One of the problems is identifying genuine constituent emails from a tide of nationally orchestrated campaigns that hits the computers of all federal MPs:

> There was one recently where a resident in Langwarrin [on the Mornington Peninsula] was most upset that my response to him wasn't of the quality and thoughtfulness – and timeliness – that he would expect for 'a swinging voter in a marginal seat'. In other words, 'You should be working

your tail off for my vote, sunshine!' I thanked him for his feedback and his critique of the quality of my response, but I asked how I was supposed to have known that – and to protect the innocent I'll change the email address – foxymama@hotmail.com was a resident in Langwarrin with a particular concern. How would I pick that out of the fog of emails that come in? That's one of the dilemmas – that you can underperform in some people's eyes without ever knowing quite what the expectation was, or that they are a local constituent. But we try to optimise our response to those people in the electorate.

When I ask Billson how many staff he would require to keep up with the incoming correspondence, he isn't able to answer. 'No matter how many we had, they would still be run off their feet.' In other words, higher levels of service would drive up the demand. Which could explain why many British MPs, who have comparatively fewer resources, manage to circumscribe their electorate contact hours (which they call 'surgery') to a few a week. Whether this lessens the democratic legitimacy of their relationship with constituents is another story.

•

The politics of the Greens may be too radical for some, but when it comes to constituency work the party's only MP in the House of Representatives, Adam Bandt, is solidly mainstream. 'I want everyone who approaches me and my office to walk away saying "Adam Bandt and his staff helped me fix my problem",' he says. 'The last thing that anyone deserves from their member of parliament is the feeling that they have just been flicked to someone else.'

Who could argue with that? MPs helping constituents has to be good for everyone, and indeed most politicians will be able to rattle off some great examples of pastoral care. For Adam Bandt it's a story of helping to get a visa arranged for someone to make it to their wedding in Australia (Bandt's electorate officer scored an invitation to the reception). Another federal MP tells me of tracking down a specialised gardener to help an eighty-two-year-old constituent who was having problems with her Australian natives.

But this goodwill on the part of the MP isn't codified. There's no job description. He or she may choose to spend all spare time available on constituency matters, or tell staff members to focus exclusively on big-picture policy. In fact, other than showing up for parliamentary sittings every so often, MPs can do as they please. Pay increases are not linked to electorate productivity benchmarks; you can tell your eighty-two-year-old constituent to find her own gardener and lose not a cent of your income.

The extent to which a politician does any constituency work is a rough-and-ready convention – arbitrary and discretionary. 'The only real performance appraisal of an MP is the election – there is nothing else,' says Stephen Bartos, a former senior public servant who is now a director of Sapere Research Group. But he also admits that the real impact of 'good' constituency work on the ballot box bottom line may be overstated.

'There are MPs whose constituency work will make a bit of a difference – one or two percentage points against a swing,' Bartos says. 'It's not a huge difference, though, so a general tide will sweep them away, no matter how hard they've worked.' This means that spending Saturdays meeting and greeting in the mall may have less of an impact on an MP's future than, say, the decision of a party leader to break a campaign promise.

So, why bother? What drives marginal-seat politicians to hand over increasingly large chunks of time to their electorates? And what kind of people do they become in the process?

•

In the mid 1990s I had two unhappy stints working for MPs. I eventually realised that it wasn't them – it was me. Whatever qualities are required to be a politician's staffer, I didn't possess them.

I had come to the job after spending my adolescence in Italy, where national politics lacks what is known as *presenza sul territorio*. There were no geographically based constituencies in the 1980s, just an impersonal system of proportional representation across often large regions. As a rule, Italian politicians don't have electorate offices (although they pocket an allowance earmarked for that purpose) and direct contact between electors and the elected is rare.

Australian politics, with its intricate topography of electoral divisions, was a breath of fresh air. I imagined a landscape of political microcosms, in which a relationship between the MP and his or her community could flourish; local issues could then resonate nationally.

On paper, it was the best political system in the world; in practice, it soon became unbearably pedestrian.

One of my bosses was an irascible, hardworking MP in a marginal regional seat who was widely acknowledged as a 'strong local member' (which I found out years later was a euphemism for someone not destined for greater things). On the second day of my employment, she stormed into my office. 'Where are they?' she shrieked. 'Where are my letters?' (I have learned to drop the expletives when retelling this story, or it sounds too unbelievable.) 'When I get to work, I want my letters!'

I was later informed that the MP, who started work at 5 am (often after a kip on the couch if she had come straight from a function the night before), liked to have constituent letters to sign and place into the out-tray. She wanted the electorate to know she was in touch. My job was to help generate that correspondence.

When she wasn't berating employees, she was barnstorming her large electorate in a van: a flag-raising ceremony at a school, a lunch at the RSL, a meeting at the local chamber of commerce ('Where's my speech about the Business Incubator?' she bellowed at me on day three, astounded that I had never before heard 'business' and 'incubator' in the same sentence).

When she was out for the day I jokingly asked the others (back then federal members only had a staff of three) if we could finally relax. They rolled their eyes and muttered something about 'generating work'. Sure enough, when she exploded back into the office at 7 pm, she had a list of things for us to 'follow up'. Letters to be written, enquiries to be made, further visits to be organised.

Practically all of her work was constituency-based – even when she was in Canberra. 'Could the minister inform the House how policy X will benefit my constituents in town Y?' was her usual contribution to question time. She would then print out the minister's predictable reply from *Hansard* and send it out to the good burghers of town Y. She didn't have to spend much time on party matters: the seat was too marginal for anyone to want to challenge her for preselection. She had a job to do and she did it well by beating the odds and holding on to a seat that would have fallen with a less single-minded local member.

The other MP I worked for was far more interested in the internal machinations of his party than electorate work in its purest form. What that meant was constituent enquiries in his suburban, marginal electorate were essentially a chance to build his reputation as a fixer – a reputation that would then echo around party branches.

But he was also deeply suspicious of everyone and everything (he once had the office swept for listening devices: none were found) and he sensed that constituent sentiment could be used against him. He hated sending people away dissatisfied and was always happy to leave them feeling that he was on *their* side, no matter what.

One of my first enquiries was from an angry man with a strong accent. 'Someone wants to know if you think Macedonia is Greek,' I said, with the caller on hold. The MP's brow furrowed, as it did when he was asked to focus on the complex issue of his self-preservation. 'Who's asking?' he snapped.

My experience working for the MPs convinced me that marginal-seat politics were creating a class of people who had to be obsessively parochial in order to survive. MPs were too terrified of electoral defeat to want to soar among the big ideas of national politics. Meanwhile, though, the picture of society emerging from their constituents' complaints was too fractured – and too biased towards discontent – to really come together as a useful mosaic of Australian society.

'That may be the case, but they have to win their seat,' says Carlo Carli, who was a state Labor MP in Victoria between 1994 and 2001. 'For a lot of MPs, they're not going to have a seat if they don't do the work ... Remember, you can't soar if you don't have a seat.'

Sure – first, you have to last. But does that imply that only MPs in safe seats can afford to drag themselves away from their electorates long enough to be intellectually engaged in running the country? Would Paul Keating have taken on important economic reforms if he had spent his spare time lurking around the Bankstown RSL?

The 2009 British satirical comedy *In the Loop* features a fictional minister for international development by the name of Simon Foster. One day, he is in Washington, arguing the pros and cons of military intervention in the Middle East, and the next he is at 'surgery' with disaffected constituents. One resident has written to demand that Foster do something about 'cyclists looking smug', while a woman is angry about the faulty septic tank which her property shares with the minister's electorate office. A discussion about who is responsible for filling the tank ends with Foster saying, apologetically, 'Of course you're not an elephant, and you certainly should not be treated as if you are one.'

Did it ever get that bad in my experience? Maybe not. And in fairness I should say that while for me marginal-seat work became an impediment to thinking about policy in more abstract terms, my bosses viewed their grounding in reality as an asset. They argued – and they might be right –

that close contact with the community made them better politicians. And better people.

•

In 1967, Labor MP Gordon Bryant argued that electorate work was all about talking to people. 'It's not that the federal member has any magic or any authority,' Bryant wrote. '[B]ut what he does have is a line of communication readily at hand into the last pigeon-hole in the most remote department. He has a phone and he uses it.'

An ability to dial may not feature prominently in modern job applications, but the late MP's idea of taking an interest in one's electorate certainly resonates with today's crop. Federal politicians find out what's going on even when it has nothing to do with the Commonwealth government – they know it could all end up being their business anyway.

Writing in 1994, British academic (and Conservative peer) Andrew Norton identified at least seven constituency roles of the member of parliament. They are: safety valve; information provider; local dignitary; advocate; benefactor; powerful friend; and promoter of constituency interests. An Australian MP would have no problem recognising all of these categories, although the home-grown edition may read more like this: information provider; local dignitary; promoter of constituency interests; powerful friend; and safety valve.

The provision of information, which Bruce Billson jokingly refers to as a 'triage or concierge' service, is straightforward. People don't always know how government works and whom they need to turn to; in fact, research that Stephen Bartos conducted in 1993 found that 80 per cent of Australians didn't understand the difference between federal, state and local government.

What usually happens is that people with a problem turn to the most prominent politician they know and ask for help. The office staff will then channel that enquiry to the appropriate bodies, while being careful not to give the impression of fobbing the constituent off (even when they have good reasons to do just that).

Under the rubric of 'local dignitary' comes the community outreach – chairing meetings, speaking at a TAFE graduation, cutting a ribbon, judging the cake competition at the local CWA. Again, it's all self-explanatory. 'Promoter of constituency interests' can have some federal implications. A constituent comes in to offer an opinion about policy or to complain about the way he or she has been treated by a federal agency.

The MP may choose to take up the issue in parliament, or informally with ministers. It's what representative democracy is all about.

But when politicians become a constituent's 'powerful friend' – a role that MPs usually take on with relish – things can become ethically tricky. Because when constituents ask MPs to intervene on their behalf, to intercede in a dispute, what are they actually asking for? And how appropriate is that relationship anyway?

Gordon Bryant, who was Bob Hawke's predecessor in the division of Wills, told the story of a constituent whose sister had emigrated from Europe to Venezuela but was now being denied the chance to migrate to Australia. Bryant was able to ascertain that the decision to deny her a visa was wrong and 'on Christmas Eve, [she] embarked for Australia'.

Heartwarming stories of this kind may have struck a chord back then, and Bryant was suggesting that MPs were playing a valuable role in the oversight of the federal bureaucracy. And indeed, MPs view the 'oversight' or 'safety valve' aspect of the job as an important part of what they do.

The question for modern readers is whether in an age of accountability, transparency and customer service, the hit-and-miss noblesse oblige of powerful politicians stepping in is still appropriate. Perhaps what constituents should be getting from their MP is the phone number of the ombudsman, or a good lawyer, rather than a promise to intervene.

In Bryant's Venezuelan scenario, for example, who told the woman that she wasn't eligible to come to Australia? What repercussions are there for bureaucrats providing misleading information? Why were the phone calls of the member for Wills answered by a departmental secretary (as Bryant eventually reveals) while the constituent's enquiries were ignored? And if Bryant had decided, on a whim, not to take an interest in his constituent's case, would the sister still be stuck in Caracas?

The same ethical question could be raised every time an MP gets a constituent a win – even for the noblest of causes. A Liberal senator for Queensland, Sue Boyce, recently told ABC Radio National that she had to lobby the immigration minister to intervene to ensure that a mildly disabled child with strong family ties to the Gold Coast was allowed into Australia. Migration rules would otherwise have prevented that child from getting a visa.

Boyce readily admits that the system in which a family's welfare hinges on the personal intervention of a politician is unsustainable and says the system needs to be changed. 'It shouldn't be the minister who has to make the decision,' she said. 'The stories that come to the ministers are often quite heart-wrenching and I think they would all like an opportunity to see this cleared up so that it's not entirely their responsibility.' As things stand however, it's only the lobbying of individual MPs that can make a difference. What happens to the families whose case isn't taken up by a politician?

In short, if MPs are being granted a real or implied power to help administer the functions of the Australian public sector then shouldn't we be able to quantify that power? If politicians see it as their role to act as intermediaries between citizen and state, how can this work be assessed and reviewed? And how do we ensure this work is being carried out ethically?

Stephen Bartos believes that aggrieved citizens who choose to go to their local MP rather than the ombudsman are doing so because the politicians are more visible, and may well offer a better service. 'What MPs have, which other agencies don't, is that much higher visibility of going around to a community event and being recognised at a bus stop.' Typically, says Bartos, politicians tell the constituent 'that they are interested in their problem and that they'll solve it in their office. And that's something a lot harder for, say, the ombudsman's office, or a consumer complaints office, to deal with.'

•

Labor MP Andrew Leigh has 125,000 voters in his ACT seat of Fraser, making it the second-largest in the country. So in spite of his comfortable 15 per cent margin, he's no stranger to the demands of constituency work, with a few hundred emails coming into his Canberra office every day. 'One of the things I find hardest about the job is drawing a line around that,' he says. 'Of not being constantly in a situation of turning away from my two-year-old who wants to be read a story in order to respond to yet another constituent email from the kitchen counter.'

But in terms of requests for MPs to intervene, Leigh argues it's not usually about pulling strings, but rather about helping the constituent through the complexities of the case. 'I would be deeply concerned if the [government] department was making an ad hoc decision based on the fact that an MP had written to them,' he says. 'But that's not the sense I get. The sense I get is that the department sees this as a chance to explain what's going on, why something appears like an anomaly when it isn't.'

But Leigh agrees that the MP's role as a 'powerful friend' can become 'awkward' unless properly managed:

There are a couple of things I won't do ... I won't write an immigration support letter for a person that I don't know. I don't feel it's appropriate for me to intervene in a complicated decision that the department is making – based on much more information than I have – in order to support a constituent who has phoned me up, over a constituent that doesn't think to phone me up.

Fintan O'Toole's complaint about 'demented ward-heelers' in Ireland refers to politicians' obsession with 'doling out "imaginary patronage"'. But in Australia, that patronage isn't always imaginary – letters from MPs supporting a constituent's cause do carry weight, particularly where ministers have discretionary room to move (immigration is the best example of that).

In Italy, a politician's offer of patronage would be seen as an attempt to create a relationship of political 'clientelism', a practice that traces its origins back to ancient Rome. Anthropologist Amalia Signorelli describes *clientelismo* as 'a system of interpersonal relations in which private ties of a kinship, ritual kinship, or friendship type are used inside public structures, with the intent of making public resources serve a private end'. *Clientelismo* has become an expression of corruption because politicians actually have access to public property (in the form of jobs) which they are at liberty to hand out to repay political patronage.

So, let's assume an Australian MP's letter of support is worth something, then that something is being given to a constituent, free of charge, purely at the whim of a politician. Yet the value of that gift does not belong to the MP – he or she is merely administering it on behalf of the Australian state. Electorate staffing jobs can also be used to pay off political debts, but on the whole our clientelism is more subtle. That's largely because MPs recognise the ethical dimension of what they're doing and are usually careful not to cross the line. Usually.

When, on 31 August 2000, the Labor member for Wills, Kelvin Thomson, wrote a 'To Whom It May Concern' letter in support of drug dealer Tony Mokbel, he claims not to have known about his constituent's colourful history. But the letter itself, which refers to Mokbel's 'successful establishment as a local businessman', highlights the mechanics of political patronage. The logic for writing these letters is that an MP's intervention (in this case, supporting Mokbel's application for a liquor licence) will tap into a broader network of support – for example, those to be employed at Mokbel's future business, or his family and friends.

In 2005, Liberal backbenchers campaigned for former immigration minister Amanda Vanstone to grant a visa to a man suspected of links to Calabrian organised crime – just five years after the department had ordered his deportation. The logic of such decisions is simple: *do ut des* – I give, so that you may give (through political support and/or party donations).

Politicians who intervene directly in what should be independent public service decisions do it in the hope of establishing networks that they will use come election time. The question that no politician is keen to answer is whether such intervention, with the inconsistencies it entails, is an appropriate form of governance.

How much would the granting of a visa have been worth, in dollar terms, to someone who may have faced prosecution in Italy if deported? And who did that amount belong to? Australia, or the Liberal Party? Who owns the value of MPs' ability to bring about ministerial intervention?

•

There's little appetite for reforming MPs' role as political patrons – particularly when politicians list examples of their direct intervention as being among the highlights of their career. There is also a strong belief that their role in offering constituents some oversight of the public service outweighs any consideration about process.

Adam Bandt, whose office in the seat of Melbourne has 250 electorate matters currently on its books, says constituent involvement is too important for it to be curtailed by regulation:

> I think that we're in a unique position ... of having a bird's-eye view of how the system works at the different levels and being in a position of being able to have access, from ministers down to departments. I think it's a good system.

Back in Frankston, even Bruce Billson is prepared to say that being on the receiving end of 800 emails a day isn't as bad as the alternative – no contact at all. 'The democratic process is untidy, we all know that,' he says. 'But there's been no better way of trying to govern through processes that are as responsive to those being governed as they can be.

'Getting an outcome for a person who is feeling that there's no one on their side is incredibly satisfying,' he says. 'So, if I can help resolve problems, or relieve a burden or a concern that's troubling someone's life, or bring about some change that makes a local person's prospects for the future better, I reckon that's pretty worthwhile.'

MARGARET THATCHER, BETWEEN MYTH AND POLITICS

DAVID HAYES

12 January 2012

This is not the kind of comeback Margaret Thatcher would ever have wanted. There was a time, in the wake of her tearful departure from 10 Downing Street in November 1990, when she seemed to be holding on to the dream of recovering Britain's prime ministership. So dominant had she been for over a decade – dominating both the country's political scene and the psyche of millions of its citizens – that it would not have been altogether fanciful to imagine her reappearing, in the manner of Norma Desmond in *Sunset Boulevard*, to declaim, 'I *am* big – it's the politics that got small!'

But the whirligig of time has its ravages, its revenges and its rewards. Now, over two decades later, a film treatment that skilfully intertwines Thatcher's past career glory and present fading memory, and thus depicts her as both powerful and vulnerable, offers her an unexpected late reprise. The formula – the exploits of a heroic personality shadowed by private tragedy and undone by lesser men – is reliably comforting, the central performance of Meryl Streep an impressive simulacrum. A success in its own terms, then, though any cultural trace will be (I would guess) almost imperceptible.

The baroness will not see, let alone cast any beady-eyed verdict on, *The Iron Lady*. In any event Margaret Thatcher always did live for politics and had little time for art in whatever form. (Her notional favourite poet was the imperial tub-thumper Rudyard Kipling – like her, a great left-hater – and she favoured Dickens' *A Tale of Two Cities* 'with its strong political flavour'.) This always marked her as a philistine to many of her adversaries, admittedly a subsidiary item in a long charge sheet. To those with some knowledge of the public world and events the film depicts – if my own reaction is any guide – the film will appear caricatural and depoliticised to an almost unwatchable degree. But if *The Iron Lady* is thus a minor indication that Margaret Thatcher is becoming ever more a mythic figure, it also invites an effort to look at its subject in the perspective of politics and history.

•

Margaret Thatcher's top-rank political career spanned only twenty years, a shorter period now than the one since that red-eyed resignation. For the first decade, moreover – even after she became leader of the Conservative Party in February 1975 following a bold challenge to the managerialist Edward Heath, and arguably even after she led the party to the election victory that made her prime minister – there was little indication of the transformative role she would play.

Margaret Roberts, born in 1925, was raised in the English East Midlands market town of Grantham, the daughter of a corner-shop grocer of Methodist religious beliefs and an instinct for public service (he served on many local associations and briefly as the town's mayor). Her 'practical, serious and intensely religious' childhood helped her win a scholarship to Oxford University, from where she graduated in chemistry in 1947 before working as a laboratory researcher, while pursuing her political interests. She contested the national elections of 1950 and 1951 as a Conservative candidate in the safe Labour seat of Dartford, south-east of London, meeting her husband Denis on the stump. She gave birth to twins in 1953, the year she qualified as a barrister specialising in taxation law. The relationships with her father, Alfred, and with Denis Thatcher (a wealthy manager of a paint firm, unstintingly supportive of his wife's career) were the vital ones of her life.

Margaret Thatcher became member of parliament for the north London seat of Finchley in 1959, a foot soldier in the Conservatives' third successive national victory. It had been a long apprenticeship for a young, ambitious, hardworking, self-assured woman seeking advancement in a party whose higher reaches and governing ethos were overwhelmingly male and upper-class (albeit with a vast female membership and a policy orientation that accorded women's perceived interests a crucial priority). In other respects, however, it was a conventional rise amid propitious family circumstances, in a conformist era in which a woman judged (not least by other women) to be of the right calibre could ascend some way up the greasy pole.

The upper extent of the climb began to be renegotiated as the revolutions of the 1960s – far slower at the time than in mediatised retrospect – got underway. The election of a minority Labour government under the wily Harold Wilson in 1964 ended the Conservatives' thirteen-year hegemony, and after its consolidation in 1966 the reformist home secretary Roy Jenkins introduced liberalising reforms (on divorce, homosexuality, capital punishment and censorship) that began to unlock some damaging social rigidities.

The prospect of a woman prime minister still seemed far distant – Thatcher herself, in a starchily filmed BBC profile in 1973, speaking of what would now be called her 'work–life balance', said that this was unlikely 'in my lifetime'. Even the national profile she earned as shadow education minister in Edward Heath's government of 1970–74 proved double-edged when, in ending the obligation for schools to provide free milk to their charges, she gained notoriety as the 'milk snatcher'. It was rather around Labour cabinet members Barbara Castle and Shirley Williams that, in the late 1960s and mid 1970s respectively, 'who will be the first?' speculation began to cluster.

What made Thatcher the favourite to win this imaginary race was her capture of the leadership of her party in the wake of its electoral defeat in October 1974. Heath had promised that a market-led economic approach would release entrepreneur energies stifled by Labour's corporatism. Instead, rising inflation led him to impose price and wage controls and to widespread strikes, of which the powerful coal miners' strike was the most disabling. Heath called an election in February 1974, asking 'Who governs Britain?'; the voters replied, albeit by a whisker, 'Not you, guv.' Wilson returned as head of a Labour minority government, winning a tiny majority the following October.

If all political careers are ultimately defined by a single moment, the decision then to challenge the gruff Heath for the Conservative leadership was Margaret Thatcher's. She was neither a senior cabinet minister nor one associated with new ideas or a fresh policy agenda. But having made her choice, she gathered support from a band of fellow discontents – notably the former intelligence operative Airey Neave, whose astute campaign won her the day.

Much of Thatcher's four years in the role of opposition leader confirms the notion that it is the most thankless job in democratic politics. She was disliked by a large swathe of her parliamentary party, less out of loyalty to Edward Heath (a brooding presence on the back benches) than because of a mix of personal antipathy, patrician disdain and doubt that she would win a national election. Labour's contingent could be more openly hostile, and its leader James Callaghan – who became prime minister after Harold Wilson's sudden retirement in March 1976 – developed an effective line in patronising avuncularity in their despatch-box encounters. Most important of all, the British people showed no sign of taking this evidently determined but fundamentally uncongenial character to their hearts. Shirley Williams – Labour education minister, daughter of the pacifist writer Vera Brittain, cheerfully agonised, attractively scatty – was much more the coming woman.

It seemed a poor hand, but Thatcher – a conviction politician with 'the second word ... as important as the first', says her best biographer, John Campbell – had assets beyond her self-belief. The support of party figures, often from the ideologically anti-communist and old-imperial right, who everywhere saw threats to Britain's national interests and unity – Irish terrorists, militant trade unionists, Soviet infiltrators, Scottish nationalists – was valuable ballast in an environment where alarm over Britain's 'crisis of governability' was spreading.

Indeed, around politics there then swirled a florid atmosphere of encroachment and impending breakdown – the 'pungent mélange of apocalyptic dread and conspiratorial fever' evoked by Francis Wheen in his vivid portrait of the 1970s.[3] The bookshops displayed works with titles such as Samuel Beer's *Britain Against Itself* (a fine work of political analysis); *The Future That Doesn't Work; Is Britain Dying?* and ominously, Patrick Hutber's *The Decline and Fall of the Middle Class*.

A newer anti-Keynesian right, much of it concentrated in emerging think tanks such as the Centre for Policy Studies and the Institute of Economic Affairs, had the answer: the development of a marketising agenda that sought to learn from the failures of the 1970–74 government and this time really change the country's economic model. Thatcher was always impatient of those who could not translate ideas into practical nostrums that accorded with her instincts ('she has absolutely no interest in ideas for their own sake', observed the Conservative intellectual Oliver Letwin). But she listened and learned, and in 1979 a version of Milton Friedman and Friedrich von Hayek's monetarist arguments became a keystone of the 'household economics' that underpinned her election message.

The Conservative leader's most potent asset was Britain's faltering economy, at the centre of the range of crises battering the Labour governments of the second half of the 1970s. The main instrument used to contain surging inflation – voluntary wage restraint dependent on agreement between ministers and trade-union leaders – was increasingly vulnerable to localised discontent.

When this spilled over in a series of public service workers' strikes in 1978–79 (the 'winter of discontent') – which followed James Callaghan's

---

3   Francis Wheen, *Strange Days Indeed* (London: HarperCollins, 2010), 9.

fateful postponement of an election he seemed about to call – the popular mood shifted. As did the intellectual: many of those who were to count out the 1980s in the spleen they vented on Thatcher had voted her in – Harold Pinter and the theatre director Peter Hall at least admitted it, while Christopher Hitchens acknowledged that his abstention was in effect a blue choice (and 'I was secretly, guiltily glad to see her terminating the long reign of mediocrity and torpor'). On 3 May 1979, after an election in which Margaret Thatcher's watch-the-pennies wisdom was complemented by slick and combative anti-Labour messages, she entered 10 Downing Street.

•

The long march of Thatcherism had begun. But to where? As so often, reaching the summit was soon to look the easy part. Thatcher's government was dominated for more than its first three years by a severe recession whose main ingredients – double-digit inflation (18 per cent in 1980), rising unemployment (to three million in September 1982) and interest rates (15.7 per cent in 1980), and regular industrial casualties, all in the context of increased consumer taxes and a strong currency – owed much to its own monetarist agenda. (The first Thatcher government 'was something unique in modern British history,' wrote Paul Hirst: 'a party led by a clique of intellectuals with a strong commitment to a radical ideology'.)

The spread of mass unemployment, especially in Britain's manufacturing heartlands (northern England, central Scotland, south Wales – which was also where Labour support was most concentrated), caused immense social damage that the government had no strategic plan to ameliorate. A series of urban riots in 1981, in parts of London as well as other English cities, was but the most dramatic expression of many-sided opposition.

It can seem, to adapt a line from Graham Greene's *The Quiet American*, that rarely did anyone for all her good intentions inflict such costs. That is not how Margaret Thatcher saw it. It was all worth it (though the journalist Hugo Young's absorbing papers do record her as saying, in 1980, both that redundancies are 'inevitable' and that she is 'conscious of the effects on people'). The pain, her acknowledgement of which was as partisan as everything else about her ('Oh, those poor shopkeepers!' was her instinctive reaction to the destruction in Toxteth, Liverpool), was necessary to reverse national decline and restore Britain's greatness. There was no alternative. And those who believe in 'consensus'? 'I regard them as Quislings, traitors,' she had told the urbane British ambassador to Tehran, Anthony Parsons, in 1978 – admittedly in the back of a taxi.

Yet, as Frank Bongiorno noted in Inside Story in November 2009, the bark was often sharper than the bite. Moreover, at this early stage Margaret Thatcher led a government far from fully 'hers', let alone committed to 'Thatcherism' (itself an elastic term which Thatcher used, albeit with levity, as early as March 1975, notes Richard Vinen in his indispensable *Thatcher's Britain: The Politics and Social Upheaval of the Thatcher Era*). Her ideological confrères, most prominent at this time the treasury minister Geoffrey Howe, were at the heart of economic policy, but many others in the cabinet were survivors of Edward Heath's cabinet and/or adherents of an older form of paternalistic conservatism that the former group believed was co-responsible for Britain's economic decline. The just-released official cabinet papers from 1981 show how acute were the intra-governmental debates over (for example) whether to pursue an active urban regeneration policy, as successfully advocated in the case of Liverpool by the party-conference favourite Michael Heseltine.

The 1979–1982 years were a test of fire in which Thatcher often felt beleaguered and her reliance on key advisers, some from outside the party-political world – always a feature of her premiership – grew. Her government was immeasurably aided in the period by Labour's slow-motion implosion after 1979, which saw the veteran leftist intellectual (and surprisingly effective government 'fixer' in 1976–79) Michael Foot elected to replace Callaghan but unable to prevent a schism that saw the leaders of Labour's right (including Roy Jenkins and Shirley Williams) create a new Social Democratic Party, or SDP, and form an alliance with the Liberal Party.

Into this mix of bleak economic news and emerging three-way politics irrupted Argentina's military occupation of Britain's half-forgotten sheep-farming colonial-era outpost in the south Atlantic, the Falkland Islands (or Malvinas). Any signals from Thatcher's government over the longstanding diplomatic dispute with Buenos Aires had been encouraging of the ambitions of the brutal *junta* there, but this history was buried as the prime minister seized the armoury of a violated Britannia and – strongly backed by the passionate Foot, who had won his journalistic spurs denouncing domestic 'appeasement' of Hitler in the 1930s – sent a naval force to recapture the territory.

An extended prelude followed by a concentrated campaign, with vital support from Ronald Reagan's administration, brought victory in the Falklands in under three months. Thatcher's men were swift to exploit the moment's ebullient patriotism, aligning disparate forms of regeneration in a cocksure narrative that sought – via the supercharging of a classic Conservative trope – to identify the party with the nation, Labour with disloyalty, and (a new element) the female warrior-leader with something approaching Britain's destiny.

The 'iron lady' – a sobriquet first bestowed by the Soviet military mouthpiece *Krasnaya Zvezda* (Red Star) in 1976 and quickly appropriated by a delighted Thatcher – had already paraded intransigence over the costs of recession and the hunger strikes by the Irish Republican Army prisoners in Northern Ireland (though here too the 1981 papers suggest a more nuanced policy was pursued behind the scenes). In the Falklands, the name acquired a new quasi-regal cast.

In June 1983, the Conservatives won a landslide election victory, with Labour – fighting on an unwieldy manifesto that one of its MPs called 'the longest suicide note in history' – only just edging into second place ahead of the SDP–Liberal alliance. In its aftermath there were, as the increasingly martial argot of those times would have it, new battles to fight. The government had already limited the trade unions' ability to call strikes and enforce a 'closed shop'. But in 1981 it had also retreated from what it saw as inevitable confrontation with the National Union of Miners, a tactical sidestep as representative of her leadership as any ideological thrust. (The historian Robert Skidelsky describes Thatcher as 'visionary in aim, cautious in method'.) By early 1984, after building up extensive coal stocks, it was readier to risk an open-ended dispute by announcing a series of mine closures.

The ensuing year-long strike, complicated by divisions among the miners (partly over the union leadership's failure to hold a ballot to give the stoppage democratic sanction), was intensely bitter (and in a few cases fatal), and ended in the miners' comprehensive defeat. The return to work was followed by staged closures that shrunk the once mighty industry and the miner's union to near vanishing point. This 'loss without limit' signalled the decline of many relatively isolated settlements created for and around a workplace whose inhabitants now had little or no prospect of alternative employment.

The victories of the second term created a strong foundation for securing a third, which followed another sweeping election win in June 1987. By then the convulsions of the early 1980s had receded for a significant portion of the population as the proceeds of Conservative largesse – or merely of public goods turned into private income streams – began to filter through: a boom in house prices (which also benefited the million-plus who had, thanks to first-term legislation, bought their rented homes from local councils), income tax reductions, an expanding consumer-leisure economy, and the revolution in the City of London symbolised by the introduction of electronic trading in October 1986 (the 'big bang').

All well and good for those (and they were very many) who floated on the bubble of 'casino capitalism', but this was not exactly the trick that Thatcherism had sought to perform. Rather, it intended – in its originating impulse at least – to solve Britain's macroeconomic problems of low growth, falling competitiveness and low productivity via rigorous application of monetarist policy. ('You turn if you want to, the lady's not for turning' was her conference pledge in the depths of the 1980 recession.)[4] The Thatcherite message was that the path to a solution lay in shrinking the state's role in the economy and allowing entrepreneurial initiative to flourish, while legislating to curb the trade unions ('the free economy and the strong state', in Andrew Gamble's pithy summation).[5]

The more that the 1980s wore on, the more elusive was this particular white rabbit. The plunge in share prices on 'Black Monday' in October 1987 was a premonition that even the boom that Thatcherism had finessed might be unsustainable. As inflation climbed, businesses were squeezed and unemployment again rose, and the question of Britain's entry into the European Union's mechanism to coordinate and stabilise currency exchange rates became a fault line dividing the government's most senior figures.

The dependency of Thatcher herself on her trusted economic adviser Alan Walters caused an irreparable breach with her (post-1983) chancellor Nigel Lawson, leading the latter to resign in October 1989. He was followed a year later by the deputy prime minister Geoffrey Howe, as Thatcher's intransigence over Europe reduced government policy to a cabal of one.

An unobtrusively scintillating speech in the House of Commons by the lawyerly Howe – whose mode of attack in the chamber had once memorably been compared by the Labour heavyweight Denis Healey to 'being savaged by a dead sheep' – proved a turning point. The flamboyant

---

4 Margaret Thatcher, "Speech to Conservative Party Conference" (speech, Brighton, October 10, 1980), Margaret Thatcher Foundation, https://www.margaretthatcher.org/document/104431.

5 Andrew Gamble, *The Free Economy and the Strong State* (Hampshire: Palgrave, 1994), 38.

Michael Heseltine, self-exiled from the cabinet since his resignation in 1986, challenged Thatcher for the party leadership. In an ill-managed campaign, she marshalled enough support among Conservative MPs to defeat Heseltine, though by an inconclusive margin. Following consultations with cabinet colleagues, she decided to resign, paving the way for her favoured successor John Major to win the prize. After a last bravura parliamentary performance, she left Downing Street on 27 November 1990.

Within days, the inflamed reaction to her implied suggestion that she would be the colourless Major's 'back-seat driver' confirmed what all outside the circle of her most faithful acolytes already knew: that after eleven-and-a-half years at the summit, it really was over.

What lay ahead was a local (and this being the United Kingdom, somewhat baroque) version of the now familiar afterlife of the world statesman: that is, not just a two-volume autobiography (heavily crafted by her adviser Robin Harris), a foundation in her name, an official website and archive, and a place on the A-list international speechmaking circuit, but also elevation to the House of Lords, state honours (including membership of the Order of the Garter and the Order of Merit) and a prominent statue – brass not iron – outside parliament.

It was never going to be an easy transition for a leader so intoxicated by the daily realities of executive governance and for so long commanding of the political scene. But Margaret Thatcher played gamely along, while gradually receding from public view – a process accelerated by the death of the stalwart Denis in 2003 and the diminishing of her own mental faculties that was quietly acknowledged by the time of her eightieth birthday in 2005.

•

Another provincial and controversial Tory who had a profound influence on Thatcher, Enoch Powell, famously wrote that '[all] political lives, unless they are cut off in midstream at a happy juncture, end in failure, because that is the nature of politics and of human affairs'.[6] Of few political leaders is the judgement more open to challenge than Margaret Thatcher, given the number and scale of the contests she won, the way she changed Britain's political landscape and language, her impact in much of the Soviet bloc and the United States, and her influence on the thinking and policy of her domestic successors, not least Tony Blair.

---

6   Enoch Powell, *Joseph Chamberlain* (London: Thames & Hudson, 1977).

Yet in so many of these achievements Thatcher also enjoyed quite extraordinary good fortune. There was luck in the character of her adversaries: Edward Heath, and the ineffectual Tory cabinet 'wets' whom she demoted or vanquished; the Argentinean tyrant Leopoldo Galtieri; the doomed romantic Michael Foot; the conceited miners' leader Arthur Scargill. And there was luck in the unfolding political arena in the 1980s: the election of Ronald Reagan, an ideological soulmate; a split centre-left in Britain, which made untrammelled governance possible; the arrival of Mikhail Gorbachev, the Soviet leader she famously 'could do business with'.

True, effective leaders also make the weather and seize opportunities, as in several of these cases. Moreover, they respond to and in turn help shape the zeitgeist, as Thatcher surely did over privatisation and globalisation, consumerism and the market. For all the enabling circumstances, she won three elections, and at the end of her decade one poll by a respected agency reported 47 per cent saying her governments had been 'good' for the country (against 35 per cent 'bad') – though the 'good for you' answers were 39 versus 41 per cent.

There were also lasting failures. Her dogmatic opposition to any devolution of power to Scotland led to the Conservatives' gradual electoral meltdown there and fuelled nationalist sentiment. (The artful Scottish National Party leader Alex Salmond once said that a statue of Thatcher should be erected outside the Scottish parliament established in 1999.) In the IRA she found an adamantine enmity to match her own. (Her narrow escape from its hotel bomb at her party's conference in 1984 could count among her luck, though it killed five others, just as another Irish republican group had killed Airey Neave in 1979.) Her wilful inflexibility in Europe (over German unification, for example) and the Commonwealth (especially over South Africa) – again, a sort of internationalisation of the esoteric British notion of absolute sovereignty – lost friends and uninfluenced people by the truckload.

On the core of what Thatcher's governments tried to achieve – a renovation of Britain's economic fundamentals – there is on most measures little evidence of success. On balance, 'a great deal of economic dislocation for a very modest amount of renewal' was Paul Hirst's judicious verdict.[7] And all this despite, and because of, the most egregious good fortune of all: the fact that the oil resources discovered

---

7   Paul Hirst, "Miracle or Mirage?: The Thatcher Years, 1979–1997," in *From Blitz to Blair: A New History of Britain Since 1939*, ed. Nick Tiratsoo (London: Phoenix, 1998).

in and extracted from the North Sea, between Scotland and Norway, in the 1970s began to affect Britain's economy and balance of payments in the year after her government came to power. (The country became a net exporter in June 1980; a trade deficit of 110.5 million tons in 1979 turned into a surplus of 31 million tons by 1988, and oil provided 8 per cent of tax returns at its peak.) The revenues, rather than being applied to a once-in-a-lifetime opportunity for wholesale modernisation – backed by the equivalent of Norway's state investment fund, for example – were in effect recycled as welfare payments for the millions Thatcher's policies discarded. Christopher Harvie's *Fool's Gold* (1994) is a brilliant telling of a near-forgotten national epic.

•

'Die before your death' goes the Sufi maxim. Margaret Thatcher's evident personal decline, the publicity surrounding the new biopic, and now a controversy over reported preparations to award her a state funeral, are naturally producing a slew of quasi-obituaries and career assessments. The reflections are fuelled by the current political echoes of her decade in power – a right-wing government imposing deep austerity during a recession, a north–south English divide, urban riots, divisions over Europe, a Scottish nationalist challenge.

The journalist Charles Moore, Thatcher's official biographer, is among the Conservative voices identifying a 'cultural change' beyond the 'Thatcher – for or against' pattern that has long framed British public debate. Boris Johnson, the mayor of London, sees *The Iron Lady* as 'the most important political film in years' which works to 'rehabilitate' its subject; he extracts from it the message that 'what really actuated Thatcher was a feminine impatience with the cosy, clubby, complacent politics of the postwar consensus – a consensus that was held overwhelmingly between men of a certain age and class'.[8]

The right's subtle repositioning of Thatcher as personalised national icon, somewhat above the partisan fray, is a familiar and effective device of conservative 'heritagisation'. The left has a different problem: how to prevent its instinctive, rooted excoriation of her memory and legacy

---

8 Boris Johnson, "Maggie's magic came from her contempt for complacent men," *The Telegraph*, https://www.telegraph.co.uk/comment/columnists/borisjohnson/9001544/Maggies-magic-came-from-her-contempt-for-complacent-men.html.

from becoming a comforting evasion of the need to think through and beyond it.

The signs here are not good. Much of the left, the metropolitan *Guardian* left especially, remains deeply in love with its hatred of Thatcher, unaware that this is the most conservative of emotions. The widespread, vicarious – and alarmingly cross-generational – nostalgia for a time of 'real battles' is another melancholy ingredient of this pathology (part of what in the 1990s I called the 'socialist heritage industry'). The outcome is a form of self-entrapment that corrodes the capacity to begin to understand the political experience of the last four decades in all its many-sidedness, contingency and complexity.

One example of the last point is my former neighbours in the Scottish council-house 'scheme' where I was brought up, who bought their home under the right-to-buy legislation. They sold it for a cosy retirement flat, and had enough left over to enjoy comfortable late years. They loathe Thatcher, and thank her.

Moreover, as Richard Vinen writes in a perceptive *Financial Times* column, 'The demonisation of Lady Thatcher reveals an extraordinary lack of context'; she 'has become a kind of voodoo doll for a left that talks as though sticking pins in the image of its enemy will be a substitute for thinking about its own problems'.

'Hatred must make a person productive. Otherwise, you might as well love.' The great Viennese satirist Karl Kraus spoke a hard and necessary truth. If the left can learn to see Margaret Thatcher's years in terms of their full political texture, rather than through the prism of its luxuriating abhorrence, their history may yet be retrieved from myth. The acceptance of complexity would be a good starting point.

THE REAL JULIA

SARA DOWSE

15 October 2014

Saturday 24 November 2007. I was one of the 1,112,000 viewers tuned to the ABC, the most-watched television channel that fateful night. Like millions of other Australians, I had had enough of the Howard government. Howard in his tracksuit, Howard pontificating, Howard's trimmed eyebrows pointed upward, conveying a spuriously avuncular worry or concern. The punitive action against Mohamed Haneef, David Hicks and desperate refugees. The lies about going to war in Iraq, the blandishments for mothers to stay at home. The blanket refusal to sign the Kyoto Protocol, to say sorry to Indigenous people whose families and cultures were ripped apart by the policies of successive governments. The massive loss of revenue through unwarranted tax cuts and inequitable superannuation entitlements for well-to-do retirees. The horror of the grossly misnamed WorkChoices, the scandal of inflated private school funding, the neglect of basic infrastructure, the dilapidation of public schools and hospitals, the long waiting lists for treatment, the disingenuousness about interest rates. The new Labor leadership had brought fresh hope that this second-longest, dismayingly reactionary and short-sighted federal government was about to come to a well-deserved end.

The two guests with Kerry O'Brien on the ABC were Nick Minchin, the government's finance minister, and Labor's new deputy leader Julia Gillard. (How symbolic this was, if we'd only known then to read the signs.) I found Gillard enchanting: bright, funny, a workaday woman in the best working-class tradition. There was nothing shellacked about her, nothing slick or polished. But sharp – my, she was sharp. In my memory this remains the real Julia. And what happened to her afterwards is, to me, the real Julia story.

It appears she agrees. *My Story*, the memoir she's produced in the fifteen months since she ceased being prime minister, opens with a snapshot of another, no less fateful night:

> I felt a sense of stillness and loneliness on the walk from
> Labor's caucus room to my office, having just been voted

180

out of the prime ministership. Around me was anything
but stillness. There was a frenzy of cameras and reporters
pushing and shoving to try and get 'the' shot, hear a
comment. Good colleagues, loyal colleagues walked with
me, yet that did not overwhelm the sense of being isolated
in the moment. My wonderful staff lined the corridor to
my office, applauding in tribute to me. Caterina Giugovaz,
a young woman on my staff who had become a close friend,
like a daughter to me, was sobbing as she clapped, her face
a picture of misery.

Gillard goes on to describe her walk to the Blue Room, where she would
face the throng and deliver her announcement, an announcement
unaccompanied by tears. She would be resilient, as she had always been.

It borders on cliché to say that a book never appears in a vacuum, that
the way it is written is the way in which its author attempts to address its
context. In this, as in so much that characterised her prime ministership,
Gillard responds quickly and comprehensively to the major criticisms,
the ones that dogged her in office and would have made it impossible for
anyone less resilient to function, let alone govern. She means to brush
them away so she can proceed to the more high-minded issues that are
the substance of the next 300-plus pages. But it's an error similar to calling
the 2013 election so far in advance, which fanned rather than pre-empted
the opposition's campaign. And by opening with a section designed to
set the record straight about how she took over the leadership, she gives
more oxygen to the controversy. True to form, the media has seized on
this part of the book and on other, more trivial, anecdotes that pepper
what is, for the genre, an unusually serious-minded, analytical and
reflective text.

Perhaps the story's most durable element is the one that Gillard was
determined to play down until well into her prime ministership. To
succumb to further cliché, this was the large female elephant taking
up all the space in the room. On that electrifying night when 'Kevin07'
carried the nation, I could never have imagined that Kevin Rudd himself
would be swept away by the woman who was revelling so in the victory or
dreamed that she would become Australia's first woman prime minister.
It was enough that there was a Labor one, even though Rudd's acceptance
speech was such a curious letdown. (His most emphatic remark on that
momentous night – the night, remember, on which Howard himself
was unseated – was that Labor couldn't party much because they had to

get down to work. Indeed, work was a constant theme for Rudd and his successor, a thorny path to the collective unconscious if there ever was one; but I'll come to that.) When the time did come for Rudd to go – and Gillard makes a near-unanswerable case for it – and we women were to be led, far sooner than we expected, by one of our gender, the circumstance of Gillard's ascendancy had many of us floundering.

I confess to being one of those. Having watched the fortunes of Labor in New South Wales, where premier after premier was shot down like so many ducks in a carnival booth, Rudd's removal filled me with dismay. Not because I was uncritical of his leadership but because of the political disaster I was certain it was. Nor was I convinced that Gillard could improve Labor's prospects. How could she hope to campaign on the government's record when the government itself had to get rid of its leader? To my mind, it was yet another instance of Labor's handing over the poisoned chalice to a woman whenever trouble was brewing.

And Gillard was changed. Her hair was restyled, her make-up impeccable; the suits came straight from Millers of Manuka, or looked like they did. To some, even the painted nails shrieked blood. Where was the bubbly, laughing, down-to-earth, sharp-as-a-tack woman who'd beguiled me, a woman who was one of our own? On this model, what's more, the unaltered working-class twang came over like a crosscut saw. The geniuses who put Gillard through this grotesque metamorphosis seemed to have forgotten what made Rudd so popular. Nerd that he was, he didn't come across as a silvertail. He was rumpled, smiling, seemingly comfortable in his skin.

If this seems unfair, especially coming from a feminist, let me be clear. What I am groping towards is a recognition of the nuances involved in projecting an image in modern democracies. The teams of specialists who groom politicians for the public can be horribly wrong when they choose mediocrity over whatever it is that makes that politician special. Perhaps the very novelty of an Australian woman prime minister had them flummoxed, so the best they could come up with was a clone of a commercial television newsreader.

•

Both Gillard's belief in herself and her purpose in entering the political sphere are better conveyed in this book than they ever were in public once she became the country's leader. This is largely due to the imperfect filter our media has become, particularly when so much of it is controlled by Murdoch, a man who relentlessly opposed her government, and her vengeful predecessor's skill at selectively leaking to key press gallery journalists, even those like Laurie Oakes and Peter Hartcher who weren't in Murdoch's stable.

Yet it owes much as well to Gillard's specific leadership qualities, which are more transactional than inspirational. A negotiator and administrator par excellence, she's a woman who gets things *done*. Like Rudd, she places a lot of emphasis on work: she had work to do in government, and she was focused on 'working families'. Whenever either of them praised the government's record it was generally in terms of the *work* it had done or was doing. How revealing this is, not only about the preoccupations of the government, especially and legitimately so when steering us through the global financial crisis, but of the kind of society Australia has become – of the transition from the land of the lackadaisical long-weekenders to a country with the longest working hours in the OECD. But how do we feel about this? What about *play*, the source of all creativity? (And by this I don't mean sport.) Why dampen our enthusiasm for creative solutions, like the National Broadband Network or the National Disability Insurance Scheme or Gonski? Have we become such dullards and plods? Is it truly the way to our hearts, to yabber on so about work?

In her chapter devoted to the subject, Gillard quotes from her first prime ministerial speech:

> I believe in a government that rewards those who work the hardest, not those who complain the loudest. I believe in a government that rewards those who day in, day out, work in our factories and on our farms, in our mines and in our mills, in our classrooms and in our hospitals, that rewards that hard work, decency and effort. The people that play by the rules, set their alarms early, get their kids off to school, stand by their neighbours and love their country.

There are certainly good things about this manifesto. Neither high-blown nor insincere, it's a genuine attempt to connect with those perceived to be ordinary Australians. It may even serve to represent the speaker as one of them. But what it isn't is inspiring. It's a profoundly conservative and frankly dull message. It seems more concerned with working for its own sake than for what work may accomplish, and for whom. And what about the people *out* of work? Or those who don't have kids to send off to school? And what about those kids? What is the message about their future? These are the words of a manager, and this, I believe, lies at the core of the problem we had with Gillard's leadership.

By now there is no question in our minds about the deficiencies in Rudd's. He was more than a poor manager. His working style was disastrous. In the infamous words of that old Labor stalwart Fred Daly, he couldn't run a bath. Gillard's own view of it has been endlessly corroborated by people with no particular axe to grind, other than to give vent to their massive frustrations. It was Canberra's open secret – the cavalier way he treated ministers, backbenchers and bureaucrats alike, not to mention the loyal minions in his office. The paperwork piled so high on his desk that the entire federal public service breathed a collective sigh of relief when he left the country so that Gillard, his deputy, could break the logjam. His grapeshot approach to issues, the indecisiveness, the lack of concentration. All this became readily apparent to the rest of us during the 2013 campaign, reinforced as it was by all the truly nasty things his colleagues had to say about him when they were still behind Gillard.

In the best of all possible worlds we might have retained them both – the man who for reasons not always fathomable could manage to inspire crowds and the woman who managed to manage. But this was not, nor is it still, the best of all possible worlds. Not for the nation, nor for the Labor Party. In February 2013 Gillard made a speech to the ACTU Congress that truly shocked me. Needless to say, the Labor Party is backed by the union movement – it would be odd if it weren't. But to insist as she did that it was fundamentally a trade union party as distinct from a social democratic one was to my mind so politically ham-fisted. This was being too pragmatic by half. How will Australian progressives vote if not for Labor, or increasingly as we've had to, for the Greens? Why would she want to exclude us? Why would she shun such a sizeable chunk of the electorate in order to retain the allegiance of trade unions? Why indeed play one against the other?

In her chapter on party reform, 'The Party Problem', she offers the reasoning behind that speech. As she sees it, at the heart of Labor's troubles has been a lack of purpose, a condition she hoped to remedy but was in office for too little time to fully effect. Central to her cure, however, was reforming the party's selection process by such measures as 'community outreach work and lower fees for new recruits, especially the young and poorly paid' and 'new structures … to revive Labor's appeal to activists within communities'. Note how at odds these words are with her remarks to the ACTU. But the crunch comes several paragraphs later when she notes that even if unions represent only 17 per cent of the workforce, that's nearly two million people. If Labor were to restrict voting to rank-and-file members, that would result in the party's being governed by a mere 45,000, 'overwhelmingly in older age brackets and generally to the left of the centre of community opinion'. That there's a contradiction here only reinforces my criticism and does little to answer the question of what the party's purpose is to be, beyond the status quo. The very question that she begs.

•

There is more I would criticise. Her thoughts on Israel, for instance, sent my blood pressure soaring. Likewise her take on single mothers and refugees. For all that, it can't be denied that Gillard is a methodical, forceful thinker. Many of her arguments persuaded me, on education especially, although even here some still don't hang together as well as she believes. But on the overall achievements of Labor in office, despite the circumstances in which they governed, she is firm:

> Finding another time in Australian history when Australia's Gross Domestic Product (GDP) growth was 4 per cent or more, inflation was 1.5 per cent or less, the unemployment rate was 5.5 per cent or less and the standard variable mortgage interest rates were 7 per cent or less, means going back to the March quarter 1964.

Why, then, Labor's poor reputation for economic management? Gillard charts the growing disconnect between Treasury's modelling and declining revenues to explain the failure to reach surplus (though going gently around the question of why surpluses were either necessary or desirable). On spending and Abbott's 'budget emergency', she rests her case:

> In financial year 2010–11, the government emerged with a net debt of $85 billion. The vast majority of it arose because revenue collapsed during the GFC, rather than being the result of expenditure on economic stimulus.

Although the economy recovered faster than elsewhere in the Western world, that meant a higher dollar and an increase in the prices of Australian exports, which affected revenue and gave rise to the Coalition's harping about economic mismanagement. By 2013, the share of the economy taken in tax was 21 per cent, well below a peak of 24.5 per cent, in 2004, under the Howard government. Moreover, 2012–13 saw 'the biggest real reduction in spending in Australia's history, edging out of first place the Hawke government's savings in 1988–89'. The problem was reduced revenue, not increased spending. The distortion in perception, however, egged on by the Coalition, was that the Howard years were 'normal', when what Howard managed was a boom.

Mirroring Gillard's role in government, *My Story* is a thoroughly researched, forensically argued, well-organised piece of writing. The warmth for which she is known to people who have seen her at close quarters, and that I had witnessed that 2007 election night, also shines through. She is a woman with heart, humour and sense, a person who notices people. (Wayne Swan's hands, for instance: 'Tanned. Expressive.') She is understandably scarred by the brutal attacks she endured, and there are those for whom she reserves her special condemnation, but she is not vindictive, nor is she shy about taking full responsibility for her mistakes. How sad for her, but more for us, that it's only in 2014 – after a year of Abbott's enthusiasm for boy's own adventure and yet more draconian legislation to protect us from a ramped-up terror, his willingness to spend billions on military hardware and expeditions while attempting drastic cuts to education, culture, health and welfare, his dismissal of the climate threat and the punitive approach in almost every respect to nearly half of the population who voted against him – that it finally dawned on us just what it is we've lost.

PERSONALITY AS DESTINY

JANE GOODALL

18 June 2015

As an elegiac piano-and-cello duet plays us into *The Killing Season*, a crow is silhouetted on a bare, wintry branch against a foreboding sky. Resonances of Edgar Allan Poe and Hitchcock set the mood: a blend of melancholy fatalism and psychological ferocity. Then comes a still image of two figures seated on a bench at the far end of a corridor, backlit by a massive window. There is something fateful about corridors and those who walk down them, and the title sequence continues with a succession of such images, releasing the figures from stillness into motion. Colour leaks in as the camera gets closer to the faces. Rudd. Gillard. A shot of her giving him a kiss on the cheek; a Judas kiss. Gillard's red hair flares as flames explode on the right of the screen. Kevin Rudd's eyes appear in extreme close-up, as if we are about to find out exactly what lies behind them.

Episode 2 of the ABC's three-part series opens with Rudd being prepared for the cameras. He adjusts his position and closes his eyes for a second as if composing himself, but it's a hard, set expression that faces the interviewer. Clearly he's beyond any attempt at charm.

'Are you enjoying the experience of doing these interviews?' asks Sarah Ferguson.

'Not particularly,' is the clipped response.

He doesn't need to say it and she doesn't need to ask. Every muscle in his face signals acute discomfort. But she presses the question: 'Why not?'

Ferguson is fast gaining a reputation as Australia's most effective political interviewer, and one of her tactics is to force every issue into the realms of the explicit. As drama, its effectiveness is unquestionable: the result is utterly compelling. But in this case a boundary is being crossed. It's not just that Rudd's discomfort communicates. He's not exactly squirming before the cameras – he's too solid a presence, in every sense – but he is visibly suffering, and doing so with a kind of stoic honesty. 'I'm a human being,' he says, and reminds her it's something they have in common.

Suddenly we have gone from the poetic symbolism of the opening titles to a confronting level of naturalism. The mythic register has become confused with that of contemporary political reality. This is too recent a past to be mythologised – it is not even history yet, and in prematurely treating it as such, critical distance is being manufactured. However intrusively the camera probes Kevin Rudd's eyes for the truths hidden from public knowledge, we can't see through his skull, and that kind of intrusiveness raises questions about what it is our business to see. Even a former prime minister has some right to psychological privacy.

The confusion of registers may be an issue in this brilliant series but it highlights a more general phenomenon in the way political events are portrayed in the media. Politicians are portrayed as cartoon caricatures engaged in extreme forms of behaviour, or characters in a melodrama working their way through a storyline. As the storylines are usually deficient in credibility and substance, political reporters need a regular supply of crises to spike their trade.

•

There's much to praise about *The Killing Season*. Executive producer Sue Spencer (also responsible for *Labor in Power* and *The Howard Years*) knows exactly how to pitch these documentaries, luring the viewer in with a promise of melodrama, deepening the lines of concentration by picking out the critical details, and then steering into turning points with unfaltering precision. She's well teamed with Sarah Ferguson, whose streamlined presence never distracts from her subject. Although Ferguson displayed the killer instinct as a political interrogator during her recent term on *7.30*, here she plays a very quiet game. The voice is low and even in tone, and the script is spare, but the quicksilver intelligence leaves no nuance unregistered.

Episode 1 begins in the winter of 2006, in a cab driving towards Parliament House with the radio news announcing a challenge to Beazley. It's the last sitting week of parliament, known by insiders as 'the killing week' because it is the prime opportunity for leadership challenges – those contests that journalists can describe only using the language of violent assassination. Leaders are wounded, or fatally stabbed. There's blood everywhere – on the floor, on the knives, on the hands of the conspirators. Rudd becomes Julius Caesar; Gillard is Lady Macbeth. If we are turning the lens of psychoanalysis onto those involved in this mix-and-match tragedy, perhaps we should also apply it to ourselves. Why do we so readily respond to metaphors of bloodshed? One answer is that we all know the killing isn't real. Our leading politicians are our leading actors, and when they've played out their roles they are no more dead than the actors in *Game of Thrones*.

'It's a very, very sobering and lonely walk down the corridor,' Rudd says, reflecting on his final approach to Beazley's office. 'You almost wish it could be a little longer than it is ... Kim had this marvellous PA sitting at the desk. She had tears streaming down her face, because she'd been in politics a long time, and she knew what this meant.' His way of recalling the scene doesn't fit with the profile of someone repeatedly accused of a lack of empathy and a pathological disregard for the feelings of others. Gillard, by contrast, offers clichéd generalities about her own experience of the fatal walk. 'It's a big emotional thing to do ...' she tells Ferguson, 'there's nothing pleasant about it, there's nothing fun about it, it's quite a horrible, gut-wrenching process.'

The Killing Season brings us close to the real human consequences of some of the things that go on in the house on the hill when it morphs into the nightmare world of *Wolf Hall*. One of the insights it offers is that politicians can have very strong human relationships, with all the associated vulnerability. Greg Combet's enduring loyalty to Beazley shapes his perspective on the whole cycle of feuding that followed under Rudd and Gillard. He is sceptical, detached, openly disgusted by the display of ambition on both sides. 'I had the shits big time,' is the crux of what he has to say.

Wayne Swan might have been expected to stand by Rudd in the same way. They'd known each other since school days, worked together on sweeping reforms in the Queensland Government, and fronted the challenge of the global financial crisis as a team. Interviews with the two of them about their last phone call – they have not spoken since that day in 2010 – are intercut to devastating effect. Swan looks barely in control as he recalls it. 'I told him I viewed his position as being untenable.' *Et tu, Brute*? Rudd's comment now is about gut feeling. 'Well – mate – you could have spoken to me.'

If references to bloodbaths and classical tragedy serve on one level to mask the human impact of all this, on another they are instructive. Tragedy taken as a classic dramatic form rather than as melodrama is profoundly structural. 'There's a divinity that shapes our ends,' says Hamlet, 'rough hew them how we will.' The divinity may not be so relevant here but the shaping certainly is. In a secular framework, personality is destiny. The protagonist is typically an overreacher, and the fatal flaw is hubris: not knowing one's limits means that the structure of the personality becomes misaligned with the shape of events. Struggles are experienced, actions are taken, and yet at each stage all the tragic character can do is tighten the net. Was there something inevitable about the configuration of personalities and events leading to the killing seasons of 2010 and 2013?

In both the first and second episodes, Rudd is absolutely the centre of the drama. Gillard's charges against him were all about personal failings; her actions can only be justified by the conviction that these failings were radical and irremediable. This is essentially the charge being examined in *The Killing Season*, and it underlies the psychological invasiveness of the series so far. David Marr's *Quarterly Essay* 'Power Trip', which was published shortly before the challenge in June 2010, engaged in a sustained interpretation of Rudd as anger-driven, a man at the mercy of a deep-seated vindictiveness generated by childhood experiences. The essay hasn't been mentioned in the series, but it set a precedent for some tendentious amateur psychology from which Gillard built her case for the prosecution.

Sarah Ferguson has said that she takes no side – she was 'a feather in the wind' when it came to judging the two protagonists – but through a minute reconstruction of the sequence of events and interactions the first two episodes of *The Killing Season* present what amounts to a case for the defence. Much of the first episode is taken up with two of Rudd's strongest achievements: the apology to the stolen generations, and his response to the global financial crisis. Jenny Macklin, closely involved in arrangements for the apology, describes his meeting with Nanna Nungala Feyo, whose story Rudd told at the start of the apology speech. 'He was incredibly respectful. He was very patient. He didn't say very much. He let her talk.' Macklin and Tanya Plibersek are still deeply moved as they remember the occasion. 'He mended broken hearts. No one can take that away from him.'

Former Treasury secretary Ken Henry, one of the most compelling interview subjects throughout, is the key witness on the handling of the global financial crisis. Rudd saw it coming in advance, says Henry, and wanted to start pre-emptive planning. 'I thought he was jumping the gun ... Two weeks later Bear Stearns collapsed ... His instincts were better than mine.' Hank Paulson, the US Treasury secretary at the time, corroborates: 'It stood out. He understood not just the politics but the economics.' Former British prime minister Gordon Brown credits him as a co-instigator of the critical summit meeting from which the G20 was born. So far so good, or apparently so, but with a stellar deputy managing the business back home while he was dealing with matters on the world stage, perhaps Rudd could have done without another major overseas crisis in his first term. And given his propensity for working twenty-four-hour shifts that left him and everyone around him exhausted to the point of dysfunction, maybe he needed to learn to pace himself.

The case for the prosecution began to gain traction in December 2009 when Rudd attended the UN summit on climate change in Copenhagen.

'I think Kevin dreamed big dreams for his role at Copenhagen,' Gillard says. 'Now would you call that vanity, or would you call that focused on the task of getting a global climate agreement?'

When you bring in the eyewitnesses from the scene at Copenhagen, no such doubts are apparent. Andrew Charlton, who accompanied Rudd as his economic adviser, confirms that he outworked everyone. By the final, critical meeting with Gordon Brown in a small upstairs room, Obama had left, Wen Jiabao had left, and most of the remaining delegates were heavily asleep in their chairs. Brown acknowledges Rudd for his unique willingness to stand up to the naysayers and credits him with brokering the compromise declaration that saved the whole summit from complete failure.

•

If this were a classical tragedy, Rudd would be the warrior who returns home from the battle, bloody and exhausted after cutting his way single-handedly through thickets of enemy fighters. He may have defended the bridge, but he failed to bring home a victory. Now he's 'spent', to use Gillard's word, and he's dogged by a tale of less than honourable conduct on the battlefield. Rudd famously used foul language to describe the Chinese delegation, and the remarks were leaked.

There's especially fine work in this part of the episode from producer Deb Masters and her editors. From the point at which Rudd, along with other world leaders, is seen arriving in Copenhagen in a snowstorm to the point where he disembarks back home in the full-blown Australian summer, the structural ironies build relentlessly. It is clear that he is moving between two worlds that know nothing of each other. In his absence, Abbott has replaced Turnbull as opposition leader and the government's carbon reduction scheme has been voted down with, of all ironies, the assistance of the Greens. There's talk of a double dissolution, which Gillard and some of her advisers think would lead to a wipe-out for Abbott. Now it's holiday time, but not for long. Gillard visits Rudd at Kirribilli House on 4 January with the prospect of a double dissolution in her sights and confirms her impressions that he is not 'refreshed'. She is 'seriously worried about his psychological state', and concludes he's in no condition to fight a campaign. 'Absolute bollocks,' says Rudd when this is conveyed to him by Ferguson, who is looking increasingly like one of the dramatis personae, the shadowy figure who always has a word in the ear of someone who is riding dangerously on fortune's big dipper.

The more experienced ministers – Macklin, Anthony Albanese, Chris Bowen, Martin Ferguson – are steadier in their judgement of Rudd. It's telling that the ministers who are the first to lose confidence in him are the newer ones – Nicola Roxon, Tony Burke, Bill Shorten. Perhaps they are a bit too easily spooked by this idea that the leader is a cot case, and the idea is very catchy to those with a taste for crisis. In a rather clunky piece of action replay, we see Mark Arbib and Sam Dastyari consulting over some polling in key marginals and starting to press the panic buttons. Rudd's approval rating is 'in the toilet'. Asked about that now, Rudd comments that it is very easy for political operatives to say the sky has fallen in, and points out that both Arbib and Karl Bitar, another of the panic merchants, are currently working for a casino. Yet somewhere around this moment, the point of no return was passed. In classical tragedy, the figures involved can never determine just when the outcome has become inevitable, but it often involves minor players messing about in matters whose larger significance is beyond their ken.

The consequences have taken some years to play out, and we still have Episode 3 to come. There's no problem about spoilers – we all know what happened. Albanese was right when he predicted that an assault on Rudd would mean killing two prime ministers. Both, in their very different ways, had the potential to make a mark as among the most distinguished in Australia's history, but neither got the chance to operate at full capacity. At the end of the day, it's the Australian people who are the losers. That's how it is in tragedy – everyone loses. But do they learn?

THE LIBERAL NONCONFORMIST FROM SYDNEY'S WEST

ROBERT MILLIKEN

8 September 2015

When Craig Laundy spoke at a reception to mark the fortieth anniversary of the *Racial Discrimination Act (Cwlth)* in June, he began by warmly acknowledging the gathered dignitaries. All except one. Finally, with a sharp sense of timing, he turned to Gillian Triggs, president of the Australian Human Rights Commission. 'Don't worry Gillian,' he said. 'I'm saving you for last.'

Whispers and nervous titters rippled through the audience at the ornate Royal Automobile Club in Sydney. Triggs had just survived public attacks from Tony Abbott and other Coalition ministers over her report on the plight of child asylum seekers in detention. It had been one of the most brutal government character assassinations of a senior statutory official Australia has seen. Was Laundy about to nettle her even more?

On the contrary. He praised Triggs for her work and encouraged her to keep doing the job that Abbott and Attorney-General George Brandis had reportedly tried to make her leave. 'My door is always open to you,' he told her. She nodded an acknowledgement as the audience applauded.

Of course, an attack on Triggs would have made Laundy an outsider in this crowd. His fellow speakers included Race Discrimination Commissioner Tim Soutphommasane and former Fraser government minister Fred Chaney, who launched Soutphommasane's book *I'm Not Racist But ...* at the same event. Mark Dreyfus, the shadow attorney-general, also spoke, and so did Penny Wright, an Australian Greens senator.

Where Laundy really has emerged as an odd man out is among his fellow conservatives since he entered parliament at the 2013 election. He stood up for Triggs in the Coalition party room in February, arguing that the real point should be to release children from detention. He threatened to cross the floor against the Abbott government's plan to change the *Racial Discrimination Act (Cwlth)* to allow hate speech; the government dropped the plan in August.

And last Friday, while Abbott was trumpeting his government's 'stop the boats' policy as Europe's refugee crisis unfolded, Laundy publicly pleaded for Australia to take more refugees from Syria. 'There but for the grace of God go any of us,' he said. His stand flew in the face of a powerful portion of the Liberal Party's conservative base that opposes bringing in more refugees, but his electoral office was swamped with emails from the public, about 90 per cent of which supported him.

Laundy is an odd Liberal out in other ways, too. He is a small businessman in a party that once identified as the champion of small business but whose frontbench is now dominated by lawyers, ex-lobbyists, political advisers and party officials. He is a liberal in a party that has shifted sharply to the right under its last two prime ministers, Abbott and John Howard. And he refuses to identify with the factions that now determine power in the Liberal Party. 'I see myself as my own voice,' he says.

•

I met Laundy in late August in Burwood, one of the inner-western suburbs that make up his electorate of Reid. Named after Australia's fourth prime minister, George Reid, the seat was for many years a Labor stronghold; incumbents have included former NSW premier Jack Lang and former Whitlam government minister Tom Uren. But Labor's comfortable margin was cut when a 2010 redistribution brought in much of the neighbouring electorate of Lowe. Three years later the national anti-Labor swing made Laundy – as he later told parliament – 'the first Liberal to hold this seat since it was formed' in 1922.

Yet the broader electoral geography still leaves him something of an outsider. Reid is surrounded to the south and west by the traditional western Sydney Labor seats held by opposition frontbenchers Anthony Albanese, Tony Burke, Jason Clare and Julie Owens. Once a working-class Anglo-Australian region, it is now a multicultural heartland. In Burwood alone, almost 60 per cent of citizens were born overseas, many in Asia, the Middle East, North Africa and Eastern Europe. Laundy reckons his seat is the second most multicultural in federal parliament, after Burke's seat of Watson next door.

Outwardly, at least, Laundy seems a classic figure of old Australia. At forty-four, he is tall and boyish-faced, and on the day we meet he is dressed smartly in business trousers and a blue pinstriped shirt with no tie. His electoral office in Burwood Road is sparely furnished, with no sign of the lavish use of entitlements that had felled Bronwyn Bishop a couple of weeks earlier.

Laundy's family story seems classic rags-to-riches. His paternal grandfather, Arthur, left an orphanage at the age of fifteen 'with just the clothes on his back' and bought a hotel lease twelve years later. The family business, in which Craig worked for twenty-three years before entering politics, now comprises more than fifty hotels in New South Wales. Laundy still seems to identify as much as a businessman as he does a politician. 'I'm a third-generation western suburbs publican,' he tells me.

He joined the Liberal Party only eighteen months before successfully contesting the 2013 election. And he reckons he is one of the first of what he calls a 'Labor family on both sides' to support the Liberals, adding yet another layer of complexity to his outsider's profile.

What attracted him to politics, and especially to the Liberal Party?

> I was very frustrated with the former Labor government. I believe in small government, low taxation and a genuine safety net. I thought that becoming an MP may be a chance to make a difference. I'd grown up in the western side of the electorate, the Labor side, and I had tentacles there through my involvement with churches, charities and sporting clubs. I have a lot of mates from my small business background who would never go into politics. They think I'm mad. So does my father!

Laundy's responses to social issues during his short parliamentary life have been driven by his practical business mind and family life, not by the ideology that drives some sections of the Liberal Party. His stand against the proposed change to the *Racial Discrimination Act (Cwlth)* angered many on the party's right. But, he says, it also reflected opposition to the change among his multicultural constituents:

> They believe that free speech is a right in Australia, and that rights also involve responsibilities. My pragmatic argument says that too. Pragmatic thinkers on both sides of parliament are in the minority. Ideological thinkers on both sides are in the ascendancy.

Laundy's support for Triggs' call to stop incarcerating child asylum seekers also won him few fans in his party. 'If there are findings of hers that allow us to run things better, we should accept them in good faith and act upon them,' he says. This hardly chimes with Abbott's dismissal of Triggs' report as a 'political stitch-up'. Laundy also wants a more inclusive approach from government to Australia's Muslim community, despite the Abbott government's pursuit of a national security policy that seems to cast them as potential enemies:

> There is a marginalised Muslim minority heading to jihad. You have to question the cause of the problem first, and I think that's been missed. The second or third generations of Australian-born eighteen- to twenty-five-year-olds have battled with education and finding jobs. That's where susceptibility is born. We have to stop them ending up at the plane gate to Syria and Iraq. The Australian public responds negatively, and the vicious circle makes them more marginalised. The role of leadership, in government and the communities, is to step in and break the circle. It's a long-term exercise.

On same-sex marriage, though, Laundy is not rocking any Liberal boats. He and his wife Suzie attend Catholic churches in the electorate with their three children, and he opposes same-sex marriage on grounds of that faith. At first, he supported a conscience vote in parliament. 'The conscience vote that the Liberal Party stands for is important to me,' he tells me. 'I would never be a member of a party that you can't vote against if you want.'

He was later reported to have changed his mind, and to oppose a conscience vote, on this issue at least. But since the bitter Coalition partyroom debate in August, which endorsed the government's opposition to same-sex marriage, Laundy says he once again has an 'open mind' on a conscience vote. He argues that the debate has become 'aggressive' on both sides, and that those who chose to vote against gay marriage could be vilified. 'On the gay marriage side, I'm criticised as a bigot and a homophobe, which I'm definitely not. But I see fault on both sides.'

A few days after our meeting, Laundy escorted foreign minister Julie Bishop to Burwood Girls High School, one of Australia's most multicultural schools, where she addressed senior students, including some from neighbouring schools. Bishop spoke about women and careers, and fielded questions from the girls about Australia's human rights record and military involvement in the Middle East. But her visit was quickly swamped by a row over same-sex partners and censorship that erupted a few days later.

The school had planned to show *Gayby Baby*, a documentary about children of same-sex parents made by Maya Newell, a former student at the school. It had already been shown at the Sydney and Melbourne film festivals, and at Parliament House in Sydney. Two days before the scheduled school screening on 28 August, *The Daily Telegraph* splashed a front-page story headed 'Gay Class Uproar', with the banner 'Parents outraged as Sydney school swaps lessons for PC movie session'.

It later emerged that parents had been informed of the screening and given the option of not allowing their daughters to attend. But the furore sparked by the Murdoch tabloid was enough for NSW education minister Adrian Piccoli to order a ban on screenings of *Gayby Baby* at all the state's schools during class times. (It passed unremarked that Julie Bishop's address at the Burwood school had also happened during class hours.)

Laundy publicly supported his state Liberal colleague's ban on the film. After talks with local parents and community leaders, he claimed 'many parents' were concerned the screening in school hours 'may create difficulties for their children on the basis of their family's religious or personal beliefs'.

•

Beyond this issue, though, Laundy finds his inherent liberalism frequently stalled by the realities of life in politics. If frustrations with the former Labor government drove him into politics in the first place, the process of achieving change as a parliamentarian troubles him just as much, if not more. Again, he comes back to a business analogy:

> In small business it's about outcomes, not process. My criticism of politics is that the focus is on process ahead of outcomes. In business, before I renovated hotels I talked to staff and customers and worked out what they wanted, then made a decision. In politics, cabinet makes the decision, but then hands the policy to the marginal backbench seat-holders and tells them to go out and sell it. That's counterintuitive. After two years in politics, the pace of change and the length of time to get decisions is frustrating for me.

The trend on both sides of politics to recruit candidates from within the party machine makes things even more frustrating for those from a broader background like Laundy's. 'They know the system from a young age and are prepared to live within it. For people like me who come from outside, it's a big change to make.'

Laundy doesn't conceal a sense of irritation over the Abbott government's inertia on economic reform. 'I get frustrated when discussions are about do we apply a GST on tampons. You should be talking about reforming the whole tax system, as well as federation, and preparing the country for the next forty years.'

The Abbott government's entrenched opinion poll deficit has rattled many backbenchers, especially those who may have nowhere to turn for lives outside politics if the government falls in 2016 and they lose their seats. On this score, Laundy once again could be an odd man out. He won Reid in 2013 with a 3.5 per cent swing. But if the still-marginal seat eventually swings back to Labor, he will be happy to say he tried. 'I'd rather lose my seat standing for something, and standing for reform, than govern for the sake of governing,' he says. And if that happened? 'I can go back to my family business job any time.'

A FORMER LEADER'S ADVICE: IN A CRISIS, HAVE THE COURAGE TO BREAK WITH THE PAST

TIM COLEBATCH

3 March 2017

In October 1970, a young Laurie Oakes interviewed an old Sir John McEwen, the legendary leader of the Country Party (now the Nationals), long-time deputy and strong right arm of Sir Robert Menzies. One of the things the old warrior had to tell him was why he so much admired his former adversary, the Labor leader John Curtin.

'Curtin found himself prime minister while we were at war, and his party was completely unprepared for the violent policies necessary,' said McEwen. 'He had never been a minister, and he had to handle the crisis by introducing conscription and wage-fixing policies completely repugnant to the Labor Party. He faced up to this without a flinch, and I admire his courage and sense of duty.'

In his memoirs, McEwen elaborated:

> Curtin had to decide whether he would go along with the historic attitude his party had taken to conscription, or pick up the responsibilities of the prime minister of a country at war. He did the latter, showing a willingness to take on people in his own party when he felt that the well-being of Australia required it. I think Curtin was a very great man.[9]

McEwen himself was likewise a man of courage, as Peter Golding demonstrated in his 1996 biography, *Black Jack McEwen: Political Gladiator*. As a young MP, he was expelled from the Victorian branch of his party for refusing to obey head office dictates; he ignored them, and head office backed down. Two years later, McEwen challenged his autocratic and feared leader, Archie Cameron, only to lose in bizarre circumstances when McEwen and a third candidate, former leader Sir Earle Page,

---

9   John McEwen, *John McEwen: His Story* (Melbourne: n.p., 1983), 34.

ended up twice tied at nine-all, with a sulking Cameron refusing to vote. A non-candidate, Arthur Fadden, was drafted to serve as a compromise temporary leader; he stayed in the job for eighteen years.

It was McEwen who drove one of the bravest, and most unpopular, decisions any Australian government has made: negotiating a trade agreement with Japan, a few years after the war that had left many Australians, including his own followers, with a deep hatred for the Japanese. Like Curtin, McEwen took on his own party because he felt the national interest required it. His proposed deal was twice rejected by Menzies and the cabinet, but McEwen persisted until they allowed him to open negotiations – and even then they distanced themselves almost until the deal was done.

Why recall this ancient history now, in 2017, at a time when the Coalition is in crisis, trailing far behind in the polls, and experienced observers are saying that Malcolm Turnbull's days as prime minister are numbered? Because we need to recognise that it is not just Turnbull who has squandered his opportunity to restore the Coalition as the natural party of government in Australia. It is the cabinet, the Coalition backbench and, above all, John McEwen's old party, the Nationals, who share the blame by not allowing Turnbull to be Turnbull.

The election is still far away. The Coalition could make its way back. But the way back is not to try to make the Coalition more like One Nation. At last year's election, One Nation stood in every state for the Senate and won 4 per cent of the vote. The latest Newspoll has them at 8 per cent, and even that relies on the Coalition's refusal to criticise Pauline Hanson and her party. This is not because Hanson has changed, as they claim; she hasn't. They are silent because they see One Nation's three Senate votes as essential to pass legislation opposed by Labor and the Greens.

It's time to take stock. This week's Newspoll reports that the government now trails Labor 45–55 on a two-party-preferred basis. That's an even worse deficit than the government had in Tony Abbott's final polls. Correct me if I am wrong, but I can't recall any government coming back from so far behind to win the next election. Turnbull's own satisfaction rating is down to 29 per cent, with a staggering 59 per cent of Australians dissatisfied with his leadership.

No realist can flick that away as merely an opinion poll. Nine of the past fifteen elections in this country have seen governments voted out; in a tenth (South Australia), the government also lost the vote, but hung on thanks to independents. The bookies rate it as odds-on that Western

Australia's election on 18 March will be the tenth of the last sixteen elections to vote the government out.[10]

Let's wind the clock back eighteen months to 2015. When the Liberals chose Turnbull to be their leader, it was because they were staring defeat in the face. They had lost thirty consecutive Newspolls, the last three of which showed the Coalition trailing Labor 46–54. Only someone as self-indulgent as Abbott could believe he was heading for victory in 2016.

The impact of the leadership change was immediate. Two months later, the Coalition had soared to a 53–47 lead in the same poll, which was a shift of 7 per cent. Abbott's net satisfaction rating in his final poll was minus 33; Turnbull's satisfaction rating after two months was plus 38. Abbott had trailed Opposition Leader Bill Shorten as preferred prime minister by 37–41; by November, Turnbull led Shorten 64–15.

By electing Turnbull as its leader, the Coalition had given itself a new lease of life. The Australian public knew him and liked him. People recognised what he stood for: he was an intelligent, forward-looking leader in the mainstream of Australian thinking, who had spoken out on issues such as tackling climate change and allowing same-sex marriage. To state the obvious, he, and the Coalition, had become popular because that is the way people thought he was going to govern.

•

But that was not the way the Coalition was going to let him govern. It was not going to let Turnbull be Turnbull. Much of the blame for this rests on the shoulders of the National Party. Even with the ultra-reasonable Warren Truss as its leader, the National Party hit Turnbull with a long list of demands in return for its support. Along with rural pork-barrelling and some mild challenges on behalf of the downtrodden, the Nationals demanded that Turnbull pledge not to reintroduce an emissions trading scheme or discard the Coalition's policy for a plebiscite on same-sex marriage.

In hindsight, we can say that Turnbull should have rejected this. Just as William Pitt the younger, then aged twenty-three, refused the prime ministership of Great Britain until he could take it with a clear majority (as he did a few months later), so Turnbull should have held out until he

---

10   In the 2017 Western Australian election, Labor won 41 seats to defeat the incumbent Coalition, with the Liberals retaining 13 seats and the Nationals 5.

could take power on his own terms. But at the time, that didn't seem a plausible course.

He had managed to haul himself over the line to become leader by winning the backing of Liberal MPs and senators who were on the conservative side of the party but saw that Abbott was fatally wounded. To defy the Nationals' ultimatum would put their support at risk, and he needed a clean handover with a minimum of fuss. So he succumbed.

At the time, the consequences weren't obvious. As Turnbull's popularity swept the Coalition back into the lead, we assumed that he would win a thumping victory at the 2016 election and that would give him the power to get his way. Instead, he allowed himself to be beaten back on tax reform, abandoned Scott Morrison's plans to limit negative gearing and made no substantial changes to the policies he had inherited from Tony Abbott, apart from secretly negotiating the refugee swap with the US, which so far has had no effect.

Australia had welcomed the arrival of Malcolm Turnbull as leader. But instead, we got Malcolm Abbott: a more articulate spokesperson with the same hard-right policies.

Take same-sex marriage. It is one of those issues on which the public has made up its mind. The latest Newspoll on the issue last September found 62 per cent of Australians – including 53 per cent of Coalition voters – support its legalisation, with only 32 per cent opposed. The Abbott policy of insisting on a non-binding plebiscite, once popular, now has only 39 per cent support.[11]

Australians just want the issue dealt with, and they expect the Turnbull government to do it. Instead, unable to win Senate support for a plebiscite, it has done nothing. And that's the Turnbull government in a nutshell. It is seen as doing nothing; it is seen as failing to lead. This isn't because Turnbull lacks the ability to do so, but because he has not been allowed to.

True, unless he is hiding a lot from us, Turnbull appears to have gone along with this. He's made his share of mistakes, as most of us do. And above all, perhaps, his obvious love of being prime minister seems to have dulled his awareness of the catastrophic consequences of being a leader who is unable to lead us anywhere.

---

11   In November 2017, the Turnbull government conducted a country-wide postal survey on amending the *Australian Marriage Act 1961* to allow for same-sex marriage. As a result of the plebiscite, the *Marriage Amendment Act (Definition and Religious Freedoms) 2017* came into effect on 9 December to legalise same-sex marriage.

•

The one person who can do most to save the Turnbull government is the man who now sits in John McEwen's place: Barnaby Joyce, the deputy prime minister and National Party leader.[12] Just as McEwen and Curtin confronted their own parties in times of crisis with the need to change deeply entrenched policies, Joyce needs to do so now. His government has allowed issue after issue to fester, trying to find political angles to exploit rather than solving the problems. Don't they ever ask themselves what voters want?

Joyce and his conservative colleagues in the Liberal Party need to give Turnbull the space to cut through on some of the issues that are wearing down the Coalition's popularity. To take a few examples:

Same-sex marriage. The political manoeuvres have failed, and it's become a dead weight the Coalition has to carry. Let Turnbull fix it by moving for a free vote in parliament.

Housing affordability. I suspect nothing depresses Australians more than the problems they or their kids face in trying to buy a home in the capital cities, especially Sydney and Melbourne. Everyone knows that negative gearing and capital gains tax breaks are a big part of the problem – and while these continue, homes in the cities will not be affordable. Turnbull's tax paper in 2005 suggested he understood that. There are many ways to tackle these twin problems, so the Coalition can find its own solution – so long as it will actually solve the problem.

An emissions intensity scheme. It's not a carbon tax or an emissions trading scheme, and it beats renewable energy targets as a least-cost way to drive emissions down. The electricity industry wants it, their big industrial customers want it, the chief scientist wants it, Turnbull's hand-picked Climate Council wants it, the Business Council and the Australian Industry Group want it ... need I go on? Do it and you solve the central problem of climate change policy. A bipartisan agreement will at last unblock investment in new generating stations, and in the long run the main beneficiaries will be Australia's farmers, who are the biggest losers from climate change.

---

12 Barnaby Joyce resigned as deputy prime minister and leader of the Nationals in February 2018, after fallout from revelations of an affair with a former staffer.

Struggling families and the deficit. Wealthy Australians have had a generation of doing it very nicely, thank you. It's time they (and we) gave something back to shrink the deficit, instead of the government forever looking for ways to take money from the poorest. Why not drop the welfare cuts the Senate opposes, and look for ways to lift revenues – not by raising taxes, but by closing the loopholes that still allow rich people to pay less than their share?

Infrastructure. Australia invests far too little for a country whose cities are adding a million people to the population every three years, with 300,000 of them in Melbourne alone. While congestion is mounting in the cities, money is being wasted on duplicating low-traffic rural highways in projects yielding negative returns. As on other issues, ministers know what to do. They would get far more credit from voters if they fixed the problems instead of trying to play politics with them.

Spreading the economic gains. And, finally, the government should find a way to take a fresh look at perhaps the biggest issue in voters' minds: who is being left out of the gains from Australia's economic growth, and what can be done about it? The Productivity Commission is the wrong body to ask, because too often its doctrinaire economics has been part of the problem. If the Nationals feel threatened by One Nation, why not respond with an honest, open look at why so many Australians, especially in regional Australia, have missed out, and what policies would work best to spread the gains.

•

Coalition frontbenchers, backbenchers, and particularly the Nationals, must be honest with themselves: by forcing Turnbull to govern like Abbott, they are driving the government towards the same cliff they faced under Abbott. Most of them share the blame for its collapsing support. Australia wants leadership. The government is not generating it.

Bill Hartley is a forgotten name now, but for years he was one of the linchpins of the Coalition's success. He was Labor's state secretary in Victoria in the 1960s, and – with a cohort of far-left union leaders – he focused almost entirely on securing their dominance of the Victorian Labor Party, rather than helping Labor get into government. That is, until Gough Whitlam and the party's federal executive intervened in 1970 to boot him off the stage.

The Coalition today seems to be increasingly dominated by its own Bill Hartleys – people focused on securing conservative dominance of the party, even if it ends the party's dominance of politics. Malcolm Turnbull's star still shone just brightly enough to win them the 2016 election; it has gone out now. If they want to win the next election, they have to step back and let it shine again. They have to let Turnbull be Turnbull.

If the Nationals are frightened of One Nation, then the Coalition needs to treat it like the opponent it is, exposing its idiocies while tackling the problems that are generating its support. But the votes the Coalition needs to win back to get over 50 per cent of the vote are not to its right but in the middle, and that is the direction the Coalition needs to move in and govern from.

Only one person can take the lead in doing that. It is John McEwen's heir, Barnaby Joyce. He needs to match the old leader's foresight, courage and sense of responsibility.

AUSTRALIA'S GREAT POLITICAL SHIFT

NORMAN ABJORENSEN

28 July 2017

Not long before he died in 1998, that veteran political warrior BA (Bob) Santamaria granted me a series of interviews. After one session, over a cup of tea, his spirits seemed low and he wondered aloud if he had achieved much. The world seemed as troubled a place as ever.

In an effort to cheer him up, I suggested that, given he'd been on the receiving end of a great deal of anti-Catholic sentiment over the years, he might be heartened by the fact that religious bigotry was no longer evident in public life.

Santamaria looked at me with sad eyes, shook his head and said quietly, 'No, bigotry has not gone. It is religious belief that has faded, but once that returns, if it does, back will come the old hatreds.'

Santamaria was blamed by many people for splitting the Labor Party in the 1950s. His largely Catholic-based industrial groups, set up to fight communist influence in the unions, expanded into a force that almost took control of the Labor Party. Now, he was conceding that religion and politics, often inextricably bound together, constituted 'an ugly mix'.

Two decades later, one of his acolytes, Tony Abbott (about whom Santamaria had reservations), is busy playing the religious card as he seeks to undermine Malcolm Turnbull and his government and avenge his thoroughly deserved toppling from the prime ministership.

Earlier this month, he spoke to a Liberal Party branch meeting in assistant treasurer Michael Sukkar's electorate of Deakin, in Melbourne. The event was billed as 'a rare opportunity to join former prime minister Tony Abbott to discuss how to navigate the political sphere as a Christian'.

According to media reports quoting a member of Abbott's audience, the 200-strong gathering was 'basically in raptures' at the end of Abbott's presentation. 'He is definitely on the warpath,' the source said. 'I have never seen him speaking so well or looking so good.'[13]

---

13 Michael Koziol, "'We're at a low ebb': Tony Abbott bashes Liberal leadership in leaked audio," *The Sydney Morning Herald*, July 5, 2017, https://www.smh.com.au/politics/federal/

A leaked recording of the address, in which Abbott criticised the direction of both the government and this year's federal budget, reveals the crude populism of the drum he is beating. The former PM implores members to heed the 'two fundamental precepts' of Western civilisation, 'both of which stem originally from the Gospel' – equality in the eyes of God ('equal rights, equal dignity, equal responsibilities') and treating others as you would have them treat you.

Never mind the former PM's own patchy record on equality (for women and asylum seekers, for example), the 'Western civilisation' that he invokes is a curious one that omits such defining features as the Reformation, the Enlightenment and religious tolerance. ('For too long,' he said, 'the good people of our country have been too tolerant of people who do not share some of the fundamental values that have made us who we are.')

Quite apart from its highly idiosyncratic reading of history, the speech raises many issues. How did such concerns come to the fore in the Liberal Party? Who is the presumed wider audience for such messages? Why is he doing this?

Tony Abbott's comments that night are a reminder of how much, and in how relatively short a time, Catholicism has come to characterise the Liberal Party.

For much of its history, the party and its non-Labor predecessors were bastions of Protestantism; it was in the Labor Party, traditionally, that Catholics found their political home. As the political historian Judith Brett has noted:

> Australian Liberals' central values and stories drew on Protestant values and stories ... Their virtues were Protestant virtues, and [in their minds] there was an easy slippage between the vices of the Labor Party and the vices of Protestantism's historic enemy, the Roman Catholic Church.[14]

This sectarian strand in non-Labor politics goes back a long way. Australia's first prime minister, Edmund Barton, ran into a sectarian storm when he visited Pope Leo XIII in Rome on his way back from receiving a knighthood in London. When the Pope presented Barton

---

were-at-a-low-ebb-tony-abbott-bashes-liberal-leadership-in-leaked-audio-20170704-gx4pee.html.

14 Judith Brett, "The Sectarian Foundations of Australian Liberalism," *Sydney Papers* 14, No. 3 (Winter 2002), 170.

with a gold commemorative medallion, the ire of Australian Protestants was raised. The fiery anti-Catholic cleric Reverend William Dill Macky organised a petition of protest that attracted more than 30,000 signatures. (Barton and the pontiff conversed in Latin during the visit. Some years ago, through an intermediary, I sought to obtain a record of their meeting from the Vatican archives, but I was informed it was 'not accessible'. This might suggest, even a century later, that the Vatican, aware of the controversy in Australia, was unwilling to fan sectarian embers.)

A decade and a half later, Labor was split by the bitter debate over whether men should be conscripted to fight in the First World War. When Catholics opposed this form of assistance to Britain, supporters of conscription accused them of disloyalty, despite the fact that British troops were being used to repress the independence movement in Catholic Ireland.

When the modern Liberal Party swept to power under Robert Menzies in 1949, John Cramer was the lone Catholic in the overwhelmingly Protestant party, and he felt it keenly. Menzies – in many ways the least sectarian of people – had a habit of joking whenever Cramer walked into a room: 'Be careful, boys. Here comes the Papist.' It was rare, even as recently as forty years ago, to find Catholics in the Liberal ranks; the party was profoundly Protestant and more than a little suspicious of Catholics and their supposed clannishness.

Menzies was aware of these perceptions and would make light of them. In 1961, after long-serving Arbitration Commission president Richard Kirby received a knighthood, Menzies quipped that he had only recently learned that Kirby was a Protestant. 'If I'd known that, Dick, you would have got your knighthood a lot earlier,' he added. 'I thought you were a left-footer.'

If there was a turning point, then it was the moment in 1988 when Nick Greiner (now federal president of the Liberal Party) became premier of New South Wales. This was the first time since a single case in the 1930s that a Catholic had led a non-Labor government. What is extraordinary, given Australia's sectarian history, is that it aroused so little interest at the time. (In fact, the next four leaders of the Liberals in NSW were also Catholics.) Something had changed, quickly and profoundly.

The sectarian politics of the 1950s, when the Labor Party split over communism and much of its Catholic conservative wing left to form the Democratic Labor Party, were ugly and bitter. No one knew this better than Bob Santamaria.

The Labor Party, once regarded as a natural home for the Irish-Catholic working class, grew increasingly suspicious of the Catholics who remained in its ranks. Meanwhile, elements of the Liberal Party fought hard against visionaries like John Carrick, the NSW general secretary of the Liberal Party, who sought to court the Catholic vote, chiefly by taking up the proposal that government funds – referred to at the time as 'state aid' – be provided to non-government, especially Catholic, schools.[15]

It's hard to exaggerate the significance of the Liberals' eventual support for state aid. It broke down barriers and opened up a major political realignment by prising the Catholic vote away from Labor. Carrick told me many years ago that Menzies entrusted the negotiations to him, knowing full well the opposition within Liberal ranks to such an initiative. 'Such things are beyond the comprehension of a simple Presbyterian,' Menzies told Carrick.

The Menzies government was already the beneficiary of a 'soft' Catholic vote through the preferences that had flowed from the breakaway Democratic Labor Party, which enabled Menzies to scrape in by a single seat in 1961. Sitting on such a meagre majority, Menzies was keen to go further – to build on that indirect support by actively courting Catholic voters.

State aid, bitterly opposed by Labor following the split, was the key. It was to prove one of the decisive contributors, along with economic recovery, to the increase in Menzies' majority in 1963. (Interestingly, when the Liberals gained power at the 1965 NSW election after twenty-four years of Labor rule in that state, Labor's most pronounced electoral decline was in heavily Catholic areas, whether working-class or not.)

It was a high-risk strategy for Menzies and an uneasy Liberal Party. Some MPs even saw a split looming, such was the intensity of feelings aroused. Protestants at large, mostly Coalition voters, opposed state aid by a margin of three to two, according to opinion polls. But there was an even greater degree of opposition evident among Protestant clergy, lay organisations and associations of state school teachers. One prominent NSW Liberal supporter of state aid, Ben Doig, lost his preselection in a bitter contest over the issue.

Behind the generic argument that Catholic parents were entirely free to avoid the double financial burden by sending their children to state schools lurked two other issues: very few Protestant schools existed, and

---

15   Dean Ashenden, "The Educational Consequences of the Peace," Inside Story, July 28, 2016, https://insidestory.org.au/the-educational-consequences-of-the-peace/.

they were mostly attended by the children of wealthy parents; and within the opposition to state aid was a measure of plain anti-Catholic prejudice. That bigotry was common. Writing in 1963, journalist Peter Coleman, later a NSW Liberal leader, described a 'traditional prejudice against Catholics' and recounted how an interview he conducted with a Liberal leader who favoured state aid led to 'a stream of abusive letters' to them both.

Yet, within the space of a single generation, all that changed. In 2009, a Catholic leader of the Liberal Party (Turnbull) was challenged by another Catholic (Abbott) in a three-way ballot with yet another Catholic (Joe Hockey). Such a scenario would have been unthinkable even as recently as the 1980s; it has been not just a religious and political change, but also a cultural transformation of some considerable magnitude. In the 1970s, Catholic Liberals such as Kevin Cairns and Philip Lynch were rare birds indeed, with Lynch once joking about being a 'token tyke'.

At the same time, the lessening of Catholic influence in the Labor Party has seen its focus veer towards more post-materialist concerns, notably in women's rights, gay rights, marriage equality and the environment – what conservatives rail against as a 'progressive agenda'.

New areas of political contestation (the 'moral' Liberals versus the 'godless' Labor Party, for instance) have opened up. The culture wars, which have dominated political discourse over the past twenty-five years, say more about conflicting sets of abstract values than about concrete policies in areas as diverse as education and immigration. Political discourse has been, to a large extent, 'valuised', with all sorts of implications for political messaging and campaigning.

Does Tony Abbott have a wider audience for a Gospel-flavoured conservatism? One might suspect not, given the declining importance of religion in Australia. In the 2016 census, the number of people reporting no religion increased noticeably from 19 per cent (in 2006) to 30 per cent. The largest change was between 2011 and 2016, when an additional 2.2 million people reported having no religion. According to a global Gallup poll in 2008, 70 per cent of Australian adults consider religion to be of no importance in their lives.[16]

International surveys have identified Australia as one of the least religious nations in the developed world, particularly among Australia's youth, who were ranked as the least religious worldwide in a 2008 survey reported by the *Christian Science Monitor*. While only 7 per cent of youths

---

16   The data from the 2016 census on the declining importance of religion in Australia can be located on the Australian Bureau of Statistics website.

internationally didn't regard life as having a spiritual dimension, that figure was 28 per cent among young Australians. This is scarcely fertile ground on which to build a wider base of support.

When Tony Abbott talks of 'the conservative base' with which he identifies, presumably he means that minority in the Liberal Party who call themselves conservatives. People join political parties for a multitude of reasons, and there is no reason to assume that party members are in any way representative of society as a whole. With membership of all political parties not much more than 1 per cent of the population, and the Liberals share a small proportion of that, his presumed base is tiny indeed.

In his speech to the Deakin electorate branch, the former PM said the Liberal Party needed help 'so that we can be what we really are', a remark as enigmatic as it is disturbing. It carries suggestions of a lone crusade, perhaps again demonstrating the flawed judgements that characterised, and eventually ended, his tenure in the job. One suspects Mr Santamaria would not be amused.

'WE'RE NOT JUST LOOKING AT WHO'S TELLING THE STORIES, BUT THE STORIES WE'RE CHOOSING TO TELL'

SOPHIE BLACK

23 March 2018

The usual shelf life of a hashtag is on par with a tub of really good yoghurt – once opened, the gratification is instant, but it spoils pretty quickly. And yet #MeToo has stuck. Months later, we're still seeing the phenomenon rippling out, way beyond the Oscars stage, beyond the media bubble, into our own workplaces, around our dinner tables. It's easy to be cynical about the limitations of this thing, but something *has* shifted, and it has a bit to do with the media lens that's been applied to this story.

Women have many reasons to be wary, depressed or downright terrified of the internet. I've sat comparing notes with bunches of female commentators and journalists about how often they're abused online (daily), how many times they've taken complaints to the police, and how many death threats they've received (in one woman's case, binders full). No guaranteed safe space exists for a woman online. Especially a lippy one.

And yet ... as a tool for social change, the internet, to the extent that we can still refer to it as a single entity, still offers immense possibilities. Algorithms may ultimately kill us all, but the sheer scale of this form of instant mass communication means the screws can be turned on the powerful – but only if enough people unite behind a single message.

Mostly, they don't. They split apart, atomise, sift into niches and talk to themselves. But #MeToo, with all its flaws and nuances, was undoubtedly a moment of relative unity. Crucially, the momentum dovetailed with a conversation about diversity that's been playing out online for years now, and has now well and truly bubbled to the surface of mainstream media consciousness.

'You can't put those stories back in a box,' *The New York Times*'s Francesca Donner said during a recent conversation at the Wheeler Centre about the media company's new Gender Initiative. 'It kind of started with Harvey, but we use words like "avalanche" and "tsunami" and "the dominos falling" to describe what happened after,' she told us. 'There was so much going on and there was so much to kind of make sense of … We didn't have the answers any better than anybody else did. We were figuring it out.'

Getting *The New York Times* to admit they don't know something would've been unthinkable twenty years ago. But we're living in an online world now, with a very online sensibility. Smart, responsive mastheads have learnt to learn from their audience, and the Gender Initiative is the latest project from a media company attempting to remake itself in the digital age.

Despite being voracious consumers of online news, more than half the population are used to seeing their own 'issues' corralled into a pink-tinted genre. Think 'women's' sections, specialist publications and curly-fonted 'mummy blogs'. Part of the intention of the Gender Initiative is to change the dominant point of view across the entire paper. 'We're working across desks to make sure that gender is this lens that we apply to the stories we're already telling,' said Donner. 'Gender as it crosses everything … culture, sport, politics.'

The scale of this ambition requires unpicking decades worth of assumptions about everything from the wording of headlines to the nuts and bolts of news angles and newsworthiness. As Donner said, 'We're not just looking at who's telling the stories, but the stories we're choosing to tell.'

One arm of the new initiative is literally rewriting history by launching the Overlooked project in the obituaries sections. The death desk is seeking to balance the ledger by telling stories of remarkable women who never rated a mention (um, hello Charlotte Brontë). As Amisha Padnani and gender editor Jessica Bennett write, 'Who gets remembered – and how – inherently involves judgement. To look back at the obituary archives can, therefore, be a stark lesson in how society valued various achievements and achievers.'

Conversations in newsrooms about 'the women problem' have traditionally centred on numbers, or the lack of them, and for good reason. The 2016 Women in Media report found that when it comes to the Australian press and broadcasters, women were only named or acknowledged as the authors of 31 per cent of coverage during 2015. Overall, they represented just 23 per cent of all sources quoted in the news, while men made up 77 per cent.

The ABC's director of news, Gaven Morris, also acknowledged this giant gap back in 2016. 'While much is changing in the media sector,' he wrote, 'one thing never seems to: white, middle-aged men continue to dominate in front of the cameras and microphones.'

But while this kind of talk used to circle back to a pretty unhelpful debate about quotas, it's now taking place under the umbrella of an even bigger conversation about diversity. The phenomenon routinely dismissed by critics as 'identity politics' has the potential to reflect and elevate a multitude of first-hand perspectives, and the mainstream media is just now catching up.

As Katharine Viner, editor-in-chief of *The Guardian*, wrote in 'A Mission for Journalism in a Time of Crisis' at the end of last year, 'If journalists become distant from other people's lives, they miss the story, and people don't trust them. *The Guardian* is not at all exempt from these challenges, and our staff is not diverse enough. Because of our history, values and purpose, we are committed to addressing these issues – but there is still a long way to go.'

All of which means that some sections of the mainstream media are starting to talk about gender very differently. As Lauren Rosewarne wrote in *Meanjin* recently, 'The rise of identity politics, our heightened awareness of, and sensitivity about, gender fluidity, race, class and ability, means that the idea of "women's media" – of readers being segmented based on assumed anatomy – is being put under greater scrutiny.'

The surge in interest can result in a deeply unhelpful call-out culture, but it's also forcing a conversation about deep-seated newsroom assumptions. If the debate used to centre on the death of objectivity and impartiality, it's now all about the (points of) view.

The diversity imperative is pushed along by the global aspirations of big media outlets like *The Guardian*, which are looking at ways to enlarge their international audiences. But it's only working for them because readers are interested. 'This is not about quotas, it's not about worthiness, checking a box for the sake of it,' said Donner. 'People are genuinely interested in this stuff.'

Australian writer Matilda Dixon-Smith, also on the Wheeler Centre panel, has found editors a lot more receptive to pieces about gender issues over the past two years, and for the same reason – because people are interested. When it comes to the #MeToo momentum, that interest equates to inviting women to tell stories about behaviour that has been unquestioned, and taking their accounts seriously. As Dixon-Smith says, 'people have found this outlet, and #MeToo is just the name we give it … it's so much more than that.'

Of course, this conversation is happening mainly in progressive media circles. For every Gender Initiative, there's Charles Wooley subjecting the 'attractive' prime minister of New Zealand to a line of questioning straight out of *Anchorman*. And there's still no shortage of headlines for journalist Jane Gilmore to take her red pen to as part of her #FixedIt campaign. But we are witnessing the beginnings of a new way of thinking about who is shaping, presenting and packaging the stories we consume, and some of the coverage of #MeToo echoes that approach.

#MeToo invites people to consider things from women's perspectives, and it turns out that they actually are. Read that sentence again, because it's more revolutionary than it sounds. The lens has blurred, refocused and suddenly we're seeing the story from the point of view of the token female character in the corner of the screen. Let's hope the camera lingers for a little while yet.

SAM DASTYARI AND THE THOUSANDS OF YEARS OF CHINESE HISTORY

ANTONIA FINNANE

4 December 2017

S am Dastyari's grasp of Chinese history must be among the least of his worries at present. He's possibly wishing that he knew less about it rather than more, or at least that he had never had occasion to mention it, especially not in a public gathering standing beside a member of a political party whose interests aren't necessarily aligned with those of his own party.

As we now know, that mention was to be his downfall. In 2016, he recalled it as a murmured or garbled off-the-cuff response to a question. When the tape emerged it showed what he had really said: 'The role that Australia should be playing as a friend is to know that we see several thousand years of history, thousands of years of history, where it is and isn't our place to be involved.'[17] What was he thinking?

On the face of things, it seems bizarre that a politician should voice approval for the policy of a foreign country on grounds not only satisfactory to the country concerned, but actually supplied by that country – in this case the 'thousands of years of history' that China commonly advances as justification for its actions in the South China Sea, and many other places as well. But invoking those 'thousands of years' has become common in the age of China's rise. Dastyari may have picked up the habit from his sometime mentor, former foreign minister Bob Carr, who has urged that 'the China story needs to be told and given credit for all that it has achieved ... It has a culture and civilisation that goes back five millennia.' Carr may in turn have been influenced by, and has certainly quoted, Henry Kissinger on the importance of paying attention to 'five thousand years of history'. On this point, all three men are in lock step with Xi Jinping.

It is difficult to understand what is meant by 'five thousand years of Chinese history'. None of the commonly mentioned linchpins of

---

17   A recording was leaked of ALP Senator Sam Dastyari's address to a Chinese media conference in Sydney on 17 June 2016.

Chinese culture were secured that long ago. The earliest forms of writing in East Asia have been dated to around 1200 BCE, or 1400 BCE at a stretch. Confucius was not alive till the sixth century BCE. A unitary state – the Chinese empire, that is – was not founded till 221 BCE, and since then, a succession of states have existed in what we now recognise as Chinese territory. Through centuries and even millennia of those five thousand years, vast areas of this territory were occupied by non-Sinic peoples.

Probably the period is best viewed as something like the four thousand years of biblical chronology: a sacred period attached to a belief system. This would explain why the line between history and mythology is blurred. 'China has a full rich history of over five thousand years,' writes Kang Ouyang. 'From ancient times when the three emperors and five sovereigns started the Chinese civilisation, national wisdom began to sprout ...' Ouyang is director of the Institute of Philosophy at Huazhong University of Science and Technology and is known for his work on the 'national spirit'. He otherwise writes on Marxism, but in this account, a recently published book on *The Chinese National Spirit,* the true believer trumps the Marxist. The 'five thousand years' is advanced at several points in the book, most fascinatingly as a label for the period within which China has been engaged in international relations.

What is the logic of the connection between the 'five thousand years' policy positions on either China's part or anyone else's? In another recently published book, *History and Nationalist Legitimacy in Contemporary China: A Double-Edged Sword,* Robert Weatherly and Qian Zhang chart the ruling Communist Party's purposeful use of history and historical memory as a legitimising strategy, to replace the foundations formerly supplied by a commitment to revolution and Marxism. The point they make is not a new one, but it is worth reiterating until it permeates general knowledge about contemporary China. Every country has its national myths, most of which are grounded in or derived from history; but in China, history alone is the bedrock. The People's Republic doesn't have a religion, and it doesn't have a constitution – or at least, not one that counts. It no longer even has a revolutionary ideology. It just has history and lots of it.

Needless to say, such 'history' cannot be freely researched and openly debated. It is more akin to a religious doctrine. Its central tenets can be recited, as if from a catechism. What is the history of the Chinese Communist Party? 'It is a history of leading the peoples of the whole country under the guidance of Marxism–Leninism–Mao Zedong Thought to undertake a socialist revolution and the establishment of socialism, with tremendous achievements ...'[18] What is the Chinese Dream?

> It came out of the great experience of the thirty years or reform and opening up, out of more than sixty years of persistent searching since the establishment of the PRC, out of the profound conclusion of 170 or more years of development of the Chinese people, out of the enduring legacy of the Chinese people's 5000-year-old culture.[19]

When Dastyari first heard mention of 'thousands of years' uttered in relationship to the People's Republic of China, his instincts should have told him that it was a mantra routinely uttered in the service of a particular belief system, with no self-evident relationship to the South China Sea. As things stand, it is hard to understand why he would have chosen to recite it, other than that he might have been talking too much to Bob Carr, whose position on the South China Sea he echoed. The rather muddled sentence quoted above, in which he actually rephrases the term, suggests that he might have been somewhat confused as to what he was saying. As a citizen of a country with sixty-five thousand years of human settlement, and as a parliamentary representative in a complex society with a different sort of history – difficult, intensively researched and much debated – he was in a position to bring quite a different perspective to bear on regional disputes. That might have required greater sensitivity to Australia's history, as well as a better understanding of China's.

---

18   Chinese government website, http://www.gov.cn/18da/content_2247082.htm.
19   *People's Daily*, 1 June 2017, 7.

THE GREAT ASSENTERS

JEREMY GANS

1 May 2018

When the US Supreme Court recently split five judges to four on a new test for deporting criminals, Trump-appointee Neil Gorsuch joined the court's four liberals for the first time. That was the court's fourth five–four split for the month, alongside three more that were either six–three or seven–two. The world's nine most powerful judges agreed just once during the month: to throw out a case that had been overtaken by new legislation.

In Australia's top court, it's a different story. All four decisions made in the High Court of Australia in April were approved by every judge who sat (even if they sometimes disagreed on the reasons). This contrast between Australia and the United States is new. The nine justices of the US Supreme Court have long divided, often sharply, in around half of their cases. Canada's top court is the same. And, just a decade ago (and two chief justices back), so was Australia's.

In recent years, though, the High Court has become like Britain's top court, whose judges agree roughly three-quarters of the time. Only in about fifteen cases a year in each court does a judge disagree with the rest. Close decisions, like the five–four decisions that are common in America, now only happen here about once a year.

Many people like our newly harmonious top court. Our current chief justice, Susan Kiefel, says that she thinks the High Court's judges should think long and hard before disagreeing with the majority: 'It could just be that one is wrong.'[20] The court reaches its decisions quickly and without rancour. Australian lawyers and law students have fewer messy rulings to deal with. But some people – I, for one – dissent.

What's not to like about judicial agreement? Nothing at all, if the judges are judging easy cases. But the top courts in Britain, the United States, Canada and Australia usually hear only the toughest, most controversial

---

20   Susan Kiefel, "Judicial Courage and the Decorum of Dissent" (speech, Supreme Court of Queensland, Brisbane, November 28, 2016), High Court of Australia, http://www.hcourt. gov.au/assets/publications/speeches/current-justices/kiefelj/KiefelCJ28Nov2017_1.pdf.

cases. If top judges constantly reach the same decision on hard cases, we're entitled to start wondering why.

The US Supreme Court learned that hard lesson eight decades ago. In the 1930s, four of the court's nine judges agreed so regularly on (often novel) constitutional challenges to the New Deal legislation that the media dubbed them 'the four horsemen'. This pointed label allowed an aggrieved Franklin Delano Roosevelt to tell Americans, shortly after his thumping second election victory, that 'in our courts we want a government of laws and not of men'.

Detailing the four's shared decisions (in majority and dissent), he declared 'a quiet crisis' and announced his plan to appoint extra judges 'who will act as justices' and 'save our national Constitution from hardening of the judicial arteries'.

No politician will ever accuse Australia's High Court of being a 'third house' of parliament (a term FDR coined long before Malcolm Turnbull used it in a different context). Our Constitution places very few restrictions on what our parliaments can do. Indeed, the High Court only makes a couple of politically important decisions a year, and the bulk of its work is made up of regular court appeals. That is why Australia's High Court has never developed political blocs like the liberal and conservative wings of the US Supreme Court.

But Australia's High Court has had a long and proud history of internal debate about Australian law, often propelled by particular judges – known as Great Dissenters – who routinely criticise the majority's approach. Past examples are Sir Isaac Isaacs (the first Great Dissenter), Sir Owen Dixon (often regarded as our greatest judge) and Lionel Murphy (whose radical views became the orthodoxy when Sir Anthony Mason was chief justice). More recently, Michael Kirby and Dyson Heydon have taken on the role of 'appealing to the future' with particular vigour, dissenting in up to half of their cases.

But no more. Since Heydon's departure five years ago, the High Court has no Great Dissenters – or even middling ones. The closest thing to a regular dissenter is former solicitor-general Stephen Gageler, who has disagreed in barely one out of eight cases.

And that's how Chief Justice Kiefel likes it. In a speech late last year, she hearkened back to a time in England when judicial dissent was regarded as 'a serious thing' reserved for the most important cases, lest it detract from the court's authority. She declared that it was 'perfectly proper' for 'senior judges' to persuade dissenting judges to tone down their language in the name of dignity and others' feelings. Dissents, she said, aren't courageous and may even be cowardly if majority judges opt not to 'enter the fray'.

Kiefel advises law students to pay more attention to 'more mundane majority judgements' and legal commentators to stop encouraging dissenters' 'self-indulgence'. (In passing, she mentions a 2016 book edited by UNSW's Andrew Lynch on *Great Australian Dissents*, which includes a chapter by me feting the dissenters in Lindy Chamberlain's failed High Court appeal).

She certainly practises what she preaches. Kiefel now dissents in fewer than one in forty cases, or just one a year. It's been more than two years since her last dissent (over the meaning of a trust deed).

•

The 'court-packing' scheme FDR proposed in 1937 never eventuated. Just as the scheme was announced, the court's two swing voters swung behind the New Deal legislation, isolating the four horsemen. Shortly after, the bloc's oldest member, Willis Van Devanter, retired to a Maryland farm and a freshly legislated pension. *The Washington Post* bid the judge a cold farewell:

> Justice Van Devanter might have been called 'The Great Assenter', in contradistinction to the term 'The Great Dissenter', often applied to the late Justice Oliver Wendell Holmes. His record up until the last or present term of the court shows that of the forty-one cases in which acts of Congress were held unconstitutional, Van Devanter assented forty-one times and dissented none.

His replacement, Hugo Black, had voted for every New Deal statute as a senator.

By *The Washington Post*'s standards, Australia's current High Court has three Great Assenters, each of whom has dissented in fewer than one in forty cases in the past four years. In addition to Chief Justice Kiefel, there are Justices Patrick Keane and Virginia Bell. Since the start of 2014, Bell has been the court's Greatest Assenter, with just two dissents out of 164 decisions.

What is different about these three judges? After all, the entire current bench is a very agreeable bunch. But these three stand out in how often they agree with each other. Most pairs of judges on the court agree between 80 per cent and 90 per cent of the time. But, in the past four years, both Keane and Bell have sided with the chief justice in 97 per cent of the cases where they sat with her (and about 95 per cent of the time they sat with each other). The three reach the same decision in nine out of ten cases where they are together on the bench.

On a seven-member court with no political blocs, three judges routinely agreeing is enough to allow them to determine nearly all of the court's orders. As a past judge, Michael McHugh, candidly admitted of his time on the bench in the 2000s:

> I regard [Chief Justice] Murray [Gleeson] and myself as irrelevant players while we were on that court together, for the reason that [Bill] Gummow and [Ken] Hayne always seemed to come together. And they usually had Mary [Gaudron] ... So, as long as those three were there, it didn't matter what they decided, they would either pick up [Ian] Callinan or pick up [Michael] Kirby.[21]

But that court's power trio was much less constant than the current one – Gummow and Hayne agreed with each other in 95 per cent of cases, but with Gaudron much less.

The upshot is that a trio of current Great Assenters – Susan Kiefel, Virginia Bell and Patrick Keane – have quietly become the three most powerful judges in contemporary Australia. Indeed, they are almost certainly the most constant (and arguably therefore the most powerful) bloc of judges Australia's High Court has ever seen. And, in a uniquely Australian twist, their bloc isn't political, either in cause or effect.

Unlike New Deal America's four horsemen (elderly, white, conservative), these three Great Assenters have little or nothing in common. Kiefel and Keane are both Queenslanders (and formerly on the Federal Court), but Bell is from the New South Wales Supreme Court. Keane and Bell are both Labor appointees; Kiefel was appointed by Coalition governments, both to the bench and as chief justice. Kiefel and Bell share no relevant characteristics at all. Unlike the horsemen, their agreement isn't limited to constitutional cases, but applies to everything the High Court decides: criminal appeals, contract disputes, administrative challenges, whatever.

---

21   Michael Pelly, "The Day Gaudron Put Chief Justice in His Place," *The Australian*, May 30, 2014, https://www.federationpress.com.au/pdf/Hughes%20appointment%20set%20an%20alarming%20precedent_The%20Australian,%2030%20May%202014.pdf.

Rather than shared policy goals, the trio simply seem to have remarkably similar minds on everything. Australia's answer to America's sombre four horsemen (who notoriously shared a car to court to plan their judgements) is a much sunnier troika (who, coincidentally – because this is determined by seniority – always sit beside each other on the bench).

Strangely, their shared dance is relatively recent. When Kiefel and Bell first joined the court, they spent some five years disagreeing with one another (and dissenting) at the same rate as the court's other judges. But, not long after Keane joined the bench in 2013, the pair's rate of disagreement and dissent fell to just one decision a year and has stayed there ever since. Whether the change is mere coincidence, or even conscious, is impossible to know.

•

Is a court in which three out of seven judges routinely agree a bad thing? The arrangement certainly brings benefits. The High Court has, for instance, been enmeshed recently in several national political controversies about the same-sex marriage survey and the validity of the 2016 federal election. It has settled these disputes speedily and unanimously, avoiding both political instability and controversy. The court's harmony on these topics is almost certainly aided by, and may have been the result of, that core alliance of three judges. The same may be true for many of the three-quarters of regular cases on which the court routinely agrees, settling hard case after hard case quickly and with little rancour or lingering questions.

But speed and stability aren't the only measures of a top court, which must deliver wise answers to hard questions. Chief Justice Kiefel's most famous slogan is 'collegiality is not compromise', but saying that does not make it true.[22] The court's last Great Dissenter, Dyson Heydon, famously disagreed, publishing a thinly veiled critique of his own bench – and especially the pairing of Gummow and Hayne – as 'the enemy within' and a threat to judicial independence.[23] While Heydon feared that strong judicial personalities were dominating weak ones, I suspect a less extreme explanation in the current bench: that three judges – consciously

---

22 Susan Kiefel, "The individual judge" (speech, Sir Richard Blackburn Lecture, Canberra, May 13, 2014), ACT Law Society, https://www.actlawsociety.asn.au/documents/item/944%3E.

23 Dyson Heydon, "Threats to Judicial Independence" in *Heydon: Selected Speeches and Papers*, ed. John Sackar and Thomas Prince (Annandale, NSW: The Federation Press, 2018).

or otherwise, and whether for personal reasons or institutional ones – desire consensus above all.

Whatever the benefits or threats posed by the troika of Kiefel, Bell and Keane, they are not long-term ones. In contrast to the US Supreme Court, Australian judges must retire at seventy. That means that the current trio will be broken up in three years and all but gone in four. With them may well go a number of legal doctrines they established only by a slim margin (such as the role of proportionality in constitutional law, whether state tribunals can hear interstate disputes, and how to assess the weight of disputed evidence).

But even the short-term situation has potentially significant drawbacks. One worry I have is that Australia will largely be deprived of the independent thoughts of seven of its finest judicial minds over the better part of a decade, lost to the banality of reflex consensus, sidelined diversity and discouraged dissent. But my main concern is for ordinary litigants with cases before the nation's highest court during this period – ranging from accused drug traffickers to private hospitals to alleged killers to restaurateurs to land councils to child abuse defendants – who have reason to worry that their disputes (and in some instances, their futures) may have been decided by a court, not of laws, but of men and women.

CLASS AND CRISIS

THE QUEEN AND THE PERFECT BICYCLE

TIMOTHY J SINCLAIR

12 August 2009

As even the most ardent republican would acknowledge, Queen Elizabeth is not one to make flippant comments about grave matters of public policy. So when, capturing perfectly the mood of public exasperation, she asked an economist why his profession had not seen the crisis coming, it became a serious matter for the British establishment. The response – which came at the end of July in the form of a letter to Her Majesty from that august institution, the British Academy – suggested that everyone had been doing their individual jobs correctly, but as a group economists had missed the big picture of a 'series of interconnected imbalances'. If economists were guilty of anything, the letter suggested, it was 'a failure of the collective imagination of many bright people ... to understand the risks of the system as a whole'. What the letter revealed was that economists are willing to take the blame for not thinking big enough, but they are not willing to accept that their 'perfect bicycle' is in need of any serious repair. This perfect bicycle is the term applied by the young Paul Samuelson – who went on to become one of the most celebrated economists of the twentieth century – to the mathematical equilibrium economics that has dominated the profession for much of the past fifty years. But it may be that the assumptions and implications of this approach to economics and to financial markets, summed up in the Efficient Markets Hypothesis, or EMH, are the problem, and that the failure to think about the system as a whole follows from this approach.

Like monetarism, another famous way of thinking about economics, the EMH originates at the University of Chicago. The basic idea is that because prices for stocks, bonds, derivatives and so on are always based on a large body of information analysed by a large number of buyers, they will therefore reflect the fundamental value of these securities. Securities will trade at an equilibrium between supply and demand, and markets will therefore operate efficiently. This is a remarkable claim about information and how it is incorporated into market prices.

The case for EMH is built on three assumptions, suggests Harvard economist Andrei Shleifer. First, investors are said to be rational and to value their potential purchases rationally. So investors are not likely to buy before finding out information about what they are buying and also thinking about how to maximise their return. Second, even if some investors are irrational, their random trades will cancel each other out, leaving prices unaffected. Irrationality is the exception and it is of no consequence. Last, even if there is a consistently irrational approach to investing among a group of investors – based on the mating cycle of cane toads, for example – rational arbitrageurs will meet them in the market and eliminate their influence on prices.

The EMH has two main implications for financial markets, argues the economist Richard Thaler. First, that 'the price is right': asset prices for stocks and bonds incorporate all information, providing very accurate signals to buyers and sellers. If this is correct, asset price bubbles are simply not possible. The very notion of a bubble or inflated price cannot survive the three processes Shleifer identified. The second implication, suggests Thaler, is that there is 'no free lunch', because traders cannot beat the market. If everyone in the market has the information then any cheap or expensive assets will rapidly be identified by traders and arbitraged away. Just as it is difficult to beat the house at roulette, it is hard to beat the market under these assumptions.

What are the general problems with the EMH? Samuelson's perfect bicycle of financial engineering is sustained by the 'ergodic axiom', which underpins the EMH. In economist Paul Davidson's words, the ergodic axiom holds that the future is 'merely the statistical shadow of the past'. In other words, financial economists calculate probable future risks based on historical data. Unfortunately, human societies are not, to use Robert Skidelsky's phrase, 'a stable and repetitive universe'. Our communities are more like living things than automobile engines. They grow, change, adjust and over time are transformed. They are non-ergodic. Adopting a fundamental axiom more appropriate for the physical world than the social world seems like a bad start.

Eliminating uncertainty from the lexicon of the financial markets has arguably been a mistake. EMH encourages altogether too much confidence in financial engineering. If more of our financial activities assumed uncertainty – and therefore that we would have to be more risk-averse – we would live in a world of more conservatively managed companies, governments and individuals. Of course, the trade-off would be a society more like that of our grandparents, in which getting a mortgage was a struggle and the standard of living was much lower. But the global financial crisis has forcibly recreated that world for many people in any case.

The EMH leads to neglect of the regulation of the key institutions like banks and credit rating agencies that actually make our markets work. It encourages this neglect, because it says that information works automatically to impose the disciplines of the market, a bit like an operating system in a computer. But in a non-ergodic world, institutions are fundamental to instilling confidence about the future in market participants. In an uncertain world we need institutions we feel we can trust in order to engage in financial transactions.

What specific role did the EMH play in the global financial crisis? The EMH led policymakers to ignore key market processes. Financial market participants do not merely integrate information coming from outside the markets in the wider, real economy, but are focused on what other traders are doing, in an effort to anticipate their buy/sell activities and thus make money from them (or at least avoid losing more money than the average). In this sense, rumour, norms and other features of social life are part of their understanding of finance.

Keynes provided what remains the best intuitive illustration of the importance of this understanding of finance and financial crises in his tabloid beauty contest metaphor, first published in 1936. Keynes suggested that finance is not, as the EMH supposes, a matter of picking the best stocks, based on an economic analysis of which should rise in value in future. Rather, anticipating what other traders in the market were likely to do was actually more relevant. Keynes compared finance to beauty contests that ran in the popular newspapers of the time. These contests were not, as might be assumed, about picking the most attractive face. Success was achieved by estimating how *others* would vote and voting with them – although, as Keynes pointed out, others would be trying to do the same, hence the complexity of the financial markets. The point is that policymakers were focused initially on fundamental issues rather than, as Keynes suggested, on what traders were doing. As time moved on, of course, the policymakers had to abandon the EMH-type approach and focus squarely on anticipating traders.

EMH led to a misunderstanding of the initial episode of the crisis, when securities markets came to a halt in late 2007 and early 2008. This was not caused by 'toxic' subprime loans. Given that the subprime securities market was worth only $0.7 trillion in mid 2007, out of total global capital markets of $175 trillion, the supposed impact of subprime assets is out of proportion to their actual weight in the global financial system. This strongly suggests that another explanation for the global financial crisis is needed. The paralysis or 'valuation crisis' that came over global finance in 2007–2009, in which banks were unwilling to trade with each other or lend money, had no specific relationship to subprime lending. It was a crisis of confidence in the non-ergodic social foundations of global finance.

Given all this, what could replace the EMH? The great attraction of the ergodic axiom and the EMH is that it allows for the construction of models of human behaviour. These models are deeply embedded in the training of the economics discipline, and many economists will be very reluctant to give them up. A more modest worldview, which allows uncertainty back into the story of financial markets, as seems necessary, would imply a more inductive approach in which experimental and other empirical techniques become more important. A great deal of research into the social foundations of finance, including trust and how institutions work, seems vital, given the experience of the crisis. Rather than focus on the little pieces of the world, economists may feel compelled to undertake more holistic studies into how things actually fit together.

•

The EMH, as it has been taken up in the financial markets and by policymakers, is clearly implicated in the global financial crisis of 2007–2009. Two very different understandings of financial crisis compete. The first, the exogenous approach in which the EMH is king, sees finance itself as a natural phenomenon, a smoothly oiled machine that every now and then gets messed up by the government or by events that nobody can anticipate, like war or famine. The other perspective, critical of the EMH, argues that the machine-like view of finance is mythic. Like all other human institutions, finance is a social world made by people, in which collective understandings, norms and assumptions give rise periodically to manias, panics and crashes. On this account, financial crises are normal.

While truly global financial crises are fortunately rare, we understand so little about the mechanisms that cause them that much greater modesty about how finance works seems sensible than is evident in the EMH. We should abandon Samuelson's perfect bicycle and embrace the lesson of Keynes's beauty contest and the valuation crisis of 2007 – that financial markets are social phenomena in which collective understandings, especially confidence, are vital. Perhaps then economists will not have to explain themselves to the Queen.

THE POLITICS OF COMPASSION

KLAUS NEUMANN

1 March 2012

In October 2009 prime minister Kevin Rudd took over control of Australia's asylum seeker policy from his immigration minister, Chris Evans, and decreed that the *Oceanic Viking* should not be allowed to off-load its human cargo of Sri Lankan asylum seekers in Australia. Since then, the Labor government's response to the arrival of 'boat people' has been a shambles. To make matters worse for the government, the Coalition's immigration spokesperson, Scott Morrison, has hardly put a foot wrong. The one significant exception happened in February 2011.

Three months earlier, in December 2010, a boat carrying asylum seekers lost engine power, struck rocks just off Christmas Island, and crashed in heavy seas against the island's cliff face. At least thirty of the passengers – and perhaps many more – died. Two months later, twelve of the victims were buried in Sydney, where they had relatives. The Australian Federal Police footed the bill for the funerals and the federal government paid for close relatives who had survived the disaster and were still in detention on Christmas Island to attend. That's when Morrison made a serious error of judgement, questioning why the funerals weren't held on Christmas Island. He told the ABC's Barbara Miller:

> If relatives of those who were involved wanted to go to Christmas Island, like any other Australian who wanted to attend a funeral service in another part of the country, they would have made their own arrangements to be there.

He also called on the government 'to understand the value of taxpayers' dollars in this area'.

On the face of it, these were innocuous comments. But many of those who heard them also saw footage of the first three funerals: of two babies and of a man from Iran, whose orphaned nine-year-old son, Seena Aqhlaqi Sheikhdost, had been flown in from Christmas Island. Seena's mother and brother had also perished but their bodies had not been recovered. His closest relative in Australia was now a cousin living in Sydney. The television news reported Morrison's remarks and showed images of the distraught boy. The shadow minister was lambasted not only by refugee advocates but also by a senior member of the shadow cabinet, Joe Hockey:

> No matter what the colour of your skin, the nature of your faith, if your child has died or a father has died, you want to be there to say goodbye, and I totally understand the importance of this to those families.

Within a day, Morrison had to admit that the timing of his remarks was 'insensitive' and 'inappropriate'. While he stopped short of apologising for the comments themselves, he said, in a rare show of self-criticism by an Australian politician, 'I had to show a little more compassion than I showed yesterday. I am happy to admit that.'

Morrison's faux pas and his subsequent contrition would have given the government a chance to score much-needed points – if not for a similar error of judgement by his counterpart, immigration minister Chris Bowen. The minister insisted not only that nine-year-old Seena should remain in detention but also that he should be flown back to Christmas Island after the funeral rather than being allowed to stay with his cousin in Sydney. In a remarkably emotional interview, Melbourne radio host Jon Faine pleaded with the minister to release the boy: 'It's the easiest of cases you'll ever get. He should be with his family, minister.' Bowen was unmoved, missing the opportunity to highlight Morrison's lack of compassion. But he relented soon afterwards and, within days of having returned to Christmas Island, Seena was released and reunited with his Sydney relatives.

Maybe Morrison and Bowen should have known better. Ten years earlier, the visible suffering of another young Iranian immigration detainee, Shayan Badraie, also elicited a strong emotional response from the Australian public. Footage depicting Shayan, filmed with a camera smuggled into the Villawood detention centre, was broadcast on ABC TV's *Four Corners*. The immigration minister at the time, Philip Ruddock, misread the public's mood when he tried to blame the parents for the boy's suffering. The arrival of the *Tampa* soon shifted the debate; but the 'children overboard' lies, which featured so prominently in the last days of the 2001 federal election campaign, could be seen as the government's belated response to the public relations debacle over Shayan's detention.

Jon Faine opened his interview with Chris Bowen with a revealing choice of words: 'To the politics second, and the compassion first.' The consensus of the Labor government and the Liberal–National opposition – that asylum seekers pose a threat to the integrity of Australia's borders or to its social fabric, that fear of asylum seekers is legitimate, and that a policy of deterrence is an appropriate response – has been questioned effectively in only two respects: by the courts' occasional insistence that measures of deterrence must not violate Australian law, and by the public's occasional show of compassion for individual asylum seekers, particularly children. Another potentially effective response, rational argument, has had very little impact. Who really cares that Australia has to deal with only a tiny fraction of the world's irregular migrants, that deterrence can't be a substitute for a long-term solution involving other countries in the region, or that Australia has the capacity to accommodate a much bigger share of refugees in need of resettlement? By contrast, who *doesn't* care about young Shayan and young Seena? It seems as if only compassion can trump politics.

Politics and compassion can hardly be separated, of course. In fact, what we have witnessed over the past fifteen or so years is the rise of a politics of compassion: a politics that refers to compassion (rather than, say, rights) for its justification and draws on the language of compassion, and which increasingly informs policymaking. In Australia, it was Kevin Rudd who began championing a greater role for compassion. Two years before he became prime minister, he nominated compassion as one of five values 'which might underpin a vision for the nation's future' (the others were security, competition, fairness and sustainability). As prime minister, he frequently invoked the language of compassion when promoting government policies.

•

Among the handful of scholars who are analysing the growing traction of the politics of compassion is the French anthropologist Didier Fassin. As he writes in his 2011 book, *Humanitarian Reason: A Moral History of the Present*, 'The distinctive feature of contemporary societies is without doubt the way that moral sentiments have become generalised as a frame of reference in political life.' What makes Fassin's work particularly interesting is the fact that his explanations of how and why people today 'often prefer to speak about suffering and compassion than about interests or justice, legitimising actions by declaring themselves to be humanitarian' are based on ethnographic fieldwork and what is usually referred to as discourse analysis. As he writes:

> We must ask to what extent the words used contribute to forming (and transforming or even deforming) the objects that constitute the world, and ... we must examine the way actors take hold of words to manipulate them.

One of Fassin's 'fields' is the bureaucracy responsible for regularising the status of illegal immigrants in France. In one of his chapters, he analyses the work of public medical officers in the *département* of Seine-Saint-Denis in the Île-de-France, north-east of Paris. He charts the shift from the 'immigrant' (the source of much-needed labour) to the 'foreigner' (whose presence is perceived as an imposition and who is of no immediate use to the French economy). In the 1990s, the state increasingly clamped down on the *sans papiers*, France's undocumented migrants. But at the same time, new legislation gave authorities the option of using a 'humanitarian reason' when deciding whether a *sans papiers* would be deported or granted a visa. If they deemed that a foreigner had a serious illness that couldn't be treated adequately in his or her country of origin, medical officers could recommend that the *département*'s prefect issue a residence permit. As a result of the new laws, the foreigner's body has become as much of an asset as the immigrant's, because it can arouse the compassion that compels the bureaucrat to make a favourable decision.

The fight against AIDS in South Africa is another of Fassin's case studies. He shows how the death in 2001 of twelve-year-old Nkosi Johnson, who had opened the thirteenth international AIDS conference in Durban the previous year, transformed the debate about AIDS. In Fassin's words, Johnson's death 'signalled the entry of the theme of childhood' into public discussion of the disease. Subsequently, AIDS campaigners focused on children who were HIV-positive and on AIDS orphans. Fassin shows how their reification as victims removed children 'from the social reality in which they lived' by neglecting the historical and social contexts of their situation, and how the mobilisation of compassion for their suffering tended to detract attention from other AIDS victims. Yet representing innocent children as the prime victims of AIDS, faced by an indifferent society and a government in denial, also allowed campaigners to compel the South African authorities and international aid agencies into action.

Did the ends justify the means? In Fassin's view, 'this emotional mobilisation is fragile and ambiguous'. The sentiments aroused by images of abused, dying or abandoned children are fickle. The orphan who deserves compassion can quickly morph into the threatening criminal youth living on the streets.

As Fassin shows, the rise of a politics and a rhetoric of compassion has contradictory consequences. Compassion is the symptom of an unequal relationship between victims and spectators who have the option of becoming good Samaritans. In Australia's case, it is the relationship between the asylum seeker and the person extending compassion as a citizen of a prosperous, peaceful and democratic country. As Fassin observes, 'Humanitarian reason governs precarious lives.' By neither questioning inequality nor exposing its root causes, compassion enshrines this inequality. And often compassion's main benefit is to make the compassionate person feel good about being able to indulge in seemingly unselfish sentiments.

But compassion can also gesture towards, and maybe prompt, a politics of solidarity. Fassin writes:

> In contemporary societies, where inequalities have reached an unprecedented level, humanitarianism elicits the fantasy of a global moral community that may still be viable and the expectation that solidarity may have redeeming powers ... This secular imaginary of communion and redemption implies a sudden awareness of the fundamentally unequal human condition and an ethical necessity to not remain passive about it in the name of solidarity – however ephemeral this awareness is, and whatever limited impact this necessity has.

What if compassion has become the most realistic means of generating such awareness? After all, images of Seena and of Shayan shifted, however fleetingly, public opinion in ways no rational argument could.

The insight that political issues are increasingly read in moral terms and that compassion has the capacity to trump politics makes the kind of critique performed by Didier Fassin all the more important. There is nothing wrong with feeling compassionate towards a suffering child, of course, particularly if the arousal of compassion is then channelled towards changing the policies that make such suffering possible in the first place. But that is neither to say that compassion on its own is the most appropriate response, nor to condone its implications. Studies like this, empirically grounded, theoretically informed and open to surprises born of relentless curiosity, demonstrate the value of scholarship that is truly critical – even if it's critical of something as 'morally untouchable' as the humanitarian reason dissected in Fassin's book.

TWO SUBURBS, 167 LIVES: HOW THE LIFE CHANCES STUDY TURNED TWENTY-ONE

MELISSA SWEET

8 October 2012

Jennifer sits poised on the edge of a large leather armchair, one of several plush lounges decorating the expansive lobby of the high-rise building where she works in Melbourne's CBD. She is composed and smartly dressed. If she's nervous about sharing the intimate details of her life with a stranger, she shows no sign of it.

She speaks quietly and surely, describing the ups and downs that have shaped her first twenty-one years, and her ambitions to move up the ladder at the call centre where she has worked for the past three years. Eventually, she hopes to establish an IT business with her boyfriend.

'If you see your parents working hard and struggling when you're growing up, it helps you realise that you do need to work hard to support yourself,' Jennifer says. 'That's why I'm the way I am. I've been financially independent since I was fifteen and I started working. I've never asked my parents for money since then. A lot of my friends don't understand that I've always wanted to work and support myself.'

Some young people might have been derailed by the events that life has already thrown Jennifer's way – her father's bankruptcy when she was a young girl, the separation of her parents, the tough times her mother had bringing up five children. But Jennifer sees her early experiences in a largely positive light, recognising that they contributed to her independence and maturity.

She stresses that many contemporaries have known worse, and cites the Life Chances study, a research project tracking the experiences of children born in inner Melbourne during a six-month period in 1990. The study began with the mothers of 167 babies, and the most recent findings – just released by the Brotherhood of St Laurence, or BSL – paint a rich and complex portrait of the study's 'babies' at age twenty-one.

The findings may not be representative of wider Australia – the subjects were sourced from two suburbs that are unusual in having high concentrations of both low-income and high-income earners – but they provide a fascinating study in contrasts. They illuminate the differences, and some similarities, between subjects whose parents are refugees, unskilled workers, or unemployed, and those whose parents are doctors, academics and other well-to-do professionals. (The researchers ask that the suburbs not be named to protect the privacy of their subjects, given the large amount of personal detail revealed in the study's reports.)

Tim Gilley, who helped establish the study but now works in education research and teaching at the University of Melbourne, says the contrast between the study's subjects is what makes the findings so powerful. 'It raises the question, if something is good for these [wealthy] children, why isn't it available for all children?'

While many families have been on the move over the years – only one-fifth still live in the suburbs where the study began – there has been less social and economic mobility. About half are in the same income bracket as they were at the start of the study, 37 per cent have improved their position, and 14 per cent are now worse off financially.

One reason Jennifer has been such an avid reader of the study's findings is that they record something of her own family's history. She began to take an interest from when she was about twelve, and says its reports have made her conscious of the positives in her life. 'They showed us what other people had been through. Some people have lost their parents, some are homeless,' she says. 'That made me appreciate the fact that I do have a family and a house; that even though we don't have the money, we still do have some things.'

The importance of growing up in a close-knit family is a recurring theme for Jennifer, who says, 'I definitely want my own family like that.' She puts more emphasis on family and relationships than material success, and says the earthquakes in Japan and New Zealand, and the 11 September 2001 attacks on the United States have had a lasting impact. 'Those made me aware of what can happen and to expect the unexpected – so to appreciate the time you do have with people that you care about.'

Jennifer acknowledges, however, that responsibility to family can have a downside. She and her siblings help support their mother financially, and 'It does feel like a burden sometimes,' she says. 'I do think, we're the children, she should be taking care of us, but we have all found our own jobs, so we're supposed to give something back to her.'

As well as helping pay her mother's debts, Jennifer is repaying a $35,000 debt incurred when she was eighteen and crashed a hire car. No one was hurt, but the accident changed the course of her life.

Only afterwards did she realise she hadn't been insured to drive the car. She gave up university to get a job to repay the debt, and says she probably would have stayed at university if not for the crash.

But the accident was her fault, she says, and she has no regrets: 'The car accident was a big part of me growing up. It's helped me gain a lot of responsibility; it was a bad situation but there was a positive outcome out of it.' One of the only regrets that Jennifer expresses during our conversation is that she didn't spend more time with her grandparents in the United States before they died. 'When I was younger,' she says, 'I didn't realise how important it would be to go and visit them.'

It's impossible not to be impressed by Jennifer, especially for those of us who don't find anyone nearly so thoughtful or mature when we look back to ourselves at her age. But is she typical of twenty-one-year-old Australians?

A clear message from the study is that searching for stereotypes about young people is foolish. Their lives are diverse, and not always predictable from their early circumstances. The 123 young people (out of the original 167) whose experiences help inform the latest Life Chances report don't even agree on whether, at age twenty-one, they are grown-up. Only 38 per cent said they would describe themselves as adults; 13 per cent said they were not yet adults and 49 per cent answered 'yes and no'.

Tellingly, there are marked differences according to their backgrounds. Those from well-to-do families are far less likely to consider themselves as adults, compared with those from lower-income and middle-income families. They are also far more likely to be living at home. Eighty per cent of those from well-to-do families receive financial help from their parents, compared with 20 per cent of those from low-income families. Those from families in which English was not the first language are also far less likely to receive financial help from their parents.

While most twenty-one-year-olds are studying or working, some already show the mark of poor health. Fourteen per cent said they had long-term health problems or a disability (anxiety and depression being the most common conditions mentioned), with almost one in five saying they had experienced mental health problems during the year they turned twenty-one. Four people – all of whom had grown up in low-income, single-parent families that had experienced multiple forms of disadvantage – had taken on the role of caring for their own parents. Of the 123 young adults, five are now parents themselves.

•

In retrospect, 1990 was quite a year. The Cold War was thawing; Germany was reunifying; Soviet leader Mikhail Gorbachev was awarded the Nobel Peace Prize. Iraq invaded Kuwait and Nelson Mandela was released from prison. It was also the year when poverty was to have been banished from the lives of Australian children – if Bob Hawke's (later regretted) 1987 election promise had been kept.

But often, the significance of historical events only becomes apparent with the passage of time. The young people born in 1990 tend to see their present circumstances as the result of their own choices, without necessarily recognising the impact of wider events or forces, whether it's a tight housing supply, changing demographics, economic crunches or world events. It is only towards the end of our conversation that Jennifer mentions that her parents are Chinese and came to Australia from Vietnam thirteen years before she was born. When I enquire further, she is vague about whether they were refugees, but then says they were. She doesn't know a lot about their history, she explains. 'They don't really talk about it much,' she says. 'They don't want us to live off their life experiences. They want us to live off our own.'

But the study's reports make it clear that the individual stories – like the factory worker whose job loss sent his family into a downwards spiral and the young people who struggle with part-time, insecure jobs – are also shaped by wider narratives, such as changes in the economy and the labour market. While the study write-up describes how 'structural inequalities of income, ethnicity and gender' influence young people's experiences, most of the study's subjects are quite positive about their early lives, often seeing good in what might be judged as hard times.

Whether they grew up rich or poor, most say their family's economic situation did not affect them. Even those who do recognise an impact tend to see it in a positive light – for example, that it taught them to be independent or to manage money. The researchers see this as reflecting 'both the need to put a good face on one's life story and the optimism of young people starting their lives as increasingly independent adults'.

Nonetheless, the study findings make it clear that financial constraints have had a very real impact, particularly on the children's access to education and healthcare. Parents from all income groups valued education, but the costs of a supposedly free public school system imposed hardship on many, reducing their capacity to support their children's education. By age eighteen, a quarter of children from low-income families had left school early, but none from high-income families had done so. As a previous report from the BSL puts it, 'the education system in many ways serves to maintain social divisions across the generations' – an observation that is particularly pertinent given recent state government education funding cuts.

Some children from poorer backgrounds did very well at school. 'This raises the challenge of predicting early school leaving from early indicators, and of finding ways to acknowledge both the impact of disadvantage and the resilience of young people in a way that avoids unhelpful stereotypes,' write the researchers:

> Our findings suggest the importance of all schools being well resourced to provide extra support at all ages for students with language and learning difficulties, but also to provide a context which does not label certain groups as low performers. The young people experienced very different learning environments, not only in government and non-government sectors, but also in differently resourced government schools.

According to Michael Horn, a senior manager in the BSL's research and policy centre, one of the study's important messages is the need for Gonski-style reforms to direct more resources towards the most needy children, particularly those from the 5 per cent of families experiencing multiple layers of disadvantage:

> For the foundational issues like education, adequate income, affordable housing, these foundational building blocks need to be addressed with strong universal services, which we currently don't have. You also need to target, ideally in an early intervention way, those students experiencing disadvantage beyond the school gate. We need to do more to prevent that group of kids who struggle from dropping out of school.

Alan Hayes, director of the Australian Institute of Family Studies, has taken a close interest in the Life Chances findings over the years – not least because he also has a child born in 1990. While it may not be as large or representative as other longitudinal studies, he says its in-depth interviews provide rich insights into the diversity of children's lives, and the unpredictability of their pathways through childhood and into adulthood:

What gives me heart out of the Life Chances study is that some of the children who looked most compromised have remarkable capacities to recover, and part of that resilience comes from those around them and the opportunities they are given. Today we can be a bit precious about the capacity of children to adapt and recover.

Hayes says the findings also reinforce the importance of providing better support to children and families at all stages of development, particularly the middle childhood and the critical years of ten to fifteen, and not only during early childhood. 'That's what Life Chances and other studies show you – how there are many important windows along the way where things can be changed for good or for ill.'

Hayes cautions against placing too much emphasis on the Jesuit maxim about the enduring influence of the first seven years of life – and warns against labelling children if they've had a tough start. 'Sometimes, it can become a self-fulfilling prophecy in a dangerous way if we change the way we interact with these kids,' he says.

•

Back in the late 1980s, when they were lobbying for support for the Life Chances study, the far-sighted researchers hosted screenings of the famous *Seven Up!* documentary series, which has followed a small group of British children since they turned seven in 1964.

Now, some of the Life Chances children feature in an educational DVD that captures glimpses of them at ages thirteen and eighteen. While there are funny moments – as when thirteen-year-old Bernard says, 'I don't really look forward to going to school but it's better than going to the dentist' – the main impression it leaves is a sadness that some children miss out on so many of the chances available to others.

Even so, money can't solve every problem. William may enjoy every opportunity available to a privileged white boy, but at thirteen it's clear in the documentary that he just wanted more time with his father. He says, poignantly, 'Money isn't the most important thing in life and I realise we are really lucky because we've got quite a lot of it. I'd rather have not as much money and spend a lot more time with my dad.' William's father, meanwhile, tells us that he never wanted to be like his own father, working long hours, but adds, 'I don't see much of my own children at all.'

Five years later, the concern still weighs on William as he considers whether to study medicine and follow in his father's footsteps. 'I have always just thought that I don't want to work as hard as Dad does,' he says. 'He works very hard to afford the lifestyle that we keep but it comes at a cost of not seeing him as much, but it also has its benefits, we have the opportunity to give back to the community.'

The film also introduces us to the musically talented Oscar, who shows impressive motivation despite a series of seemingly insurmountable obstacles – on top of having no job, no transport and no significant qualifications, he is socially and geographically isolated. He seems determined to create a future, however, and is set on getting a driver's licence so he can find an apprenticeship.

I watch the film with a friend, Daniel Clements, who has worked with disadvantaged youth for many years. He is impressed by how it lets us hear the voices of the young people (something that the study's reports suggest agencies like Centrelink and schools often fail to do). 'The natural strength of the kids' voices comes out,' says Daniel, 'from the anxieties to the optimism.'

That contrast also strikes Janet Taylor, a researcher on the project since its conception. She says that twenty-one is an age of both anxiety and anticipation, citing one man who spoke of the 'quarter-life crisis' but also saw the twenties as 'the golden years'. Taylor says many young people worry about studies and job opportunities, and that their lives are completely different from when she was their age. 'When I went to uni, there was definitely a job at the end, or at the end of school,' she says. The years do not seem to have dimmed Taylor's passion for her work. When we meet one morning in a cafe near her office in Fitzroy, her gestures are intense and her eyes alight as she describes the families whose stories she has come to know so well, and what might help improve their lives.

She says that there needs to be a rethinking of policies built on the assumption that young people follow a linear transition from school to higher education or training to employment. These days, for many, the journey is more one of stops, starts and backward steps.

While Taylor is delighted by the resilience of some of the young people, she worries about others, including those young men who left school early with learning and/or behaviour problems and possible mental health issues, don't seem to have found a niche in life, and have not been engaged in any meaningful way by support services.

'The government's "earn or learn" policy does not seem to usefully reach these young men,' she says:

I also have concerns about the isolation of a couple of the young mothers in public housing who don't feel they have friends. And while here I am talking about a few individuals, we know that there will be a much larger number of young people in the wider community facing similar issues.

Taylor nominates housing and the need for youth-friendly mental health services as two other critical areas requiring more policy attention.

Tim Gilley also stresses the importance of housing policy to wider societal well-being. 'If housing wasn't so expensive, people would have more resources,' he says. 'Housing has an enormous, distorting effect on where people live, go to work, on quality of life and stresses that affect children.'

Any number of reports and inquiries have shown the impact of disadvantage on health and well-being. Recent examples include an Australian Council of Trade Unions inquiry into insecure work; a report from the Australian Social Inclusion Board, which revealed that 33 per cent of Australians in the lowest income group experience fair or poor health, compared with 6.5 per cent of those in the highest income group; and a report from the Council of Australian Governments Reform Council showing significant inequities in both health outcomes and access to health services.

What Life Chances adds to statistics like these is the power of storytelling, says Taylor. She and her colleague Malita Allan hope the study will focus more attention on the often untold stories of those experiencing hardship. Says Allan: 'I do think the story of these kids growing up, missing out on school excursions, textbooks etc., just goes unnoticed.' Taylor agrees. 'By trying to tell some of the young people's stories and the families' stories from their perspective,' she says, 'we hope to give people in our wider society more understanding of what some members of the society are going through.'

•

When the latest Life Chances survey arrived at Lucienne's family home, her mother wasn't keen to continue sharing the family's details. But Lucienne insisted she complete the form. 'I was like, "You have to do it,"' she says. 'It's extremely important because I'm studying psychology and I really believe in the benefits of longitudinal studies.'

Lucienne, who is thoughtful and articulate, has had plenty of life chances – both parents are professionals and she enjoys good relationships with them and her younger sister. Her parents have been very supportive, helping her financially when she moved out of home, and taking the family on many overseas trips.

Only after we've been talking for some time does it emerge that there was a time she hated school so much that she wanted to drop out. She was bullied and felt excluded, both at primary and at high school. 'I didn't fit in,' she says. 'I was kind of a ratty kid. I wanted to be a writer and a musician and didn't want to waste any more time studying.'

Her attitude changed towards the end of Year 8, when she started going out with a boy who was academically inclined. 'I needed to impress this guy so I decided I wanted to take school a bit more seriously,' she says. 'I don't even know if I would have graduated if I hadn't have met him.' Eight years later, the pair are saving so they can travel overseas when uni is finished.

Looking back, Lucienne feels her difficult times at school led to her interest in psychology, and, if she could go back in time, she would reassure her fifteen-year-old self that 'life gets better'. 'I think I wanted to be the school counsellor,' she says, 'and sit in that room and talk to me and say it's going to be better when you get to uni.'

Back in the high-rise lobby, Jennifer's childhood experiences seem worlds away from Lucienne's. But she also had to deal with tough times at school – suffering exclusion because of her Chinese appearance. 'It definitely made me feel left out,' she says. It was a relief to leave school and find less discrimination in the workplace.

While Jennifer stresses that she doesn't let racism bother her, it clearly has had an impact. 'Even though people try to overlook it and say Australia is multicultural, in truth there are a lot of racist people and it's hard, it's really hard,' she says. 'I've grown up here my whole life … Some people treat me very poorly because they don't think I belong here.' When I ask her what she would like to see flow from the study, Jennifer says a greater acceptance and understanding of diversity, and a 'society that helps everyone'.

What Jennifer has learned in her first twenty-one years is, to some extent, what the researchers have learned from the study at this landmark stage in its history. 'It's about what sort of society do we want to live in?' says Janet Taylor. 'As a society, how can we give all our kids every opportunity?'

THE REMARKABLE PERSISTENCE OF POWER AND PRIVILEGE

ANDREW LEIGH

18 April 2014

If you want to know who made up Australia's elite in the nineteenth century, a useful place to look is the *Australian Dictionary of Biography*. In its many volumes, you'll find the business leaders, scientists, media barons and politicians who featured among the upper echelons of Australian society.

Now, suppose we take the first cohort of significant Australians – those who died before 1880 – and identify those with unusual surnames like Ebden or Maconochie. People with those names were over-represented among the elite in the nineteenth century. Are they still at the top of society, or are they mixed through?

The answer to this question will depend on the level of social mobility we have in Australia. In a very mobile society, privilege dissipates quickly. Children of doctors become labourers, and children of cleaners become lawyers. 'Class-jumping' is the norm. Conversely, in an immobile society, we should expect to see privilege perpetuated across generations. If wealth can easily be passed down to one's children, if education is costly, and if jobs are based on old school ties rather than ability, then the same surnames will stay at the top across generations.

For Australia, it turns out that if we look at the register of modern-day medical practitioners, we find the privileged names of the nineteenth century over-represented by a factor of nearly three. In other words, if your ancestor was at the top of Australian society six generations ago, you are three times more likely than the average Australian to be a doctor today.

In *The Son Also Rises: Surnames and the History of Social Mobility*, economist Gregory Clark uses rare surnames to learn more about the extent to which societies are fluid or static. Take the case of Samuel Pepys (1633–1703), the famous diarist who was secretary of the English Admiralty. Pepys has been a rare name since it entered the ranks of the elite in the late 1400s. And yet in the past 500 years, Pepyses have attended Oxford or Cambridge university at a rate at least twenty times that of the general population. On average, those of them who've died over the past decade left wealth of at least five times the British average. Four of the eighteen living Pepyses are medical doctors. Only in a society with extremely low levels of social mobility would we expect a name to persist among the elites in this way.

Analysing mobility in medieval England, Clark finds that people with names derived from jobs (Cook, Butler, Thatcher and so on) were more likely to move upwards, while those with names that derive from towns (including Baskerville, Pakenham and Walton) tended to move downwards. And not much changed after the industrial revolution. Surnames of Oxbridge graduates in the early 1800s, for instance, are three times as common among British MPs in the late 1900s.

In the United States, tax return data for the top taxpayers was publicly reported in 1923–1924. Nearly a century later, people with the same surnames as those who featured on the list are three to four times as likely to be doctors or lawyers, while those with lower-status names are under-represented. People with the high-status surname Katz are twelve times as likely to be doctors or lawyers as those with the low-status surname Washington.

In Japan, samurai surnames date back to before the 1868 Meiji Restoration. Even today, they are over-represented at least fourfold among doctors, lawyers, professors and writers. In China, Qing surnames over-represented among the nineteenth-century elite are over-represented among today's corporate board chairs and government officials. In Chile, surnames over-represented among landowners in the 1850s are still over-represented among high-earning occupations.

Strikingly, Clark finds persistence even in Sweden, one of the world's most egalitarian societies. The 1600s and 1700s saw the creation of a set of 'noble surnames', which today have twice their expected share of doctors, five times their expected share of lawyers and three times their share of members of the top 1 per cent of income earners. This degree of persistence of status across ten generations demonstrates the power of inherited privilege.

•

Gregory Clark's analysis of intergenerational mobility signals a marked shift in the way economists think about social mobility. In his 1988 presidential address to the American Economic Association, Gary Becker argued that 'earnings are not strongly transmitted from fathers to sons'. Four years later, Gary Solon showed that prior researchers had been overestimating the degree of social mobility because they were using just a single year of data.

To see how this happens, imagine a high-earning barrister who happens to take six months off work in the year of the survey. Now suppose his son becomes a high-earning barrister too. A study that used just one year of data might wrongly assume that this was a case of someone moving from rags to riches. But a study that used several years of data would see that both father and son were well-off.

At this point, I need to introduce a few numbers. The standard measure of mobility across generations is the 'elasticity' of children's earnings with respect to their parents' earnings – in other words, how closely the former reflects the latter. Because women have tended to have much lower rates of paid work, researchers have focused on the father–son earnings elasticity. An elasticity of zero means there was no relationship between the earnings of fathers and sons, while an elasticity of one would mean that a 10 per cent rise in fathers' earnings was associated with a 10 per cent rise in sons' earnings. The closer the elasticity gets to one, the less mobile the society.

Elasticity measures aren't confined to income. The elasticity of height, for example, is about 0.5, which means that if a father is ten centimetres taller than average, then we expect his sons to be five centimetres taller than average. Sure, there are tall fathers with short sons (and vice versa), but basketball dads are generally taller than gymnast dads.

In the case of earnings, economists' best estimate of intergenerational elasticity went from 0.2 when they used a single year of earnings (as did the studies Gary Becker was relying on) to 0.4 when they used a few years of earnings (Gary Solon's approach). Over the next decade, US researchers threw better and better data at the problem, and each time they found less and less mobility. Using more than a decade of earnings data, Bhashkar Mazumder estimated in 2005 that the intergenerational earnings elasticity for the United States was 0.6. That would put it higher than the father–son height elasticity. Among American sons, fathers had a larger impact on their earnings than on their stature.

Using similar techniques, researchers began estimating father-son earnings elasticities for other countries. As one survey showed, Scandinavian nations tended to be extremely mobile, with elasticities below 0.2. In Latin America, there was much less class-jumping, with elasticities over 0.5. Compared with other nations, the United States is extremely immobile, a fact that Barack Obama has thankfully switched from denying ('In no other country on earth is my story even possible') to decrying ('It is harder today for a child born here in America to improve her station in life than it is for children in most of our wealthy allies').

In 2006, while I was working as an economist at the Australian National University, I produced the first (and so far, only) estimates of the father–son earnings elasticity in Australia, putting the intergenerational elasticity at around 0.25. This means that a 10 per cent increase in a father's earnings translates to a 2.5 per cent increase in his son's earnings. My estimate implied that we are more socially mobile than the United States but not as mobile as Scandinavia. Looking back through the twentieth century, I found no evidence that we had become markedly more, or less, mobile.

So what does the surname approach add to our understanding of mobility? Simply put, there are two reasons for using surnames. The first is that we only have good data on earnings (from surveys or administrative records) for the relatively recent past. If we want to understand mobility in centuries gone by, surnames may be the best torch for seeing into an otherwise dark statistical corner.

The second, and more important, reason for using surnames is that they may help to take out some of the transitory fluctuations. Recall how we got more precise estimates of the intergenerational earnings elasticity when we used data that smoothed out the fluctuations in an individual's earnings over a career? Call it the 'odd year' problem. Now let's think about a different problem: a family where the social status dips down for one generation, before reverting to the long-run average. You might call this the 'black sheep' problem. By looking at surnames, we are able to look not just at single father–son pairs, but also at patterns for entire lineages.

So, once we take out the odd years and black sheep, how easy is it to jump between classes? Several assumptions need to be made in order to estimate an intergenerational elasticity from surnames. But if we accept Gregory Clark's methodology, his results imply a very static society. For Britain, the United States, India, Japan, Korea, China, Taiwan, Chile and even Sweden, he concludes that the intergenerational elasticity is between 0.7 and 0.9. This would mean that social status is at least as hereditable as height. It suggests that while the ruling class and the underclass are not permanent, they are extremely long-lasting. Erasing privilege takes not two or three generations, but ten to fifteen generations. If you cherish the notion of a society where anyone can make it, these results are disturbing.

How do we break the pattern? Part of the answer must lie in a fair tax system, a targeted social welfare system, effective early childhood programs and getting great teachers in front of disadvantaged classrooms. We need banks willing to take a chance on funding an outsider, and it doesn't hurt to maintain a healthy Aussie scepticism about inherited privilege.

Yet Gregory Clark's results also remind policymakers that this is no easy nut to crack. Part of the transmission of social status occurs through genes. On top of this, people tend to marry those with similar levels of education; and researchers have also documented significant differences in parenting approaches among different social groups. Making the system a bit fairer is within our reach – but a complete transformation may prove elusive.

'AUSTRALIA HAS BROUGHT OUT THINGS ABOUT MYSELF THAT I THOUGHT WOULDN'T EXIST'

PETER MARES

4 January 2016

When Camilla Pivato walked around Melbourne on her first day in Australia, she felt she was finally in the right place. 'I just fell in love with Australia and the Australian way of life,' she tells me by Skype from Rimini, on the Adriatic Coast. 'It's a really, really happy country and coming from Italy you can really feel the difference.'

After two years in Australia as a working backpacker, she was hoping to settle permanently. She had a job offer from an employer willing to sponsor her on a four-year 457 skilled worker visa and sought expert migration advice to assist with the application.[1] Thousands of dollars later, though, she was forced to leave Australia at short notice and was banned from coming back for three years.

Pivato was a twenty-nine-year-old costume designer, struggling to find steady work in her field, when she decided to take an extended break in Australia. Like more than 210,000 other young visitors in 2013–2014, she arrived on a working holiday visa. Under reciprocal agreements with nineteen countries, Australia allows travellers aged between eighteen and thirty to live and work here for up to a year, with the possibility of a second twelve-month visa if they undertake at least eighty-eight days of 'specified work' (in agriculture, forestry, fishing, mining or construction) in a regional area.

When Pivato arrived in March 2013 she intended to remain only until July, when her return flight was booked. But as the months ticked by, she postponed her departure. With the expiry of her first working holiday visa drawing closer, she decided to work for eighty-eight days to secure a second year's stay. She's far from alone in making that decision: since the option of a second visa was introduced ten years ago, the

---

1   In March 2018, the 457 skilled worker visa was abolished by the Australian government and replaced by the Temporary Skill Shortage (TSS) visa.

number of travellers taking it up has grown steadily, from fewer than 8000 in 2006–2007 to more than 45,000 in 2013–2014.[2]

Pivato took a job packing fruit in Shepparton in central Victoria – a town, as she puts it, with 'more cows than people'. At the start of the harvest season she was packing cherries, then peaches and plums, and at the end of summer, apples and pears. If not for the possibility of securing a second visa, she would never have considered doing this kind of work, let alone sharing accommodation and her private life with thirty other young women. 'I thought I was too old for that,' she says. She was surprised to find herself enjoying both the job and the lifestyle.

Other Italian visitors have had this experience too. 'I would never have imagined in my whole life that I would be working as a watermelon picker,' says a backpacker in *88 Giorni* (*88 Days*), a film documenting the experiences of young Italians working in Australian agriculture. In Italy, he says, harvesting watermelons would be 'discredited as a job that no one would do'. Harvest work is hot, dirty, difficult and poorly paid; in Italy, as in Australia, it is largely reserved for migrants. 'I now understand how foreign workers feel,' says another visa holder in the film. 'Here I am the immigrant.'

Like backpackers from other countries, some of the young Italians report being abused, exploited and underpaid. 'Mildura's farms are the worst thing that has ever happened in my life,' says Antonio in *88 Giorni*. A young woman remarks that if you work this hard, at least you should be treated with respect.

Yet if the interviews for *88 Giorni* are anything to go by, many young Italians find their work picking pumpkins or driving tractors enjoyable, in some cases even liberating. Some, like Camilla Pivato, who also features in *88 Giorni*, decide they want to settle here. 'Australia opens your horizons and makes you feel incredibly young,' she says in the film. 'Australia has brought out things about myself that I thought wouldn't exist, such as the ability to adapt that I thought I didn't have any more.'

•

Young Italians are not just helping to harvest produce in rural Australia, they are also staffing city restaurants and cafes. Postwar migrants who came to Australia in the 1950s and 1960s gave the Melbourne suburb of

---

2 Department of Immigration and Border Protection, *Working Holiday Maker Visa Programme Report* (ACT: Department of Home Affairs, June 2014).

Carlton its genuine Italian flavour. As the Italian community aged, though, the Lygon Street coffee strip risked becoming a caricature of its former self, its reputation hanging by a slender thread of marketing. But thanks to the latest wave of Italian migrants, Lygon Street is getting its zip back. When I ate lunch at a self-proclaimed *Gastronomia Italiana* in November, a waiter told me that all the stylish young staff in the establishment were recent Italian migrants. Some (I suspect most) are here on temporary visas; others have made the transition to permanent residence.

The same phenomenon is evident in Sydney. Over dinner in a chic new pizzeria in Walsh Bay, Michele (Mike) Grigoletti and his colleague Silvia Pianelli have fun guessing by their accents which regions of Italy the waiters hail from. Both Grigoletti and Pianelli settled in Australia relatively recently, and they devote much of their time to gathering data and stories from the new wave of Italian migration of which they are a part.

Grigoletti and Pianelli formed the independent study group Australia Solo Andata (Australia One Way), which has embarked on a research project called 'From Temporary to Permanent: The New Migration of Young Italians in Australia'. With sponsorship from the Fondazione Migrantes, the Italian Bishops' Conference's reference body on migration, they have published reports on migration issues as well as shooting and editing *88 Giorni*, which is due to be screened in Rome early this year.

Grigoletti links the surge in temporary migration to Australia to economic problems in Italy triggered by the global financial crisis, which left more than 40 per cent of under-twenty-five-year-olds unemployed. He points out that Italian backpackers are, on average, at the older end of the working holiday spectrum, and that many are highly qualified university graduates unable to find work in their chosen field. 'They tend to come when they are twenty-eight, twenty-nine or thirty,' he says. 'This shows that they are not taking a gap year, but come because they have given up. Their spirits have been crushed.'

This was Pianelli's experience. She had several unpaid internships after graduating from university but none that led to ongoing work. So she came to Australia on a temporary visa. 'I couldn't live in Italy any more,' she says. 'It is better to pick vegetables or do whatever basic job in Australia than to stay in Italy and be told you are too young and need to learn and not good enough to get a job.'

A recent report by the Migration Policy Institute supports this assessment. It says that southern European nations like Italy have 'in some ways returned to their earlier, more traditional roles, as significant countries of emigration'. The difference is 'that migrants today are younger, better educated, and more skilled than past waves, with a high proportion of professionals among those leaving'.[3]

•

When she arrived in Shepparton, Camilla Pivato was the only Italian in town, but after clocking up her eighty-eight days and securing her second visa, she decided to stay on. 'I didn't mind Shep at all,' she says. 'It's a simple life. Why not? It was much easier than living in Melbourne.' Pivato had previously spent four months working in a cafe in Moonee Ponds. 'It was fine but people were quite fussy about their coffee,' she says.

Life was also cheaper in Shepparton, enabling Pivato to save more towards the cost of a student visa. She was contemplating a degree in business management – a course that could put her on the path to permanent residency, something that neither fruit packing nor costume design was going to do.

The owners of the fruit packing business came up with an alternative. They offered to engage Pivato as the company's human resources co-ordinator and sponsor her for a four-year 457 temporary skilled work visa.

Pivato grabbed the opportunity and started work immediately. She travelled to Melbourne to help select workers and supervised all aspects of their employment in Shepparton. 'I would choose the girls, hire girls, fire girls, train them in the work in the packing shed, do quality control, look after their wages and collect the rent every Monday,' she says. (The business runs two on-site hostels for its workers.)

She was very happy with the arrangement. 'It was much easier than getting a student visa,' she says. 'Besides, I am thirty-one and I have already studied a lot.' She liked and trusted her employers – European migrants from an earlier generation – who she says were like family to her. But they didn't have much experience with sponsoring visa applicants, so, on the recommendation of a work colleague, she engaged registered migration agent Dennis Allan, owner of Prestige Migration Services in Melbourne, to help with the paperwork.

Pivato says that she first met with Allan in late January 2015, about six weeks before her second working holiday visa was due to expire, and that she signed the service agreement for him to prepare the 457 sponsorship and visa applications in his presence on 2 February 2015. She jumped

---

3   Demetrios G. Papademetriou, *Rethinking Emigration: Turning Challenges into Opportunities* (Washington, DC: Migration Policy Institute, 2015).

through the other required hoops, like passing an English language test, and paid Allan $8000 in fees. Then she returned to work in Shepparton and waited for a call to say her visa had been lodged.

No news came. Pivato says she called Prestige Migration Services repeatedly and was told not to worry. When the 19 March expiry date of her existing visa passed, she became more anxious, but she says Dennis Allan told her everything was in hand. When she repeatedly asked for a copy of her visa application, though, he gave a variety of reasons why that wasn't possible, including computer problems and alleged difficulties with the departmental website, or promised he would send the documentation the next day. Finally, on 7 May, an exasperated Pivato called the immigration department directly to clarify the status of her application. An officer told her that no documentation had been lodged in her name and that she was in Australia unlawfully. Pivato was told to report immediately to the department's Melbourne office, where she was given a four-week bridging visa and told to leave the country before 4 June.

When Pivato confronted Dennis Allan, she says he told her that it was 'just a little mistake' and tried to convince her to pay him even more money to sort it out. Pivato refused and demanded her $8000 back. In the weeks that remained to her, she turned up at Allan's office almost daily asking for her refund. 'He kept making up excuses,' she says. 'Like he shows me a receipt, telling me that he had transferred the money into my bank account, but could not explain why I did not receive it.'

Allan was not the only person who sought to take advantage of Pivato's desire to stay in Australia. One day, Pivato was pleading her case at the Department of Immigration and Border Protection in central Melbourne. The interaction left her distressed and tearful. At that moment a stranger approached and asked her what was going on. He then encouraged her to go outside, where he identified himself as a migration adviser and offered to lodge a partner visa on her behalf – for a fee of $12,000. Luckily, she didn't take the bait. She was in a relationship at the time, but not one that would have met the relevant criteria.

Besides, says lawyer Melinda Jackson, who represented her at the time, Pivato's application would have been rejected outright, because by the time she got in touch with the department she had already overstayed her visa by more than twenty-eight days.

'Her timing was unfortunate,' says Jackson. If Pivato had called within those twenty-eight days, immigration department staff may have been able to make allowances for her circumstances and enable her to submit the 457 application late. Once that time threshold had passed, however, she fell foul of 'public interest criteria 4014' of the migration regulations, which made it all but impossible for her to obtain any other visa onshore. What's more, the over-stay activated an automatic three-year ban on her returning to Australia on any other temporary visa.

The ban can only be waived if there are 'compelling circumstances' affecting Australia's interests, or 'compassionate or compelling circumstances' affecting the interests of an Australian citizen or permanent resident. In the eyes of immigration department officials, being ripped off or deliberately misled by a migration agent does not meet this test.

Jackson tried to argue that Pivato's case does affect Australia's interests, because it involves potential fraud committed by a migration agent working in an industry regulated by the federal government. But her closely argued twenty-page submission was rejected with a dismissive half-page response. An internal appeal to the delegate's manager also failed. After this, Pivato and her lawyer had nowhere left to turn.

'This is administrative decision-making with no recourse to the courts,' says Jackson. 'You get arbitrary, terrible decisions and can't do anything about it.' There is not even the possibility of intervention by the immigration minister, because ministerial discretion can only be triggered by the decision of a court or tribunal.

•

When I was growing up just outside Adelaide in the 1960s and 1970s, I would sometimes meet my father for lunch in the city. After the meal he would invariably take me to a small Italian cafe in the ornate Adelaide Arcade, where he would order a short black and I would have a cappuccino. In those days it was one of the rare places equipped with an espresso machine. If we went out in the city in the evening, my father might indulge me with *tartufo* or *cassata* from the Flash Gelati Bar in Hindley Street. Gelato and espresso were novelties – a gift to the tastebuds of Adelaide courtesy of the postwar wave of Italian migrants.

In the years between 1947 and 1954, Australia's Italian-born population more than tripled in size. It doubled again between 1954 and 1961 and continued to grow for several more years, peaking at around 290,000 people in the 1971 census. For at least thirty years, the Italian-born were second only to the British as the largest overseas-born group in Australia.[4]

---

4   Janet Phillips, Michael Klapdoor and Joanne Simon-Davies, *Migration to Australia: A Guide to the Statistics*, Parliamentary Library (ACT: Department of Parliamentary Services, 2010).

When Mike Grigoletti tells me that the scale of *temporary* Italian migration to Australia today rivals the permanent migration that changed the flavours of my Adelaide childhood, I am surprised. But when I do my own calculations, I find the numbers bear him out, although the time frame to date is far shorter, and it remains to be seen if the trend will continue.

Over the two and a half decades from 1947, Australia's Italian-born population increased by an average of about 11,000 people per year; during the peak period between 1954 and 1961, that number was 15,000. By comparison, around 13,000 young Italians have come to Australia as first-time working holiday-makers annually since 2012.[5] A few thousand more have been granted temporary visas as international students[6] or skilled workers.[7] And the data suggests that, like Camilla Pivato, a significant proportion of these young Italians will extend their stay or settle – if they can.

•

Pivato's lawyer, Melinda Jackson, helped her to lodge a complaint against Dennis Allan with the Office of the Migration Agents Registration Authority, or OMARA, the immigration department's division responsible for regulating professional standards and integrity in the migration advice industry. Six months later, the only evidence of progress on Pivato's complaint is a letter from OMARA informing her that the regulator would 'shortly be sending a notice to Mr Allan under Part 3 of the *Migration Act 1958 (Cwlth)* and giving him the option of making a submission in response to the notice'.

Jackson suspects that Pivato isn't alone, and that Allan has been 'doing similar things to people in similar circumstances'. She believes it is quite possible that OMARA is compiling a set of complaints against the agent before proceeding. (When I attempted to confirm this, I was told that the *Privacy Act 1988 (Cwlth)* prevented OMARA from disclosing whether

---

5 Department of Immigration and Border Protection, *Working Holiday Maker Visa Programme Report* (ACT: Department of Home Affairs, June 2014).

6 Department of Immigration and Border Protection, *Student Visa and Temporary Graduate Visa Programme Quarterly Report* (ACT: Department of Home Affairs, June 2014).

7 Department of Immigration and Border Protection, *Subclass 457 Quarterly Report* (ACT: Department of Home Affairs, June 2014).

a complaint has been made about a migration agent because this is 'personal information'.)

But even if OMARA upholds a complaint against Allan, it will be largely symbolic. The regulator can't cancel Allan's registration as a migration agent because that lapsed on 9 March 2015, ten days before Pivato's visa expired. The best OMARA can do is bar Allan from *re-registering* as a migration agent.

'It's a pretty feeble complaints investigative body,' says Jackson. OMARA cannot even get Pivato's money back from Allan. In its letter to Pivato, OMARA noted that 'the Authority can recommend a refund, but we cannot order it'. For that, Pivato must take civil action before the courts.

With the help of Melinda Jackson, Pivato tried to go down this route too, and on 4 September 2015, the Victorian Civil and Administrative Tribunal, or VCAT, ordered Allan's firm, Prestige Migration Services, to pay Pivato 'the sum of $8000'. Her chances of ever seeing this money are remote.

'The order itself can't do anything,' says Jackson. 'In any civil process, enforcement becomes the question.' The next step would be to launch proceedings in the Magistrates' Court to enforce the VCAT order. But this would require Pivato to be present in Australia.

Even if Pivato were able to return to Melbourne to commence court proceedings, tracking Allan down and serving him with court papers could be a challenge. Allan did not turn up to the VCAT hearing, and the Australian Securities and Investment Commission, ASIC, has since given notice that it is proposing to deregister his company.

An online search for Prestige Migration Services threw up two different business addresses and two different phone numbers, both of which had been disconnected. My calls to the mobile number listed on the company website went unanswered.

I did, however, get a response to my attempt to contact Dennis Allan via the company's online contact form. A woman called Pauline called me back and, when I explained my inquiry, she told me that Allan was 'not really working at the moment'. She said she would pass on my contact details when he came back. When I asked if Prestige Migration Services was still a going concern, she said it was, and that the threat of deregistration by ASIC was 'being sorted out by the accountant'. She confirmed that Dennis Allan's registration as a migration agent had lapsed and told me that other registered migration agents were now handling the firm's work. My follow-up calls and emails seeking comment from Allan himself did not elicit any response.

With two and a half years of her ban on returning to Australia remaining, Pivato is finding it hard to live back in Italy. She feels stuck, as if her future is on hold. She misses her job, her friends, even the smells of Shepparton. 'It is hard to live anywhere else after Australia,' she tells me. 'Australia is just so organised and clean and fair.' Then she pauses and reconsiders. 'Well, I thought it was fair, but I don't think that anymore.'

If anyone has broken the rules, it is her migration agent. 'All I have done, every single paper I have signed and money I have paid is legal,' she says. 'But fine, the real criminal is me, and I have been punished.'

Despite her setbacks and disappointments, Pivato is determined to return. 'It's time to settle down for me,' she says. She has embarked on a master's degree in Italian language teaching in the hope that this will give her a qualification that is in demand here. She is even planning to do her final six-month placement in New Zealand in order to be one step closer to returning when her ban expires.

'I can't help it,' she says. 'I miss Australia a lot. My life is there.'

After this article was published in Inside Story, other victims of Dennis Allan's poor migration advice got in touch with Peter Mares, and he followed up the issues for Radio National's Law Report in July 2016. Seven clients of Dennis Allan, including Camilla Pivato, lodged complaints about the migration agent with OMARA, the Office of the Migration Agents Registration Authority. OMARA eventually upheld all seven complaints, finding that Dennis Allan had been 'dishonest and reckless' and had 'systematically' taken payments for 'work that he did not do'. OMARA banned Dennis Allan from registering as a migration agent for five years, the stiffest penalty available.

IN THE NAME OF THE PEOPLE

RODNEY TIFFEN

27 April 2017

Republican candidate Donald Trump and Democratic aspirant Bernie Sanders have both been labelled populists. So have the left-wing Occupy Wall Street movement and the right-wing Tea Party, along with Marine Le Pen, Geert Wilders and an array of other far-right European party leaders. So too was Venezuela's left-wing president, Hugo Chávez, as well as heads of government as different as Hungary's Viktor Orbán, Turkey's Recep Tayyip Erdoğan and the Philippines's Rodrigo Duterte.

That list tells us two things: there's a lot of it about, and it seems to cover an astonishingly wide variety of leaders and movements.

In political commentary, populist is often a derogatory term, excusing the writer from giving a person or a party any serious consideration. It is popular at *The Australian*, where it has been used to criticise Labor's calls for a royal commission into banking and its opposition to tax cuts for big business. When the Gillard government called a royal commission into institutional sex abuse in 2012, the headline on Paul Kelly's column called it a 'Depressing Example of Populist Politics'.

While 'populist' comes from the same root as 'popular', it elicits a very different value judgement: popular good; populist bad. But how are the two linked? Isn't all democratic politics populist? Isn't being responsive to public concerns and outlooks a democratic virtue? Passing judgement by calling something populist – even when it's an accurate description, unlike Kelly's headline – is no substitute for explaining it.

Part of the problem lies in the concept itself. Populism cuts across the usual ideological constructs of left and right, which rest on different views about the role of the market and government. Populism is anti-market, especially in its hostility to free trade, transnational corporations and 'money power'. In American parlance, it is pro–Main Street and anti Wall Street.

In the past, populist movements were often agrarian, attracting farmers whose struggles against the vagaries of the seasons were compounded by the fickleness of the market. They felt entitled to a fair price for the labour they had invested in the production process, and resented the seeming arbitrariness of broader economic forces. Reflecting these contending pressures, populism often seems to support government intervention – explicitly or implicitly – yet resents bureaucratic interference and red tape, and views welfare recipients with suspicion.

Populism may be a useful concept for explaining the activities of economically nationalist governments in the Third World, or the appeals that dictators use to extend their powers in countries with fragile democratic institutions. But it is not always helpful to think that everything labelled populist is sufficiently similar to come under one umbrella. Here, I'll focus on contemporary right-wing populist movements in economically advanced and politically stable democracies.

In practice, analysts generally reserve the term 'populist' for two types of conventional electoral politics. One involves politicians who try to pit a unified 'people' against outsiders – migrants, minority groups, terrorists and so on – using essentially symbolic gestures that demean or threaten outsiders, like the Turnbull government's toughening of the process for immigrants to become citizens.

The other brand of conventional populism is practised by politicians who pander to misconceptions among segments of the population or urge courses of action they know will be ineffective. Populists can be simultaneously in favour of increased government spending and lower taxes, for instance. A trivial example of this kind of populism was Kevin Rudd's promise during the 2007 election campaign to launch a website called Grocery Choice, which was designed to dramatise the fact that Labor shared the public's concern about cost-of-living pressures. The party no doubt knew that it would have little effect on prices, and, in the event, it was quietly dropped a year or so into government.

The sterility and cynicism of mainstream political debate in Australia is depressing in itself, and contributes to the growth of populism. But full-blown right-wing populism goes well beyond the frustrations of party politics by adopting four key elements.

THE IN-GROUP VERSUS THE OUT-GROUP

The central characteristic of all populism is the sharp division between us and them. As Jan-Werner Müller writes in his 2016 book, *What Is Populism?*, populism sets a morally pure and fully unified people against all others, whether they are elites, foreigners or other enemies of the people. The view that the people speak with a single voice makes populism anti-pluralist. If 'the people' have a common interest and outlook, then dissent can easily be portrayed as disloyalty or betrayal.

This leaves populist rhetoric with the problem of extracting 'real people' from the total sum of the citizenry. Nigel Farage, leader of the UK Independence Party, called the Brexit referendum a 'victory for real people', as if the 48 per cent who voted to remain were not real. Right-wing Republican populist Sarah Palin used to refer to the 'pro-America areas of this great nation'. The populist strand of the Republican Party called itself the Tea Party, after the Boston Tea Party incident of 1773, a pivotal moment in the build-up to the American War of Independence; yet the modern Tea Party is not pitted against British colonialists, but against its fellow Americans.

UPWARD, DOWNWARD AND OUTWARD RESENTMENT

The main animating force of populism is anger. Its proponents are determined to confront forces that threaten or betray 'the people'. Betrayal by the 'elites' – the perfidious and corrupt wielders of self-seeking power – is an ever-present motif.

Donald Trump encapsulated this theme in his inauguration speech:

> Today we are not merely transferring power from one administration to another ... We are transferring power from Washington, DC and giving it back to you, the people. For too long, a small group in our nation's capital has reaped the rewards of government while the people have borne the cost. Washington flourished but the people did not share in its wealth.

During the campaign he had argued that 'the establishment, the media, the special interests, the lobbyists, the donors, they're all against me. I'm self-funding my campaign. I don't owe anybody anything. I only owe it to the American people to do a great job.'

While disgust with elites is a recurring motif in populism, at least as important is hostility to outsiders, especially immigrants. In 1996, Pauline Hanson was primarily aggrieved by Aborigines and by the Asian migrants who were allegedly swamping Australia; by 2016, her primary target had shifted to Muslims. What remained constant was her need for an alien enemy. Among the elderly Britons and others who voted for Brexit, studies found that the common thread was hostility to immigration and the fear of even greater immigration to come.

In France and several other West European nations, similarly, immigration has been the major target for the populists, gaining momentum from the association of a small number of Muslim immigrants with terrorism. Immigrants are seen as a security threat, and are blamed for crime and economic difficulties: in a simple equation, a French National Front poster dating back to 1978 declared, 'Two million unemployed is two million immigrants too many!'

Less obvious than upward and outward resentment is downward resentment. Supporters of populism are not usually from the very poorest sectors of society, and while many populists support the welfare state, they are often also hostile to those they see as undeserving recipients, including unemployed people and refugees. Often, too, weaknesses in the welfare state are blamed on the usual targets, as when Marine Le Pen asserted in a 2015 campaign appearance that 'they are pulling out all the stops for the migrants, the illegals, but who is looking out for our retirees?'

Only in the United States is a more sweeping disapproval of the welfare state still apparent. 'You are not entitled to what I have earned,' declared one bumper sticker. Journalist Mark Danner quotes one Trump supporter describing himself as a member of 'the white working class in America. The ones paying for all the others. Finally we're getting someone who'll do something for us.'[8]

HOSTILITY TO DEBATE AND DEMOCRATIC PROCESSES

Populism transforms the complexities and ambiguities of the contemporary world into a search for enemies and culprits. This allows its proponents to argue that simple solutions championed by strong leaders are the answer. Their policy prescriptions are liberated from the real world of trade-off and compromise, of limited resources and unintended consequences, to the realm of simple solutions obvious to anyone with common sense. All that is needed is strong leadership; further debate is unnecessary, and simply a means of avoiding action.

Populists often use simple, strong slogans – 'Make America Great Again', or the pro-Brexit 'Take Back Control' – to avoiding discussing specifics or

---

8   Mark Danner, "The Real Trump," *New York Review of Books*, November 16, 2016. https://www.nybooks.com/articles/2016/12/22/the-real-trump/

to discredit critics. British Conservative minister and Brexiteer Michael Gove used the most sweeping dismissal: 'People in this country have had enough of experts.'

As Jan-Werner Müller argues, populism is inherently hostile to the mechanisms and values of constitutionalism. It is scornful of the need for checks and balances, of the protections and inhibitions that stem from due process. It often manifests an impatience with – and even a disdain and disgust for – proper procedures and conventions. The judges in Britain who ruled unanimously that Brexit could only proceed with parliamentary approval were labelled 'Enemies of the People' by the *Daily Mail*.

BAD MANNERS

In the most nuanced and comprehensive recent book on populism, *The Global Rise of Populism*, Benjamin Moffitt argues that we need to move from seeing populism as a particular set of policies, and view it more as a political style that thrives on crisis and confrontation. Populists have succeeded in shaping the public agenda and generating media attention, often by going outside or defying political conventions – by being provocative and aggressive and trying to generate a sense of crisis and scandal. Donald Trump was a 'chaos candidate', Jeb Bush complained, as the insurgent's tactics unbalanced other Republican contenders.

The political scientist Pippa Norris has observed that Trump and his allies introduced a new 'brutalism and intolerance, altering what's speakable in American politics'.[9] Populists nearly always resort to coarse and culturally vulgar appeals, says Moffitt, with many swearing and directing offensive taunts at opponents. (Marine Le Pen has accused political rivals of being paedophiles.) Their followers often see this coarseness as plain talking, which cuts through the suffocating inhibitions of political correctness to tell it like it really is. Offensiveness becomes proof of authenticity, says Moffitt; other politicians are seen as self-seeking and hypocritical. In Australia, as Moffitt reports, political scientist Sean Scalmer found people who saw Hanson as a 'dinkum stirrer' bringing views shared by many Australians into the public realm.

9   Pippa Norris, "It's Not Just Trump. Authoritarian Populism is Rising Across the West. Here's Why," *Washington Post*, March 11, 2016, https://www.washingtonpost.com/news/monkey-cage/wp/2016/03/11/its-not-just-trump-authoritarian-populism-is-rising-across-the-west-heres-why/.

It is often said that populism comes as a response to crisis. But populists have an interest in fomenting a sense of crisis, Moffitt argues. They need to show that politics as usual is failing – that the country is out of control and needs to change direction. This can be seen, for example, in Trump's use of false data to exaggerate the crime problem in the United States. Populists also seek to create an aura of drama around themselves, as was on bizarre display when Pauline Hanson made a video that included the words 'If you are seeing me now, it means I have been murdered ... You must fight on.'

•

So populism isn't just a case of more politics as usual. Nor is the answer to 'bad' populism 'good' populism. A left-wing Alan Jones isn't the answer; a political discourse that doesn't reward the Joneses is. The key – much more easily stated than achieved – is for political debate to become more grounded in the real options facing societies, and for clashes between parties to be disciplined by empirical realities.

Is populism the way of the future? Especially since the victories of Brexit and Trump, the seemingly irresistible rise of right-wing populism has been a running story in the media. This narrative downplays several counter-examples. Justin Trudeau won a smashing victory in Canada in 2015 on an economically progressive and culturally tolerant platform. In May last year, Londoners made Sadiq Khan their mayor, the first Muslim candidate, and the first person from an ethnic minority, to be elected. Earlier this year, Pauline Hanson's One Nation Party was expected to win 15 per cent of the vote in the WA election, but support fell to just over 8 per cent in the electorates her party chose to contest. In Austria last year, many expected to see the election of the country's first far-right president; in the event, the victor was a Green. And just last month, many Dutch voters were fearful that the party of the far-right Geert Wilders would sweep the country; on election day, it increased its vote slightly to win twenty of the 150 seats, fewer than it won in 2010, or that its forerunner won in 2002.

Yet both the Dutch and Austrian elections show a splintering of political support and significant disillusion with the established parties. In the Netherlands, the top three parties together won 85 per cent of the vote in 1986; but by 2017, the figure was just 45 per cent. In Austria, the most interesting aspect of the presidential election was the collapse of the centre. In the first round of the election, the two parties that have dominated postwar Austria and provided every president, the Social Democratic Party and the Austrian People's Party, each polled just 11 per cent of the vote, trailing not only the Freedom Party and the Greens, but also an independent. This splintering of loyalties brings a greater likelihood of legislative deadlock; mixed with increased polarisation, it is a recipe for continuing political frustration and more populism.

For these reasons, populism surges, but its support usually collapses eventually. Distaste for major parties, and for politics as usual, drives people to populist parties, rather than any intrinsic appeal of their own. Once these parties are under scrutiny, it becomes clear that they are usually unable to articulate or defend their policies. Much depends on the leader, the one who claims to embody the people's will: it is often his or her newsworthiness that thrust the movement into the media limelight.

Not only are their feet commonly made of clay, but they also often run their parties in an authoritarian manner and become prone to defections and internal discontent. Since Pauline Hanson's party returned to prominence last year, it has been plagued by disputes and disaffections. 'I've been in this for twenty years and to have a new kid on the block telling me what to do is absolutely ridiculous,' Hanson said during her contretemps with the soon-to-be-disqualified One Nation senator Rod Culleton.[10] In fact, far-right parties (like their mainly defunct left-wing counterparts) appear to have an inherent tendency to split.

What this all demonstrates is that right-wing populism is a far-from-irresistible force. History shows that its surges are often followed by collapses. Given the dysfunctions in current politics and ongoing economic stresses, though, it is likely to keep disfiguring democratic politics for some time, and to have a disproportionate influence on policy and public debate.

---

10   Henry Belot, "Pauline Hanson Says Rod Culleton 'Not a Team Player' for Voting Against Party on Backpacker Tax," *ABC Online*, December 6, 2016, http://www.abc.net.au/news/2016-12-06/pauline-hanson-launches-spray-at-rod-culleton/8095944.

HAS LIBERALISM FORGOTTEN WHAT IT DOES BEST?

ROB HOFFMAN

11 July 2017

'All under heaven is great chaos.' So observed Mao Zedong, with evident satisfaction, when the West was wracked by social upheavals in 1968. Half a century on, and three decades beyond Francis Fukuyama's 'end of history', Western democracy seems to have come to another crossroads. The psychodrama that is the Trump administration grips our attention; Britain's messy divorce from Europe continues along its uncertain path; upstart populists threaten the establishment across the globe, claiming to speak for a forgotten people cast aside by the diktats of modern liberalism.

Politics may offer an imperfect reflection of society, but there are unquestionably fundamental forces at play. Nearly ten years after the global financial crisis, inequality has persisted, if not deepened. Refugee populations continue to grow, straining our capacity to respond, or even to hold them at bay. Automation threatens the very nature of our economies, and with it the future of work. The climate continues to warm. The health of Western democracy has come into question, and with it the liberal philosophies that underpin our way of life.

Financial Times chief US columnist Edward Luce attempts to interpret all this in his concise but broad-ranging new book, *The Retreat of Western Liberalism*. Western democracies, he argues, are facing an existential crisis. The Brexit referendum and the Trump election are obvious indicators, but they reflect a broader trend. Imitators across Europe might have failed to match these successes, but that is almost beside the point. As Luce persuasively argues, the fact that anti-establishment politicians who would have been nonentities just ten years ago are capable of running a healthy second in major democracies is sign enough that times have changed.

More importantly, this new demagoguery is symptomatic of deeper structural tensions and represents an entirely rational backlash against establishment liberalism. Indeed, in one of the book's finer passages,

Luce argues against characterising those who vote in support of populist causes as anti-democratic, and he offers a stinging and well-deserved critique of those who do so.

Compounding these challenges are evolving global conditions that have brought the presumed dominance of liberalism into question. While recent United States administrations have been wilfully soiling liberalism's claims to global legitimacy through ill-planned and ill-fated Middle Eastern adventures, the centre of global economic power has been steadily shifting towards a decidedly illiberal but equally ill-understood China, and automation threatens to amplify the impact this is having on Western societies.

The capacity of our way of life and its political systems to survive this global shift in power is the question Luce says he is seeking to answer, though he also explores more fundamental questions about the nature of liberalism and liberal democracies. The crisis of liberalism, he argues, reflects a complacency and ignorance of history on the part of liberals, politicians of most stripes and voters themselves. Collectively, we have forgotten what made Western democracies a success in the first place, and with the end of easy economic growth – a historical oddity born of unique circumstances – we have perhaps lost the capacity to repeat it. In its place, an arrogance towards the have-nots of society has set in, dividing our societies at their moment of greatest vulnerability.

•

If there is one lesson we should learn from the history of liberalism, it is that sharing economic spoils does not come easily. Indeed, as Luce points out, liberalism's pretensions to universality have rarely been reflected in how societies actually function. Though he draws this thread right back to the 'year zero' of the *Magna Carta* – a short-lived document that enshrined the privileges of the aristocracy and restricted the rights of women and Jewish people – the modern history of liberalism is sufficient to demonstrate the point.

The great democratisations of the eighteenth and nineteenth centuries were inherently restrictive, with women, the unpropertied, Indigenous peoples and the enslaved excluded by design. Where the franchise expanded, it did so largely in response to a crisis. From the nascent organised labour movements of the nineteenth century, through the social demands of the world wars, to the women's suffrage movement and the postwar civil rights struggles, liberties were, as Aldous Huxley put it, taken rather than given.

These concessions reflect an innate strength of liberalism: the flexibility and capacity for reform that saw it outcompete and outlast its great twentieth-century rivals, fascism and Soviet communism. But it also means that the era of true liberal democracy has been far briefer than we might think. In most Western democracies, the franchise has only been truly universal for a century at most, and in many – including Australia's – for far less. That the Swiss, aspirants to the title of the world's oldest modern democracy, only guaranteed women the vote in 1970 says it all.

This flexibility is a function of the liberal state's reluctance to exert force against its own people. And so, when desperate times have called for desperate measures, the response has been to spread the benefits of the status quo more widely so that the stake in defending it is also shared. But the fact that this has generally occurred in response to crisis reflects the tension at the heart of liberalism and the liberal society.

Regardless of their origins, liberal societies have been a marked success. They have produced the greatest material prosperity enjoyed anywhere at any time (leaving aside unaccounted-for externalities). Despite an increasing preoccupation with security within the state and society, liberal principles do still remain the best defence against the arbitrary abuse of power, and liberalism is the societal model least likely to rely on the logic of secret police and concentration camps.

The legitimacy of liberal societies rests on their capacity to enhance the lives of their people on a broader level. Where this capacity is diminished, consciously or otherwise, so goes that strength. Indeed, the lesson we can draw from the past century is that while individual freedoms may be a necessary precondition for a healthy society, they are not a sufficient one. As Lucius D. Clay, US military governor of postwar West Germany, once wrote, there was little choice between becoming a communist on 1500 calories and a democrat on 1000.

Luce draws out much of this. He acknowledges the episodes during which privileges (the franchise, the welfare state, or the broader fruits of economic growth) were extended, and he recognises the relative health of those states that established and have retained the equalising structures of social democracy. He perceptively highlights the fundamental reality that has granted liberal societies this capacity, suggesting that while 'we are taught to think our democracies are held together by values' – a myth fuelled by our faith in history – 'liberal democracy's strongest glue is economic growth'.

•

Where Luce's argument about liberalism runs into trouble is in his failure to satisfactorily explain why privileges were extended to growing numbers of citizens, and why our societies no longer engage in that process to the same degree. This is the fundamental question posed by the problems he discusses: liberalism has shown a capacity to reform in the past, so why not lately, and why not in response to the present crisis?

However, Luce's emphasis on the perils of the automation of our economies is warranted. He also makes a persuasive argument that these perils will affect China and India just as much as they do Western democracies, though he doesn't fully explore the underlying forces. Any society is ultimately dependent for its legitimacy on its capacity to make the lives of its members better – or, at least, not worse. This is the true lesson of the age of easy growth, and of its end.

While Luce's observations are often perceptive, the most cogent and coherent sections of *The Retreat of Western Liberalism* are those in which he discusses other observers' ideas. Between these diversions, he tends to skip across the challenges facing our democracies without demonstrating underlying connections, adding articulations of his contentions seemingly as afterthoughts. This rapid-fire argument becomes disconnected, at times contradictory and ultimately half-formed.

And when he moves into contemporary politics and the possibilities for the future, the analytical power of the book softens markedly. While the myopic Clinton campaign is an apposite example of the elite arrogance that has fostered and then ignored anti-establishment revolts, Luce's explanations here, too, fall short. Framing 'identity politics' and immigration as fundamental problems, he fails to explore the history of either.

Identity politics has its root in those groups who remained excluded from society even at what might be called the time of peak equality for the broader mass of people. The fact that sections of liberal societies have needed to engage in collective action to formally attain the rights that liberalism theoretically already guaranteed to all individuals highlights the nature of the system. Curiously, Luce doesn't look at how that history can help us understand the white working-class anxiety and millennial resignation that has fed the present climate.

Like Australia, the United States is a settler society, a nation built on the back of successive waves of mass migration. That a stable society could be fashioned in such circumstances demonstrates liberalism's capacity to reconcile divided societies when circumstances demand – and permit. That identity politics and immigration are now points of contention around which populist movements rally, ironically often through a competing identity politics of their own, says little about the innate nature of either impulse. Rather, Luce again poses the question of what has changed, and why, but then leaves it unanswered.

Not surprisingly, Donald Trump figures largely in the second half of the book. Luce clearly demonstrates Trump's inability to resolve these tensions (and, indeed, the likelihood he will heighten them) but offers little on the ends we might pursue instead. As he argues, Trump is merely a symptom of a far deeper malaise, and as likely to be replaced by someone worse as someone better. Yet, in framing the president as a function of a disenchanted, reality television culture, Luce abandons his previous arguments, and to his own disservice. Neoliberalism offers no shortage of distraction and, if anything, Trump is living proof of the inherent limitations of bread and circuses. Without a deeper and more systematic analysis of his causes, the prescribed treatments are equally limited.

The challenges Luce outlines are unquestionably real. Deepening inequality, global power shifts, environmental degradation, the automation of work, an elite unwilling to take responsibility – all these threaten the foundations of Western democracies. How, or even if, we can sustain our way of life is one of the pressing questions of our time, and there are unquestionably important books to be written on the topic. *The Retreat of Western Liberalism*, an intriguing but unsatisfying read, is not quite one of them.

THE COMING BOOM IN INHERITED WEALTH

JOHN QUIGGIN

26 July 2017

I t's hard to pinpoint an exact date, but sometime early in the years after the global financial crisis the problem of inequality moved to centrestage. Evidence that had once been discussed mostly in academic seminars found a wider audience among people trying to understand what had gone wrong in Western economies. What the figures showed were striking disparities in income and wealth, particularly in the United States, where they challenged the longstanding self-perception of a land of opportunity unshackled by the social rigidities of 'Old Europe'.

Among all the research, two findings were crucial. First, French economists Thomas Piketty and Emmanuel Saez went back to the raw evidence about the income share flowing to the top 1 per cent of households. This detail had been buried – for statistical or privacy reasons – in the broad categories used by data collectors, or had been obscured by sampling problems. Piketty and Saez found that the share of income going to these households was substantially larger than had previously been supposed, and was growing rapidly. Most of the benefits of economic growth were flowing to a relatively small part of the population; living standards for everyone else were stagnant or even declining.

The second finding, from a wider range of researchers, was that social mobility – the chance that someone born to poor parents would become wealthy, or vice versa – was declining in the United States, and was now lower than the more egalitarian European countries. Because comparisons across time are difficult, the most reliable way to quantify this trend is to look at relativities between countries. By this measure, the chance that a person with parents at the top (or bottom) of the income distribution will end up in the same or a similar position is now higher in the United States than in Europe. Until at least the late twentieth century, the evidence had suggested the opposite to be true.

Low social mobility is partly a predictable result of inequality. With relative equality, a modest lift in income is all that's needed for an individual to move up the scale.

But inequality is also self-reinforcing, making a mockery of the common distinction between 'equality of outcomes' and 'equality of opportunity'. The greater the disparity in resources available to families, the easier it is for the better-off to give their children a head start. Since the desire to look after your children is both natural and admirable, there is no real way to offset this tendency, except to resist the rise of unequal outcomes.

Together, these two sets of findings yielded a new and much gloomier picture of inequality in the West. They were presented most clearly in Thomas Piketty's *Capital in the Twenty-first Century*, which became a surprise bestseller in 2013.

Unfortunately, the debate sparked by *Capital* was diverted into a largely sterile discussion of Piketty's claim that the growth of inequality depended on the formula $r > g$ (in other words, that the rate of return on capital exceeds the rate of economic growth). This obscured Piketty's more crucial observation that, in the absence of political action to counter it, growing inequality would ultimately restore the 'patrimonial' society that prevailed in the nineteenth century.

Wealth and social position in a patrimonial society are primarily obtained, as the name implies, through inheritance. Patrimonial societies preserve their structure against the fissile tendencies of inheritance by encouraging the combination of fortunes through marriage. Piketty illustrates this tendency through reference to portrayals by Jane Austen, Honoré de Balzac and other classic nineteenth-century novelists.

In these novels, every possible marriage is graded in terms of the wealth and annual incomes of the prospective partners. Romance might require that the relatively impoverished heroine should succeed in winning the affections of the wealthy hero, but financial calculation usually triumphed. Balzac presents a darker view, with his protagonist Rastignac plotting a loveless marriage in pursuit of an inheritance.

This point is even more evident in the 'industrial novels' of the later nineteenth century, where the impossibility of ascending the social scale through hard work and intelligence is at the core of the class divisions that drive the plot. As the protagonist of David Lodge's twentieth-century novel *Nice Work* observes, the authors of the industrial novels were unable to contemplate a political solution, and so the dilemmas of the characters could be resolved only through 'a legacy, a marriage, emigration or death'. Play by the rules of patrimonial society and win, or leave once and for all.

Is this the future that awaits us? If so, what will it look like? The years since the publication of *Capital* have seen a modest recovery from the Great Recession. But that recovery hasn't been sufficient to prevent the breakdown of the old political order, which relied on a consensus favouring some version of market liberalism.

To understand occurrences like Brexit and the Trump presidency, it's useful to look at the most recent developments in the unequal distribution of income and wealth. The clearest evidence is from the United States – but where the United States leads, the rest of the world is likely to follow. Piketty finds evidence of growing inequality in Britain and France; and even in Australia, where the shift has been moderated by relatively progressive tax and welfare policies, similar trends are emerging.

The news on inequality in the US is nearly all bad. The top 1 per cent lost more than most during the global financial crisis but that was just a blip. Between 2009 and 2015, the top 1 per cent of families earned more than half of total real income growth per family. As a result, their share of total United States income reached 22 per cent, one of the highest values since records based on income tax returns were first collected in 1913.

The top 1 per cent have attracted most attention, but focusing on that group can be misleading. Within the top 1 per cent, the pattern of unequal benefits is replicated, just like a set of Russian nesting dolls or a fractal pattern in mathematics.

The top 0.01 per cent, which may be seen as 'the 1 per cent of the 1 per cent', has done much better than the remaining 0.99 per cent. Within this group (made up of about 16,000 families), the top 1 per cent (the top 0.0001 per cent of households, amounting to a few hundred people) own substantially more than the bottom 50 per cent of *all* households. In the racially divided United States, it's worth noting that the top 0.0001 per cent own more wealth than the entire African-American population, even including billionaires such as Oprah Winfrey.

Looking beyond the top 1 per cent, have the benefits of increased income inequality flowed to high-income professionals and business owners as a group? To some extent they have, but not nearly as much as is often imagined. For a recent report, *Striking It Richer*, Emmanuel Saez divided the top decile (or 10 per cent) of the income distribution into three groups, the top 1 per cent, the next 4 per cent and the next 5 per cent. The top 1 per cent have done very well indeed. Their share of total income bounces around because much of it takes the form of capital gains, but the upward trend is clear and strong. The next 4 per cent have also done well, adding around five percentage points to their share since the 1980s.

The next 5 per cent have not done nearly so well. Their share of total income has barely changed since the 1980s and now appears to be falling. The incomes of households in this group have grown in line with the average growth of total income in the United States, which has been considerably slower in recent years than in the 1950s and 1960s. In other words, this group did better in postwar decades of relatively equal income and strong economic growth.

For the rest of the population, the picture is much worse. Households outside the top 10 per cent have seen their share of total income decline consistently. For many, income has declined in absolute terms. These disastrous outcomes are reflected in and reinforced by a variety of social stresses, including an epidemic of opioid addiction and declining life expectancy for large sectors of the population.

The one apparent bright spot is that those at the top were more likely to earn than inherit their riches. In particular, most of the very wealthiest Americans have made their fortunes from the technology boom that began in the 1990s. This might seem like a refutation of Piketty's prediction, but in reality it mostly reflects the time lags involved in the process of building dynastic fortunes.

The fact that currently wealthy Americans have not, in general, inherited their wealth follows logically from the fact that, in their parents' generation, there weren't comparable accumulations of wealth to be bequeathed. More generally, starting from the position of relatively equal income and wealth (relative to earlier periods and to the current one, that is), which prevailed between about 1950 and 1980, growing inequality of income must precede growing inequality of wealth. Wealth is simply the cumulative excess of income over consumption (and American high-income earners have not been notable for restrained consumption).

So, given highly unequal incomes and social immobility, we can expect inheritance to play a much bigger role in explaining inequality for the generations now entering adulthood than for the current recipients of high incomes. That inheritance will include direct transfers of wealth as well as the effects of increasingly unequal access to education, early job opportunities and home ownership.

Counterintuitively, this process is further advanced in Australia. Of the top ten people on *The Australian Financial Review*'s 'Rich List 2017', three inherited their money. Two are foreign businessmen, listed because they hold dual citizenship in Australia, so we can put them to one side. Of the remaining five, some of them members of the talented generation of Jewish refugees who came to Australia and prospered in the years after the Second World War, only one (Andrew Forrest) is under eighty. When they're gone, the rich list will be dominated by heirs, not founders.

The same point is even clearer with the paper's list of rich families. As recently as twenty years ago, all but one of these clans were still headed by the entrepreneurs who had made the family fortune in the first place. Now, all but one of the families are rich by inheritance.

Meanwhile, for the mass of the population whose financial wealth is limited to a superannuation account, a different form of inherited inequality is becoming evident. With median house prices over $1 million in Sydney, it is essentially impossible for young people on average or below-average incomes to enter the housing market unaided. Far more commonly, they rely on parental assistance to provide a deposit and, in many cases, to guarantee a loan. Malcolm Turnbull's suggestion that wealthy parents should 'shell out' to buy houses for their children, and that anyone who had problems with this idea was engaged in 'class warfare', illustrates the point.

What will a patrimonial society look like? Most obviously, it won't be pleasant for those born to families who lack the resources to give them a head start in life. More generally, it is likely to be economically and socially stagnant. A patrimonial society inevitably wastes much of its talent, often putting its privileged children into positions of power and influence for which they may have little aptitude.

As was notably observed by Thomas Gray in his *Elegy Written in a Country Churchyard*, in a society of this kind, most people's opportunities are circumscribed from birth:

> *Full many a flow'r is born to blush unseen,*
> *And waste its sweetness on the desert air.*
>
> *Some village-Hampden, that with dauntless breast*
> *The little tyrant of his fields withstood;*
>
> *Some mute inglorious Milton here may rest,*
> *Some Cromwell guiltless of his country's blood.*

This does not mean that no one can ever rise to the top. Given even the smallest opportunity, those of exceptional ability will rise in any society, as did both Oliver and Thomas Cromwell. But the odds against such an achievement are long.

Indeed, we have probably already passed the point where the growth of inequality and the accumulation of massive fortunes, particularly in the financial sector, have become a drag on economic growth. Even such staunch advocates of liberalisation as the OECD recognise that the financialisation that allowed the accumulation of massive fortunes has reached the point where it reduces growth, makes economies more vulnerable to crises, and undermines the living standards of most households. In Australia, the governor of the Reserve Bank has expressed alarm at the consequences of stagnant or declining wages.

What, if anything, can be done about this? The policies that reduced inequality in the twentieth century, notably including inheritance taxes and progressive income taxes, are widely assumed to be off the table in the current economy. But if the political events of the last couple of years have shown anything, it is that it is a mistake to write off any political outcome as impossible.

The fact that Labor, led by a man as cautious and instinctively centrist as Bill Shorten, can campaign on a platform of increasing the top marginal tax rate suggests that the appeal of 'trickle down' theories of income fairness has been erased by the actual experience of an unequal society. The forces pushing us towards a patrimonial society are powerful, but not irresistible.

JUMPING THE GATE

JACK LATIMORE

23 August 2017

Talk to people in Indigenous new media and you'll probably hear the story of a $200 online survey that realigned the debate about the constitutional recognition of First Nations people in Australia. At first blush, it's a tale about a niche Indigenous-led media outlet that distinguished itself sharply from a multimillion-dollar, government-sponsored publicity campaign. And it has a happy ending, because the community it represents went on to validate its work. Go deeper, and it's also the story of potentially more profound shifts.

Talk to people involved in new media more generally about how it is influencing news and political communication in Australia, and you might hear about IndigenousX, the group that commissioned that survey. You may hear that the poll was a welcome and long-overdue intervention in the debate about constitutional recognition, particularly in the face of the mainstream media's repeated assurances that black support for the proposals was a given.

The slow-burning disruption commenced when the mainstream media got around to reporting on the survey data, close to a week after IndigenousX published the findings on 15 June 2015.[11] Independent news site *New Matilda* had covered the story earlier, though, publishing 'Online Poll Finds Majority of Black Australia Opposed to Recognise Campaign' on 16 June. The article, by Indigenous journalist Amy McQuire, was distributed widely by black social media networks, yet was ignored by the same mainstream outlets that had chewed over the results of earlier polls on the topic.

Three days later, a report by Celeste Liddle, another Indigenous writer and that week's @IndigenousX Twitter account host, was published by Guardian Australia with the title '87 Per Cent of Indigenous People Do Not Agree on Recognition: You'd Know if You Listened'. The only other mention of the survey during those first five days was a forty-three-

---

11 Celeste Liddle and @IndigenousX, "Constitutional Recognition Survey," @IndigenousX (blog), June 15, 2015, https://indigenousx.com.au/blogx/constitutional-recognition-survey/#.VzPu62R94sl.

second radio interview with IndigenousX founder Luke Pearson, which aired on the National Indigenous Radio Service.

Only on Saturday morning did the results get a nod in News Corp's *Weekend Australian*, where Phillip Hudson, writing an 'exclusive' report about a fresh Galaxy/Newspoll on the subject, made a cursory reference to the IndigenousX data at the tail end of his article. Hudson's fleeting mention was enough to stir up minor interest from Australia's other traditionally dominant news organisations.

Since 2012, the agenda-setting mainstream media had largely been interested only in the broader Australian public's generally favourable view of constitutional recognition. Opposition to the proposal was mentioned occasionally, but assumed to exist only among ultraconservatives rallied by commentators like News Corp columnist Andrew Bolt, South Australian senator and Australian Conservatives founder Cory Bernardi, and former Labor minister Gary Johns.

Generally, these media outlets uncritically reported the views of Recognise, an organisation formed in 2013 by Reconciliation Australia and seeded with $10 million from the federal government. Recognise's objective was to promote broad public support for constitutional amendment. Both as an organisation and a public relations campaign, it enjoyed strong bipartisan support from the two major parties, as well as from the Greens. Combined with sizeable corporate support, the almost universal political goodwill gave Recognise preferred status in mainstream coverage and public discussion of constitutional change.

•

Scepticism about the constitutional recognition proposal had existed among some First Nations people even prior to the appointment of the Gillard government's Expert Panel on Constitutional Recognition of Indigenous Australians in 2011. As the recognition process developed, so too did black dissent begin to emerge, but mainstream news media exhibited next to no interest.

As the increasingly unpopular Tony Abbott led federal government poured another $15 million into Recognise while cutting around $534 million from Aboriginal community services in the 2014 budget, grassroots cynicism spiked. The weight of mistrust and suspicion was almost immediately directed at Recognise. Numerous Indigenous-led opposition pages were launched on Facebook. Long threads of conversation on the topic trailed through the twittersphere.

Australia's mainstream news media appeared to be oblivious. With their own resources shrinking, these outlets were increasingly reliant on media releases, and most of these were coming from Recognise. They often included details of what appeared to be overwhelming survey support for a constitutional amendment. In May 2015, for instance, Recognise released poll results showing that 87 per cent of Indigenous respondents would vote 'yes'.

It was less than a month later that IndigenousX's poll yielded a figure of just 32.3 per cent Indigenous support for a 'yes' vote, and even that level of support was contingent on the amendment's including every one of the 2012 expert panel's recommendations. Less than 13 per cent of Indigenous respondents said they would vote for recognition even if the changes didn't include a clause banning racial discrimination. A very modest 14.7 per cent indicated that they would vote 'yes' if the final model was symbolic, with no genuine, substantive changes to the Commonwealth's founding document. Arguably, the most damning figure of the IndigenousX survey was the low level of support for Recognise, with only a quarter of Indigenous respondents falling in behind its campaign.

'The level of disparity between the two surveys surprised me,' says IndigenousX founder Luke Pearson:

> We made a lot of effort to make sure we got it out to as many different people and groups as we could. So I expected that the on-board people would rally their troops and that the anti-Recognise people would rally their troops. I wasn't trying to stack the deck one way or the other.

In fact, Pearson says that he expected the results of the two surveys to be closer:

> If the Recognise survey had come out and said 65 per cent of blackfellas supported it, I would have been, like, 'Well that's not my experience, but okay' ... But they came out with 87 per cent. I was, like, 'That's impossible. It's too high.' If you randomly asked a hundred Aboriginal people, to have eighty-seven of them say yes to it – that just wasn't what I was hearing at the time.

The ABC got around to reporting on the contradiction ten days after IndigenousX released the survey results, when journalist Bill Birtles interviewed Luke Pearson for a story broadcast on ABC Radio's *AM*. Later that day, National Indigenous Television, an auxiliary channel of SBS, ran a similarly structured story on its evening news bulletin. Then the big news organisations lost interest again.

Engagement with the story continued online, however. It was primarily driven by Indigenous people on social media who, according to research conducted by McNair Ingenuity Research in 2014, use Twitter and Facebook at rates about 20 per cent higher than non-Indigenous Australians.[12] So much so that a former member of the expert panel, Indigenous constitutional law expert Megan Davis, has noted:

> If anyone wants to know what Aboriginal and Torres Strait Islander people are thinking on any political or legal issue, you go to social media. Since 2011 the message has been clear. Communities eschew recognition. They seek concrete reform to achieve practical outcomes.

With the attention of the mainstream media directed elsewhere, Celeste Liddle's *Guardian Australia* article attracted around 25,000 page views and over 10,000 shares on Twitter and Facebook, with similarly keen interest in her data analysis, published by IndigenousX.

The significant differences between the two surveys went beyond the raw results. As Liddle wrote:

> Questions were asked by Aboriginal and Torres Strait Islander people all over social media: who did Recognise survey? What did they ask them? What were the respondents actually indicating that they supported? The media release was big on the figures and light on the details.

In contrast, IndigenousX made every effort at transparency, with Liddle's analysis detailing the eight survey questions posed, all responses for each question and all sample sizes for each question. It included repeated disclaimers about the shortcomings of self-selected surveys of this kind, as well as open acknowledgement that the overall sample size of 827 Indigenous respondents was not representative of the diversity of views

---

12 McNair Ingenuity Research, "Media usage amongst Aboriginal and Torres Strait Islander People," *McNair Ingenuity Research*, August 2014, http://mcnair.com.au/wp-content/uploads/Media-Usage-amongst-Aboriginal-and-Torres-Strait-Islander-People-McNai....pdf.

of all blackfellas. In comparison, the initial release of the Recognise poll results made no such details available to the public, other than its sample size of 750 Indigenous respondents.

In a blog post on Recognise's website written in response to Liddle's analysis and the Guardian Australia article, campaign co-director Tim Gartrell provided more detail about the question put to respondents and the methods deployed by Polity Research, who conducted the poll. 'We have never denied there is dissent nor that there are critics of the movement,' wrote Gartrell. 'We simply disagree on the scale of it. We listen to our opponents and we respect their right to a different view.'

The initial omission of details, however, was enough for opponents to vehemently dismiss the findings. And, says Luke Pearson, the ongoing lack of any discernible model of proposed amendment only contributed to the increasing suspicions and frustrations within the ranks of the Indigenous opposition:

> When they said 87 per cent of Indigenous people would vote 'yes' if the referendum was held tomorrow, it was completely meaningless ... It was like Recognise were saying, 'Eighty-seven per cent of Indigenous people would sign their name to a blank bit of paper that the government is going to fill in later.' Really? Aboriginal people have said that? That's not possible, because us blackfellas do not sign our fucking names to blank bits of paper for the government to fill in later.

•

As Indigenous digital networks kept the story alive on social media, the IndigenousX survey data was beginning to have a wider impact. On 25 June it entered *Hansard* when Senator Nova Peris alluded to it in a speech on the report of the Joint Select Committee on Constitutional Recognition of Aboriginal and Torres Strait Islander People. Around the same time, Cape York lawyer Noel Pearson, another former member of Julia Gillard's expert panel, used the data in an interview with Brisbane's 98.9FM to argue for a series of Indigenous-only community conferences.

'That IndigenousX survey confirms to me,' Pearson told listeners, 'that the whole process going forward has got to allow Indigenous people to have the debate and have the discussion right across the country.'

The following month, prime minister Tony Abbott invited forty hand-picked Indigenous delegates to Kirribilli House in Sydney to devise an acceptable way to proceed with the issue. The brimmed hats of Noel Pearson and Pat Dodson were prominent among the invitees.

During meetings with the PM and opposition leader Bill Shorten, the Indigenous leaders rejected a symbolic, 'minimalist' approach to recognition and sought substantive constitutional change. The PM rejected their proposal, later describing it as 'something akin to a log of claims unlikely to receive general support'. He also roundly rejected Pearson and Dodson's push for a series of Indigenous conferences. They would soon go ahead anyway, however.

'Until that point, pretty much the only thing we were seeing from Recognise were things like the Long Walk and sponsorship,' says Celeste Liddle:

> It was very much this corporate-focused entity that seemed more interested in getting the big millionaires to sign-on and don the R-logo than actually consulting with the community. The survey made people think, *Well, hang on. A bunch of community members really don't seem that happy with this at all. What's going on? Maybe we need to talk to them?*

Tanja Dreher, who teaches communications and media studies at the University of Wollongong, describes the survey as a savvy intervention. Her own research has focused on community media, experiences of racism, and news and cultural diversity. She says the survey 'cut through' because it took the form of an opinion poll:

> Though we can argue that the methodology was not as robust as it should be, playing the numbers or working those marketing techniques is the absolute bread and butter of legacy media ... And that's why it did finally cut through and shift how that debate is now made public, who's involved, and what's happening. Even though, at that moment, you still see evidence of the legacy media really playing catch-up, slow to realise what was happening in other channels, particularly Indigenous new media and social media channels.

•

Until the publication of the survey results, IndigenousX was known only as a Twitter account engaged in cultural activism. Its website, launched in September 2014, mainly functioned as a repository for interviews with each of its weekly hosts. In the early years, host Aaron Nagas took Aldi and Big W to task over culturally offensive T-shirts, compelling them to remove the items from their shelves. Best & Less was soon caught out over the same issue, and it too removed its stock. Another success came when the *Macquarie Dictionary* corrected its entry for the word 'boong', and yet another when IndigenousX raised around $10,000 for the Indigenous Literacy Foundation.

More recently, IndigenousX has become an influential voice in a loose coalition of activist organisations and individuals pushing to change the date of Australia's official national day on the basis that 26 January represents a history of violent dispossession for First Nations people.

'There was a time there for a year or two, where people were just reaching out on social media going, "Hey, just letting you know there's a golliwog in a shop, or there's a racist dude who said something," or whatever it was,' says Pearson. 'If somebody saw something racist on social media or had put it up on Facebook or Twitter, someone would say, "Tell IndigenousX!" And we would do something about it to try and change it.'

Before IndigenousX, Pearson and his older brother ran what he describes as 'mini-campaigns' to raise the profiles of Indigenous Twitter accounts belonging to organisations such as the National Aboriginal Community Controlled Health Organisation, the Healing Foundation, and Yindjibarndi. In those days, the account went under a different handle and Pearson was working on it twelve to eighteen hours each day.

'My older brother Sean joined up just to back me up, because I was still fighting with racist trolls back then. But we got around to helping out other Indigenous accounts,' he says. 'I had 4000 followers or something, which was big back then. One day I thought, *Why should I have 4000 following me when people actually doing shit don't have that?*'

It was during this period that the Pearson brothers played a little-known role in advocating the eventual 'act of partnership' between international surf-clothing giant Mambo and fledgling surf brand Mabo, a commercial venture by Malcolm Mabo, son of the renowned land rights campaigner Eddie Koiki Mabo. The 2011 brand dispute resulted in the re-release of Mambo's 1992 '100% Mabo' T-shirt, with sale proceeds going towards kickstarting Malcolm Mabo's new project. The brothers were also behind Google's decision to alter its search algorithms to stop racist jokes appearing at the top of Aboriginal-related search results. 'That was the first thing we did where I was like, "Wow. I can effect real-world change doing this,"' says Pearson.

The idea of IndigenousX had been on Pearson's mind for six months before he finally, and coincidentally, launched it at a 2012 youth-led constitutional recognition conference at the National Centre for Indigenous Excellence in Redfern. Pearson was to speak on a panel alongside former NSW senator Aden Ridgeway and Kirstie Parker, who was editor of the Indigenous-owned newspaper the *Koori Mail*. A room full of young future leaders had assembled to hear about media and communications campaigning strategies. When it was Pearson's turn to speak, he says he threw away his talk and, instead, sent a sheet of paper around the room:

> I got up and said, 'Fuck it. I'm doing it. I'm going to pass this around and you fellas put your name down on there and you will be the first round of IndigenousX' … I'd been sitting on the idea for ages, not confident I could sustain it, but in that room there was all these deadly young fellas who were already on Twitter.

Pearson donated his substantial Twitter following and shuffled his own name across to a personal account. Rotating curator accounts were far from common on Twitter at the time:

> By the time I actually launched it there was @Sweden, which is run by the Swedish government with a different Swedish citizen each week. Technically they are the first rotating account on Twitter in the world. @IndigenousX is the second.

Rotating accounts like @EduTweetOz and @WePublicHealth followed, each acknowledging the influence of @IndigenousX.

'I did it because I had a platform and I could do it,' says Pearson. 'When I realised that the account was working, I leveraged it. I messaged all the organisations I'd helped out along the way to just say, "Hi, I might be in your town sometime soon. I want to come in and say g'day." And, though no one knew who I was then, most went, "Come on in, we'd love to meet you."'

•

In 2013, Pearson was approached by Guardian Australia, a new entrant on the Australian media scene. Katharine Viner, its founding editor, had been following @IndigenousX on Twitter and says she was intrigued by the range of experiences covered via the mechanism of rotating hosts. She asked her opinion editor, Jessica Reed, to find out who was behind the account and talk to them about a partnership.

'When I arrived in Australia in January 2013, I was looking for gaps in what was covered by the media,' says Viner:

> It seemed to me that the gaps then were around asylum and immigration, political policy, and Indigenous issues. As someone fascinated by Australian history, the issue of the rights of Indigenous Australians seemed to me to be glanced over. I wanted to find a way for *The Guardian* to cover that, and was keen that it wouldn't be top-down reporting. The account was one of the most interesting things we could see in the Australian media and we thought if we collaborated we could perhaps find ways for the work to reach even more people – readers all around the world.

Pearson was invited to *The Guardian*'s office in Sydney, but says he was so unaware of media generally that he had no idea it was setting up in Australia. 'I thought they were doing an Australian-focused single edition and wanted to interview IndigenousX,' he says.

Viner recalls that Pearson was full of ideas and it quickly made sense to work in tandem with IndigenousX and effectively hire Pearson as a content curator. They decided that Guardian Australia would profile the weekly @IndigenousX hosts with a Q&A about their lives and the issues they were interested in. Viner believed this simple approach would reveal a broad Indigenous experience for the *Guardian*'s predominantly non-Indigenous readers.

Anticipating a hostile reception by Australia's long-established news media players, says Pearson, *The Guardian* group seemed determined to do Aboriginal affairs well. 'They were quite open about it,' he recalls. 'They had ideas about how they wanted to go about it, but I suppose they knew if they didn't do something significant, organisations like *The Australian* would have destroyed them.'

Viner was impressed by the diversity and range of Indigenous perspectives delivered by the partnership, which she says included community organisers, students, professionals, public figures and little-known activists:

> The stories were powerful. They were affecting and revealing
> ... We also found good writers that way, such as Kelly Briggs

and Siv Parker. It gave space to so many different angles and lived experiences – the kind we didn't see anywhere else. We understand that a lot of stories are better told by the people who are living it, or who are close to their communities and what is happening every day. Our job, as journalists, is to go out and find those stories – and collaboration is a great tool to get this done.

•

In the half-decade since the launch of IndigenousX, new media entrants and social media have had a revolutionary impact on journalism and the relations between news media and civic and political communication. New journalistic and organisational values and practices have rapidly replaced the old ways, and continue to evolve. For the most part, media observers agree that Australia's legacy news organisations have been slow to react and have subsequently suffered through a combination of short-sightedness and obstinacy. Guardian Australia was the first international new media news venture to land on the local mediascape. Digital media behemoth *BuzzFeed* followed in 2014, and *HuffPost* arrived in August 2015 in partnership with Fairfax Media. Then, in May 2017, *The New York Times* bustled onto the scene.

Add in small news and opinion outlets like *Crikey, New Matilda* and *Independent Australia,* plus the hard pivot to online news at the ABC, and the local news market has opened up a profusion of opportunities for otherwise marginalised voices. Meanwhile, social media has enabled a proliferation of Indigenous news and opinion 'participant-users'.

'Everything was just moving that way, towards blogs or blog-style op-eds,' says Pearson. 'I had my own blog, and there was Celeste, Amy McGuire, Leesa Watego and other people. We had already been getting recognised by various institutions.'

Celeste Liddle, who now regularly writes for Fairfax Media in addition to her popular blog *Rantings of an Aboriginal Feminist,* says big media outlets have responded to the way many people prefer to seek out new online spaces and the perspectives filling them. 'The ability for us to create spaces for our own voices using these online platforms was the key starting point,' she says:

> *Guardian* and Fairfax and the rest saw that most people were shifting to online and social for their news. They knew that

if they were smart about it, they could recruit these sorts of voices which had been ignored before, but generated some online pull because they were seen as alternatives.

While acknowledging that these new outlets can provide strong paths to self-determination and greater diversity, Tanja Dreher warns that they also create what she describes as 'tensions' for traditional community media. 'There's an enormous amount of excitement and enthusiasm about the opportunities enabling First Nations in terms of social media,' she says. 'But one of the reasons to be wary is because government funding bodies are very happy to use that enthusiasm as a rationale for stepping back from, or cutting funding for community media.'

Community radio and community television remain vital, Dreher argues. 'For many First Nations communities, Indigenous community media is actually *the* mainstream media: it's not a marginal kind of extra or whatever. It is *the* crucial information and cultural communication resource.'

Dreher believes that parts of the community media model can't be easily replicated by social media. She describes the development of relationships at routine times and at a set location as the sorts of strong ties that are too often neglected in the social media sphere:

> Building a relationship with the station as well as with the community, as well as with other broadcasters has certain values in terms of sustainability, in terms of collective action, in terms of building an ongoing project that might have a charter ... This is where there are central values that you sign onto, and commit to. And that you contribute to.

•

The week after IndigenousX successfully campaigned to have Aldi and Big W remove clothing bearing the slogan 'Australia Est. 1788' from their shelves, Indigenous businessman and conservative commentator Warren Mundine was approached by the *Daily Telegraph*'s Jason Morrison for comment. Asked about his views on IndigenousX's intervention, Mundine was reported to have described it as a 'load of huffing and puffing about rubbish' before adding, 'We've got Aboriginal kids with health problems and kids not going to school – if you want to get fired-up about something, try that ... not a bloody T-shirt.'

Luke Pearson responded to the comments on his own blog at the time:

> During that same week on Twitter Aaron talked about a huge range of issues, including the fact that he helped establish the Australian Indigenous Basketball Championships, Marriage equality, everyday racism, Climate Change, education as well as help raise awareness for many Indigenous Organisations/ events by giving them a plug, and I myself was promoting a fundraising campaign trying to raise funds to print and distribute an independently made Elders Report into Indigenous Youth Suicide.

Warren Mundine recalls that while he didn't see the Aldi and Big W actions as 'greatly important' at the time, they did highlight for him the potential of new media for effecting change for Indigenous people:

> It said to me, 'Hey, we can get our message out there and we can bring our people along with us without having to go through the old media, or the mainstream media' ... That message wouldn't have got out before. But it showed that through new media you could reach a lot more people who could then put pressure on big firms, challenge big organisations and make changes.

Mundine says he now accesses new media for his news because it provides him with things he wouldn't otherwise hear about, except along the traditional 'black grapevine':

> You see something in the Indigenous new media and then a day or so later you might pick up a story in the mainstream media about it ... I'm seeing things that I wouldn't usually see, stories that I would normally not hear of. Previously, you couldn't get our voices out there because the mainstream media only went to a few select people, and I'm one of them. They'd come looking for a story, but now we can bypass that gatekeeping.

Katharine Viner, now the London-based editor-in-chief of *The Guardian*, says the success of the IndigenousX collaboration has recently led to a similar initiative in its US newsroom:

> We've started a project which is a collaboration with smaller newsrooms across America to find stories that national

outlets either undercover or miss completely. This project was driven by Jessica Reed, the opinion editor who got in touch with Luke Pearson in the first place. Their work together in 2013 has paved the way.

Viner sees the trend in journalism increasingly shifting towards collaborative partnerships as news organisations become more globally focused and financially stretched:

> Whether it's 400-plus journalists working together to produce the Panama papers or Guardian Australia and IndigenousX, it produces better journalism, of course, and much greater impact … In the case of IndigenousX, it means that the work can get a large audience in Australia and also a large audience around the world, connecting with interested communities in places like the US, the UK, Canada and Europe.

Luke Pearson says that IndigenousX's collaboration with the *Guardian* simply aims to open up a new, more inclusive discussion. That endeavour is still a work in progress, but it is clear that it has already helped a rapidly changing media landscape to amplify under-represented voices. 'It's fair to say that in Australia, *The Guardian* did it and then everyone else did it,' he says:

> All the dominoes didn't tip over at the same time. I can say with confidence that IndigenousX was a significant part of the shifting landscape and that the collaboration with *The Guardian* was one of the first major positive changes in that media landscape.

THE CRUELLEST OPTION

TESSA MORRIS-SUZUKI

6 November 2017

I n her first meeting with Malcolm Turnbull on 5 November, the New Zealand Prime Minister Jacinda Ardern behaved with admirable tact and diplomacy. She offered the Australian government a partial way out of its self-made disaster on Manus Island, and when her proposal was instantly put on ice by Mr Turnbull, she expressed understanding for his position and assured Australia that the offer was still on the table. Such are the diplomatic courtesies of meetings between heads of government.

But ordinary members of the public need not be so diplomatic: whether through design, weakness or sheer incompetence, Malcolm Turnbull has chosen a particularly cruel response to the gift that Ardern brought across the Tasman. He could graciously have accepted it, and opened the way to a rapid and safe resettlement of a quarter of the refugees from Manus Island to New Zealand. Or, had he been adhering to the line that his own government has insistently repeated in recent months, he could have said that the refugees on Manus Island are no longer Australia's responsibility but Papua New Guinea's, and that New Zealand should address its offer to the PNG government, which would probably have accepted it with alacrity.

Instead, he chose to reassert Australia's responsibility for the fate of the refugees, at the same time ensuring that the opportunity for 150 desperate people to escape from limbo and find a new life is postponed indefinitely, until after the completion of the 'US deal'.

But that 'dumb deal', as Donald Trump called it in one of his more insightful moments, is going nowhere. Having accepted a very small proportion of the refugees, the US officials concerned have departed with no assurances that they are going to complete the processing of the remaining asylum seekers, let alone allow any more into the United States.

Meanwhile, the Australian Government, which has enough control over the refugees to ensure that none goes to New Zealand for the foreseeable future, simultaneously denies all responsibility or control when it comes to providing them with the basic necessities for survival. A large proportion are so unwell that they need to be on regular medication, but their medical supplies will cease this month because the Australian Government no longer takes responsibility for them, and PNG is not picking up the slack. This has left underfunded and understaffed refugee support groups with the almost impossible task of trying to navigate the medical chaos on Manus Island and raise the substantial donations needed to prevent suffering and quite possibly deaths.

If we are to believe Peter Dutton and other cabinet ministers, of course, it is the refugee supporters themselves who are somehow responsible for this whole debacle. The Turnbull government's approach to offshore detention, we are told, is a compassionate way of stopping the people smugglers, and thus preventing deaths at sea. But that rhetoric wears thinner with every passing day.

It is the government's policy of turning back boats, and not the miseries on Manus Island and Nauru, that has prevented arrivals of people-smuggling boats on Australian shores. Boat arrivals dropped drastically, not when Julia Gillard reintroduced offshore processing, but following the start of the Abbott government's 'Operation Sovereign Borders', or OSB, in September 2013. But then again, just how many lives are actually saved by boat turnbacks, and by the Coalition's entire policy of 'being cruel to be kind'?

No one knows the answer, of course, since the government has no interest at all in finding out what happens to refugees either before or after the moment their boat is turned back from Australian waters. Despite the veil of secrecy with which OSB is shrouded, though, there have been reports of turned-back boats running out of fuel or being left aground on the borders of Indonesian waters. The Kaldor Centre for International Refugee Law at the University of New South Wales notes that refugees returned to Sri Lanka and Vietnam under OSB have been interrogated and imprisoned, and torture has been alleged in at least one Sri Lankan case.

Nor do we have any idea how many turned-back refugees have simply gone on to board other dangerous people-smuggling boats in desperate attempts to reach other safe havens; and we have no idea how many of those deterred from attempting to reach Australia by boat have been imprisoned or killed in their own countries or en route. The government's policy does not make refugees safe. It simply ensures that they do not die in Australian waters.

If there is one good thing that has come out of the meeting between Ardern and Turnbull, it is an end to the bipartisan support for the chaos and cruelty of the Coalition's refugee policy. Labor is finally beginning to find an alternative voice on the issue. The urgent task now is for opposition parties to join forces with the growing number of government politicians showing queasiness at their own party's policies, and to demand answers to a few basic questions.

What evidence can the government provide to show that its cruelty on Manus Island saves lives elsewhere? What assurances can the government give that any more refugees will be processed and resettled under the US deal, and when might that happen? Why can the government stymie refugees' chances of going to New Zealand, but be incapable of working with PNG to provide the refugees with the basic necessities for safety and survival? And when will the misery, shame and chaos of Manus and Nauru end?

Meanwhile, it's surely time for Jacinda Ardern to start talking directly to the government of PNG.

UP TO A POINT, PROFESSOR HAMILTON

FRANK BONGIORNO

8 March 2018

Hardly a day goes by without another tale emerging of the apparently malign influence of the People's Republic of China on Australian life. The growing power and assertiveness of China in the region and the wider world has become the grand narrative of our times, the single immutable fact around which all else must be arranged. What we cannot change, we must learn to live with.

Clive Hamilton is having none of such fatalism. It will only be a Chinese world if we decide that it should be; to suggest otherwise is capitulation or appeasement. Hamilton, an uncompromising critic, seems to mean this literally. In an essay published online in April 2017, he compared high-profile academic Hugh White's views about China to an imaginary Oxford don arguing in 1938 that Britain's response to Germany should ignore 'the fact that Germany is ruled by a dictatorial, expansionist party bent on European domination'.[13]

Silent Invasion: China's Influence in Australia is a call to arms; not literally, but a plea to Australians to resist Chinese interference in their democracy. Hamilton argues that China's efforts to influence Australian politics, business, media, academia and the Chinese-Australian community shouldn't be treated as business as usual. They do not resemble past and present efforts by the United States to influence Australian political and cultural life. Australia and the United States share fundamental values, Hamilton suggests, but China is a one-party state whose ideology and practice are inimical to our own. And increasingly, he claims, they are also a threat to our own.

Silent Invasion's publication has become a news event in itself. It was widely reported in 2017 that Allen & Unwin had withdrawn from publishing

---

13 Clive Hamilton, "China Capitulationism: What's Missing from Hugh White's China Calculus," *Asia & Pacific Policy Society*, April 28, 2017, https://www.policyforum.net/china-capitulationism/.

the book because it feared vexatious defamation action. Given the state of Australian libel law, one can understand their lawyers' concerns. Eventually, Hardie Grant – run by Sandy Grant, who published former British spy Peter Wright's *Spycatcher* in the face of the Thatcher government's efforts to suppress it – took on Hamilton's manuscript and published it with a cover picture of Parliament House flying a Chinese flag.

The book has done well on the back of such publicity, apparently enjoying a second printing within a few days of its release. Two former prime ministers, Paul Keating and Kevin Rudd, have criticised, indeed insulted, Hamilton, Keating calling him a 'pedlar of prejudice' and a 'nincompoop' and Rudd labelling him a 'third-rate academic' who supports the views on China of 'a second-rate prime minister', Malcolm Turnbull. (I would have thought that commenting on the quality of recent prime ministers is dangerous territory for Rudd.) Former Labor senator and right factional chieftain Graham Richardson sounded a bit like a well-trained party cadre himself when he argued in the national broadsheet that 'the good ship Australia should shove Hamilton out the back with the other irritating flotsam and jetsam which pollutes our thinking'.

Hamilton's reputation will probably survive Richardson's censure; and his standing will scarcely be harmed by Beijing's reaction. A Chinese foreign ministry spokeswoman, responding to a shameless Dorothy Dixer from a 'journalist', condemned *Silent Invasion* as 'completely meaningless', 'slander' and 'good for nothing'. The ever-reliable *Global Times* published a picture of the book apparently about to be flushed down a toilet.

•

Silent Invasion is a challenging book, especially for anyone with an appreciation of the long history of Australian alarmism about Asian and communist threats to Australia. The title itself is disturbing – the trope of Asian invasion stretches from the anti-Chinese agitation of the gold rushes, through invasion fantasy novels and the cartooning of the fin-de-siècle nationalist and labour press, to Geoffrey Blainey's accusation, made during the rancorous Asian immigration debate in the mid 1980s, that the Hawke government was pursuing 'Surrender Australia' policies. The 'invasion' theme was implicit in Pauline Hanson's warning in 1996 that Australia was 'in danger of being swamped by Asians'.

Hamilton explains carefully at the outset that his concern is about the Chinese government, not about Chinese. He is right to point out that the accusation of 'racism' or 'xenophobia' is a useful weapon at the disposal of those who wish to deflect attention from the character of their own connections with Beijing and, more particularly, their receipt of Chinese money. But there is a supplementary accusation: that Hamilton is reviving Cold War paranoia; that, in the words of reviewer David Brophy, he has produced a 'McCarthyist manifesto'. Certainly, Hamilton's suggestion that we shouldn't defend the free speech of those who aim to suppress free speech is a reprise of the kinds of arguments that circulated in favour of banning the Communist Party in Australia in the early years of the Cold War.

Nonetheless, Hamilton has not invented the problem to which he draws attention. Much of what he has to say draws on the painstaking investigative reporting of journalists such as Primrose Riordan and Nick McKenzie. Respected Sinologists – such as John Fitzgerald, who provides an endorsement on the book's cover – have expressed serious concerns about the extent of Chinese government penetration of Australian academic life. The intelligence services and leading public servants have warned against complacency about espionage, to the point that the federal government is moving to strengthen its legal instruments for dealing with foreign political influence. And almost everyone seems to be able to acknowledge that China has entered a new phase in its domestic and global politics, one in which it is more assertive in its foreign policy, more hostile to the basic freedoms valued in the West, more concerned with displaying its rising wealth and military power, and more preoccupied with demonstrating national greatness in compensation for past humiliations.

Still, my unease about aspects of Hamilton's argument remains. Central to his case about the aggressive 'United Front' strategy of the Chinese government is the critical role that it sees for its diaspora – including Chinese students abroad, who are now, in Hamilton's telling, carefully choreographed by embassies and consulates – in promoting its interests and outlook. This, says Hamilton, extends to 'intelligence gathering and technology theft'. 'The large and growing number of highly qualified Chinese-Australians now working in science and technology labs around the country provide fertile recruiting grounds,' he tells us.

Is there not a danger that anyone of Chinese ancestry might come to be regarded as untrustworthy, a potential spy, and therefore suffer baseless suspicion, job discrimination and social marginalisation? Especially so given that, based on conversations with Chinese-Australian friends, Hamilton produces some remarkably crude and unsubstantiated guesstimates of the proportions of the Chinese in Australia who are pro-Beijing, anti-Beijing or neutral. Is it really so simple?

There are points in the narrative where the analysis seems to me to go over the top entirely. Hamilton is worried by the sight of 'a group of PRC men in suits' wandering around the campus of the Australian Defence Force Academy in Canberra taking photos. He seems concerned that ADFA's cleaning contract 'is staffed by ethnic Chinese'. He gives us the proportion of CSIRO staff – it is 'close to 10 per cent' – who were born in China. 'It is fair to assume that the results of every piece of scientific research carried out by the CSIRO become available free of charge in China,' he claims.

We are in danger, he warns, of becoming 'a tribute state of the resurgent Middle Kingdom', which is 'a totalitarian regime bent on dominating Australia'. The Chinese leadership has 'asked the embassy in Canberra to formulate a strategy to subdue us'. The book is littered with examples of overstatement of this kind. I defy anyone raised on Sunday morning screenings of *Point of View* not to think of Bob Santamaria when they read that 'Beijing has its eye on Australia's north' and 'China plans to dominate the world, and has been using Australia and New Zealand as a testing ground for its tactics to assert its ascendancy in the West'.

This kind of claim can be demonstrated by quotation from this or that official Chinese source, rather as Soviet sources could once be quoted to prove the existence of the desire to expand Soviet power to promote global proletarian revolution in every corner of the globe, not excluding Australia. But this was never really the best way to understand Soviet foreign-policy behaviour. Is it the best way to discern Chinese intentions?

•

Hamilton brings together much information that should worry Australians who care about the quality of our democracy. The Dastyari affair was not an isolated instance of a politician getting far too close for comfort to a wealthy Chinese donor interested in using his money to advance the Chinese regime's foreign-policy goals, as well as his own prestige and influence in Australia and China. Expatriate Chinese businesspeople are generous donors to Australian politicians and political parties, while a number of ex-politicians seem to have done rather well for themselves as lobbyists, consultants and advisers to Chinese firms. The interval between the end of their time in politics and the beginning of their business careers has often been very short.

But in isolating Chinese influence from the wider problem of influence-peddling in Australian politics, Hamilton falls into the trap of viewing Communist China as uniquely demonic. He is very relaxed about the influence that the United States exercises, and has long exercised, in Australia, seeing in the strengthening of that relationship one antidote to Chinese domination. On this subject, I'm sure I wouldn't be alone among Hamilton's readers in thinking, 'thanks, but no thanks' – and perhaps simply 'no thanks' while we have a dangerous charlatan in the White House. At least up to this point, subservience to the United States and complicity in some of its more egregious foreign-policy decisions have done a great deal more harm to Australia than its relationship with China.

There is an all-or-nothing aspect to this book – for Hamilton, China watchers either see with perfect clarity the danger to our sovereignty and values, or they are moral relativists. Few sit in between, and there is little respect for honest differences of perspective. For instance, I found myself sometimes unable to recognise Hugh White's views as they were caricatured by Hamilton. White is a foreign-policy realist who makes no pretence of being otherwise, and his understanding of the implications for Australia of growing Chinese power reflects this perspective. When Hamilton criticises White for failing to give sufficient weight to the ideology of the Communist Party in his assessment of the Australia–China relationship, he is really criticising a particular way of understanding international relations. That's fine – the realist tradition has long had its critics – but that doesn't mean White is a 'capitulationist', as Hamilton calls him.

•

No doubt there are too many commentators in Australia who are willing to cite China's economic achievement as if it more than compensates for the tyranny of one-party rule and the absence of basic human rights and freedoms. Australian business, academic and political leaders see China as a vast goldmine and many care little about the undemocratic nature of the Chinese political system. There are Australian scientists, funding bodies, universities and research institutes that have asked too few questions about the end users of their collaborations with Chinese partners, reassuring themselves that work with obviously military applications would also have civilian uses – even if that 'civilian' use might be a contribution to more effective mass surveillance of the Chinese population.

Quite apart from the vulnerability of universities (such as my own, the Australian National University) to Chinese government coercion in the context of their dependence on the Chinese student market, some have compromised their ability to stand up for academic freedom. The enterprise university of the post-Dawkins era has been only too eager to accept Chinese money – whether in the form of funding for Confucius Institutes or as donations for academic buildings and research centres from well-connected Chinese businesspeople.

The University of Technology Sydney clearly has some work to do in managing its relationship with Chinese donors in a manner that doesn't damage confidence in its autonomy. Its Australia–China Relations Institute, or ACRI, is led by former Labor foreign minister Bob Carr, who was appointed at the request of the Chinese-Australian donor Huang Xiangmo, who in turn was made an adjunct professor of the UTS. All of this would be bad enough, but it's even worse when you consider the piddling sum, $1.8 million, that Huang donated to establish the institute. That would be just enough to endow a rather junior lectureship, with little change left over. There must be further money coming from somewhere.

Nonetheless, with Carr at the helm, ACRI provides reliably pro-Beijing commentary to the Australian media. As I was preparing this review, I heard Carr on ABC Radio discussing China's recent constitutional changes, which have removed the ten-year, two-term limit on Chinese presidents, thereby possibly allowing Xi Jinping to rule for the rest of his life. To be fair, Carr didn't defend the change, describing it as likely to be 'disappointing' to many observers. But Xi would surely not have been upset that Carr, in the same interview, raised the spectre of an authoritarianism that until recently was assumed to have died with Chairman Mao. Such a comparison passes for flattery these days.

•

It is no pleasure to carp about *Silent Invasion*'s flaws, not least because it is, without question, one of the important Australian publishing events of recent years and a truly significant contribution to the debate about Australia's future relationship with China. Hamilton is a brave commentator who was always going to incur pain for venturing into this territory. On balance, he and his publisher have done us a service in bringing together a great deal of information about Chinese influence on Australia, as well as guiding us towards the questions that need to be asked in our dealings with the PRC across a range of domains. I find it hard to disagree with Hamilton's suggestion, made towards the end of the book, that since the 1980s Australians have 'set the economy before everything else and put power in the hands of those who tell us we must sacrifice everything to it, including our sovereignty as a free country'.

Or rather – as so often during my reading of this book – I think I can agree with him up to that last clause. I am not sure that our sovereignty and freedom are really in danger at present. But I do agree that in treating for so long a rather ruthless one-party state as, in essence, just another business opening, we have been storing up some serious problems for ourselves as a liberal democracy. The rapid growth of the Chinese economy, China's rising global power, and its increasingly authoritarian and centralised political turn have magnified the scale and increased the urgency of these problems. Hamilton's book suggests that, at the very least, China spruikers who tell us there is nothing to see here should have their views subjected to the most careful scrutiny – especially if, as 'friends of China', they have grown rich and powerful on lucrative consultancies, political donations, research grants and business opportunities.

AMERICA'S DEADLY EXCEPTIONALISM

LESLEY RUSSELL

28 May 2018

'America's strength has come from the love and courage and devotion of our mothers,' Donald Trump tweeted on Mother's Day this year. It would have been an inoffensive sentiment if he and his administration had demonstrated an awareness that too many American women aren't around to provide love, courage and devotion because they die in childbirth or soon after, or that too many infants who could have basked in that love, courage and devotion die before their first birthday. American women are more likely to die from pregnancy-related causes than women in any other developed country, and the country's infant mortality rate is about 70 per cent higher than the average among comparable countries.

In 2015, according to the latest figures, America's maternal mortality rate (defined as deaths due to complications from pregnancy or childbirth) was 26.4 per 100,000 live births. Australia's rate was 5.5 and Western Europe's was 7.2. Even more shockingly, the statistics have worsened over time. While most countries have made major inroads, the United States has gone backwards. In 1990, its maternal mortality rate was 16.9 per 100,000 live births.

Despite the marvels of modern medicine, and despite huge expenditure on healthcare, bearing a child is still one of the most dangerous things an American woman can do. Among women aged twenty to thirty-four, it's the sixth most common cause of death. Yet at least 60 per cent of those deaths are preventable. And for every woman who dies in childbirth, seventy more come close.

The tragedy of maternal mortality is intertwined with the tragedy of infant mortality. Again, the United States is out of alignment with comparable countries. In 2014, its infant mortality rate was 5.8 per 1000 live births, compared to around 3.4 in Australia and comparable countries. Not surprisingly, neonatal deaths – deaths within twenty-eight days of birth – are also higher. While both rates have improved since 2000, advances in the United States have been slower than in similar countries. Countries like Iceland, Japan and Singapore have infant mortality rates of around one per 1000 live births, highlighting what can be achieved.

As always, more complicated – and, in this case, much worse – stories lie behind the national data. The most recent data, released in 2018 by America's Health Rankings, put the maternal mortality rate for African-American women at 47.2 per 100,000 live births (comparable to the rates in Brazil, Iraq and Mongolia). The rate for Native American and Alaskan Native women was also high, at 38.8 per 100,000 live births. The rates for white, Hispanic and Asian/Pacific Islander women were 18.1, 12.2 and 11.6 respectively. The worst rates are generally found in the southern states. In Texas, African-American mothers account for 11.4 per cent of births but 28.8 per cent of pregnancy-related deaths.

Researchers have struggled to understand why. Much is made in other fields of 'American exceptionalism', but in this case the difference can only be shameful and concerning. We know that factors like socio-economic status, nutrition and affordable access to healthcare services (including prenatal care) play a key role. So too do obesity, rising rates of chronic health conditions and, most recently, the opioid epidemic.

The health of the mother is a key factor in the health of the child. African-American mothers are much more likely to be poor, uninsured and very young, and their babies are much more likely to be born prematurely. Black babies are more than twice as likely as white babies to die before their first birthday – a disparity that is wider now than in 1850, before the end of slavery.

But even after accounting for demographic differences, including education, employment, medical histories, insurance status and prenatal care, African–American women are still more likely than their white counterparts to have babies born early and of low birth weight. Education is only a mildly protective factor: a black woman with an advanced degree is more likely to lose her baby than a white woman with an eighth-grade education. While biomedical factors – including higher rates of hypertension and pre-eclampsia – play a part, intergenerational stress, racism and discrimination are also thought to be involved.

Why, then, despite high levels of social disadvantage, including low rates of health insurance, low levels of education, and young maternal age, do Hispanic women and their babies have better outcomes than those in other disadvantaged groups? One explanation for this 'Hispanic paradox' might be the strength of culturally protective social support networks, including informal systems of prenatal care. Understanding the paradox and implementing this approach could offer one solution to the current crisis.

Clearly, an essential part of the solution is improved access to healthcare. Obamacare included a range of measures that specifically benefitted women and their children and tackled health disparities. These include a guarantee of maternity coverage, free preventive services (including breastfeeding support, contraceptives and contraceptive counselling), and screening of pregnant women for gestational diabetes, hepatitis B, Rh incompatibility, HIV and iron deficiency. Interventions to stop alcohol consumption and tobacco use during pregnancy are also covered, as are folic acid supplements to prevent infant birth defects.

Obamacare's policies to increase health-insurance and Medicaid coverage delivered dramatic gains. The proportion of women of reproductive age who were uninsured dropped by 41 per cent between 2013 and 2016. With both the Trump administration and Republican states seeking to wind back Medicaid and federal support for insurance exchanges, these gains are under threat, with obvious consequences. It's no coincidence that Texas, with the largest number of uninsured people in the United States and substantial cuts to women's health programs, has the nation's highest maternal mortality rate.

Little data is yet available on the benefits of Obamacare for maternal and child health. But a very recent report showed that the mean infant mortality rate in states that haven't expanded Medicaid rose slightly between 2014 and 2016 (from 6.4 to 6.5 per 1000 births) but declined in states that have expanded it (from 5.9 to 5.6 per 1000 births). The 14.5 per cent decline in the infant mortality rate among African-American infants in states that expanded Medicaid was more than twice the 6.6 per cent seen in other states.

The Trump administration's policies – enacted and planned – will adversely affect nearly every government program that offers benefits to pregnant women, mothers and their children, with the largest impact falling on the most vulnerable. It is significant that Republicans now include Medicaid, food stamps and housing assistance in 'welfare reform', making it easier to justify cuts and changes to these programs as merely affecting the undeserving welfare recipients they routinely demonise. Ultimately, the impact is racist.

Trump's campaign promise that he would not cut basic social welfare programs and his inauguration pledge that 'the forgotten men and women of our country will be forgotten no longer' evidently didn't apply to all Americans, especially those of colour. This is most egregiously demonstrated in Trump's executive order directing federal agencies to consider adding work requirements to federal assistance programs.

Republican states looking to implement this policy are seeking federal Medicaid exemptions for counties with predominantly white populations.

The administration and congressional Republicans have proposed deep cuts and structural changes to the Supplemental Nutrition Assistance Program (food stamps) and the Special Supplemental Nutrition Program for Women, Infants and Children, which offers food assistance and support to pregnant and postpartum mothers. These changes are planned despite a large body of evidence showing that access to these two programs is linked to positive outcomes for mothers and infants that carry into adulthood. Nearly a quarter of African-American households experienced food insecurity in 2016, compared to 9.3 per cent of white households.

Trump has also moved to limit women's access to reproductive and preventive health services provided through the Title X Family Planning Program. This is a vindictive strike at Planned Parenthood, which has long been prevented from using any federal funding for the provision of abortions. Now the administration has announced restrictions that effectively bar caregivers at facilities receiving Title X funds from providing any services, referrals or information about abortions.

With these facilities providing an array of essential healthcare services, the ramifications go well beyond affordable access to abortions. The proposed rule overrides an Obama administration initiative that mandated the federal funds for services related to contraception, sexually transmitted infections, fertility, pregnancy care, and breast and cervical cancer screening to qualified health providers, regardless of whether they also perform abortions.

This move is just one part of the restrictions being systematically imposed on women's reproductive health. In October 2017 the administration rolled back the Obamacare mandate that schemes must cover contraception at no extra cost, allowing virtually any employer to claim a religious or moral objection to providing that option. Ongoing legal actions from both sides can be expected.

These restrictions also have international implications. On day three of his presidency, Trump signed an executive order reinstating the 'global gag rule' and extending its application to all international health assistance – not just maternal and child health, but also HIV/AIDS and tuberculosis programs. Trump's 2019 budget proposal would severely cut United States funding for global women's health and halve funding for reproductive health.

The only good news on the horizon comes from states that have assessed the economic and social costs of unacceptably high rates of maternal and infant mortality and morbidity and are taking action. A prime example, the work of the California Maternal Quality Care Collaborative, shows that changes aimed at improving birthing procedures and follow-up care can deliver real gains.

California has reduced its maternal mortality rate by more than half, from 14.0 deaths per 100,000 births to 6.2 in four years. This was achieved primarily by identifying common but preventable causes of death (like haemorrhage) and recognising that many of the most dangerous childbirth complications can be solved with simple fixes, such as giving hospitals clear, step-by-step instructions on what to do in emergencies and having the necessary equipment on hand. The state's maternal mortality rates (deaths per 100,000 births) for African-American, white, Asian/Pacific Islander and Hispanic women are 17.4, 4.7, 4.1 and 3.1 respectively.

When Trump announced the latest effort to limit access to federal family-planning dollars, the White House said the proposed rule would fulfil his promise 'to continue to improve women's health.' These words may come back to haunt him. Polls show that healthcare is a key issue for many voters. Women, who constitute more than half the population, have cast between four and seven million more votes than men in recent elections, and African-American women have the highest turnout rate.[14]

---

14 References for all the data in this article are available in the online version, at insidestory.org.au/americas-deadly-exceptionalism/.

CREATORS

LUCKING INTO THE ZEITGEIST

IAIN TOPLISS

17 February 2011

Jules Feiffer is an all-but-forgotten name today, but his influence is discernible in every contemporary comedy of anxiety, whether on the stage, in the cinema or (especially) on television. *Seinfeld, Frasier, My Family, Two and a Half Men, How I Met Your Mother* and a host of similar programs owe a sizeable debt to the weekly cartoon strip Feiffer drew for *The Village Voice* in New York from 1956 to 1998. He was also a playwright (*Little Murders, Elliot Loves*), a novelist (*Harry, the Rat with Women*) and a screenwriter (*Carnal Knowledge, Popeye*). Along with other dimly recalled figures connected with the stage, the nightclub and the off-Broadway review – the comedians Mort Sahl and Shelley Berman and the improvisers Mike Nichols and Elaine May among them – he discovered that urban angst was the modern comic mother lode.

Indeed, Feiffer claims to have invented the Jewish Mother Joke, and one variant of it from *The Village Voice* is a good introduction to his work for anyone unfamiliar with it. It is a strip cartoon in which the panels show only the face of the mother in question, a face redrawn ten times over with small variations in expression. As is customary in Feiffer's cartoons the drawing is balanced, at first glance over-toppled, by a substantial text, here nearly 200 words – so many that one might think that it was in the words that all the work was being done. The penultimate panel upsets any such idea. There the mother's eyes engage silently with our eyes, as we weigh up the implications of all that has been said. The subtle changes from one drawing to the next – 'moment-to-moment' rather than 'action-to-action' transitions – draw our attention to character, mood, motive and predicament rather than to situation, deed, narrative and comic payoff: in fact there is a payoff, and a good one too. But, as so often in Feiffer's work, instead of dismissing us into laughter it invites us into thought.

Feiffer must have drawn nearly 2500 cartoons like this, more if one counts his work for other publications like *Playboy, The Observer* – Feiffer had an early success in London – and latterly *The New York Times*. But his heyday was undoubtedly the ten years between the mid 1950s and the mid 1960s. It was then that he refined his peculiar mixture of angst and kvetch, material that now discloses itself as the negative space, the psychic dark energy, of America's affluence, self-confidence and hegemony over its half of a bipolar world. He covered everything: male inadequacy, the pretensions of modern dance, the battle of the sexes (pre-feminism), the bomb, the new narcissism, the organisation man, psychosomatic stomach-aches, phoney Village bohemianism, through a series of dramatic monologues in which the speaker arrived at a much worse position than where he or she started. These confessional strips were first collected in the bestselling *Sick, Sick, Sick* (1959) – a phrase that described not Feiffer's kind of humour, but the people he depicted, and the society that produced them.

Backing into Forward is Feiffer's lively, funny, fresh, frank, informal memoir, comprehensively illustrated, and beautifully produced in the manner of the best American publishing – an inviting dust jacket, stylish but restrained layout, elegant typeface, high-quality paper, deckled edging, copious illustrations, a credit to the Nan Talese imprint from Doubleday. Feiffer deftly switches his attention back and forth from life to times to career, and one of the book's many virtues is the way the author helps us grasp the ceaselessly alternating flow between all three.

Backing into Forward also reminds us on every page that Feiffer's gift is verbal as much as pictorial. His modesty is particularly appealing: advised by a well-meaning uncle that he mustn't put all his eggs in one basket, Feiffer observes that the trouble is he has only one basket and in any case only one egg. Loosely chronological at first, the book becomes more associative in its organisation, leaping from one topic to another. The story is told in a series of vivid, short chapters that are verbal equivalents of the cartoonist's clearly delineated panel: 'Idol' (artist Will Eisner), 'Camp Gorgon' (the army), 'My Candidate' (a vignette of Democrat Gene McCarthy at the 1968 California presidential primary, preferring to trade lines of poetry with Robert Lowell rather than take a campaign-boosting interview with James Reston), and so on.

Feiffer was a child of the Depression whose parents – Dave (passive) and Rhoda (aggressive) – were genteel-poor, lower-middle-class Jews from the Bronx. A failure academically, he defends himself from the local toughs by chalking up drawings of Popeye bashing up local toughs, and indulges his secret taste for radio serials and action comic books – the work of Milton Caniff, Alex Raymond and others celebrated in his *The Great Comic Book Heroes*. (*Backing into Forward* includes samples of the author's early work as well as that of his favourite illustrators.) The politics of Feiffer's generation were uniformly left-wing: Feiffer's sister, Mimi, is a Stalinist,

Feiffer himself a socialist, and both quarrel with the local Trotskyites. He brings his ideological disposition into the McCarthyite fifties and has some informative tales to tell about the betrayals of playwright Clifford Odets, director and choreographer Jerome Robbins and director Elia Kazan. With no obvious career in sight, he parlays himself into an unpaid 'job' as a gofer in Eisner's studio, where he discovers he can't draw figures, can't draw backgrounds, and can't letter. He does, however, eventually persuade Eisner to let him write the storyline for his comic strip, *The Spirit*.

There follow some dispiriting years in the army and some equally dispiriting years in an East Village bedsitter, where he struggles unsuccessfully to make his mark in the art departments of advertising studios and magazines, and even in animated cartoons. Finally he presents himself at *The Village Voice* (then a year old) and repeats the Eisner episode. The editors look at his drawings, inform him that they will publish anything he brings them, but won't edit him and certainly won't pay him. They don't pay him for the next eight years, the years of his astonishing early fame. So ends Part One, 'Gunslinger'.

Particularly interesting in Part Two, 'Success', is Feiffer's account of working on the various productions of *Little Murders* with Robert Brustein and Elliott Gould (he has his share of failure and rejection, and the chapter on the play is simply titled 'Flop'), and with Mike Nichols, Jack Nicholson and Art Garfunkel on *Carnal Knowledge*. Here – perhaps inevitably – the story tends towards anecdotes about the great and famous, with whom Feiffer now starts to hobnob. He has his criticisms to make – of Woody Allen's late-developed taste for 'conspicuous shyness', for example – but he never conceals his wonder at where his talent has taken him. At one dinner party he listens to Kenneth Tynan explain to Marlene Dietrich how he and Ernest Hemingway are no longer on speaking terms. Dietrich shakes her 'no-less-beautiful-because-of-the-years-head' and like a very convincing Dietrich imitator huskily croons, 'Oh no Ken. No no no, Ken. We can never be mad at Papa.' Ken! Marlene!! Papa!!! Feiffer cannot believe what the boy from 1225 Stratford Avenue, Bronx, is witnessing.

•

Any artist has to make it new not just in material but in form and *Backing into Forward* is most interesting in showing from the inside the formal revolution that underpins Feiffer's work. Simplifying a little one can say that this occurs around 1950–1951 with the shift from *Clifford* to *Munro*. Clifford was the hero of a comic strip that Eisner allowed Feiffer to draw for the last page of *The Spirit* lift-out syndicated across US newspapers. Munro was the hero of the first truly Feifferesque comic story, dreamed up during Feiffer's miserable time in the army in 1951, a story he couldn't get published for eight years.

Clifford stands somewhere between Pogo and Charlie Brown. That is to say, he is a standardised, cute, lovable child cartoon character of the period. He is delineated in the crisp, professional style favoured by the Eisner studio – deftly inked-in, or brush-flicked, character outlines set against a realistic background. His story is told in a series of nine or so bordered panels with conventional speech bubbles filled with lettering probably done by a lettering specialist and the rapid action-to-action transitions characteristic of the classic comic strip. It is droll, but controlled, conventional and off-the-peg.

Munro, a four-year-old boy drafted into the army, is idiosyncratically and authentically Feiffer. He is drawn in an exhilarating free and informal style that owes something (Feiffer tells us) to the effect on him of seeing the work of Saul Steinberg, William Steig and André François. What Feiffer liked about Steinberg was the cultural critique Steinberg's art implied (his line 'indicted', he says; it was a form of cultural anthropology); what he liked about Steig (later the author of *Shrek*), especially the Steig of books like *Till Death Do Us Part*, was the fusion of Freud, Reich and cartooning; what he liked about François was the careless, improvised, confident freedom of his line:

> It was François's sense of the moment ... immediacy on paper ... drawing as if it were coming from inside the page out, a scrawl by an invisible hand announcing itself on the page without consciousness of layout, composition or design ... art that just happened ... that's what I was after.

It is an apt description of where Feiffer ended up. What he contributed was that overabundance of words – the narrative of inner states of being.

Munro represents a complete rejection of Eisner's cartoon world: both as to draftsmanship (Feiffer comments admiringly on Eisner's mastery of anatomy, pose, expression, point of view, his melodramatic contrast of light and shade, but admits these effects are quite beyond him), and as to subject matter (in Eisner's case a noir-ish, melodramatic, quasi-allegorical storyline, for which Feiffer substituted an acute psychological realism). One gradually comes to see Eisner as Feiffer's 'strong predecessor', an artistic father figure whom he had to confront, overcome and repudiate.

His success depended, as so often, upon a combination of rebellion, self-acceptance, and innovation. Feiffer's strengths never lay in the direction of his heroes like Milton Caniff, Alex Raymond, and Will Eisner: in the tough, disciplined world of professional cartooning Feiffer was a flop and he had to give up his investment in it. He couldn't even draw a convincing gun; 'my guns were made of melting butter', he confesses. His breakthrough came when he took that melting-butter style, accepted it as his own, and applied it to the depiction of the mid-century unhappy consciousness.

•

Crucial to Feiffer's story is the story of his mother, Rhoda Feiffer. Rhoda is the cartoonist's antagonist in this book; although she has been dead for many years you sense that much of the book is directed to her, that the quarrel, the need to defy, justify, explain and reject is still strong in him. (Dave, gentle, irritable, ineffectual, is dispensable.) Rhoda is affectless, accusatory, dominating, lacking maternal warmth: 'Not a hugger, a holder, a kisser, a squeezer, or a pincher. She didn't go in for bodily contact, certainly not with my father. I've suspected for a long time that mine was a virginal birth.' She was, he says, 'a control freak ... a micromanager who managed ineptly', who sought some perverse justification for her position by welcoming acts of defiance by others: 'endless letdowns, betrayals ... weakness on the part of men who left her holding the bag'. Among many stories of betrayal, Feiffer relates the story of his adored dog, Rex, whom Rhoda gives away to a 'fairy tale farmer and his daughter' without telling Jules what she is doing (he is at school when the dog is taken), on the grounds that while the boy might take care of the dog for the moment he will eventually 'fall down on the job'. Feiffer remembers the phrase, says that Rhoda 'patented it', and, after all these years, still flinches from its assault.

Feiffer's sense of his mother's implacable hostility to her children continues to the end of the book. In Feiffer's account, she engineers her own death with one eye on how it will affect her children: 'It was her breath. I believe she was driven to hold it. "I'll show you, I'll hold my breath till I die." She did show us. "I'll die and then you'll be sorry!" She died. We weren't sorry.' Near the front of the book is a cabinet photograph of Jules, aged nine, a beautiful, adored child – but we see the photograph has been folded, torn and ripped: we can only guess at the history of that disfigurement, and guess too at the circumstances of the photograph's rescue.

Rhoda's sad story is a Depression-era counterpoint to her son's Age of Affluence success. The child of immigrant Jews who settled in the mid-West, she returns to New York conscious of her superiority to the *shtetl* Jews around her – unlike them, unlike Dave, the third-best man she settles for as a husband in the name of security, a man who mixes up his double-u's and vees, she speaks in a perfect 'accentless English'. Rhoda has talent, artistic taste, ambition. She hopes to succeed as a fashion stylist, a term she believes she invented. Her aim is to get her designs adopted by dress manufacturers, and when Jules sets off on a coming-of-age trek across America he travels with samples of her designs in his rucksack to show to dress manufacturers en route. They throw him out and copy the designs. Success eludes her. All that remains is her resentment, her sense of entitlement, her fierce ambition, qualities that Jules himself, for all his *nebbish*-ness, his hatred of his mother, has inherited, along with her artistic talent. What else drives him to present himself, unannounced and barely nineteen years old, at the door of Eisner's studio to ask for a job? To work for Eisner just as, later, he works for *The Village Voice*, for no pay? In both cases he is convinced he has something – something – to offer, not as the inheritor of Eisner, but as the founder of a new comic style. This could be presented heroically of course, but more modestly, alert to the role of accident, chance and contingency in even the most driven personality, it is for him just 'lucking into the zeitgeist', or the 'backing into forward' of his title.

Rhoda is a monster, and a late chapter details a truly astonishing incident late in her life concerning Feiffer's younger sister, Alice. But she is also the book's tragic, unlovable, offstage anti-heroine, her fall the counterweight to her son's rise, and for that son, you feel, a piece of unfinished, and unfinishable, business. The stories of Jules and Rhoda go together and give the memoir a satisfying if discomforting coherency – negative space again – and exemplify, comically, tragically, triumphantly, DH Lawrence's observation about the huge mountain of failure that American success is built on.

WOMEN BEHAVING BADLY

JILL KITSON

16 May 2011

No literary classics have a greater claim to 'Englishness' than the novels of Jane Austen. Set among the gentry of the southern counties during the Regency period, Austen's six novels depict the minutiae of daily life as she herself observed and experienced it in the Hampshire villages of Steventon, where for more than half her life her father was the rector, and Chawton, where she lived with her widowed mother and sister Cassandra for the last nine years of her life. It was a narrower existence than that of the Brontë sisters a generation later. They left home – a Yorkshire rectory – to work as governesses or schoolteachers; Charlotte even ventured abroad to teach in Belgium. Jane Austen's years in Bath, where the Austen family moved after her father retired, and Southampton, where she and her mother and Cassandra lived for a time after his death, expanded her horizons but not the focus of her attention.

In September 1814, in the midst of writing *Emma* in the parlour at Chawton, she offered this insouciant advice to her niece Anna: 'Three or four families in a country village is the very thing to work on.' In another light-hearted letter written the same year to her brother Edward, she likened herself to an inept portrait miniaturist: 'the little bit (two inches wide) of ivory on which I work with so fine a brush, as produces little effect after much labour'.

That Austen, with her witty self-deprecation, is – like her novels – so very 'English' is a clue to her continuing popularity in England, but what about the United States, where Jane Austen is a multimillion-dollar industry, giving employment to academics, actors, filmmakers and writers? Rachel M. Brownstein's platitudinous answer to this question concludes her new book, *Why Jane Austen?*:

> Jane Austen is the focal point of nostalgia ... not only for
> heritage England ... but also for a world that seemed more
> comprehensible and coherent, and for the novel itself
> in its youth and vigour, the novel endowed (as it appears

in retrospect) with an integrity, innocence, health and prosperity, a hopefulness and seriousness of purpose, that has been or is being lost.

Brownstein and William Deresiewicz, author of *A Jane Austen Education: How Six Novels Taught Me about Love, Friendship, and the Things that Really Matter*, are among the latest American writers to capitalise on the popularity of Jane Austen in the United States. Their claim on our attention, however – that their subject is Jane Austen – is a ruse to buttonhole us about themselves. Both write with the breezy informality of a blog.

So we learn that throughout Professor Brownstein's long academic career, she has been teaching courses on Austen's novels and keeping abreast of what she calls 'Jane-o-mania' in all its manifestations. Part memoir, part 'biographical criticism', part catalogue, her book characterises Jane Austen as a teacher whose books impart lessons about life: 'In *Pride and Prejudice*, Elizabeth had learned to put thinking above feeling, and so did I, by reading about her.' Brownstein's free-flowing prose, studded with rhetorical questions (like her title) and digressions, brings to mind the garrulous Miss Bates of *Emma*. She says that she tells her students 'about the coteries of so-called Janeites, a term coined by the English literary critic George Saintsbury, and the gallant gentlemen Virginia Woolf wrote about who felt about criticism of their darling as they would feel about an insult to one of their aunts (these were gay guys, they guess)'.

William Deresiewicz's book is a chatty memoir about the self-transformation wrought by reading Jane Austen. The banalities Deresiewicz learned from each of Austen's six novels are summed up on the back cover:

> *Emma*: Pay attention to the everyday things; *Pride and Prejudice*: You aren't born perfect; *Northanger Abbey*: Stay awake: don't take things for granted; *Mansfield Park*: Being entertained is not the same thing as being happy; *Persuasion*: Be honest with your friends; *Sense and Sensibility*: Love is about growing up, not staying young.

The idea of reading Jane Austen to learn lessons about life is totally repugnant to me. Equally repugnant are memoirs about lessons learned from reading her. I read Jane Austen for pleasure, for the instant delight of, say, the opening of *Persuasion*:

> Sir Walter Elliot, of Kellynch Hall, in Somersetshire, was a man who, for his own amusement, never took up any book but the Baronetage; there he found occupation for an idle hour, and consolation in a distressed one ...

The poised irony of this character sketch, the rhythm of the sentence with its paradoxical tone – Jane Austen's style – makes me laugh out loud. Vladimir Nabokov, in his 1950s Cornell lecture on *Mansfield Park*, ends by reflecting upon Jane Austen's style, and particularly what he calls 'the epigrammatic intonation, a certain terse rhythm in the witty expression of a slightly paradoxical thought. The tone of voice is terse and tender, dry and yet musical, pithy but limpid and light.'

That style is what gives endless pleasure to readers of her novels, not the 'life lessons' touted by Brownstein and Deresiewicz. Austen's style is what is lacking in film or television adaptations of her novels, however faithful they are to the dialogue and the plot. So in the 2008 BBC version of *Persuasion*, Sir Walter is portrayed as a vain snob, just as Jane Austen declares him to be, but not as foolishly comic, which her irony renders him. Underpinning the style is her command of language, the acuity of her observations, her finely nuanced moral sensibility and her natural wit.

All six of her novels are about love and marriage among the county gentry. To find 'lessons' in them is to lose sight of them as comedies of manners, in which bad behaviour keeps breaking out. If the comedy arises from human folly, the drama, the excitement, the plot itself springs from bad behaviour, incivility, and its consequences. In *Mansfield Park*, it is the bad behaviour of the two Bertram sisters; in *Pride and Prejudice*, it is the bad behaviour of the two youngest Bennet sisters – as well as that of the young men they flirt with – that animates the plot. Austen's most engaging heroines, Emma Woodhouse and Elizabeth Bennet, in addition to being witty, intelligent and spirited, are at crucial moments breathtakingly badly behaved. Emma wounds Miss Bates, behaves cattily to Miss Fairfax and, in her arrogance, almost ruins her protégé Harriet. Elizabeth bluntly tells her suitor Mr Collins: 'You could not make me happy, and I am convinced that I am the last woman in the world who would make you so'; she replies insolently to Lady Catherine de Bourgh's rude questions about her upbringing; and when Darcy, proposing to her, refers to her social 'inferiority' as a 'degradation', she rounds upon him: deploring his manners, accusing him of dividing his friend Bingley from her sister Jane, of ruining Wickham's life, and declaring him to be 'the last man in the world whom I could ever be prevailed upon to marry'.

Even docile Fanny Price, in *Mansfield Park*, dares to defy her uncle, Sir Thomas Bertram, to whom she is totally beholden. In the face of his anger, she refuses to marry Henry Crawford and has to bear her uncle's lengthy condemnation and the consequences: 'Self-willed, obstinate, selfish and ungrateful. He thought her all this. She had deceived his expectations; she had lost his good opinion. What was to become of her?'

Elizabeth Bennet even believes it was her bad behaviour that caused Darcy to fall in love with her. When Darcy cannot recall exactly what set him off, Lizzie jogs his memory:

> 'My beauty you had early withstood, and as for my manners – my behaviour to you was at least always bordering on the uncivil, and I never spoke to you without rather wishing to give you pain than not. Now be sincere; did you admire me for my impertinence?'
>
> 'For the liveliness of your mind, I did.'
>
> 'You may as well call it impertinence at once. It was very little less. The fact is, that you were sick of civility, of deference, of officious attention. You were disgusted with the women who were always speaking and looking, and thinking of your approbation alone. I roused, and interested you, because I was so unlike them. Had you not been really amiable you would have hated me for it; but in spite of the pains you took to disguise yourself, your feelings were always noble and just; and in your heart, you thoroughly despised the persons who so assiduously courted you. There – I have saved you the trouble of accounting for it; and really, all things considered, I begin to think it perfectly reasonable. To be sure, you knew no actual good of me – but nobody thinks of that when they fall in love.'
>
> 'Was there no good in your affectionate behaviour to Jane, while she was ill at Netherfield?'
>
> 'Dearest Jane! Who could have done less for her? But make a virtue of it by all means. My good qualities are under your protection, and you are to exaggerate them as much as possible; and, in return, it belongs to me to find occasions for teasing and quarrelling with you as often as may be ...'

'Style like this,' writes Nabokov, 'is not Austen's invention, nor is it even an English invention: I suspect it really comes from French literature where it is profusely represented in the eighteenth and early nineteenth centuries. Austen did not read French but got the epigrammatic rhythm from the pert, precise, and polished kind of style which was the fashion. Nevertheless, she handles it to perfection.'

SILENCE MADE VISIBLE

SYLVIA LAWSON

13 November 2013

Ivan Sen's *Mystery Road* is a Western which observes the conventions of its genre: conflict of law and lawlessness in a remote setting; visible wide landscapes; a central character, the man who rides into town with a mission, a man who holds experience and emotion in reserve; a climactic shootout; laconic dialogue all round. Seen from behind, Aaron Pedersen's Jay Swan has a John Wayne kind of walk; and this film, like many Westerns, looks outward across a realm of historical loss. But it's not about the domains of pioneers and frontiersmen, we're not in Monument Valley, and the lawman isn't on horseback. Horses do appear, but as the prized possessions of David Field's wonderfully poisonous Sam Bailey, one of the story's thriving villains. The detective drives an unpretentious sedan. The music is significantly unheroic: a few barely noticeable passages of long-held electronic lament in low and higher registers. Like the cinematography and editing, the music is Sen's own; there is a sound design credit, well deserved, to Lawrence Horne.

You notice the music only if, on a second viewing, you're deliberately alert for it. In those sounds, however, the sadness is unequivocal. Detective Swan has returned after ten years to the small town of the film's main action. He and the film are silent on his past in 'the city', a place which, like the town we're in, goes unnamed. In his unfolding relations with his fellow policemen and the locals, 'the city' works as the absent source of his superior authority and skill, and also as the reason why he must be thwarted, choked-off whenever possible, taken down a peg. At the place of the first murder, he asks the local sergeant (superbly performed by a wry Tony Barry) why the area hasn't been roped off as a crime scene; the answer, a rebuff, is that this kind of thing just happens around here, no big deal. This victim, like the next one, is a black girl, and the question hangs: how different would the response have been if she'd been white? The town is mostly an Aboriginal community, and Jay Swan's Aboriginality is at the psychological centre of the story. If there's going to be any sort of an investigation, he's an essential presence; at the same time, his status makes him a traitor among his own kind, since he's going to subject them to the white man's law. The word 'coconut' isn't used, but the accusation is actively in play.

Another charge hits him harder; he has failed to be a father to his daughter Crystal, who understandably doesn't want to talk to him; nor do her friends, and Crystal's mother Mary gives him no quarter when he tries for a conciliatory meeting. Sticking implacably to her routine, beer and the pokies, she tells him that she at least knows who she is. They all know more than they'll tell him about the drug circuits, and about the girls who, it is said, 'go with' the truckies for their supplies. Among the police, Hugo Weaving's Johnno taunts him; Johnno, self-described as 'a sad case', is always one jump ahead with the dealers and informers; he is inveigling, mocking, complex, and a part of him would like Jay to get the case together. Weaving could be a great Hamlet, indeed an Iago. As Crystal and Mary, young Tricia Whitton and Tasma Walton give performances of equal subtlety. Aaron Pedersen finely negotiates Swan's double aspect, the wordless personal unease beneath the intent professionalism on the job. His character too is generic; the mean streets of the classic detective tale become these long, forking dusty roads and the grid of the town, seen in aerial shots as his car makes purposeful turns in pursuit – of just what, we're kept unsure. As a Western, this is also a thriller; from the dark opening on the road, with the long track along the culvert underneath, the tension is extreme.

The uncertainties, the silences and broken-off exchanges, the crazy set pieces in which Jack Thompson does dementia and Jack Charles does the scheming old know-all, all compose a world in which nothing's going to be wrapped up. There will be the ominous passage with the roo-shooters, intimations of evil right out of Boorman's *Deliverance*. There will be moments of lightness, even of promise, with the kids playing in the dust, and in the comedy of Swan's strung-out negotiation with the boy who found a lost mobile phone. There will be the second murder, while the great rigs, the Titans of the outback world, go thundering along the highway; the speed and noise are relentless. Here, as in *Beneath Clouds*, the roaring juggernauts signal the forces against which the people of this town – any town – can do so little. As they loom up, drug dependence, petty trafficking and beer-soaked idleness make a terrible kind of sense; this account doesn't even let in the struggling schoolteacher whose kind we saw last year in Sen's *Toomelah*.

In that film, too, a small town has its place on the drug trails, a network criss-crossing outback Australia; Ivan Sen is giving us parts of a map we would rather not recognise as our own. It has been said that within every strong feature film there's a documentary, the whole film's grip on the world, and it's true of *Mystery Road*. Some commentators have found it lacking for leaving those loose ends, the open gaps in Swan's and the audience's knowledge. If you pay close attention to the final quarter of an hour, there aren't in fact so many gaps; but in any case, the kind of detective work that wraps the case up completely, with all the ends tied off, belongs with Agatha Christie and Poirot. Tight plots can be part of cinema, but the richest and most interesting cinema makes doubt and silence visible; Ivan Sen has acknowledged the influence of Andrei Tarkovsky.

The town in *Mystery Road*, not far from Massacre Creek and Slaughter Hill, belongs in Australian history, past and present. It inherits – and with the two murders indeed continues – what Henry Reynolds has recently named as 'the forgotten war' between black and white, and the destruction of Aboriginal society over two centuries.[1] The banal desolation of the town, with its untended yards, littered interiors and boredom, is wreckage from exactly that war. Some will say that this response calls into the film too much that lies outside it; but it's exactly the inconclusiveness, the supposedly unanswered questions, that hold the story open on to history: consider those huge skies. This film is a small masterpiece.

---

1   Henry Reynolds, *Forgotten War* (Sydney: NewSouth, 2013).

PETER SCULTHORPE, A COMPOSER IN AUSTRALIA

ANDREW FORD

11 August 2014

Peter Sculthorpe's friends had been expecting word of his death for some weeks. He had been in hospital for much of 2014, and close to the end more than once. Still, when word finally came on 8 August, there was an immediate feeling of absence. People that day spoke of a hole, even a chasm, in our musical life. They were not exaggerating.

For fifty years, Sculthorpe wasn't simply at the heart of Australian music, he was its heart. From the mid 1960s, along with Richard Meale and Nigel Butterley, he had been part of a modernist triumvirate in the concert hall. Meale's music brought intellectual rigour and cosmopolitan brilliance, Butterley's a sort of private ecstasy, but it was Sculthorpe's pieces, painted from the start in broader brushstrokes, that captured the public imagination. In orchestral works such as the *Sun Music* series (1965–69), *Mangrove* (1979), *Earth Cry* (1986), *Kakadu* (1988) and *Memento Mori* (1993), Sculthorpe addressed a wide audience, communicating with them in a direct manner similar to the way in which Aaron Copland had addressed American audiences. However, there was a difference. At the height of Roosevelt's New Deal, Copland had deliberately set out to find an American style, assembling it from hoedowns and hymns. Sculthorpe, at least initially, was far less deliberate in his methods.

Peter Sculthorpe was, above all, an instinctive composer and an extremely individual one, his music always deeply personal. His childhood was solitary, in that he was happiest with his own thoughts – perhaps that is true of all composers – and accordingly he made his own musical technique, finding confirmation in the work of composers who had gone before him. His boyhood discovery of whole-tone scales, for instance, readied him for the influence of Debussy, whose music is full of those scales. He was also drawn, early on, to melodic lines that moved at a different rate from their harmonies, and particularly to pedal points – bass notes that continue to sound even as the harmony above them shifts. He recognised them in Schoenberg's *Verklärte Nacht* and

Mahler's *Das Lied von der Erde*, which he heard on ABC Radio. One is seldom influenced by things to which one is not already receptive, and so Sculthorpe's embrace of those composers – and, later, Japanese court music and Balinese gamelan, and later still, Aboriginal music – was made possible by his musical personality; it did not form it.

Of course, when you are a major public figure, as Sculthorpe was, the public feels it knows you and, to some extent, owns you. Your life and work are rolled into one, and both are mythologised. For that to happen, the story must first be simplified, and in Sculthorpe's case this came down to a belief that his music was somehow drawn from the Australian landscape, extracted, as it were, from the very rocks.

You can see how this happened. First, there were Sculthorpe's titles, which often seemed to tie his music to a particular place. Then there was the character of his music, which generally unfolded slowly, like the eye travelling across a wide expanse of outback. His melodic lines had rather narrow ranges, keeping close to the earth, resembling the undulating landscape itself. And those pedal points: were they not really drones, even didgeridoos? Perhaps, if Sculthorpe had been more of a Copland, he might have thought in such terms. But Sculthorpe did not draw on Australia so much as Australia drew on him. He gave us music that was *echt*-Sculthorpe, and we heard our land in its notes.

Peter's personality was in his music, but also his music was in his personality. There was even something about the way he spoke – a measured pace, a sonorous delivery – that seemed an extension of the slow unfolding of melody in a piece such as *Earth Cry*. That said, the man and the music were not the same. Perhaps we could say that the music contained Sculthorpe's essence, but the composer himself – like the rest of us – was a tangle of contradictions. For example, although he had apparently led Australian music away from its colonial past by accepting influences from Asia and Indigenous Australia, he was quite the Anglophile. I was astonished to discover, late one night in 1999 over a little too much to drink, that this musical 'voice of Australia' was actually a monarchist.

At the end of the twentieth century, Sculthorpe began to use the didgeridoo. He included it, most memorably, in the *Requiem* he composed for the 2004 Adelaide Festival, but he also added it to a number of his earlier pieces. Those who had always believed they heard the didgeridoo in his use of pedal points now heard the real thing, as the instrument suddenly turned up in *Mangrove*, *Earth Cry* and *Kakadu*, as well as a number of the later string quartets. These were among the composer's best-loved works, and some of Sculthorpe's colleagues were less than charitable in their belief that he was being tokenistic.

But you only had to listen to the music to know this was not true. The extraordinary thing about the collaboration between Sculthorpe and William Barton was not just that the latter seemed instinctively to know what was needed – there were never any written parts for the didgeridoo – but also that these works accepted his contribution so readily. It never sounded tacked on; on the contrary, those pedal points accommodated Barton almost as though the works had, hitherto, been incomplete and were only now properly finished. These new versions cemented the music's reputation as the sound of the land and Sculthorpe's as our national composer. He was happy to accept this role and the adulation that came with it. He loved being loved.

At the Sydney Symphony Orchestra's concerts for his eightieth birthday in 2009, Peter was a little too frail to get out of the audience to take a bow. (At the Opera House concert hall, you have to leave your seat, leave the auditorium and run down several flights of steps in order to emerge on stage with the orchestra.) It was put to Peter that he might prefer just to stay where he was sitting and stand to acknowledge the applause. But instead, he remained backstage both evenings, thus missing the actual performances, before walking on at the end to receive the cheers of the young Meet-the-Music crowd. I was backstage with him on those nights and he was clearly very tired, but both times I saw him return from the stage restored by the applause and glowing with happiness.

In the end, if people believe that Sculthorpe's music symbolises Australia, then it does: there can be no greater achievement for any artist than to produce a body of work that people feel to be their own. Peter himself probably came to believe it. But whether or not his work reflects our landscape, it was undeniably a shaping force of our musical landscape. When Sculthorpe came along, Australian music changed; now that he's gone, it will change again. For the time being, though, there's just that hole, that chasm. Fortunately, we have his music to help fill it.

ON LITERARY AWARDS

SUSAN LEVER

30 May 2016

In late February, Helen Garner found an email in her junk folder telling her she'd been awarded the Windham Campbell prize for nonfiction writing. Each year the prize awards US$150,000 to each of nine authors who write in English, regardless of nationality, across the genres of nonfiction, fiction and drama. There are no submissions and the writers are judged anonymously, with the aim of calling attention to their achievements and giving them an opportunity to work free of financial concerns. Apart from the award announcements in major papers, the 'calling attention' part of the award comes with a literary festival at Yale University several months after the announcement; there, the writers come together for a formal ceremony and a few days of discussions and public lectures. It sounds like a writer's dream.

Garner is not the first Australian to win a Windham Campbell award; the playwright Noelle Janaczewska was awarded a prize in 2014, its second year. Janaczewska may be little known outside Australian theatre circles, but she works across a range of genres, including what she calls 'performance essays'. The award announcement mentions her play *This Territory*, written in response to the Cronulla riot of 2005, alongside a wide range of theatre works and collaborations. The acknowledgement of Garner mentions not only *This House of Grief* but also her remarkable ability to shift between fiction and nonfiction. The prize's interest in different genres reflects the fact that Donald Windham was a writer of short stories and essays, and his life partner, Sandy Campbell, was an actor and theatre reviewer. The awards are funded from their carefully managed legacy, and they seem directed by the interests of writers rather than the concerns of publishers or the desire for publicity.

Here in Australia we have more modest literary awards, some of them also funded from the legacies of writers and their families. Of these, the Miles Franklin, the Patrick White and the Barbara Jefferis awards are the best known. The Kibble and Dobbie awards for women writers are the legacy of a librarian, Nita Dobbie, who wished to honour her librarian aunt, Nita Kibble. As well as these named awards, literary societies, journals, publishing groups, libraries and communities offer a range of other rewards to writers each year.

With less reliability, we also have publicly funded awards, such as the Prime Minister's and the Premiers' prizes. Curiously, though they are funded from the public purse, these awards attract less public criticism than a private award such as the Miles Franklin. In fact, the Miles Franklin appears to be pre-eminent in terms of reputation and controversy. *The Sydney Morning Herald*'s recent obituary for Leonie Kramer gave more space to her role in the awarding of the Miles Franklin to Helen Darville (Demidenko) than to her years of teaching and supervising university students, let alone her decades of uncontroversial chairing of the award. Though the judges now get a small honorarium, in Kramer's day they were lucky to get a free drink as recompense for the long hours spent poring over the entries.

As Ivor Indyk has commented, the Stella Prize 'shadows' the Miles Franklin award. It was established as a response to the perceived failure of the Miles Franklin to acknowledge the writing of women. It looks for winners who are 'excellent, original and engaging' and also runs a supporting program of book talks and events to promote the work of women writers. Three of its four winners have been novels, the fourth a history book. Though it is too soon to know whether a 'Stella' genre will emerge, this year's winner, Charlotte Wood's *The Natural Way of Things*, certainly raises questions about misogynist culture in Australia, suggesting the prize may take a position close to the Jefferis award's search for an excellent work of fiction that depicts women and girls in a positive way 'or otherwise empowers the status of women and girls in society'. The Jefferis winner can be written by a man, though none has won the prize (just as no non-Australians have won the Miles Franklin, though they are not precluded). Whether or not the Stella has influenced the Miles Franklin judges, the Franklin has gone to a woman each year since the Stella's inception.

•

This plethora of prizes may be overwhelming to readers, but for writers in Australia, an English-speaking country with access to the literary publishing of the rest of the world, they offer a little financial support and, sometimes, help in building a reputation and boosting sales. It remains difficult for a literary writer to make any kind of living from publishing in Australia. With an estimated mean annual income for writers of about

$12,500 from creative work, a serious literary author may well be grateful for any award that brings annual income closer to the $50,000 of the average Australian worker.

The catch is in the process of staggered longlist and shortlist announcements that goes with most Australian literary awards. Writing begins to look like a competitive sport, with losers eliminated in each round. (In practice, judges often find the winner at a first or second meeting, so shortlists are sometimes announced after the final decision has been made.) The desire for a big announcement ceremony means that organisers may keep the winner secret so that the shortlisted 'losers' won't be discouraged from attending. If you've been present when a prize has been announced and noticed unchosen writers carefully composing their faces or slipping speech notes back into a pocket, you will understand their reluctance to attend. The decision by some awards to give consolation cheques to shortlisted authors at least recognises this difficulty.

Some award managers seem to want books, like paintings or singing recitals, to be a communal public experience subject to a voicing of popular opinion. I recently took the opportunity to vote in the People's Choice category of the NSW Premier's prize for a novel; I had read only three of the six shortlisted novels, but that's probably two more than many other voters. Promoting readers' participation in this way seems harmless but it shouldn't be mistaken for promoting the interests of writers. It would be fairer to them to release a long and inclusive list of all the good books that have a chance of the award, then simply announce the lucky winner. For the winner will, indeed, be as much lucky as deserving. Judging panels are not absolute in their taste, and often harbour deep disagreements about the final choice. One forceful personality on a judging panel can drive everyone else into submission. In my various experiences as a judge, complete agreement usually came only on two-person panels. Once three or more judges are involved, the winner is likely to be a compromise candidate, and a safe one. Award managers sometimes seem ignorant or careless about the reputations of the judges they choose: the divided Prime Minister's award for fiction in 2014 revealed a dispute between members of the judging panel, though some innocents seemed to believe that the prime minister had intervened to reward his personal favourite. As it happened, the Man Booker Prize judges later agreed that Richard Flanagan's *The Narrow Road to the Deep North* was a winner.

Perhaps commentators take it quietly when odd things happen with politicians' awards because they know that these awards are regularly endangered by political change. The Queensland Premier's awards, for instance, disappeared when Campbell Newman came to power. A range of wonderful artists benefited from Paul Keating's Creative Fellowships in the early 1990s, but the fate of the scheme was sealed as soon as the prime minister's name became attached to them. Arm's-length arts funding through the Australia Council was set up for good reason.

Judges will always have subjective taste, whether because of their academic training, their own reading experience or their place in the market; and in Australia's small literary world, outright prejudices occasionally attach to particular writers. Despite any declared political commitments, though, judges are likely to be individualists rather than ideologues, and Australian literary judges have never been shy about publicly resigning on principle or declaring their abstention from a judgement. (Carmen Callil took this to an international level when she resigned from the judging panel that awarded the Man Booker International Prize to Philip Roth in 2011.) This is one of the ways that such awards stay in the news and gain extra publicity for writing. But it also detracts from the purpose of supporting writers to do their work. In my view, the funds for the various politicians' awards would be better added to the severely depleted coffers of the Australia Council or to the state arts funds as part of their regular grants to writers.

•

In his survey of the Miles Franklin award in *Australian Book Review* a few years ago, Patrick Allington called for the publication of complete lists of all entrants, and more openness about the decision-making process. To me, the tactful approach of the Windham Campbell prize is more appealing because I can't see that the public has any right to know how a private award is decided. It is all very well to barrack for the different possible winners, but we can hardly call for 'freedom of information' rights. Why shouldn't the prize go to an excellent novel about 'Australian life in any of its phases', for instance, if that is the kind of writing its benefactor wanted to promote?

If there has been a Miles Franklin genre, it has been the kind of monumental historical novel that Franklin herself wrote in her middle years: winners from Patrick White's *Voss* to Thomas Keneally's *Bring Larks and Heroes*, to Peter Carey's *Jack Maggs*, to Roger McDonald's *The Ballad of Desmond Kale* and Kim Scott's *That Deadman Dance* conform to this genre.

It does seem that this kind of novel is usually written by men. A glance down the list of past winners shows that the prize on occasions has gone to more eccentric writing by Thea Astley, David Ireland, David Foster and Elizabeth Jolley, and to domestic novels like Jessica Anderson's *Tirra Lirra By the River* and *The Impersonators*. But women have been less frequent winners, and first-novel winners are rare. (The controversial Darville was both a woman and a first-time novelist.) The striking thing is that so many Miles Franklin winners have been excellent novels. And this is the real test of a literary prize. The judges and their processes don't really count. It is whether the novels stand up when read and re-read over time.

By this standard, the Miles Franklin has picked more winners than losers over the years – which is not to say it hasn't picked some weak novels from time to time. Occasionally there are years when there are several excellent novels in contention, and others when there are hardly any. Domestic novels have been rare winners, and comic novels rarer still. In fact, the absence of satire and humour has been a weakness across all Australia's literary prizes. Andrew McGahan's serious consideration of Australian history, *The White Earth*, won the Miles Franklin in 2006, but I doubt that his wonderfully funny *1988*, published ten years earlier, was even entered. Fortunately, a farmer called Peter Wentworth Russell noticed this gap, and has left a legacy to fund a prize for an Australian work of humour, so far to be awarded every second year. (Bernard Cohen's novel *The Antibiography of Robert F. Menzies* won the inaugural prize last year.) So, if you feel inclined to leave your estate to support literary writing in Australia, learn the lessons of these various awards. The admirable Patrick White award takes no submissions, with its judges quietly reviewing the body of work of living Australian writers before announcing the winner. There is no need to insult any other writers by shortlisting and elimination, as their chance may well come the next year. There is no need even for a recent book to promote, as the prize is based on a body of work.

If you want to promote a certain kind of writing by setting guidelines beyond excellence, then you will create difficulties. Changing attitudes change definitions: sixty years after Miles Franklin's death, 'Australian life in any of its phases' is not such a clear-cut ideal; and one can debate at length what constitutes a positive image of women, or a contribution to their improved status. Even humorous writing is a subjective category. The biographical/biological qualification for writers may not present immediate difficulties – young writers, women writers, new writers, Indigenous writers – but the possibility for imposture lies forever in wait (remember Paul Radley and Wanda Koolmatrie?). Surely the only way to avoid difficulties is to concentrate firmly on the writing, not the writer.

The Windham Campbell prize offers another idea worth considering. For all the public celebrations of writing at literary festivals, there is a paucity of deep critical engagement with contemporary Australian writing. Our literary life would benefit immensely from some sustained critical discussion of the work of winning authors. This might not be possible for individual prizes where first books often win – but surely some enterprising literature department at an Australian university could organise a seminar for the serious study of the work of the winner of the Patrick White award each year, perhaps addressing the backlog of winners by considering three or four at a time.

ONCE WERE A WEIRD MOB

BRETT EVANS

11 November 2016

For that old-style Jaffa-rolling movie experience, you can't go past the State Theatre in Sydney's Market Street. Built in 1929, it seats over 2000 patrons in the faux classical opulence favoured by early designers of picture palaces.

Today, this glorious temple to cinema hosts music, ballet, stand-up comedians and the annual Sydney Film Festival. But on a wet winter's night back in 1966, a film that would help reactivate Australia's moribund motion picture industry had its premiere there. Amid flashing bulbs, a procession of local celebrities and dignitaries tramped up a sodden red carpet. Foreign glamour arrived in the shape of the movie's star, the Italian actor and comedian Walter Chiari. In spite of the weather, *They're a Weird Mob* was being launched onto the world stage in some style.

Based on the bestselling novel by a former pharmacist called John O'Grady (writing under the pseudonym Nino Culotta), *They're a Weird Mob* tells the – ever so slightly satirical – story of an Italian journalist's encounter with the strange manners, language and rituals of postwar Australia. It's a benign portrait of the migrant experience in Australia, and gently mocks the nation's dominant Anglo-Saxon suburbanite culture. Published in 1957, it sold in its millions.

Besides its humour, the book probably found favour with Australian readers because it portrayed them in such a flattering light. Nino never encounters prejudice; he is accepted easily into Australian society because he accepts so easily its habits of speech and thought. Reading the book today, you have to consciously remind yourself that it, and the film, were released at a time when Italian migrants would have been referred to in polite circles as 'New Australians' but in the nation's public bars they were 'wogs', 'dagoes' and 'eyeties'.

Standing nervously backstage that night, 'freshly made up with big hair and lots of eye make-up' and wearing a pair of fashionable culottes bought specially for the occasion, was a teenaged Jeanie Drynan. Fresh out of NIDA, she played Betty, the newlywed wife of Nino's friend, Jimmy. Today, after a long and illustrious acting career, she is best remembered

330

for her roles in classic Australian films like *Don's Party* and *Muriel's Wedding*.

'It was a big deal, a very big deal. There was lots of excitement about this film,' she told me recently by phone from her home in Los Angeles. After the film was shown that night fifty years ago, Drynan joined her older, more experienced cast mates up on stage: Chiari, Chips Rafferty, Ed Devereaux and Slim de Grey. A little bit of Hollywood hoopla had come to Market Street.

Also in the audience that night was a budding filmmaker in his twenties called Anthony Buckley. He was working for the newsreel company Cinesound, helping to capture for posterity the damp celebrities on the red carpet. Buckley doesn't rate the film highly, but he remembers it fondly. 'We were starved for seeing something of ourselves,' he tells me, 'even if it was a bit ocker.' Now retired from filmmaking, he went on to become the award-winning producer of films like *Caddie* and *Bliss*.

Though it wasn't the best film ever to grace the screen at the State, *They're a Weird Mob* contributed significantly to the idea that an Australian film industry revival was neither a fanciful idea nor a national folly. What we would call today a 'co-pro' – partly funded with money from overseas – it was one of the very few Australian feature films that actually got made in the 1960s. It showed that Australia had actors and technicians talented enough to make films. Just as importantly, its financial success revealed that Australian audiences would pay to watch local films – if given the chance.

They're a Weird Mob played to sellout audiences at the State for six months and made over $2 million at the Australian box office nationally. (Perhaps not surprisingly, it bombed overseas. Maybe you had to live here to get the jokes.)

'*They're a Weird Mob* woke the politicians up,' says Buckley, particularly the Liberals' John Gorton and Labor's Gough Whitlam. 'Gorton led the push for film schools and film funds to be established, which was later followed up by Gough. And you can thank films like it for setting up Australia's film renaissance in the 1970s.'

Like that other pioneering work that helped re-awaken Australia's slumbering film industry – *Wake in Fright*, directed by the Canadian Ted Kotcheff – *They're a Weird Mob* was also the work of an outsider. In fact, the man who made it was a very English Englishman.

•

In 1960, the veteran British filmmaker Michael Powell released a masterpiece that pretty much destroyed his career.

Peeping Tom is a Hitchcockian thriller featuring a serial killer who likes to film his victims in their death throes. It's as much about the voyeurism of cinema as it is about the act of murder. Contemporary critics hated the film with a rare vehemence. It was widely dismissed as evil pornography. Maybe the critics objected to seeing their profession explained away as a brigade of psychopaths sitting in the dark. The film was even banned in Finland.

Today, *Peeping Tom* is widely considered to be one of the most important films of the twentieth century, but at the time it seemed as if Powell had sabotaged his ability to get films financed – which had been considerable.

With his partner, the screenwriter Emeric Pressburger, Powell had established a production company they called The Archers, which became a byword in British filmmaking achievement. The Archers produced many of its best films for the Rank Organisation, including the Oscar-winning films *The Red Shoes* and *Black Narcissus*. Martin Scorsese has called this body of work 'the longest period of subversive filmmaking in a major studio, ever'.

But that was in the past. By his own estimation, Powell spent the two years after *Peeping Tom* 'floundering about'. The only project he had on the boil was a musical about an island paradise transformed into a nuclear power station, called *E=mc2*. It sounds like box office radiation poison – and probably would have been.

Around this time, a friend gave Powell a copy of *They're a Weird Mob*. He read it on a flight from London to the south of France, where he owned a famously unprofitable hotel called La Voile d'Or. He later recounted that he laughed all the way to the French Riviera and fell in love with O'Grady's steatopygous hero. (Nino Culotta, loosely translated, means 'Johnny Big-Bum'.) He was particularly taken by the language of O'Grady's 'Sinnyites', which he described affectionately as 'a highly spiced mixture of cockney and Liverpool Irish'.

By the time his plane touched down in Nice, Powell had decided that a film of the book had to be made. But when he rang the author's agent in London, Powell was bemused to discover that the film option had already been taken by an unlikely party: the Oscar-winning actor Gregory Peck.

'This was too easy,' Powell writes in his (digressive and somewhat unreliable) memoir, *Million Dollar Movie*. 'Greg was staying in Saint-Jean-Cap-Ferrat with his family, about a hundred and fifty yards up the road from the hotel. I caught him at home.'

When Peck had been in Australia filming *On the Beach* for Stanley Kramer, his co-star Fred Astaire had lent him a copy of O'Grady's novel. Peck thought the book was a hoot. 'It was so wonderful reading it in Australia, and having all the people around us just like they are in the book,' Powell reports Peck telling him. His plans had stalled, though, and so Powell eventually acquired the rights and took up the long battle to put *They're a Weird Mob* on the screen.

As any honest auteur will tell you, the greatest of all filmmaking arts is the art of finding the cash. The energetic Michael Powell had the soul of an artist but the spirit of a carnival spruiker; and like the proverbial shark he was always on the move, sniffing out deals.

'What showman wants to be financially independent?' he once pronounced. 'Half the fun is coaxing money out of other people's pockets into your own.'

Within weeks of reading the book, he was winging his way to a country he had never visited and knew little about. But he had the whiff of a movie in his nostrils, and nothing else mattered. Years later, after the film was finished, a critic asked Powell what possessed him to make it. 'Oh, because I had never been to Australia before, and I liked the book,' he replied airily.

•

In November 1962, Australia was still in the grip of the tyranny of distance. On his first marathon trip to Sydney, Powell flew from Rome via Teheran, New Delhi, Bangkok, Singapore and Perth. At the end of this slog through the skies, Powell arrived at Mascot Airport stupefied by jet lag, but optimistic and ready for action. Australians were flattered by the interest shown in their culture by this world-renowned director. For his part, Powell found his hosts to be pleasingly similar to O'Grady's portrait of them.

During his stay, Powell took a crash course in the mores of Australia. One evening, O'Grady escorted Powell to Sydney's famous Marble Bar. The unlamented six o'clock swill was approaching its apogee when Powell was accosted by a local:

> A very drunk man said to me, 'Excuse me, sir, but you are impeccably dressed.'
> I said, 'Thank you.'
> He said, 'You are the most impeccably dressed man that I have ever seen.'

I began to feel self-conscious, and drank some beer.

He said, 'That tweed, I'll bet it's made from the best tweed in Scotland.'

I said, 'From Donegal.'

'That's what I said.'

Following up on a tip from Peter Finch, Powell had already found his Nino – Chiari, a man of great charm who also spoke perfect English. Powell renewed an old acquaintance with the actor John McCallum, who fortuitously was now working for JC Williamson, Australia's foremost showbiz empire. The two men were kindred spirits: McCallum wanted to kickstart a broken-down Australian film industry; Powell wanted to make a film – anywhere, even in Australia.

But now he needed a script. So he wrote one. It was no good. O'Grady wrote another. It would have run four hours, according to Powell.

Powell then approached his old partner in crime, Emeric Pressburger. According to Powell's account, Pressburger quickly identified the problem.

'There is no story, Michael.'

'Isn't there?'

'Oh, Michael, Michael … How many times have I told you that a film is not words. It is thoughts, and feelings, surprises, suspense, accident.'

'When could you start?'

Ten days later, Powell got a new script – 114 handwritten quarto pages – and there was now a story. Right at the very start, in Pressburger's version, Nino meets an Australian beauty called Kay (played by Claire Dunne), whom he courts throughout the film. In the novel, Kay doesn't arrive until the last quarter of the book.

So an Australian comic classic was now being directed for the screen by a Pom from a script by a Hungarian-born Jew (mysteriously credited as 'Richard Imrie') who had never been in the Southern Hemisphere, let alone to Australia. It took three more years – and three more marathon plane trips by Powell – but in November 1965 the indefatigable director was back at the Marble Bar, surrounded by real-life extras drinking real-life schooners, filming Chiari (as Nino) being introduced to the rituals of beer drinking in 1960s Australia.

•

The critics have never really warmed to *They're a Weird Mob*. Writing in *Nation*, Sylvia Lawson offered a typical contemporary view, calling the film 'tenth-rate', 'slap-dash' and 'very scrappy-looking'. But the acerbic Lawson also pointed out that Powell's movie is 'a frustrating glimpse of what it would be like to have our own film industry, of how it might be to have your city given back to you on the screen'.

In this glimpse a lot of dreams were born. A critical mass was developing in Australian film culture. Within a decade of the premiere of *They're a Weird Mob*, the Australian film industry had produced *Sunday Too Far Away*, *Picnic at Hanging Rock*, and *The Devil's Playground*.

It could also be argued that the commercially successful Barry McKenzie films made by Bruce Beresford in the early seventies owe a debt to Powell's early stab at the 'ocker comedy'. Later comedies like *Muriel's Wedding* and *Strictly Ballroom* are also in a direct lineage.

Powell's sojourn in Australia is usually ignored when his life story is written up in the media. The traditional narrative assumes his filmmaking career disappeared into a deep hiatus in the wake of *Peeping Tom* until he popped up again as a mentor and friend to Martin Scorsese and Francis Ford Coppola in the 1970s.

In fact, Powell worked again in Australia. He directed the feature *Age of Consent*, based on a Norman Lindsay book, starring James Mason as an ageing artist and a very young – and occasionally naked – Helen Mirren as the muse who gets him back to the paintbrushes. A still young Anthony Buckley worked as the film's editor on Dunk Island in Queensland, where it was shot.

The film marked the beginning of Buckley's long friendship with Powell. Buckley visited him many times at his home in England and received numerous postcards from Powell in the remaining years of the director's life. Powell even visited the set of *Caddie*, which Buckley made with the director Donald Crombie in 1975.

Buckley remembers him as a highly skilled and disciplined director. 'If he didn't need it, he wouldn't shoot it,' he told me. 'There are not many directors who are that sure of themselves, but he was so economical. He was a true artisan.'

It's an aspect of Powell's legacy in Australia that is rarely commented on: his mentoring of young Australian filmmakers. He brought skills and ideas to our local industry at a time when it needed them.

Like most filmmakers, Powell abandoned more films than he managed to make. In the years after *They're a Weird Mob*, he had wanted to make another film in Australia called *The Coastwatchers*, set during the Second

World War. He wanted to make a film called *Taj Mahal* with Rudolf Nureyev. He wanted to make a film in Russia about the ballerina Anna Pavlova. But he made none of them. Many more projects were cast aside for want of finance or studio interest.

Powell made his last movie in 1972. *The Boy Who Turned Yellow*, a short film for children, was his final collaboration with Emeric Pressburger, who wrote the script. Michael Powell died in 1990 at the age of eighty-five. That's nearly twenty years without making a movie. It must have driven him crazy.

As Buckley says, 'He was all the time going somewhere to do a deal to get a picture up and he died doing that. He didn't stop dreaming.'

JOHN CLARKE AND THE POWER OF SATIRE

MATTHEW RICKETSON

11 April 2017

The *Oxford English Dictionary* defines satire as 'the employment, in speaking or writing, of sarcasm, irony, ridicule, etc. in denouncing, exposing or deriding vice, folly, abuses, or evils of any kind.' That's fine if a little flavourless, but then most dictionary definitions are. Most but not all. John Clarke, the New Zealand-born satirist who arrived in Australia in the 1970s and acquired a nasal local accent that he then deployed deadpan to devastating effect, once tried his hand at a definition of satire: 'Noun: a reaction to the process whereby politicians and public figures hold the community up to ridicule and contempt.' This is much better, not least because the definition itself makes a satirical point.

It also offers a key to the power of Clarke's satire: his brilliance in adapting forms, especially media forms, for satirical purposes. This can be seen in his remoulding of staple journalistic forms, ranging from standard news reports to sports commentary and the interview.

If all Clarke did, though, was parody journalistic forms, his work would not have risen above the level of a television sketch show and his death this week would not have had such an impact. Instead, he inverted these journalistic forms to ask questions and critique those in positions of power and authority. According to conventional understandings of the news media's fourth estate role, scrutinising power and authority is exactly what journalists do. Clarke was not a journalist; indeed, the failings of journalism were a common target of his satire. Yet his adapting of journalistic forms carried the bite both of satire and of revelation.

His work was genuinely subversive, though he was careful never to advertise it as such. It took the trained eye of Barry Humphries to point this out. In a foreword to a selection of Clarke's work, the creator of Dame Edna Everage writes:

John Clarke sees the skeletons in our closets, and I am amazed he has not grown very rich on offshore hush money. In Australia the Powers that Be are very powerful indeed and are protected by draconian laws of libel that would make an Australian *Private Eye* unthinkable. The press bullies, hoods and monomaniacs who hold, or have recently held, high office demand critical immunity. Fortunately for John Clarke he can always be dismissed as a harmless wag, an amusing ratbag and an anodyne parodist. If he told us what he sees and what he knows about Australian society in any other way but his Jester's guise he would, long ago, have met with a very nasty accident.

FROM GUMBOOTED CLODPOLL TO NATIONAL TREASURE

Born in 1948, Clarke grew up in Palmerston North, a small town in country New Zealand for which he had fond memories but which, as he used to say, was 'not exactly Vienna at the turn of the century'. At university he took to writing and performing in revues, where he slowly developed the character of Fred Dagg, originally a gumbooted, singlet-wearing clodpoll who spoke plain truths about those in power. He described the conservative NZ prime minister in the 1970s, Robert Muldoon, simply as a 'well-known gross national product'.

Dagg became extraordinarily popular in New Zealand, but Clarke found the experience suffocating and migrated to Australia in 1977. Here, he spent time learning about the country before offering his work anywhere. 'As a satirist I wanted to have a grip on things before I opened my mouth,' he said. When he did, Dagg had been transformed from a physical presence on television to a voice on radio. In the process, the contrast between the gumbooted yokel and the pithy truths he spoke became a contrast between a broad Australian-accented voice and a collection of truths expressed far from pithily. Instead, the language was by turns indirect, ornate, blunt and inventive, as this 1981 Fred Dagg commentary on home buying makes clear:

Like so many jobs in this wonderful society of ours, the basic function of the real estate agent is to increase the price of something without actually producing anything, and as a result it has a fair bit to do with communication, terminology and calling a spade a delightfully bucolic colonial winner facing north and offering a unique opportunity to the handyman.[2]

Operating out of the mythical Dagg Advisory Bureau, Clarke's ninety-second monologues were soon syndicated across the ABC's many local stations. They ranged from topical comments on, say, progress or lack thereof at the Strategic Arms Limitation Talks, to dissections of particular industries, such as advertising. ('We kicked off with a light lunch that lasted about five hours.') At the height of its popularity, however, the segment was taken off air by ABC management for reasons that were not at all clear but clearly infuriated its creator.

Clarke nevertheless became one of Australia's most successful satirists, much loved by audiences and revered by peers. His work appeared in newspapers including *The Age* (his mock newspaper quizzes) and *The National Times* (in a column entitled 'A Month of Sundays'), *The Bulletin* (early versions of his question-and-answer interviews) and Brian Toohey's *Eye*, where he adopted Damon Runyon's style and argot to portray politicians as gangsters. Much of his work has been reprinted in books and on his website. He was part of the pioneering satirical television series *The Gillies Report*, which broadcast in 1984 and 1985. In recent decades, he was most often identified with the mock question-and-answer interviews he produced with Bryan Dawe, which first appeared in print and on ABC Radio in the late 1980s and were then aired on television, on Channel Nine's *A Current Affair* between 1989 and 1996 and on ABC television, mostly on *7.30*, since 2000.

Apart from writing and performing his own material, Clarke worked with many other artists: as an actor (with Sam Neill in *Death in Brunswick*, in 1990), as a collaborator (with Paul Cox on the Australian Film Institute award-winning feature film *Lonely Hearts*, in 1981), as co-author (with Ross Stevenson of the stage production *A Royal Commission into the Australian Economy*, in 1991), as an adaptor (of Aristophanes' *The Frogs* for Belvoir Street Theatre in Sydney, in 1992), as dramaturg (for Casey Bennetto's *Keating: The Musical*, in 2006) and as the creator of documentaries (such as *Sporting Nation*, in 2012). Sometimes, he worked on the writing, producing and performing of a program, as in the mockumentary *The Games*, which examined

2 John Clarke, "Real Estate," Fred Dagg Anthology, released January 1, 2012, https:// mrjohnclarke.com/projects/fred-dagg.

bureaucratic ineptitude and political chicanery during the two years of planning for the Sydney Olympics. He and Andrew Knight also co-wrote a satire, *Blockbuster,* about how films are funded in Australia; not altogether surprisingly, it found little favour with film-funding bodies and has never been made.

THE CLARKE TECHNIQUE

The breadth of Clarke's career is clear; what is less evident from this brief summary is the nature of his humour and how it sits in the broader Australian tradition. Though he rarely discussed his ideas about satire, he did open up in *Wanted for Questioning,* a 1992 collection of interviews with thirty Australian comedians by Murray Bramwell and David Matthews, perhaps because the authors were academics and he judged the book would be read by few. In any case, what he said is worth quoting at length:

> You could argue, as I have done, that Australians are very pungent, disrespectful of authority … and that they give the people in power a constant caning … But you could argue that the government in this country, by and large, is not that powerful and that there have been a series of recent prime ministers who have been failures and tragedies of almost Shakespearean dimensions. That the real power in Australia is held more obviously by a small group of billionaire bullies than is the case in Britain – and they are not the people that get the caning. So it could be said that satirists, about whom it is often said that they are such great snipers, are constantly shooting the messenger.

Clarke is referring partly to the entrepreneurs who made a killing after the Hawke Labor government deregulated the financial system in Australia in 1983, but primarily he is talking about the concentration of media ownership in Australia, which in many ways has become worse, not better, since that interview. What is also clear in the quotation is his high ambition for satire. In a review of *The Oxford Book of Humorous Prose,* Clarke criticised the editor, Frank Muir, for describing Jonathan Swift as a bitter character who 'could hardly be called a humorous writer'. For Clarke, Swift was among the greatest satirists because 'he attacked greed and corruption wherever he saw them and he smote the authorities hip and thigh' while Muir 'does everything he can to defuse any effect humour might have other than to amuse the clergy'.

In Clarke's view, satire needed to have a social purpose. It should go beyond a prime minister slipping on a banana skin, and shouldn't simply blow raspberries at those in power. 'I think satire is helpless if it doesn't have a positive aspect,' he told Bramwell and Matthews. The book's title was Clarke's but readers didn't know that, which illustrates not only his subversive wit but his generosity and tendency to small-note himself. (That's a grateful homage to Mr Clarke, by the way, who taught me the bite of inverting a common phrase.)

Clarke thought that a satirist should think about solutions as well as problems. He never kicked somebody because they were down, but he also thought there was little point kicking somebody simply because they were up. 'I do think there are issues and paradoxes and I think it is hard to express an idea without conceiving its opposite.'

One-time collaborator and long-time Clarke friend Andrew Knight once told me, 'I think the yardstick of any satirist is how much they are disliked [by their targets] but he is the most generous and encouraging person in an industry that is cancer-ridden with people who want to jump on you.' The wonderful humanity attested to by Knight and many others this week does not mean Clarke viewed the world's woes with bland equanimity. Andrew Denton, himself a well-known satirist, has said, 'At the heart of all great Australian comedy is a red-hot kernel of anger.' He could have been speaking about Clarke who, to meet – and I met him and wrote about his work on several occasions – could seem like a roiling well of outrage.

Clarke shied away from direct confrontation, however, which to him 'is very often an affair where people repeat their positions and become polarised, which makes it difficult for either party to back down'. Instead, he expressed his 'red-hot kernel of anger' about the world indirectly through satire and, within that, indirectly through elaborate metaphors. Unlike, say, John Oliver or *The Chaser* team, who attack their subjects front-on and at full throttle, Clarke compressed and recalibrated the intense emotions he felt into satirical conceits that appeared to have no animus, as Barry Humphries has written, but still knocked the target akimbo.

Paradoxically, despite the range of roles Clarke played and projects he participated in, he almost always presented a version of himself. He was not a character actor. Whether he was playing Alan, a stage hand for a decidedly amateur theatre company in *Lonely Hearts*, or Dave, Sam Neill's offsider in *Death in Brunswick*, he was pretty much the same: deadpan of face, laconic of voice, alternately world-weary and stroppy (Alan) or world-weary and stoically wry (Dave). For *The Games*, he dispensed with all pretence. His character, head of the Logistics and Liaison team, is called John Clarke and was, by turns, world-weary, stroppy, stoically wry and knowing. The other characters in *The Games* retained their own names, too, which added to the frisson of national anxiety that Australians felt about staging a global event such as an Olympic Games.

But while for *The Games'* Gina Riley playing a version of herself was an exception – she is best known for playing Kim in the satirical comedy *Kath & Kim* – for Clarke playing himself was part of a continuation. You might deduce from this that Clarke was not a good actor, but he has said that in his childhood, when his mother used to take him along to an amateur theatre company she belonged to, he developed a suspicion of actors being actorly; he much preferred his mother when she was being herself. He was actually a very good performer but he insisted, consciously or otherwise, on doing it on his own terms.

UP-ENDING THE QUESTION-AND-ANSWER INTERVIEW

Just what were Clarke's own terms? Well, you can see them most clearly in the mock interviews he did with Bryan Dawe. The Q&A interview is a journalistic staple in which politicians, celebrities and sportspeople have been trained – usually by former journalists – to avoid journalists' questions or to verbalise at length. It has been pretty much spun dry. Where Clarke's former colleague Max Gillies made his reputation for the uncanny precision of his impersonation of former Australian prime minister Bob Hawke and other politicians, Clarke never made any effort to impersonate the politicians and celebrities he satirised. Instead, he fielded questions from Dawe, as himself, while maintaining he was someone else. In the 1980s, the initial surprise at seeing a middle-aged, balding man wearing no make-up or wig speaking as if he is British prime minister Margaret Thatcher or actor Meryl Streep was funny enough in itself, especially when the latter engaged the interviewer in chitchat about the 'natural' colour of her/his hair and whether 'Meryl' would wear a wig for her role as Lindy Chamberlain in the upcoming film *Evil Angels*.

More importantly, though, the decision *not* to impersonate the subjects allows us to focus on what they are actually saying. For example, in an interview in 1990, Clarke, as Bob Hawke, is asked about the science and technology minister, Barry Jones, who had just lost his place in the ministry because he did not have the backing of the Labor Party's factions:

Dawe: The Hobart conference seems to have gone very well.

Hawke: Fabulous success, standing ovation I got; they all got on their feet and ovated, right at me ...

Dawe: How did the Barry Jones decision this week help with that healing process?

Hawke: I'd like to say something about Barry Jones if I may. He's a very remarkable fellow. He it was who warned ten years ago that we had no manufacturing basis in this country and that the sunrise new technology industries gave us an excellent opportunity to get one. He it was who also warned of the greenhouse effect.

Dawe: Did we get any of those new technology industries?

Hawke: No, but the countries who listened to Barry Jones did ...

Dawe: So how did Mr Jones help with this healing of the wounds within the party?

Hawke: By standing aside for a dumber man.

The first thing to notice is Clarke's attack on Hawke's vanity, underlined in the use of the arcane word 'ovated'. The second is that good policy is no match for factional alignment (crystallised in the acid line: 'By standing aside for a dumber man') and the third, at the distance of twenty-five years now, is just how prescient Jones – and Clarke – were in identifying the importance of new technologies and the need for Australia to take action on climate change. Nor is this prescience an isolated event. Clarke's commitment to examining issues in detail before satirising them means he consistently shot up warning flares.

Running to about two and a half minutes each, the mock interviews usually contained one main satirical point that is prosecuted throughout.

There is no space for digressions and no interest in providing a rounded or balanced view of the subject or issue.

Some of the most successful mock interviews turned on a comic conceit, such as one with Sir Joh Bjelke-Petersen, a National Party figure who owed his longevity as premier of Queensland to an electoral gerrymander and a garrulously folksy manner that cloaked a ruthless political warrior who had courted property developers and sent police on to the streets to crush any political dissent. In 1987 Sir Joh finally and fatally overreached, launching an ill-conceived tilt at transferring to federal politics that succeeded only in derailing the election campaign of his federal National colleagues and their coalition partners, the Liberal Party, as they sought to win office. Bjelke-Petersen had long been regarded (and underestimated) as something of a buffoon but, instead of making that obvious joke, Clarke's satirical conceit was to write a script for 'Sir Joh' as if he had *always* aspired to a career in the front rank of comedy:

> Dawe: Are you the sad clown? The commedia dell'arte clown?'
>
> Sir Joh: Well, I think I'm a very Australian clown. I think I'm a very Australian clown. I'm not immune to life's bleaker side, obviously, but I don't think I'm consumed by it either. I frequently find, for instance, the things which worry people a lot ... I find very funny. Personally, I find them very, very funny, and I wouldn't want that to sound as if I don't care.[3]

The interviewer then presses 'Sir Joh' to nominate a favourite joke he has played on the Australian public. For sheer laughter and audience response, 'Sir Joh' can't go past his 'Joh for PM' campaign:

> Dawe: Why do you think it actually worked as well as it did?
>
> Sir Joh: Various factors. First of all, let me say that it had been done before. It wasn't an original idea, people had been ...

---

3 John Clarke and Bryan Dawe, "A Great Man: Sir Joh Bjelke-Petersen, Premier of Queensland for a Very Long Time," *Great Interviews of the Twentieth Century* (Sydney: Allen & Unwin, 1990).

Dawe: But you brought something to it didn't you?

Sir Joh: Well I like to think so. I had a lot of luck with the timing. For instance, for a start I announced I was running for prime minister when there wasn't an election on.

Dawe: Yes.

Sir Joh: Pretty funny. Pretty funny.

Dawe: Yes it was.

Sir Joh: Right from the kick-off, I mean that is pretty funny. Then, an election was called, and where was I?

Dawe: Disneyland.

Sir Joh: Pretty funny. Pretty funny. Pretty funny. You've got to say that's pretty funny. I had a lot of luck with the timing. It couldn't have been better for me. There I am running for prime minister when there's no election and then there is an election and I'm at Disneyland, being photographed with big-nosed people in the background and speaking of my personal ... I mean it was pretty funny.

Dawe: Couldn't believe your luck.

Sir Joh: Couldn't believe my luck. On a plate. Literally on a plate.

Dawe: Sir Joh, thank you very much for your time.

Sir Joh: Thank you, you've been a wonderful audience.

Pretty funny indeed. You notice how Clarke mimics a conventional chat-show style so that the interview gradually becomes a conversation which leads us to notice the contrast between the smoothness of the chat and the stumbling circumlocutions we were used to with Sir Joh. And, finally, we see that the mock interview does not aim to capture Sir Joh's character but draws our attention to the impact of his behaviour on ordinary citizens.

Just as it is commonly said that newspaper cartoonists can achieve with a few brush strokes what it takes journalists hundreds of words to say, so the same has been said of the mock interviews. For the everyday person who alternates between feeling powerless to influence governments and anger at being told lies about what they have done, there is something particularly satisfying in satire such as Clarke's. Either the politicians' dissembling is pierced by his laser-like scrutiny or they become puppets controlled by the satirist and made to reveal their behaviour.

So, when Australia's federal treasurer in the 1980s, Paul Keating, a man who had long been on very good terms with himself, led Australia into what he described as 'the recession we had to have', he was made to say in a mock interview the very words he would never have uttered: that the state of the economy was his fault and 'Tell the people I'm sorry.' This is a distinct advantage satirists enjoy over journalists. As Peter Meakin, former head of news and current affairs at Channel Nine, once commented, 'When Ray Martin [then the host of *A Current Affair*] is interviewing Paul Keating, he is dependent on what Keating says.'

THE UNIONISATION OF CHILDHOOD OR THE CHILDISHNESS OF UNIONS

If Clarke's inversion of the question-and-answer interview is his best-known satire, and his invention of the mythical sport of 'farnarkeling' one of his most loved creations, I'd like to finish by reminding readers of his reworking of the standard news report to portray the particular pleasures and perils of raising children. The impersonal style and formal tone of the news report have long been the subject of parody and satire; Clarke's contribution was to use it to report the activities of the Federated Under Tens and the Massed Five-Year-Olds. Writer Shane Maloney has said these pieces of Clarke's are a commentary on the childish behaviour of many trade unions, which is certainly plausible, but for me the tone is of an exasperated but loving parent rather than an aggrieved citizen. As you will see, I trust:

> Australia ground to a virtual halt on Tuesday when the Federated Under Tens' Association withdrew services, stating that in their view it was an unreasonable demand that they wear a sun hat in the sun. They further suggested that the placement of sunscreen lotion on or about their persons was an infringement of basic human rights and was 'simply

not on'. Wednesday saw the dispute widen when an affiliated body, the Massed Five-Year-Olds, showed their hand by waiting until management had about a hundredweight of essential foodstuffs in transit from supermarket to transport and then sitting down on the footpath over a log of claims relating to ice cream. The Federated Under Tens, sensing blood in the water, immediately lodged a similar demand and supported the Massed Five-Year-Olds by pretending to have a breakdown as a result of cruelty and appalling conditions.

The problem had been further exacerbated by a breakage to one of the food-carrying receptacles and some consequent structural damage to several glass bottles and a quantity of eggs, the contents of which were beginning to impinge on the well-being of the public thoroughfare.[4]

As far as I know, only three of these short monologues have been reprinted in Clarke's anthologies, but what is striking about them is the precise use of jargon (industrial in this case), the satirical conceit (of parenting as a never-ending negotiation) and the deliciously chosen words ('beginning to impinge on the well-being of the public thoroughfare'). With a topic like parenthood, which taps many people's deepest feelings of love as well as frustration, Clarke doesn't express his feelings directly but deflects and reshapes them into monologues that convey, albeit indirectly, something essential and well-nigh universal about how it feels to raise children.

This appraisal has covered only a portion of Clarke's work and does little more than begin mapping his satirical brilliance and influence. If it is undeniably tragic that he died at such a relatively young age, it is equally true that his forensic intelligence is needed now more than ever. The bullshit-detection business has lost one of its finest exponents.

---

4   John Clarke, "Entire Country Held to Ransom" in *Tinkering: The Complete Book of John Clarke* (Melbourne: Text, 2017).

BETWEEN THE COVERS

DIANA BAGNALL

20 March 2018

In early January I asked a couple of old friends to help me think my way back into the magazine industry. I sweetened the deal by offering to cook, which was the least I could do. There was a lot of ground to cover.

It wasn't that I'd gone into snooze mode over Christmas and New Year and needed a quick reboot. It had been years since I'd paid close attention to what was happening in magazine publishing. I'd taken my get-out-of-jail-free card and shot through to another life. It's a common-enough story among journalists of my generation. In my case, I accepted a redundancy from *The Bulletin* in 2006, and in May 2009, after one last glorious assignment for *Australian Geographic*, I said I was going sailing. People say that all the time, but that's what actually happened.

But the sailing was over and now, out of the blue, had come a commission that invited me back on my old turf to look at the woes of Bauer Media and more generally to consider the state of magazines. I doubt there has ever been a trickier time to delve into this topic but I told myself, in my Protestant way, that this would be good for me. It would force me to take a measure of myself.

I'd ride out a force eight gale any day over working in magazines again. I know my limits. But since that long summery lunch, when I engaged my friends Kathy Bail and Bobbi Mahlab to take me through a professional warm-up routine, I've made up a fair bit of ground, and covered some more. (It is humbling to realise how much of a habit thinking is, and how quickly you can lose it.)

What follows is far from complete, but I've drawn pleasure from reconstituting myself as a magazine writer. Pleasure is not incidental to this story, by the way. Magazines are a business and, under the normal rules of engagement, they need to keep turning a profit for their product to survive. Everyone knows how hard it is to get people to pay for information now. They will pay for pleasure, though, which is the most promising way for magazines to find an edge. Or it may be that the normal rules of engagement will not prevail. Who knows?

•

I had a few lucky breaks in journalism over the years, but the luckiest was the timing of my exit. By complete chance, I avoided the worst of the trauma that began to break over Australian Consolidated Press, or ACP, after the death of Kerry Packer in December 2005, and has not let up since.

Of course, I shouldn't pretend that the end of my three-decade career came as a complete relief. My identity was tied up with being a journalist, and letting go wasn't as painless as banking the redundancy payment. What helped most was getting out of town, a long way out, on a boat.

This isn't the place for recounting tall tales about the sea. What's relevant is how being a sea nomad for several years affected my knowledge and understanding of how magazines were facing down the perfect storm brewed by tech and telephony. By magazine, what I mean, at least to begin with, is the printed product with its distinctive heft and touch, the treat you look forward to taking on a plane or to the beach or curling up with on a couch after work.

I'd stopped writing for magazines, but I hadn't stopped wanting to read them. On our first voyages to the tropics on our boat, my husband Alex (also a big reader) and I were on short rations in the magazine department. But in 2010 Apple launched its iPad and by early 2011, when we were preparing for our second and more ambitious voyage, magazine publishers were offering apps for tablets. We bought an iPad mainly so we could pick up our digital subscriptions to *The Economist* and *The New Yorker* while we were afloat.

We spent nearly five years cruising and crossing oceans, and though we were frequently off the grid, we didn't miss an issue of either magazine. Every time we found a free wi-fi connection, we'd download the backlog (and pick up emails, post on our blog and so on). On remote atolls, where internet service is fragile, that process could take several hours and involve many beers, but so be it.

The publishers of these two magazines were among the first to adapt their print format to the tablet, and they did it well. I shifted gratefully into reading on a screen. Who doesn't enjoy opening *The New Yorker* cartoons anywhere at any time, but especially after a four-week passage from Panama to the Marquesas?

In March 2016, we put the boat up for sale in New Zealand and came back to our house in Sydney. We didn't bother downloading digital issues any longer, even though we now had cheap, fast and unlimited internet. One of the pleasures of having a fixed address was having magazines come through the letterbox again. Sometimes there'd be a long wait then a pile-up in the post, but I didn't mind, and still don't. I don't read magazines for news anymore – who does? And there is still, for me at least, excitement in tearing open the wrapping ... all that tactility.

In the euphoria of being back among print and paper, it took me a while to notice how much thinner the selection of magazines had become, especially in newsagencies that had always carried a decent range. Instead of aisles of titles, the magazines were pushed against a back wall. And what was there didn't grab me as much. That was the strangest part.

If I scroll back to my working life, choosing a magazine had never been a problem. At an airport, for example, nine times out of ten I'd have reached for a glossy – *Vanity Fair*, American or British *Vogue*, or even *Tatler* in its heyday – and known it would hit the sweet spot. I'd get my fix.

But now, in the same situation, I floundered. More often than not, even having got down on my haunches to check the lowest shelves, I'd end up walking out empty-handed.

The first few failures to scratch my old magazine itch rattled me. From what I could see, magazines hadn't changed that much. Must be me, I figured. My interests had drifted, of course. And I was old (well, getting older). Perhaps I was just over the glossies. It happens.

But it wasn't just me. What I was seeing – or rather, not seeing – spoke to a profound disorientation of the culture. My own maladjustment probably didn't help. Dazed and confused doesn't begin to describe those early months living back in the city.

I wasn't a complete Luddite. I'd managed to work out how to make regular blog posts even from the middle of the ocean. I was familiar, theoretically, with notions like disruption and streaming. But ironically the one word I'd failed to register the significance of was 'mobility'.

The smartphone revolution had begun for real while I was preoccupied with peripherals like weather systems and sea state and how much anchor chain would keep a twenty-tonne boat from dragging in a deep Pacific anchorage. Meanwhile, back home and all over the world, people had begun carrying their lives in their pockets.

Global smartphone sales advanced fairly slowly from the launch of the iPhone in 2007 until 2009, but from 2010 sales began to pick up serious momentum, with the biggest surge between 2011 and 2013. In most advanced markets smartphone penetration is heading for between

80 and 90 per cent this year. Mobile internet use has doubled since 2011, and is expected to account for three-quarters of online use by 2019. 'For most consumers and advertisers, the mobile internet is now the normal internet,' Jonathan Barnard, head of forecasting at media agency Zenith, has said.

That story is backed in Australia by the 2017 Sensis Social Media report, which found smartphone penetration above 80 per cent, and rising, while use of laptops (59 per cent), tablets (45 per cent) and desktop computers (51 per cent) was falling. Smartphones are by far the most common way that Australians access social media and, just to end this drum roll of statistics, eight out of ten Australians use social media.

It wasn't just the internet that kneecapped traditional magazine businesses; it was the smartphone and Facebook. It's a chicken-and-egg thing, but the huge uptake of smartphones triggered a stampede towards social media with its myriad communities. Until then, people had found and demarcated their tribes in all sorts of different ways, but magazines were an important one. People gravitated towards magazines as much to endorse their idea of themselves as for information and entertainment, as ex–British *Vogue* editor Alexandra Shulman wrote on *Business of Fashion*. 'You chose to be seen with *Vogue* instead of *Cosmopolitan*, with *World of Interiors* instead of *House Beautiful*, with *Grazia* rather than *Hello*. Or vice versa.' Now, through Facebook groups, Instagram, Twitter feeds and the like, there are easier and cheaper ways of achieving many of the ends that magazines once served. The consumer magazine market is 'reaching an existential threshold' and publishers 'face a crisis of purpose', London-based media research group Enders Analysis warns.

Print is far from dead, but the analysts and consultants are having a field day. Data is cut every which way. There are summits and reports galore, mostly forecasting more pain ahead. You've heard it all before. The old business model is shot. The ads have gone elsewhere, and the expectation that everything you read online should be free is proving difficult to dislodge. Magazine circulation (where it's still counted) and readership slide month by month, particularly among mass-market magazines that, as London-based media consultant Colin Morrison recently tweeted, 'still shout the loudest, even in free fall'. It all happened so quickly, didn't it? One moment we were paying the extra for our airfreighted copies of *Vanity Fair* and the next we were mourning the passing of the golden age of magazines that Tina Brown documents in her *Vanity Fair Diaries*. When Condé Nast owner Si Newhouse and *Playboy* founder Hugh Hefner died within a week of each other last October,

The Financial Times ran what was effectively an obituary for the glossy era. The balance of power between technology and media had 'shifted irrevocably', the *FT* pronounced, and the question was how long magazine publishers would survive the new era.

•

And so to the Bauer Media Group, Europe's largest magazine publisher, which bought ACP in September 2012, and may now regret it ever set foot Down Under. *May* regret, I stress, because the Bauer family, which has managed the company for five generations, rarely makes statements about its business. The local boss of Bauer in Australia, Paul Dykzeul, doesn't have a problem with that. 'The Germans are intensely private, and so they should be,' he told me. '[The business] is theirs.'

Even when the news is good, the parent company releases results infrequently, with a minimum of detail. In September 2016 the company revealed that for the fiscal year 2015 it had posted a turnover of €2.3 billion (A\$3.6 billion), the second-highest in its history. Classic (aka print) magazine sales showed a gentle downward trend over the previous two years, but in 2015 still made far and away the greatest contribution to the group's turnover, with sales of €1.3 billion. The company is active in twenty countries and sales outside Germany that year accounted for two-thirds of total turnover. In Germany, Bauer published twenty-seven of the top one hundred magazine titles. 'Print is the platform for our success,' publisher Yvonne Bauer said at the time. The group's digital division accounted for €122 million of turnover and achieved 16.2 per cent growth. This, as far as I can establish, is the most recent public statement from Bauer Media Group on its financials.

For the sorrier story of its Australian business, I rely on reporting from *The Sydney Morning Herald*. In December, the paper's Colin Kruger got hold of the most recent financial accounts lodged by the local arm of Bauer Media for the financial years 2014 and 2015, and wrote that they showed reported losses of \$116 million and liabilities exceeding current assets by \$51.6 million. The local operation was kept afloat by a \$30 million loan from its German parent, Kruger reported. Dykzeul responded by saying that the company was private, and did not comment on its financial business.

In February, I got in touch with Colin Morrison, whose blog *Flashes and Flames* tracks the fortunes of global media companies. I recognised his name from the old days. Morrison once sat in the seat that Dykzeul now occupies. He ran ACP for Kerry Packer from 1995 to 1999 but he's also been CEO of media companies owned by Hearst, Axel Springer, Future, EMAP and others. These days he holds no executive role, though he's involved in various digital media and information companies. He sees the big picture.

Bauer, he tells me by email, is a rich and profitable company with a strong track record over the past thirty years in Germany, Eastern Europe, Britain and the United States. It is clearly shocked by its experience with the former ACP. 'There is no doubt that Australia has been a very cold shower for a company which is simply not used to getting it so wrong,' writes Morrison. But he cautions against assuming the company is terminally lost Down Under. The Bauer family, he says, has built its global media business by being patient and long-term. Indeed, he says, if his old boss Kerry Packer were still alive, he wouldn't be finding it easy either. But nor, he adds, would KP be feeling sorry for himself as some of his successors have been doing in the past twelve years:

> He would be noisily in hot pursuit of a new long-term strategy without worrying too much about the short-term distractions of declining revenues. Salami-slicing costs and tweaking teams and business models is no substitute for a real plan. That's the message for Bauer.

The short history of how Bauer Media came to own ACP goes something like this. In 2007 James Packer sold his media interests, which included the Nine Network and the magazines, to the private-equity company CVC Asia Pacific for around $5.3 billion. A critical detail of the deal was that rights to the digital content of ACP titles would be held by Nine's digital arm, Ninemsn. Later, when the print magazines were sold off separately, this became a significant problem for their new owner.

CVC's investment in Nine Entertainment did not turn out well, not least because in 2008 the global financial crisis hit and advertising revenues tumbled across all media – but also, for those who could see it, because the smartphone had begun its rampage. CVC became desperate to off-load its media assets, and in September 2012 it found a buyer for ACP. Bauer Media paid approximately $500 million to enter the Australian and New Zealand markets.

At the time, some people thought they'd paid too much; others believed they'd picked up a bargain. Nobody can say, except the Bauers. There was certainly much trilling about the fact that this was a family-owned company – and 'not somebody who is only intent on buying into the company to make money', as Ita Buttrose told *The Sydney Morning Herald*.

But still, $500 million isn't chickenfeed. ACP represented Bauer's largest investment since late 2007 when it had paid more than A£1.1 billion for EMAP's radio and magazine businesses in Britain. It was also the first major roll of the dice for Yvonne Bauer who, barely twenty months earlier, had been anointed by her father Heinz (over her three sisters) as his successor. The chosen Ms Bauer, then in her mid thirties, was jubilant about her company's expansion, and a month after the ACP deal was clinched she launched a new slogan: 'We Think Popular'. She came out to Australia in February 2013, gave unprecedented interviews in which she emphasised Bauer's commitment to and love of print, and that's where things started to get interesting.

Before Inside Story contacted me, I'd heard a little about Bauer Media from the few people I came across socially who were still involved with the company. 'The Germans' (as everyone called them) weren't easy to work for, they said. The years of private-equity ownership hadn't been a walk in the park, but when Bauer came to town, everything changed overnight. There was a cultural mismatch between Hamburg and Sydney. Bauer had a different management style (the family is notorious for micromanagement) and didn't understand how to sell the magazines they'd bought. Right from the start there had been pushback from the local staff, who fought for their own ideas. The Germans didn't understand that either. They were used to their editors doing what they were told.

People weren't happy, that much was obvious – though frankly, people were often not happy during my fourteen years of working at ACP, even when the place was buzzing and its 'iconic' magazines were making money hand over fist. The culture was awash with anxiety. But things were now much grimmer. In every traditional media company people feared for their jobs, but at Bauer expressions of fear and pessimism were amplified.

The company couldn't keep out of the news. *Mumbrella*, the media and marketing industry news site, has been tireless in its reporting of the 'nightmare' at Park Street (as Bauer headquarters in Sydney is known). Fairfax columnists, some of them ex-Bauer themselves, have kept close tabs on the carnage too, building a dossier of the closure and sale of magazines, the sudden resignations of popular editors and unexpected departures of executives, the forming and dissolving of divisions and partnerships and, most diligently collected of all, the churn at the top. Five CEOs in the past six years. That's a company in shock, as Morrison says.

And then there is the trouble with Rebel. The 2017 $4.5 million defamation win by actor Rebel Wilson was a huge story. On 8 March she announced she wanted Bauer Media to pay a further $1.3 million to cover her legal costs. (Bauer's appeal against the amount of the damages was successful.)[5]

•

It's a humid and grey Tuesday afternoon when I go in to Park Street to meet Paul Dykzeul. The front foyer, which I remember as a thoroughfare for loudmouthed sexy young women and big-swinging-dick types, is deserted. I wondered how many of those women have moved over to Surry Hills to work for Mia Freedman, who was the epitome of the company It Girl when she became the youngest-ever editor of *Cosmopolitan* in 1996. Freedman's immensely popular digital women's network Mamamia, which evolved out of a blog she began in 2004, is something Paul Dykzeul frankly envies. 'It's bloody brilliant,' he tells me. 'I just wish I'd thought of it.' I believe him. Bauer's own digital network, Now to Love, is a work in progress, to put it kindly.

Dykzeul (Mr Dykzeul to his German colleagues, who prefer formality in both dress and form of address) sees me in his office on the third floor. That's the floor where Kerry Packer held court, and it still holds the Packer imprint. Dykzeul is another kind of man altogether, slightly built, nervy and – as I discover over the course of an hour's conversation – astonishingly cheerful given the nature of the job he's been handballed. (When I mention this to a mutual Kiwi friend, *NZ Life & Leisure* editor and publisher Kate Coughlan, she replies, 'Paul is wonderfully upbeat like our prime minister, "relentlessly positive" – maybe it's in the water.')

Dykzeul was running the New Zealand end of things for Bauer when he was called back to Sydney last June to replace Nick Chan, who had lasted only a year as chief executive. Chan had replaced David Goodchild, a Brit who didn't ever make Sydney his home, and Goodchild had replaced Matt Stanton, who'd led the company through the first two tumultuous years of Bauer's ownership and then left at the end of 2014 to work for Woolworths. Dykzeul, who is sixty-five, wasn't busting to be Bauer's next

5 On 14 June 2018, the Victorian Supreme Court reduced the damages payout to $600,000 and ordered Wilson to repay Bauer $4.1 million.

Australian CEO. He had settled back in Auckland after spending many years in Sydney, and was doing a good job for Bauer there, from several accounts. 'I needed this like a hole in the head,' he says.

Coughlan thinks Australians are 'bloody lucky to have him', but Bauer's internal appointment didn't set the Sydney media alight. Mumbrella called it uninspired, which seems to have hurt. 'You can call me anything but don't call me dull,' says Dykzeul. He also takes umbrage at the persistent criticism that Bauer cops from other media. The attacks on its performance are 'so dumb and ill-conceived that I shake my head in disbelief', he tells me. He maintains that a lot of the damage to the company's business was done during the CVC period. 'People say Bauer have done it, which is an extraordinary leap, based on complete ignorance of the position.' Moreover, he says, if ever there were a time for media companies to stand together and be proud of what they do, it's now. (A month later, when six major media companies announce they'll support Bauer's appeal over the amount of the Rebel Wilson payout, I find myself wondering if Dykzeul's wounded feelings are mollified.)

So why did he come when the Bauers whistled? He's loyal, that's why. To the magazine industry in general but to ACP (and, because of the changing circumstances, to Bauer) in particular. He got his start with ACP in distribution and worked his way up through management ranks. At one point he worked for the competition (Murdoch Magazines, Pacific) but he came back to ACP. 'I love the company,' he says. 'I'm not talking about loving the Bauers ... I thought the challenge of trying to put the business back on an even keel, of plotting a path forward, was not too much for me to take on.' He seems to search for the right way to say this. 'I would rather that people thought of the company ...' He pauses. 'In some ways I wish it wasn't called Bauer.'

But it is, and Morrison thinks that Dykzeul – 'the cheerful, practical, no-nonsense guy' – might be the one the Bauers have been looking for all along, the one who will stabilise their business in Australia 'as long as he is given the freedom to rationalise the business on the way to developing truly versatile media brands'.

Since his arrival, Dykzeul has slimmed down the executive team ('the business couldn't afford the structure it had') and not only closed four consumer titles, including *Yours* and *Men's Style*, but also pulled the plug on Bauer's custom publishing business. Just recently he sold yet another of Bauer's smaller titles, *Australian Geographic*. 'We have tried that stuff, and we are terrible at it. Big companies cannot publish niche titles in my view.' (Bobbi Mahlab, one of my lunch companions and a custom publisher herself, offers the opinion that Bauer didn't recognise where the jewels were – 'the whole world has gone niche', she says.)

What Bauer is hanging onto are mass-market titles, including *Woman's Day* and *The Australian Women's Weekly* which, in its heyday, was famously the most widely read magazine in the world on a per capita basis. With *The Bulletin* gone, the *Weekly*, founded in 1933, is the oldest magazine left in Australia.

Personally, I'm not heavily invested in whether the *Weekly* has a future. My mother didn't read it, and nor do I, though I believe I missed a time when I might have. I've heard it said that Helen McCabe, who was editor-in-chief for six years from 2009, published some great covers. When she left suddenly in January 2016 she said all the right things, then resurfaced six months later at Nine Entertainment as head of lifestyle, and is now Nine's digital content director. She's preparing a new subscription site, Future Women, aimed at professionals and entrepreneurs – 'a highly attractive female premium advertising demographic', as she says. The content will be longer-form and 'curated'. McCabe's obviously still in the magazine business, but without the 'legacy' millstone around her neck.

Bauer has appointed two new editors to the *Weekly* since McCabe's departure, most recently Nicole Byers, who came to the magazine in July after seven years at the helm of *OK!*. She's bagged the Prince Harry–Meghan Markle romance and the magazine has a discrete section for the royal engagement on its website. By chance, I have an old copy of the *Weekly* at home, dated 30 June 1971 (my artist daughter found it at a local market and was going to use it for collage). In that issue, the bride on the cover is American royalty, Richard Nixon's elder daughter, Tricia. What knocks me for six is not how much has changed in the magazine in forty-seven years, but how much has stayed the same.

When Dykzeul assures me that the *Weekly* is 'still one of the great cornerstones of the publishing industry in Australia', I am reminded of the swanky party that ACP threw for the 125th birthday of *The Bulletin*, where similar kinds of things were said about that 'iconic' magazine. Three years later it was gone, closed by the accountants at CVC, who obviously did not see any future in the brand.

Even after an hour's conversation with Dykzeul I'm not clear what he plans to do next with the *Weekly*. He tells me it has 'years and years to go … and it is under no pressure'. He uses the word iconic. He also says the *Weekly* is 'socially extremely important'.

I refrain from telling him that a man further down the line but closer to the market than him, a newsagency owner in Victoria called Mark Fletcher, has told me that the magazine looks 'lost'. Fletcher also writes a very lively blog for newsagents, and is a software developer for newsagency businesses. He gets to see a lot of magazines, though like all newsagents he sells many fewer than he'd wish these days. He feels a strong residual loyalty to the *Weekly*, but from what he sees its audience has changed and left the magazine behind. 'If I was influential at Bauer, I would say that the magazine needs to be exploded and dramatically altered for it to have a future beyond 2018.'

Several weeks later, Bauer Media launches a *Female Future* strategy that pledges, among other things, to publish ten million words about women across all its platforms before 2019. Dykzeul tells the breakfast audience of marketers and the like that Bauer Media's 'understanding of what women think, feel and want is unmatched across the publishing industry'. I remain underwhelmed. What is the meaning of all those words? (At least Dykzeul speaks plain English, unlike Melissa Overman, executive editor of News Corp's freshly minted women's site, the With Her in Mind Network, or WHIMN, who struggled to do so in an interview with *Mumbrella*: 'Next year is really trying to understand the female digital consumer and what drives her to purchase products, or consume content, and then making sure we are innovating for that.')

The *Weekly*'s star shines much less brightly than it once did, though independently audited circulation figures are no longer available. Bauer pulled out of the Audited Media Association of Australia in December 2016. News Corp and Pacific Magazines followed shortly after, arguing that circulation stats don't recognise online and mobile readers or, as News Corp's (then) chief digital officer Nicole Sheffield phrased it, no longer reflect the breadth or depth of the 'brand reading audience'.

The latest magazine readership stats I can find were released on 9 February 2018. They show print readership of *The Australian Women's Weekly* down by 7.7 per cent in the year to December 2017, about the same decline as *Better Homes and Gardens*. Survey company Roy Morgan put a positive spin on the release – fifteen million Australians read magazines across print and online, it headlined. That's a big figure, but it doesn't speak as loudly as a figure published a week later: the first lot of Standard Media Index, or SMI, data for 2018 shows a 42.5 per cent decline in ad bookings for print magazines in the year from January 2017, with magazines' digital properties also suffering a 40.5 per cent decline in the same period.

I read this after I've met with Dykzeul. That news was worse than the earlier SMI data I'd put to him, to which he had countered that the SMI doesn't reflect the direct revenue from clients, small agencies and PR organisations that is now 'a significant proportion of revenue'. When I ask exactly what the proportion is, I get no further response.

I don't press Dykzeul unduly over Bauer's stop–start progress into digital either. If Pacific wants to trumpet about outpacing Bauer Media's digital performance 'for the first time', as it did just before Christmas, well, it's still early days for everyone in the digital journey, as even Pacific admits.

Dykzeul says that if digital 'migration' is not happening at Bauer as fast as he'd like then the same goes for everyone. 'A lot of the big publishing companies are not that much more advanced than we are in this space.' He confirms that Bauer didn't exit the deal that had locked up digital rights of magazine content within Ninemsn until June 2015 and that Pacific Magazines got out of a similar deal with Yahoo at about the same time.

None of this is very long ago. Time moves so fast in a digital world and I recall what Mahlab told me over lunch: Bauer didn't move fast enough, but even the groups that did move early into digital publishing didn't know how to make money out of it 'because the revenue isn't there'.

In a digital world, with its emphasis on content, Morrison explains to me, the large company has to work hard to build any kind of competitive edge. The economies of production, distribution, sales and marketing have all been undercut. 'That's why all over the world magazine companies are changing ownership.' For the large companies, he believes, the future is likely to be much leaner. They won't own nearly as many titles, and they will concentrate on key brands that can become much more than magazines.

Brands, brands, brands. It's how the future is configured. When Morrison talks of the 'sheer untapped power' of the *Weekly*, he's imagining how, based on its decades of selling millions of cookbooks, the *Weekly* might put its name to a range of high-margin products and services. He cites as a model for this kind of diversification the *Weekly*'s major competitor in the Australian market, *Better Homes and Gardens*. *BHG* is owned by Meredith Corporation, an Iowa-based publisher that about twenty-five years ago came to an agreement with Walmart to stock branded *BHG* products in its homewares and garden centres. Today Walmart stocks around 3000 *BHG* products in more than 4000 stores and online, according to Morrison; and on the back of this single monthly magazine, Meredith is second only to Disney in global licensing. And though you may not recognise its name or its other titles, Meredith has just bought Time Inc.

Kathy Bail, my other lunch companion, tells me she doesn't think Bauer has an executive team that 'knows how to maximise the power of [its] brands across different platforms'. Bail is usually very diplomatic, so I suspect she knows more than she's letting on. These days she runs UNSW Press but she's spent a lot more of her working life editing magazines. (I worked under her for seven years at *The Bulletin*.) She's one of the smart ones who saw the future before it arrived at ACP. In 2006 she put up a blueprint to management for a different way forward for *The Bulletin*. She wanted to take it away from news and capitalise on its rich historical and literary associations (anybody think *The New Yorker* doesn't do that?). Nobody wanted to know. She's philosophical about that now. 'Magazines do have eras, and sometimes time's up.'

And sometimes their time arrives. Recently I read about a magazine called *The Party Next Door*, which is presented like a twelve-inch vinyl record, with an inner sleeve and a gatefold outer sleeve. *The Party Next Door* is an extreme example of the kind of magazine I was hinting at when I said that perhaps there might be a time when the rules don't apply. Mahlab had suggested as much to me. 'Because there isn't a commercial model, non-commercial models are springing up.'

The indies are hiding in plain view. You may have seen some of the bigger titles, like *Apartamento* or *Kinfolk* or *Cereal* or *The Gentlewoman* for sale in bookstores or cafes or art galleries or hipster clothing shops. I doubt you will have come across *032c*, or *Anxy*, which won launch of the year at last year's Stack awards, but you may well have seen some of the Australian indies that have made the Stack award shortlists: *Dumbo Feather*, *The Lifted Brow*, *New Philosopher* or *Womankind* (the last two out of the same pod in Hobart).

This is the countercultural magazine movement, a deliberate and slow form of magazine publishing that rejects and in some cases actively agitates against mainstream media values. The British magazine *Delayed Gratification*, for example, prides itself on being 'last to breaking news'. I can lose myself for hours in these beautiful products. They are carefully printed on delectable paper, and feature smart writing, stylish photography and a purist design ethic (always). Some appear monthly, but more are quarterly or even biannual. They shun news and celebrity and rely on social media to spread the word. They have websites, but the physical magazine is the thing they treasure. Some, like *Womankind*, deliberately don't carry advertising. Others carry 'partnered content' or 'native advertising' (that's a whole other subject).

Megan Le Masurier, a University of Sydney media academic who has been researching indies for ten years, says she doesn't think there is one indie magazine that survives on the cover price alone, though cover prices are comparatively high. Hardly any make enough money to pay their makers, who generally have day jobs. 'Some of them are so idealistic it breaks your heart,' she says.

She is not being condescending. There is a chance that one of these small titles might become the next *Frankie* magazine, or thinking bigger, the next *Dazed and Confused*, the British fashion and culture magazine founded in 1991 by Jefferson Hack and the photographer Rankin. *Dazed and Confused* has not only survived the digital firestorm, but in its latest manifestation as Dazed Media has teamed up with Chinese luxury publisher Modern Media to form a new network, Modern Dazed. Hack is its CEO. Modern Dazed is the new home for Nowness, the video channel screening arts and culture that Hack founded in 2010 in conjunction with luxury brand conglomerate LVMH. You could never accuse Hack of being stuck in the past, and yet when he talks about the community-based culture of magazines, he sounds positively artsy.

Hack goes back to the ancient Greek root of the word, which means a container or storage unit, and from there surmises that a magazine can be in any format. 'It can be a shop, a club, it can be in print, it can be people, or a city … As long as that container of knowledge is something that is accessible, and you've got that ability to step into it as an audience, then the format is valid in whatever shape it comes,' he told *1 Granary*, a biannual European art-school magazine and blog.

If you've seen *Monocle* magazine, you'll perhaps get what Hack is talking about. *Monocle* was launched in 2007 by Tyler Brûlé (who created *Wallpaper* magazine in 1996 and sold it to Time Inc. in 1997 for a small fortune). I wrote for *Monocle* briefly in 2008, and at the time its London editor explained that the magazine's target readership was cashed-up globetrotting young professionals. I didn't really get it or them, and I fully expected *Monocle* to be gone within a year or two. But Brûlé had identified his community, and he knew how they saw the world. As the best magazine editors always can, Bail reminds me.

That *Monocle* didn't fail is an understatement. It comes out in print ten times a year and around it Brûlé has built a twenty-four-hour radio station, a website, a special-issues publishing division, events and retail businesses and cafes. In 2018, *Monocle* is expanding into mixed-use residential developments in Bangkok. In November, Brûlé sold a 12.5 per cent stake in the business for US$6 million to Thai property developer Sansiri. The plan is to build houses that reflect the urban architectural designs that appear in the magazine. *Monocle* is much more than a magazine, and while I baulk at calling it a global brand, others don't.

Like his contemporary, Hack, Brûlé seems to be able to remake magazines at will. They move remarkably fast for middle-aged men, as someone has commented. But they're not media barons in the way we've come to know them, and you sense they won't be passing the baton on generation after generation, as the Bauers have done. That time is up.

THE LOST PORTRAIT

SYLVIA MARTIN

23 April 2018

Detail from Madge Hodges' 1938 portrait of Aileen Palmer.
Courtesy of Penelope Pollitt

'I suppose you'd like to see the portrait before we have coffee.' The smiling woman who had greeted me at the door of her elegant Art Deco flat, typical of 1930s Melbourne, gestured towards the living room and ushered me in. On the wall next to the window overlooking the front garden, I saw a group of four framed portraits. Three were of the same man painted by different artists. The fourth was of a striking young woman with short hair and high cheekbones, cigarette in her raised hand, caught as if in earnest conversation with someone just out of view. I knew every line of this portrait but the immediacy of seeing the original, in colour, made my skin prickle and my eyes blur.

During the research in the National Library of Australia for *Ink in Her Veins*, my biography of poet and political activist Aileen Palmer, I had found a snapshot of her parents, Australian writers Vance and Nettie Palmer, taken in their living room in the 1950s. On the wall behind them I could see a large portrait in a heavy gold frame of a young woman. Realising it must be a portrait of Aileen, I hunted through the realia in the Palmer archive. I found two framed portraits painted in an impressionistic style by Peggy Maguire in London around 1939: one in brown tones of Aileen's sleeping figure and the other in shades of blue in which she is reclining on a bed, reading, a red cushion at her back and shadowy outlines of books at the bedhead. Neither was the one I saw in the snapshot taken at Ardmore, the Palmer family home in Kew, just a few kilometres from where I was now standing.

I began my biography with an account of the missing portrait, describing Aileen's appearance in it as 'androgynous' and 'bohemian':

> The portrait is so immediately striking ... you want to know who she is and when it was painted. Where could she be? In a cafe, in Paris perhaps? You feel almost as though you could meet such a young woman walking along a city street today ...

I outlined what I knew of the portrait from Aileen's letters to her parents from London, where she was living in 1938. She had recently returned from two years on the frontlines of the Spanish Civil War working as an interpreter and administrator for medical divisions of the International Brigades. A passionate communist from her university days in Melbourne, she had joined the fight to save the elected Republican government in Spain from General Franco's fascist rebels.

Aileen wrote to her mother on 25 July that Australian artist Madge Hodges, a former student of Max Meldrum, had asked her to sit for a portrait. Madge was a neighbour with a top-floor studio in Charlotte Street, Bloomsbury. According to Aileen, she was 'quite a decent Meldrumite painter ... She seems rather frail and limp, but is quite awake to things'. A month later, on 25 August, Aileen reported:

> I spent part of two evenings this week sitting as a model for Madge Hodges, who painted you once in Australia ... She asked me if I would sit for her, as she didn't think I would be the kind of sitter who would ask her to lengthen my eyelashes, etc. thus more or less inducing her to falsify her work as some sitters do.

Nettie Palmer's diary also mentions the portrait, noting that it had been brought back to Australia by a family friend in 1940 and was framed and ready to hang in the living room at Ardmore ten days later. 'Remarkably good' was her verdict. 'Rather dominant – Napoleonic, conducting the world with a cigarette.' She reported that Vance too was impressed.

•

Seeing the portrait in colour for the first time made me aware of how closely Madge Hodges had followed the strictures of Meldrum's 'Tonalism', in which the light or darkness of colours and how they relate to each other was the defining feature. The palette was restricted to five tones and outlines were forbidden. According to art critic John McDonald, writing about the *Misty Moderns* exhibition in 2009, the paintings that resulted were 'remarkably similar in their blurred edges and smudgy, atmospheric surfaces'. A 'penchant for gloom' seemed to be a temperamental preference among Meldrum's students, he added. In Madge Hodges's portrait, Aileen's head emerges from a dark background while the deep blue of her dress almost disappears into it. All emphasis is on her face and the raised hand holding the prominent cigarette. The effect is anything but gloomy. The glowing portrait is arresting in its strength and vitality.

In her published diary, *Fourteen Years*, Nettie Palmer recalls going to an exhibition at the Meldrum Gallery in 1933 where there was 'a good mixed show':

> ... Jorgensen, Colahan, Leason, and some younger ones, also Meldrum himself. All displayed by strong electric spotlights, the rest of the Gallery correspondingly dark. Good method for their kind of tone-values; other painting might be flattened by it.

Max Meldrum was a charismatic teacher and Melbourne was the heartland of his 'school' in the early decades of the twentieth century. Clarice Beckett was his most favoured student; his other female students have been mostly forgotten. Beckett, who never left Melbourne, died at the age of forty-eight in 1935 but several of Meldrum's best-known students, including Colin Colahan and Percy Leason, went to Britain and the United States and never returned. Little is known about Madge Hodges, but she was still in Melbourne in 1936 when she illustrated an article for anthropologist Ursula McConnel in the journal *Oceania*. A painting of hers is listed in an exhibition of Australian expatriate artists at the Imperial Institute Art Gallery, London, in 1956, which indicates that she remained in London after she painted Aileen Palmer in 1938. Colin Colahan exhibited paintings and sculptures there, and other artists listed in 1956 include Arthur Boyd, William Dobell, Sidney Nolan and Rolf Harris.

Nettie and Vance Palmer were caring parents, proud of their elder daughter's fierce intelligence and the linguistic abilities that saw her receive a first-class honours degree in French language and literature, with a thesis on Marcel Proust, at the age of twenty. They supported her political activities too, although Nettie wished she would settle down and concentrate on her writing. But when Aileen returned to Australia in 1945 after a decade on war fronts she was unable to adapt to her homeland. She felt 'a foreigner', she said, even though her parents provided the support for her to write. As her life began to unravel, she suffered a first breakdown in 1948 and was then in and out of mental institutions until she died in 1988.

The missing portrait seemed to symbolise for me the tragedy of Aileen Palmer's life. All I was able to see in the small snapshot was a glimpse of a dynamic young woman pinned like a butterfly on the wall behind and between her well-known parents. This was the woman who vowed to get out from under what she called 'their august and all-pervasive shadows' when she joined the British Medical Unit in London in 1936 and set off to war in Spain. Ironically, after driving ambulances during the Blitz in London, she returned to the family fold when she came back to Australia, and Vance, and Nettie's shadows were to blight the rest of her life. That the portrait painted in the 1930s, when Aileen was at her most liberated, was lost added another symbolic dimension.

•

Ink in Her Veins: The Troubled Life of Aileen Palmer was published by UWA Publishing in early 2016. I had just returned from overseas engagements talking about Aileen Palmer's involvement in the Spanish Civil War when I received an email from a Penelope Pollitt. Her surname caught my attention because Harry Pollitt had been the general secretary of the British Communist Party when Aileen was co-opted into the first medical unit to travel to Spain. The unit was, in large part, formed under the auspices of the party. It turned out that Penelope's former husband was Harry's son, but that was not why she was writing to me. She said she had 'read and re-read' my book, adding that 'Aileen Palmer was a presence, not always a welcome one, in my life during the 1950s when I was a teenager'.

Penelope's parents were members of the Kew branch of the Communist Party, which she described as 'an active, engaged, argumentative, inclusive branch of the party'. Her father Cedric Ralph was a lawyer who had led the Victorian legal effort against the Menzies government's push to outlaw the Communist Party. In her memoir *The Hammer & Sickle and the Washing Up*, Amirah Inglis – who was working as a clerk for Cedric during the royal commission into the Communist Party in Victoria in 1949 – described him as 'a lean and elegant man with lively bright blue eyes and the gentlemanly manner of the son of a Melbourne professional family':

> He had left the family law firm and set up on his own, married the beautiful daughter of a wealthy Melbourne business family and lived in Kew; but with that, and their cultivated voices, ended the similarity to the neighbours. Cedric and Rhea Ralph were devoted Communist Party members; their fine Georgian house was the setting for meetings, 'cottage' lectures and concerts, and their three daughters were schooled at progressive Preshil.

Aileen Palmer was a member of the Kew branch and regularly attended the meetings and socials at Penelope's family home. 'She showed no interest in me,' Penelope wrote, 'and I found the pervasive smell of cigarettes and her uncared-for appearance very off-putting but the fact that she was a poet impressed me.' Penelope's friend Muriel Arnott, the daughter of branch member Muni Bowen, remembered Aileen as 'always around', 'cantankerous' and often ill, being looked after by her mother and others in the branch. Penelope was surprised that the Kew branch did not feature more in my biography:

> The party was a powerful influence in most areas of life in those days. Its influence extended to relationships, friendships, even marriage. Its network was so extensive it determined which doctor you consulted, which lawyer you went to, which trade union you joined, even in some cases which business you dealt with.

I had been aware that Aileen belonged to the branch and I knew that she had given a talk to the Kew Peace Group when she returned from a peace conference in Tokyo. But she didn't write about her time in the Kew branch in any of the autobiographical fragments in her archive, although she was, as Penelope remembers, 'so much part of this world'. The 1950s were difficult years for Aileen and she spent lengthy periods in Sunbury and Royal Park mental hospitals. She found writing difficult when she was depressed, as she was during much of this time.

It appears that Vance and Nettie, who were left sympathisers but not Communist Party members, did not altogether approve of the influence of the Kew branch members on their daughter. When Aileen was asked to be part of the delegation going to a world conference against atomic and hydrogen bombs, to be held in Tokyo in 1957, she stopped taking the medication she had been prescribed to control her mood swings. She was also drinking heavily and the situation at Ardmore was grim. Vance wrote to his younger daughter Helen in Sydney:

> There are a lot of loyal friends around her but they haven't much sense ... The night before she left was rather a wallow with all sorts of people coming to Muni's and bringing bottles. The truth is they seem to enjoy her when she's het up and pouring out words.

While it is understandable that Vance found any encouragement of her drinking distressing, Aileen's friends at the Kew branch do appear to have provided her with an alternative 'family' where she was able to be herself free from surveillance. As Muriel Arnott remembers, her mother Muni and others in the branch 'were always there for her'.

Towards the end of Penelope's letter I was surprised to read this: 'All my memories of Aileen are of the 1950s. But she is still a presence in my life as I am the possessor of the portrait you refer to in the opening paragraph of your book.' She signed off soon after without further explanation of how she came to possess the missing portrait, but her email did contain an attachment.

•

Cedric Ralph, Penelope's communist lawyer father, began his autobiography at the age of eighty-two on his first computer. He died aged one hundred in 2007 and the attachment Penelope sent me was a few pages from his unpublished memoir, in which he writes about his friendship with Aileen Palmer.

Their friendship began after Aileen returned to Australia in 1945. Cedric remembers picking up 'the girls' (Aileen and Helen, who was still living at Ardmore then) to take them to the monthly party meetings:

From about 1947 on, Aileen and I became real friends. She was an extraordinarily warm-hearted creature, of very deep feelings, maybe too deep ... On those short car journeys we often talked, sometimes at length. I thought her emotional approach to political questions often led her astray, often we did not agree.

When Aileen suffered her first breakdown in 1948, she underwent a gruelling series of interventions in a private psychiatric hospital, including insulin coma therapy and electroconvulsive shock treatment, without sedation. She also began psychiatric treatment with Dr Clara Lazar Geroe around that time. Her psychiatrists diagnosed Aileen as a manic depressive, but Cedric did not accept a division between the mental and physical, believing that 'so-called mental illnesses have a direct physical basis'. He writes movingly about her periods of deep depression, which tended to last just a few weeks:

> Sometimes in her periods of depression, she would drop me a note demanding I take her to lunch. It appeared to me I gave her comfort simply because I treated her as being normal in a way that I gathered few others did. It was indeed sometimes difficult to be in her company while she gave no response at all. Often she would say nothing, just nod occasionally or give a tolerant glimmer of a smile. For all that, as she left after such a lunch, her thanks were warm.

On the other hand, when a 'high' came on 'she was fond of writing sonnets and these she could compose faster than I can write a quarter page of these memoirs'. Most were directed towards political and social issues, but some were personal and Cedric was the recipient of one of Aileen's sonnets. 'In 1961, a few days after I told her I planned to go to London, she asked me to call on her,' he writes. 'Rather shyly, she was too straightforward to be really shy, she gave me an envelope.' It contained the following sonnet:

> To C.R.
> You gave me courage once that was denied
> To those that fed on flowers of phantom seeming:
> To those whose only courage was their
> dreaming: You gave me courage permanent and wide.

You gave me courage, that is worth a lot
At this dull moment, in this arch of time
Courage is all my heart puts into rhyme
Courage, the plant we grow in this neat plot
The plant that seemed to perish when the wind
Blew swift and hard across Hungarian steppes:
Our world then seemed to shatter, to its depths
Among those who lived harder: though you'll find

A love of life, that clings, just like a burr:
A depth of knowing, that no breeze can stir.
A.P.

'I could not have been more moved,' Cedric responded:

The differences in our political appreciation of current events troubled me not at all, the general motif of the lines made me realise, perhaps for the first time, that each of us has influence and that influence we can use for better or for worse. And that it takes thought to use it for the better.

Not all recipients of Aileen's personal poems were as generous. Dorothy Hewett's first novel, *Bobbin Up*, was published in 1959, but only after it had caused a stir among Communist Party officials. Although it depicted the lives of working-class women in a Sydney spinning mill, it was criticised by the moralistic party men for its frank depiction of sex and its 'language'. In an autobiographical article in *Overland* in 1960, Dorothy wrote that at the launch party she 'was presented with a very soppy poem written to me by Aileen Palmer, the daughter of Vance and Nettie'. She was clearly disturbed by Aileen's appearance, continuing, 'The next day Aileen in an old and tatty overcoat took me out to lunch and afterwards to meet her mother.'

Cedric Ralph's and Dorothy Hewett's contrasting reactions to Aileen's poetic gestures contain a certain irony: the older man who saw himself as Aileen's non-judgemental friend understood something new, while the young woman celebrating the publishing of her controversial novel saw only a dishevelled madwoman 'looking like a bag lady'.

On the last page of the excerpt Penelope Pollitt sent me from her father's memoir, I finally found out how the portrait of the young Aileen Palmer came to be in her possession. Cedric Ralph wrote:

I felt myself extremely lucky to call on Aileen just as she was organising for sale her old home in Ridgeway Avenue Kew. She was getting rid of unwanted furniture. I asked her 'What is to happen to your portrait?' (It was a painting in the Meldrum style and had been hanging for years in her workroom.) She replied 'It is for sale.' The price she mentioned as that of her valuer's was I thought very modest; so I was very happy that it came into my prized possession.

The question that immediately came to my mind on reading this was why Aileen was selling her portrait, painted at a time when she was living in London among friends and writing a novel about the Spanish Civil War. She seemed to be thriving then in a way she never did after she returned to Australia. It is not a question I can answer. Interestingly, two other portraits of her did end up in the National Library. Perhaps it is significant that she kept this portrait with her at Ardmore after her parents died, apparently shifting it from the living room to her 'workroom', where Cedric had seen it. It is likely that after Nettie died in 1964 she moved her study to the closed-off upstairs verandah where Vance had always worked, the room that caught the sun and was less gloomy than the rest of the house. As she took in boarders to supplement her finances, she probably saw friends there rather than in the shared living room.

Ardmore was sold in 1977 when Aileen was in her early sixties. Helen stayed living in Sydney until her death in 1979 while Aileen moved into a flat in Reservoir on the other side of Melbourne. The move was not a success and she was to spend much of her remaining years in a ward for long-term patients at Larundel mental institution, dying in 1988 in a psychiatric nursing home in Ballarat, the last of the Palmer family.

•

Unlike a novel, a biography is never finished, complete within the pages of the text. Writing biography is risky: new material can shed a different light on aspects of the life one has written and conclusions the biographer has drawn may be altered or even debunked; on the other hand, unexpected rewards may come even years after a book is published. It is as though the biographer is in a continuing conversation, if not with, then certainly about, the people she has spent years researching.

Finding Aileen Palmer's lost portrait did not reveal any crucial new 'evidence' about her life, but it has enabled me to cover what Penelope

Pollitt saw as an important missing piece of it, that is, the importance to Aileen's life of the Kew branch of the Communist Party. Cedric Ralph's memoir – especially his poignant account of the silent lunches he spent with her at her request when she was in a state of depression – adds richness to Aileen's story. They are a testament to the importance of friendship, even if the 'lean and elegant' Cedric and the chain-smoking Aileen in her 'old and tatty overcoat' must have appeared an odd couple to the other diners.

When Penelope invited me to come and see the portrait I thought she might bring it out of storage for the viewing. Instead, I found it hanging on her living room wall with three portraits of her father by different artists. The portrait of Cedric Ralph immediately above Aileen's is by Noel Counihan, who was a friend of the Palmers and who painted the well-known portrait of Vance that accompanies the entry on him in the *Australian Dictionary of Biography*. The other two portraits are by AR (Rem) McLintock (painted because McLintock disliked the Counihan portrait) and Miklos Szilagyi. Looking at the lost portrait in full colour hanging in the company of this friend, a member of the party she devoted her life to, it struck me that Aileen had finally moved beyond the shadow of her parents into the light.

INSIDE STORY
CONTRIBUTORS

NORMAN ABJORENSEN of the ANU Crawford School of Public Policy is the author of *The Manner of Their Going: Prime Ministerial Exits from Lyne to Abbott* (2015) and several books about the Liberal Party and its leaders.

DEAN ASHENDEN, an Honorary Senior Fellow at the Melbourne Graduate School of Education, has been an educational adviser in every state and territory and at the national level.

DIANA BAGNALL worked as a staff writer for *The Bulletin* magazine, *Vogue Australia* and *The New Zealand Herald*.

SOPHIE BLACK, a former Editor-in-Chief at Private Media, is Head of Publishing at the Wheeler Centre in Melbourne.

FRANK BONGIORNO is Professor of History at the Australian National University.

PETER BRENT, an Adjunct Research Fellow at Swinburne University of Technology, is Inside Story's polling and politics columnist.

JUDITH BRETT is Emeritus Professor of Politics at La Trobe University.

BRONWYN CARLSON is Professor of Indigenous Studies at Macquarie University. This article was adapted from her book *The Politics of Identity: Who Counts as Aboriginal Today?*, published by Aboriginal Studies Press.

TIM COLEBATCH is a former economics editor and columnist for *The Age*.

GRAEME DOBELL is Journalist Fellow at the Australian Strategic Policy Institute.

ANDREW DODD is Director of the Centre for Advancing Journalism at the University of Melbourne.

SARA DOWSE, a former head of the federal Office of Women's Affairs, is a Sydney-based writer.

BRETT EVANS is a Sydney-based journalist.

ANTONIA FINNANE is a Professor of History at the University of Melbourne, specialising in Chinese history.

ANDREW FORD, Inside Story's music writer, is a composer, writer and broadcaster.

JEREMY GANS is a Professor in Melbourne Law School, where he researches and teaches across all aspects of the criminal justice system.

JOCK GIVEN is Professor of Media and Communications at Swinburne University of Technology.

JANE GOODALL, Inside Story's TV critic, is an Emeritus Professor with the Writing and Society Research Centre at Western Sydney University.

TOM GREENWELL is a Canberra-based teacher and writer.

TOM GRIFFITHS is Emeritus Professor of History at the Australian National University.

DAVID HAYES, Inside Story's UK correspondent, was a co-founder of *openDemocracy*.

ROB HOFFMAN teaches politics and history at Swinburne University of Technology.

SHAKIRA HUSSEIN researches and writes about multiculturalism and Muslim studies at the National Centre for Excellence in Islamic Studies at the University of Melbourne.

RICHARD JOHNSTONE is an Emeritus Professor at the University of Technology Sydney.

JILL KITSON (1939–2013) was a writer, editor, literary journalist, book reviewer and broadcaster, best known for her programs on books and language on Radio National.

SHINO KONISHI is a Senior Lecturer in History at the University of Western Australia. Her essay in this anthology is based on a chapter in *Transgressions:*

Critical Australian Indigenous Histories, edited by Ingereth Macfarlane and Mark Hannah, published by ANU Press and Aboriginal History Incorporated.

JACK LATIMORE is an Indigenous researcher with the Centre for Advancing Journalism at the University of Melbourne.

SYLVIA LAWSON (1932–2017), Inside Story's cinema columnist from 2009 to 2016, was a Sydney-based writer and critic.

ANDREW LEIGH, a former Professor of Economics at the Australian National University, is Shadow Assistant Treasurer.

ANNIKA LEMS is a postdoctoral research fellow in the Institute of Social Anthropology at the University of Bern.

SUSAN LEVER, general editor of the Cambria Australian Literature Series, is a literary critic.

SHANE MALONEY is a writer and the author of the Murray Whelan series of crime novels.

PETER MARES, contributing editor of Inside Story, is a senior moderator with the Cranlana Programme for ethical leadership and an Adjunct Fellow at the Swinburne Centre for Urban Transitions.

SYLVIA MARTIN is the author of three biographies, one of which, *Ida Leeson: A Life*, was awarded the Magarey Medal for Biography in 2008.

ROBERT MILLIKEN is a Sydney-based journalist and author, and a correspondent for *The Economist* magazine.

STEPHEN MILLS is an Honorary Senior Lecturer in the School of Social and Political Sciences at the University of Sydney.

DRUSILLA MODJESKA is a writer and critic. Her books include *Stravinsky's Lunch* and *The Mountain*.

TESSA MORRIS-SUZUKI is Professor of Japanese History at the Australian National University.

KLAUS NEUMANN works for the Hamburg Foundation for the Advancement of Research and Culture and is an Honorary Professor at Deakin University.

MARIA NUGENT is Fellow in the Australian Centre for Indigenous History in the School of History at the Australian National University.

JAMES PANICHI is Australasian Managing Editor for *MLex*.

ANNA CRISTINA PERTIERRA is a Senior Lecturer in Cultural and Social Analysis at Western Sydney University.

JOHN QUIGGIN is Professor of Economics at the University of Queensland.

MATTHEW RICKETSON is Professor of Communication at Deakin University.

LESLEY RUSSELL, an Adjunct Associate Professor at the Menzies Centre for Health Policy at the University of Sydney, has been a Visiting Fellow at the Center for American Progress and a Senior Adviser to the US Surgeon General.

MARGARET SIMONS is a freelance journalist and Associate Professor of Journalism at Monash University.

TIMOTHY J. SINCLAIR is Associate Professor of International Political Economy at the University of Warwick.

MELISSA SWEET is a health journalist and an editor of the health policy blog *Croakey*.

RODNEY TIFFEN is Emeritus Professor of Politics at the University of Sydney.

IAIN TOPLISS is an Honorary Associate in the English Program at La Trobe University.

MARIA TUMARKIN teaches creative writing at the University of Melbourne.

INSIDE STORY
ACKNOWLEDGEMENTS

Warmest thanks, first of all, to Inside Story's extremely talented group of regular and occasional writers, whose enthusiasm and hard work has made Inside Story what it is today. Many of them are represented in this collection, and the work of many more can be found on our website.

Thanks especially to publisher Mark Baker, who joined the project at a vital moment, bringing enthusiasm, expertise and a remarkable journalistic background; contributing editor Peter Mares, who has provided ideas, support and many of our best pieces; and the late Sylvia Lawson, whose generous bequest to Inside Story enabled us to commission more ambitiously during 2018.

Inside Story wouldn't have been launched without the support of Swinburne University of Technology, where initial funding was arranged by Heather Crosling, Michael Thorne and the Institute for Social Research's Julian Thomas. Over the years, colleagues at Swinburne – particularly Brian Costar, Jock Given, Klaus Neumann, Kerry Ryan, Eleanor Hogan and the late Scott Ewing – have been enthusiastic supporters and contributors.

At *The Canberra Times*, Peter Fray, Rod Quinn and James Joyce were obliging partners, helping Inside Story reach a new audience in the Saturday feature section and then via a bimonthly supplement.

Swinburne continues to support Inside Story, and we're especially grateful to Michael Leach, Robbie Robertson and Scott Thompson-Whiteside. More recently, the University of South Australia has begun making a generous annual contribution; our thanks go especially to Denise Meredyth and Jason Bainbridge. The Copyright Agency's Cultural Fund is gratefully acknowledged for funding assistance for the articles here by Margaret Simons and Jack Latimore.

And, of course, thanks to the capable, enthusiastic team at Grattan Street Press, who so speedily took the raw material and turned it into this book.

A NOTE ON THE TEXT

How to choose from the 3000-plus pieces we've published over the past decade? In the end, the fifty-one pieces published here fit into two strands: either they help to trace the main political, economic and social policy developments of the decade, or they deal with more perennial social and cultural subjects. This means that many topical pieces missed out despite their quality, and it also means that reviews in general are under-represented. Two of our three fine film reviewers, Brian McFarlane and Julie Rigg, aren't represented here, for instance, and we could have assembled an anthology entirely of book reviews – Robin Jeffrey's superb appreciation of Amartya Sen and Jean Drèze's *An Uncertain Glory: India and Its Contradictions* spring to mind.

Also on the longlist were Kerry Ryan's analysis of successive governments' changes to Australia's citizenship laws, John Fitzgerald on the hazards of collaborations between Australian and Chinese universities, Gabrielle Appleby on the Indigenous Voice proposal, James Murphy on the state of the Victorian Liberal Party, John Besemeres's essays on Russia and Eastern Europe, Mike Steketee on the National Disability Insuance Scheme – in fact, far too many to mention. All of them can be read at insidestory.org.au.

GRATTAN STREET PRESS
PERSONNEL
SEMESTER TWO, 2018

EDITING AND PROOFREADING
David Churack • Elizabeth Doan • Clarissa Lancaster • Sarah Layton
Rachelle Moulic • Mariano Trevino • Bailey Wall

DESIGN AND PRODUCTION
Jacinta Dietrich • Tiziana Forese • Rachelle Moulic • Gladys Qin

SALES AND MARKETING
David Churack • Elizabeth Doan • Samantha Mansell • Tony Ryan

SOCIAL MEDIA
Janice Lieng

SUBMISSIONS OFFICERS
Sarah Layton • Lucy Mackey

WEBSITE AND BLOGS
Daisy Feller • Lucy Mackey • Samantha Mansell

EBOOK PRODUCTION
Daisy Feller • Tony Ryan • Bailey Wall

ACADEMIC STAFF
Mark Davis • Katherine Day • Aaron Mannion • Sybil Nolan

GRATTAN STREET PRESS
ACKNOWLEDGEMENTS

Given that Inside Story has been quietly and efficiently informing and entertaining Australians online for just over a decade, it's surely just an oversight that a collection of IS's articles has not been published in book form before now. As things have turned out (quite in keeping with IS's origins within the university sector), the book project when it finally arrived has presented a terrific real-world publishing experience for the student staff of Grattan Street Press, the teaching press in the School of Culture and Communication at the University of Melbourne. But it wouldn't have been possible without the enthusiasm and hard work of Inside Story's Peter Browne and Kate Manton, who in the way of these things found themselves with double the workload just as the national political scene began to experience one of its all-too-frequent irruptions.

At GSP, Gladys Qin and Jacinta Dietrich led the editorial production effort, which included Clarissa Lancaster, Bailey Wall, Sarah Layton and Mariano Trevino. Rachelle Moulic produced the magnificent cover, and the whole GSP team got involved one way or the other, through editing and proofreading, or through sales and marketing. Mark Davis (not just a pretty brain) created the handsome text design, while managing editor Katherine Day wrangled a book that gradually turned into a tome more than 400 pages long, and Tim Fluence helped out with the pages. Thanks to all these people and also to Cameron Duder, our indexer; Kerin Forstmanis, from the University's legal department, who handled the contract with her usual helpful efficiency; to IngramSpark, our printer; and to Jason O'Leary, marketing manager in the Faculty of Arts, for his interest and assistance in promoting the Grattan Street Press project. Finally, of course, our deep gratitude to our Head of School, Jennifer Milam; our School manager, Charlotte Morgans; and the School Engagement Committee, for their continuing support of our work.

Sybil Nolan, coordinator, Grattan Street Press

ABOUT GRATTAN STREET PRESS

Grattan Street Press is a trade publisher based in Melbourne. A start-up press, we aim to publish a range of work, including contemporary literature, trade nonfiction, and children's books, and republish culturally valuable works that are out of print. The press is an initiative of the Publishing and Communications program in the School of Culture and Communication at the University of Melbourne, and is staffed by graduate students, who receive hands-on experience in every aspect of the publication process.

The press is a not-for-profit organisation that seeks to build long-term relationships with the Australian literary and publishing community. We also partner with community organisations in Melbourne and beyond to co-publish books that contribute to public knowledge and discussion.

Organisations interested in partnering with us can contact us at coordinator@grattanstreetpress.com. Writers interested in submitting a manuscript to Grattan Street Press can contact us at editorial@grattanstreetpress.com.

INDEX

www.ingramcontent.com/pod-product-compliance
Lightning Source LLC
Chambersburg PA
CBHW060020030426
42334CB00019B/2118